New Canadian Readings

SPORTS IN CANADA

Historical Readings

New Canadian Readings

SPORTS IN CANADA

Historical Readings

Edited by
Morris Mott

Copp Clark Pitman Ltd.
A Longman Company
Toronto

ISBN 0-7730-4928-2

Editing: Barbara Tessman
Design: Kathy Cloutier and Susan Coull
Cover Illustration: William Laughton
Typesetting: Carol Magee
Printing and Binding: Alger Press Limited
Illustrations for this volume were acquired with assistance from the Brandon
University Research Fund.

Canadian Cataloguing in Publication Data

Main entry under title:
Sports in Canada

(New Canadian readings)
Bibliography: p.
ISBN 0-7730-4928-2

1. Sports – Canada – History. I. Mott, Morris Kenneth, 1946– . II. Series.

GV585.S686 1989   796'.0971   C89-093389-8

Copp Clark Pitman Ltd.
2775 Matheson Blvd. East
Mississauga, Ontario
L4W 4P7

Associated companies:
  Longman Group Ltd., London
  Longman Inc., New York
  Longman Chesire Pty., Melbourne
  Longman Paul Pty., Auckland

Printed and bound in Canada

FOREWORD

New Canadian Readings is an on-going series of inexpensive books intended to bring some of the best recent work by this country's scholars to the attention of students of Canada. Each volume consists of ten or more articles or book sections, carefully selected to present a fully-formed thesis about some critical aspect of Canadian development. Where useful, public documents or even private letters and statistical materials may be used as well to convey a different and fresh perspective.

The authors of the readings selected for inclusion in this volume (and all the others in the series) are all first-rank scholars, those who are doing the hard research that is rapidly changing our understanding of this country. Quite deliberately, the references for each selection have been retained, thus making additional research as easy as possible.

Like the authors of the individual articles, the editors of each volume are also scholars of note, completely up-to-date in their areas of specialization and, as the introductions demonstrate, fully aware of the changing nature of the debates within their professions and genres of research. The list of additional readings provided by the editor of each volume will steer readers to materials that could not be included because of space limitations.

This series will continue into the foreseeable future, and the General Editor is pleased to invite suggestions for additional topics.

J.L. Granatstein
General Editor

CONTENTS

INTRODUCTION

Canadians have always been fond of sports, but until about twenty years ago professional historians of the country all but ignored this fact. On a personal level some historians regarded sports as trivial and therefore unworthy of study.[1] More of them were professionally interested in national history and the political, economic, or military themes that complemented that interest. They had little reason to study sports or other recreational activities. If they mentioned sports at all it was only in passing.

By the late 1960s, however, what Carl Berger has called the "transformation of Canadian historical writing" was underway.[2] The number of graduate students in the discipline was increasing dramatically. These students were "expected to explore new subjects or revise old ones."[3] Furthermore, both they and many of their supervisors believed there were two serious and related shortcomings in what earlier historians had written. First, there had been failure to acknowledge sufficiently that communities based upon ethnicity, class, gender, or region possess integrity and are as worthy of study as the national community. Second, inadequate attention had been paid to the experiences of ordinary people as opposed to elites. For these reasons a growing number of historians often studied the smaller communities that make up Canada, and they wrote "social history," a field described by the original editors of the Canadian Social History Series as "the history of the full range of human life."[4]

The study of the history of sports in Canada now became respectable, and in the 1970s and 1980s historians produced stimulating and useful items on the subject. For example, in an article entitled "Sport and Class Values in Old Ontario and Quebec," S.F. Wise drew attention to the popularity of sports in mid- to late-nineteenth-century Central Canada, and he explored relationships between developments in these activities on the one hand and the economic conditions or social attitudes of certain ethnic groups and classes on the other.[5] In collaboration with Douglas Fisher, Wise also provided a volume that represented a valuable historical introduction to virtually every group of sports that has had a significant following in the Dominion.[6] Carl Betke wrote two articles on sports in Edmonton. He paid particular attention to the manner in which sports stimulated a feeling of "Edmontonness" at the same time as they reflected or created religious, ethnic, or other divisions among the residents of the city.[7] Robert F. Harney suggested ways in which the history of ethnic groups in

Canada could be enlightened by examining sports. He was especially enthusiastic about the possibilities of using sport as a "cultural artifact" through which a "deeply textured analysis" might be written of the "problems of immigrant integration in Canadian society and of the constant encounter of immigrants and their values with the host society and its ways...."[8]

Wise, Betke, Harney, and other historians wrote directly on the history of sports and did so at some length. However, the new respectability of the subject was revealed not only in complete articles and books, but also in the manner in which historians often integrated information on sports into discussions of general social developments. To provide examples one could point to work by Paul Voisey, Bryan Palmer, Doug Baldwin, and Jack Bumsted. Voisey studied boosters of small Southern Alberta communities in the first three decades of the twentieth century. He discovered that as a "gimmick to distinguish their town from countless others" certain promoters were "excited...most of all" by semi-professional baseball teams. He also noted the "surprisingly large number and variety of sports and games played on the rural frontier," and provided a convincing explanation of how the economic and social rhythms of farm and small-town life encouraged participation in some sports and discouraged it in others.[9] Palmer revealed the popularity of baseball among skilled workers in Hamilton in the late-nineteenth century and said that baseball games "lent strength to the working-class community, providing a coherence and stability that had important ramifications in other [non-recreational] realms."[10] Baldwin looked at the life of silver miners in Northern Ontario in the late-nineteenth and early twentieth centuries. He said that "the most popular mode of escapism" for these people was sports; in fact the managers of the mines organized sports teams and social clubs in a manner calculated to "dissipate unrest" and foster "good working habits."[11] Finally, Bumsted studied Canada's "National Sport," and said that the failure of Canadians "to repatriate ... hockey from the American entertainment industry" in the 1950s was consistent with their acceptance of an American "stranglehold" over popular culture in that decade.[12]

All of these developments in the writing of Canadian history were anticipated or paralleled by similar trends in other countries so that, from the 1960s on, good sports history was produced virtually all over the world. Especially instructive to Canadian historians were some excellent books and articles published on the United States, Great Britain, and several countries that, like Canada, once had been part of the British Empire.[13] As a consequence, even if Canadian social historians did not themselves write about sports, they knew that by examining these activities one could make insightful remarks on relationships within and between classes or ethnic groups, on the values that educators tried to instill in the young, and on other important themes.

As professional historians became more aware of the possibilities that the study of sports might hold, the sports history of Canada was being written by others who had shown an earlier interest in the subject. It was written by amateur historians, sports sociologists, journalists, and especially by physical educators. These people studied and wrote about the history of sports either because they realized there was a great deal of popular interest in this topic, or because they were keen observers of the contemporary sports scene and required background historical information in order to make sense of their surroundings. The publications that appeared from members of each of these groups had certain characteristics that may be outlined briefly.

Amateur historians wrote local history books by the hundreds after the mid-1960s. These usually contained a chapter or at least a few pages on sports. Occasionally, too, amateur historians produced full volumes on a particular sport or on sports in a specific community. Too often what they wrote represented a collection of facts that did not add up to a coherent argument and that meant little to people from outside the local community. However, serious scholars could use the data and the illustrations to acquire knowledge on such themes as the popularity of particular sports at different times and in different places, the demographic make-up of participants in various sports, and the implementation at local levels of government policies or recommendations on physical education and fitness.[14]

In the 1960s sports sociologists emerged as specialists within the discipline of sociology[15] and began to produce a good deal of sports history. They often wrote on issues and in an argot that made their work uninteresting and even incomprehensible to historians or the general public. However, without the sociologists, historians frequently would have had to dive into primary sources with only a vague awareness of what might be found in an ocean of material. In Canada the leading sports sociologist was and is Richard Gruneau. He and individuals once associated with him at Queen's University wrote very stimulating articles and books although, from an historian's point of view, they were too satisfied simply to suggest rather than demonstrate that certain developments had occurred in the past.[16]

Journalists had been writing Canadian sports history of a kind in their columns since late in the nineteenth century, but beginning in the 1960s they published, more frequently than before, lengthy historical interpretations. Frequently they did not pull their ideas together into a story.[17] Furthermore, they rarely addressed the kinds of questions academics regard as significant. Which games were played or supported by which groups of people, when, and why? How did developments in sports relate to demographic, economic, political, or intellectual trends? How did sports fit into or reflect a cultural milieu? Their work contained few answers. However, the journalists excelled at biography and autobiography, and if they did not provide new information on Canadian society they offered insights into human character and behaviour.[18]

After the mid-1970s most of the valuable publications on the history of Canadian sports were written by physical educators. Early in the 1960s an Australian named Maxwell L. Howell came to the University of Alberta. He was aware that the history of sports and physical education was a subject receiving more and more attention in education faculties of American universities. He established masters and doctoral programs at the University of Alberta; the first Ph.D.s were awarded in 1969. Graduate programs offering masters degrees in the history of sport were founded within the next five years at the University of Windsor, Dalhousie University, and the University of Western Ontario.[19] By 1975 an impressive number of theses and publications had emerged from physical educators associated with these four institutions as well as others.[20]

At this time, the history written by physical educators was not of high quality. Howell's publications in particular were crammed full of facts about developments in various games, but the social contexts in which these developments occurred were only briefly and inadequately summarized from a few general textbooks.[21] However, Howell himself recognized that physical educators must acquire a detailed knowledge of the political, economic, and social history of the society whose sports they wanted to describe.[22] So did his colleagues in physical education faculties across the country, most notably Alan Metcalfe at the University of Windsor.

In the early 1970s, Metcalfe founded the *Canadian Journal of History of Sport and Physical Education*. By the mid-1970s this bi-annual journal was the most important avenue of publication for physical educators and other academics interested in the history of Canadian sports. In the 1980s the title of the journal became the *Canadian Journal of History of Sport/Revue canadienne de l'histoire des sports*, and the articles that appeared in it were, on balance, more skillfully written and much more informative than those that had appeared in the early volumes.[23] That this was the case was in large part due to Metcalfe's own efforts. Over the years he and several associates, notably Don Morrow at the University of Western Ontario, had pleaded and argued with physical educators, attempting to push them beyond what Morrow called "descriptive chronologies" of sports developments and motivating them to publish material that provided insight on the "relationship between sport and society." Metcalfe, Morrow, and others who thought as they did often explicitly utilized theories developed by social scientists in their own efforts to explain what had happened in the past. In fact Morrow suggested that historians of Canadian sports should strive to use concepts and build models that could be applied internationally and even universally.[24]

Individuals of varying backgrounds, then, have contributed to the knowledge we have on the history of sports in Canada and the ways in which that history has related to broader developments in the country. It is possible to outline briefly the events and the themes they have identified and analysed.

Native peoples had inhabited the northern half of North America for thousands of years before whites arrived. The different groups of Natives were fond of sports, although as a rule they did not take part in these activities nearly as often as they did in games of chance. The Natives' sports usually tested skills and personality traits required in hunting or warfare: endurance, speed, toughness, marksmanship, courage, to name a few. Men and boys were the main participants. Females played variations of the males' games, but did so infrequently. This was partly because in most Native societies females possessed little disposable property. The Native peoples were not inclined to play games without wagering on the outcome.

The Europeans who came to Canada between the early seventeenth and mid-nineteenth centuries were familiar with forms of almost every category of sport. They participated in, watched, and arranged combat sports such as wrestling or boxing; ball games; lifting contests, jumping contests, races, and other relatively straightforward trials of speed, strength, agility, or other physical qualities; sports in which animals raced or fought each other; sports in which objects such as boats were raced or controlled. In the New World the Europeans were more likely to play these sports if they lived in towns or cities rather than in small villages, on farms, or on the resource frontier. Only rarely did they set aside buildings or pieces of property for sporting activities; normally competitions occurred in open fields, on convenient stretches of rivers or lakes, and in warehouses or taverns or other structures used for everyday purposes. If equipment were necessary it was usually manufactured locally from available materials. Early nineteenth-century curlers, for example, made their "rocks" from iron or wood. The kind of granite from which rocks were constructed in Scotland usually could not be obtained in Canada, and to import stones from Britain was too expensive.

The immigrants of the seventeenth, eighteenth, and early nineteenth centuries came from every part of Europe and occasionally from other continents. The ones who most emphasized sports were of English, Irish, and Scots background. For a host of reasons, since medieval centuries sports and games had become more important in the British Isles than in other parts of Europe; it followed that these forms of recreation would be more important to British peoples who moved to the New World than it was to other Europeans who did so. It was also people of British origins who were the first Canadians influenced by the great Victorian transition in sports that occurred in the last half of the nineteenth century. In fact they contributed to every facet of that transition.

The most important feature of this transition was a phenomenal rise in popularity of ball games, especially team ball games. Forms of cricket, baseball, golf, tennis, bowling, lacrosse, hockey, curling,[25] and other ball sports had been played for centuries before the Victorian era, but had not been nearly as prominent as they became in the half century after 1840. By the 1890s ball games were the most popular sports of all, for spectators as well as participants.

A major reason they became so attractive was the effect the Industrial Revolution had on sports. The equipment in general and especially the balls became more kinaesthetically satisfying to use. Moreover, the athletes who used the new equipment became more aesthetically pleasing to watch. Charles Goodyear's vulcanized rubber, Elias Howe's and Isaac Singer's sewing machines, Henry Bessemer's better quality steel, John B. Dunlop's pneumatic tire, all had an impact upon equipment that is not difficult to imagine. So did improved glues, cloths, hides, as well as better tools with which to make golf clubs, tennis racquets, baseball bats, and other items. In the second half of the nineteenth century certain manufacturers began to specialize in sporting goods, and their products became available throughout the settled parts of Canada and the Western world because the Industrial Revolution was in large part a revolution in means of communication and transportation. Another example from curling illustrates what happened. By the 1880s, curlers in both Western and Eastern Canada were discarding their home-made iron and wooden stones and ordering granite ones from Scotland. Their new rocks arrived in a few weeks, having travelled thousands of miles by steamship and rail.

The standardized equipment and the revolution in communications and transportation led to a second important feature of the Victorian transition. This was the creation and acceptance of standardized rules. Canadian athletes could now travel hundreds of miles to compete. They possessed equipment similar to that used by their opponents; perhaps it was manufactured by the same company. They were aware of the rules by which specific sports were played in different parts of the world. Local rules gave way to standardized rules that applied at least at district and often at provincial or regional levels.

A third important aspect of the Victorian transition was the development of a well-articulated philosophy of sports. One of the attractions of sports is always the enjoyment received from them. One "loses" oneself while playing or watching them — in other words one *has fun*.[26] However, Victorian Canadians of British background tended to be suspicious of doing things just for fun. They looked for "higher" motives for playing sports. In the mid- to late-nineteenth century, individuals associated with English public schools were influential in creating and spreading the idea that sports were educational in the best and broadest sense. Sports tested personal attributes and skills that were desirable not only in games but in all of life. By doing so, they inculcated these qualities and dramatized both their beauty and their importance. The team ball games in particular seemed to test a wide variety of admirable traits and skills. This was another reason these activities became so popular.

A fourth important feature of the transition was the growth of *organized* sports. Prior to the mid-nineteenth century, sports occurred normally at picnics or holiday celebrations, or they were arranged "on the spot" as the result of a challenge. They took place on grounds or in buildings used for many events and functions. During the Victorian years competitions were increasingly arranged by formal organizations such as clubs, leagues, and associations. Moreover, they were held in facilities prepared for and set aside for sports; usually these facilities were built and maintained by clubs or joint-stock companies. By the 1890s impromptu matches still occurred, of course, and sports remained an attraction at community celebrations, but clubs, leagues, associations, and companies organized and accommodated most events.

By the 1890s, then, sports were much more popular and important than they had been fifty years earlier. They had become sufficiently so, in fact, that a few highly skilled young men made their living or at least supplemented their income by playing games. Normally these professional athletes were rowers, boxers, or competitors in other individual sports. They tried to win wagers or prize money. But already some of the professional athletes were salaried men in the team sports. They were hired by a community to play a game with skill and dedication. The team sports tested socially acquired qualities such as ability to work with others as well as "natural" qualities such as strength. A good baseball team reflected the vitality and the ideals of a whole community to a degree a good shot-putter did not.

The changes that occurred in the Victorian years had a permanent impact on Canada's sports culture. In the twentieth century, ball games remained the most popular group of sports, especially for spectators. Sports continued to be justified and promoted as activities that developed or dramatized "character." Clubs, leagues, and associations remained the most important means of arranging competitions; and facilities continued to be built specifically for sports, often by joint-stock companies. Although there were always minor variations in the rules followed across the country in the different games, sufficient standardization had occurred to make it reasonably easy to create more provincial, regional, and even national and international events.

If the main Victorian developments continued to have a great impact, there were also many twentieth-century changes in the look and feel of sports as well as in the meanings or functions of these activities. New technological innovations caused many of these changes. Historians sometimes say that the first Industrial Revolution took place between the late-eighteenth and mid-nineteenth centuries, and that it was followed by a second and even a third industrial revolution. It is simpler and more accurate to say that rapid technological change was a fact of life in the twentieth century as it had been in the nineteenth. With regard to sports, some technological innovations resulted in the development of new activities such as automobile racing, water skiing, and parachute jumping; other improvements resulted in safer, more efficient, more attractive skates, shoes, skis, bats, sticks, pads, uniforms and other items used in the old activities. Perhaps most important of all, technological innovations made possible the huge stadia and arenas that were built in every large city in the country, which increasingly made major spectator events "weatherproof."

Broader participation patterns represented a second important change in twentieth-century Canadian sports. Until the 1890s middle- and upper-class males of British background had been by far the most prominent participants. This changed thereafter as working-class people became more involved. They applauded essentially the same skills and attributes that middle- or upper-class individuals did, so it is not surprising that they were drawn to many of the same sports. Workers could not afford to play games such as polo, and they could not play others such as golf as often as they might have wanted, but they became far more prominent in sports overall.

Women also became more active. In the Victorian years they had been encouraged to watch men compete; in fact many sporting occasions were not complete or satisfying unless attended by women spectators. In the 1880s and 1890s women began to take part in golf, curling, tennis, basketball, gymnastics, swimming, and other activities that involved beneficial exercise but highlighted the "feminine" qualities of grace and modesty as opposed to the "masculine" ones of courage and aggressiveness. By the 1960s a few females were engaging in rugby and other body-contact sports, and in tennis, golf, speed-skating, and a host of others they were competing at a level of intensity that would have seemed most unladylike a hundred or even fifty years earlier. Their spectatorial role had always remained important, however. The presence and the actions of cheerleaders at football and other games revealed this.

The British majority often said that other ethnic groups could become good citizens if they learned to play "Canadian" games such as cricket, baseball, or hockey. The encouragement and the pressure they received from British people was one reason French-Canadians, Scandinavians, Ukrainians, and other groups began to participate in sports in significant numbers after the 1890s. However, another reason they did so was in order to maintain ethnic identities and communities. This latter consideration was especially prominent among the post-World War II immigrants who arrived from countries in which sports had become a more important part of daily life than they had been in the late-nineteenth or early twentieth centuries. In the 1970s or 1980s, when West Indians played cricket or Italians played soccer or bocce, they were not so much adopting Canadian culture as maintaining a culture they associated with their homelands.

Greater participation on the part of minority ethnic groups, women, the working class, and others — notably the handicapped after the 1960s — was encouraged in the twentieth century by the use of public money to foster sports. Through the years, governments supported sports indirectly, of course, by building road systems, for example, or by placing fewer restrictions on Sabbath-day activities, or by establishing hospitalization or medical care schemes. Mostly they supported sports directly by creating physical education and public recreation programs, and especially by helping to build and maintain facilities. In the early decades of this century it was primarily municipal and provincial governments that promoted sports but, after World War II, federal governments joined them. In the 1970s the three levels of government spent millions annually. Virtually every significant city had a parks and recreation department; provinces already had or soon would have departments of recreation and amateur sport; the federal government established a ministry of state for sport. The governments acted because businesspeople, the clergy, and other influential groups were convinced that the valuable lessons learned through sports could be applied in everyday life, and because the programs and facilities these people supplied as private citizens or through their corporations and churches were not sufficient to meet the demand.

Governments utilized resources to assist elite athletes as well as recreational ones. Beginning in the 1890s truly national champions were identified in a number of sports. Furthermore, international competitions became more and more numerous. Because the reputation of a city, a district, a province, or the whole nation seemed at stake, competitors were supported by public money. By the 1980s a few amateur athletes were in fact employees of the state. The support of different levels of government was indispensable also if communities hoped to host Briers, Olympic Games, or other major events.

The large facilities built with public money frequently accommodated professional sports. Early in the twentieth century the appearance and subsequent growth of pro sports seemed lamentable to many observers, especially educators, clergymen, and social workers. They associated professionalism with the gambling and "fixed" matches that had been too common in nineteenth-century boxing, rowing, and track and field. Whenever they could, executive officers of amateur associations banned paid men from competing. They also "professionalized" individuals who played with or against paid men and thereby became "contaminated." By doing so the committed amateurs created a good deal of difficulty for serious athletes who wanted to test themselves against other top competitors. However, by the interwar years it was obvious that strict amateur principles could not be upheld, at least in the popular spectator sports. Thereafter, it became increasingly irrelevant to the public in general and to businesspeople in particular whether or not the athletes were paid. It was more important to observe and to be identified with superior athletic performances.

Those superior athletic performances became more and more visible as the decades passed. This was primarily because of the amount of coverage given to sports by the mass media. Between the 1890s and World War I, the sports page became an important part of daily newspapers, and magazines began to feature stories on top competitors. In the 1920s radio and then in the 1950s television began to offer regular summaries of occurrences in sports. More important, they offered live broadcasts of Saturday night hockey games, Grey Cup football, and other major events; people from across the country could "be present" at a match. Newspapers, magazines, radio, and television made virtually all Canadians familiar with Tom Longboat, Lionel Conacher, "Sandy" Somerville, the Edmonton Grads, Barbara Ann Scott, the Montreal Canadiens, Nancy Greene, Gaeten Boucher, and other great individuals and teams. Sometimes Canadians were motivated in their own lives by these performers, which meant the athletes were very useful heroes.

The items contained in this collection address in some detail one or more of the events and topics just outlined. The main purpose of the volume is to introduce undergraduate university students as well as members of the general public to a variety of important themes and developments in the history of Canadian sports. An effort has been made to include items on the different regions of the country, although only English-language selections are incorporated. Not every subject receives attention. This is partly because of space limitation, partly also because some of the themes and some sports are not treated skill-fully in the literature. Readers should be able to spot likely sources of information on specific topics by looking through the Notes that are part of most selections, and by using the Further Reading section at the back of the volume.

Notes

1. See S.F. Wise's comments on A.R.M. Lower's attitudes toward sports, in "Sport and Class Values in Old Ontario and Quebec," reprinted in this volume.

2. Carl Berger, *The Writing of Canadian History: Aspects of English-Canadian Historical Writing since 1900*, 2nd ed. (Toronto: University of Toronto Press, 1986), 262. See the whole discussion in chapter 11 of Berger's book, as well in his "Introduction" to *Contemporary Approaches to Canadian History*, ed. Carl Berger (Toronto: Copp Clark Pitman, 1987), 1–3.

3. Berger, *The Writing of Canadian History*, 262.

4. S.F. Wise and Michael S. Cross, "The Canadian Social History Series," announcement in Alison Prentice, *The School Promoters: Education and Social Class in Mid-Nineteenth Century Upper Canada* (Toronto: McClelland and Stewart Ltd., 1977), 5.

5. S.F. Wise, "Sport and Class Values in Old Ontario and Quebec" in *His Own Man: Essays in Honour of Arthur Reginald Marsden Lower*, ed. W.H. Heick and Roger Graham (Montreal: McGill-Queen's University Press, 1974), 93–117. It is worth noting that Wise had been writing brief but historically informed essays on sports since early in the 1950s. See "Canadian Football," *Canadian Forum* 30, 258 (Nov. 1950): 175–76, and his article written with D.M. Fisher, "Hockey and Hokum," *Canadian Forum* 31, 372 (Jan. 1952): 224–26.

6. S.F. Wise and Douglas Fisher, *Canada's Sporting Heroes, Their Lives and Times* (Don Mills, Ont.: General Publishing and Canada's Sports Hall of Fame, 1974).

7. Carl Betke, "The Social Significance of Sport in the City: Edmonton in the 1920s" in *Cities in the West: Papers of the Western Canada Urban History Conference - University of Winnipeg, October 1974*, ed. A.R. McCormack and Ian MacPherson (Ottawa: National Museums of Canada, 1975), 211–35; Betke, "Sports Promotion in the Western Canadian City: The Example of Early Edmonton," *Urban History Review* 12, 2 (Oct. 1983): 47–56.

8. Robert F. Harney, "Homo Ludens and Ethnicity," introduction to *Sports and Ethnicity* issue of *Polyphony: The Bulletin of the Multicultural History Society of Ontario* 7, 1 (Spring/Summer 1985): 1–12.

9. Paul Voisey, "Boosting the Small Prairie Town, 1904–1931: An Example from Southern Alberta" in *Town and City: Aspects of Western Canadian Urban Development*, ed. Alan F.J. Artibise (Regina: University of Regina, Canadian Plains Research Centre, 1981), 155; Voisey, *Vulcan: The Making of a Prairie Community* (Toronto: University of Toronto Press, 1988), especially 163–65.

10. Bryan D. Palmer, *A Culture in Conflict: Skilled Workers and Industrial Capitalism in Hamilton, Ontario, 1860–1914* (Montreal: McGill-Queen's University Press, 1979), especially 52–54, 58–59, 241.

11. Doug Baldwin, "A Study in Social Control: The Life of the Silver Miner in Northern Ontario," *Labour/Le Travailleur* 2 (1977), especially 99–101, 106.

12. Jack Bumsted, "Canada and American Culture in the 1950s" in *Interpreting Canada's Past*. Volume II. *After Confederation* (Toronto: Oxford University Press, 1986), especially 408–10.

13. A few of these are mentioned in the Further Readings section at the back of this collection.

14. See Wakaw History Book Committee, *A Land Harvested By Faith 1884–1984, Wakaw [and surrounding school districts]* (Wakaw, Sask.: Wakaw Heritage Society Inc., 1984), especially 797-805; Brenda Zeman, *88 Years of Puck Chasing in Saskatchewan* (Regina: Saskatchewan Sports Hall of Fame, 1983); Brian Flood, *Saint John: A Sporting Tradition 1785–1985* (Saint John: Neptune Publishing, 1985).

15. See John T. Talamini and Charles H. Page, *Sport and Society: An Anthology* (Boston: Little, Brown, 1973), 11–13; Wilbert Marcellus Lemard II, *A Sociological Perspective of Sport* (Minneapolis: Burgess Publishing Company, 1980), 14–20.

16. See Richard Gruneau, *Class, Sports, and Social Development* (Amherst, Mass.: University of Massachusetts Press, 1983); Gruneau and John G. Albinson, eds., *Canadian Sport: Sociological Perspectives* (Don Mills, Ont.: Addison-Wesley, 1976); Gruneau and Hart Cantelon, eds., *Sport, Culture and the Modern State* (Toronto: University of Toronto Press, 1982); Cantelon and Bob Hollands, *Leisure, Sport and Working Class Cultures: Theory and History* (Kingston, Ont.: Centre for Sports and Leisure Studies, Queen's University, 1984); Cantelon and Jean Harvey, eds., *Not Just a Game: Essays in Canadian Sport Sociology* (Ottawa: University of Ottawa Press, 1988).

17. See Vince Leah, *A History of the Blue Bombers* (Winnipeg, n.p., ca. 1979).

18. See Jim Coleman, *A Hoofprint on My Heart* (Toronto: McClelland and Stewart, 1971); Trent Frayne, *The Mad Men of Hockey* (Toronto: McClelland and Stewart, 1974); Eric Whitehead, *Cyclone Taylor: A Hockey Legend* (Toronto: Doubleday Canada, 1977); Scott Young, *Hello Canada! The Life and Times of Foster Hewitt* (Toronto: Seal Books, 1985).

19. Alan Metcalfe, "Canadian Sport History, 1969–1982: An Assessment" in *Proceedings, 5th Canadian Symposium on the History of Sport and Physical Education* (Toronto: University of Toronto School of Physical and Health Education, 1982), 275.

20. The theses, at least, are listed in Brian T.P. Mutimer, comp., *Canadian Graduating Essays, Theses and Dissertations Relating to the History and Philosophy of Sport, Physical Education and Recreation* (Canadian Association for Health, Physical Education and Recreation, 1975).

21. See Nancy Howell and Maxwell L. Howell, *Sports and Games in Canadian Life: 1700 to the Present* (Toronto: Macmillan, 1969).

22. Maxwell L. Howell, "Toward a History of Sport," *Canadian Journal of History of Sport and Physical Education* I, 1 (May 1970), especially 14–15.

23. Among the best articles published in the *Canadian Journal of History of Sport* in the 1980s were the following: Bruce Kidd, "In Defence of Tom Longboat," XIV, 1 (May 1983): 34-63; D. Brown, "Sport, Darwinism, and Canadian Private Schooling to 1918," XVI, 1 (May 1985): 27–37; Patricia Vertinsky, "God, Science and the Marketplace: The Bases for Exercise Prescriptions for Females in Nineteenth-Century North America," XVII, 1 (May 1986): 38-45; Barbara Schrodt, "Taking the Tram: Travelling to Sport and Recreation Activities on Greater Vancouver's Interurban Railway — 1890s to 1920s," XIX, 1 (May 1988): 52–62.

24. Alan Metcalfe, "Some Background Influences on Nineteenth-Century Canadian Sport and Physical Education," *Canadian Journal of History of Sport and Physical Education* V, 1 (May 1974), especially 62; Metcalfe, "Canadian Sport History," 275–81; Don Morrow, "Canadian Sport History: A Critical Essay," *Journal of Sport History* X, 1 (Spring 1983): 67–79.

25. It is obvious that hockey and curling are ball games in which the ball has been shaped to make it easier to play with on ice.

26. See Mihaly Csikszentmihalyi, "Play and Intrinsic Rewards," *Journal of Humanistic Psychology* XV (1975): 41–63.

SECTION 1

COLONIAL SPORT, 1600–1850

What is a sport? The most satisfying answer to this question is suggested by the work of the philosopher Bernard Suits. Suits says that a sport is a type of game. A game is a "voluntary attempt to overcome unnecessary obstacles." A sport is a competitive game that tests physical skills or attributes.[1]

This definition is much simpler than those normally offered by scholars. It is especially simpler than those devised by sports sociologists. But as Klaus V. Meier has pointed out, sociologists' definitions of sport are "fraught with numerous inadequacies."[2] One of the significant shortcomings of most sociological definitions is that "institutionalization" is viewed as a necessary component of sports. That is, activities do not qualify as sports unless they possess some or all of the following: formal organizations such as clubs or leagues that arrange and administer matches; rules of play that are widely recognized and utilized; written records of past performances and other developments.

As Meier says, it is both "arbitrary and erroneous" to make institutionalization an essential aspect of sport.[3] One negative consequence of doing so is the logical necessity of denying that sports existed before the industrial revolution of the nineteenth century. Actually, human beings in pre-industrial societies engaged in many activities that today almost everyone would call sports.

Certainly this was true of the human beings who lived prior to the mid-nineteenth century in what we now call Canada. The articles in this section on colonial sports indicate the kinds of sports that were then prevalent. They also identify the contexts in which these activities occurred and some of the functions or meanings they had for those who participated in them.

The Indians of Canada were not colonists, of course, but our knowledge of their sports and other games really only begins with the colonial period. The first item in this section deals with the sporting activities of the Natives who lived approximately in what is now Manitoba. Morris Mott identifies some of the differences in types of sports played by various tribes not only in Manitoba but in other parts of Canada, and he offers suggestions about the "cultural significance" of these activities.

We know surprisingly little about the recreational aspects of life among the European colonists who came to Canada from the early seventeenth to mid-nineteenth centuries. This is especially true of the French colonists who inhabited the southern part of the modern-day province of Quebec. Nevertheless, it is clear that the kinds of sports in which colonists participated and the contexts in which they did so were determined in large part by where they lived.

Robert D. Day discusses the contributions made by military personnel to the sporting life of Halifax from the mid-eighteenth to the mid-nineteenth century. From what he and others have written, it is obvious that cities with a substantial military population were likely to feature both a large number of sports and many occasions on which sports were played.[4] Even if cities did not have a military garrison or naval base, however, there were government officials or a wealthy business class with enough time and money to promote aristocratic sports such as fox-hunting or horseracing. Moreover, in cities common people lived sufficiently close to each other to engage in foot-races or other contests frequently, as well as to arrange fights between animals.

Normally people who lived on farms or in small villages were familiar with all the sports found in the large centres. They simply had fewer opportunities to participate in them. As the selection from Edwin C. Guillet's *Early Life in Upper Canada* suggests, rural people in what is now southern Ontario were always busy and often isolated; some of them also were opposed on moral grounds to certain amusements. For all these reasons sports were not as prevalent in the country as in the city. In fact, sports tended to be peripheral or secondary activities on social occasions such as bees, weddings, and fairs.

The final selection in this section deals with men on Canada's fur trade frontier in the eighteenth and nineteenth centuries. As Michael Payne reveals, among fur traders sports were not as prevalent as were other forms of recreation. Nevertheless, these people frequently enjoyed races, gymnastic competitions, boxing or wrestling matches, marksmanship contests, and other sports. Evidently workers in pre-Confederation Canada's other major resource industry — timber — enjoyed similar activities, although a thorough study of the recreations of those involved in the timber trade has yet to be written.[5]

Notes

1. See Bernard Suits, *The Grasshopper: Games, Life and Utopia* (Toronto: University of Toronto Press, 1978); Suits, "What Is a Game?" in *Sport and the Body: A Philosophical Symposium*, ed. Ellen W. Gerber (Philadelphia: Lea and Febiger, 1972), 16–22; and Suit's less satisfying "The Elements of Sport" in *The Philosophy of Sport*, ed. Robert G. Osterhoudt (Springfield, Ill.: Charles C. Thomas, 1973), 48–64.

2. Klaus V. Meier, "On the Inadequacies of Sociological Definitions of Sport," *International Review of Sport Sociology* 2, 16 (1981), 81.

3. Ibid., 88.

4. See also Peter Lindsay, "The Impact of the Military Garrisons on the Development of Sport in British North America," *Canadian Journal of History of Sport and Physical Education* 1, 1 (May 1970): 33–44; Derek Swain, "The Impact of the Royal Navy on the Development of Sports in British Columbia" in *Proceedings, Fourth Canadian Symposium of the History of Sport and Physical Education,* ed. Barbara Schrodt (Vancouver: University of British Columbia School of Physical Education and Recreation, 1979); Elinor Kyte Senior, *British Regulars in Montreal: An Imperial Garrison, 1832–1854* (Montreal: McGill-Queen's University Press, 1981), 174–83.

5. See Joshua Fraser, *Shanty, Forest and River Life in the Backwoods of Canada* (Montreal: John Lovell, 1883), 313, 335. Michael S. Cross's dissertation on the timber trade is suggestive on the theme of recreation, but only peripherally concerned with it. See Michael S. Cross, "The Dark Druidical Groves: The Lumber Community and the Commercial Frontier in British North America to 1854" (Ph.D. dissertation, University of Toronto, 1968).

GAMES AND CONTESTS OF THE FIRST "MANITOBANS"*

MORRIS KENNETH MOTT

Cultures without a few games and sports are, and seem historically to have been, extremely rare;[1] it is therefore not surprising that they were present among the people who lived in "Manitoba" before the province was established.

The first of those people were of course the members of various Native "tribes" of the Canadian Northwest.[2] Although these individuals moved around extensively, they did inhabit more or less identifiable areas, and those who occupied the territory that became known as Manitoba may be specified — at least for the years just prior to and following white contact, about which we can speak with much greater certainty than about previous centuries. In the extreme north-east of the province, as at present defined, were the Eskimo. To the south and west of the Eskimo, in the region bounded approximately by Hudson Bay, the Churchill River, and Great Slave and Athabasca Lakes, were the Chipewyan. Further south lived the Woodland Cree, who occupied an immense territory extending from what is now Northern Ontario to the area west of Lakes Winnipeg, Manitoba, and Winnipegosis. There were also a smaller number of Cree bands, known collectively as the Plains Cree, who moved back and forth between the woodlands and plains in what is now southwestern Manitoba and southeastern Saskatchewan. Inhabiting the same general region, and also territory further to the south and west, were the Assiniboine, with whom the Plains Cree were on very good terms. The Ojibwa, also know as the Chippewa or the Sauteux, were latecomers to the Northwest. In the early eighteenth century they migrated from the Lake Huron–Lake Superior area to the country between Lake Superior and the Red River; as fur and game diminished in the latter environs, they migrated further to the north and west. Members of these

* Morris Kenneth Mott, "Manly Sports and Manitobans, Settlement Days to World War One" (Ph.D. dissertation, Queen's University, 1980), 17–32.

tribes, and of certain Sioux bands who lived south of the forty-ninth parallel but often appeared farther north while on hunting or warring expeditions, constituted the vast majority of the Native population of what is now Manitoba.[3]

The writings and observations of early explorers and fur traders, and the work of anthropologists and ethnologists such as Stewart Culin, whose "Games of the North American Indians" provides the most comprehensive study of the subject,[4] reveal that games and contests played a very important part in the lives of the Natives. They were especially fond of games whose outcome was determined by chance, and which in all likelihood had emerged, at some point in the history of their societies, "from the divinatory aspect of religious ceremonials."[5] One group of the games of chance may be called "guessing games." A version of these was similar to the sleight-of-hand, hidden-object games that we often see at fairs or circuses and, as most commonly played by Natives, consisted of guessing under which of four moccasins an object had been hidden.[6] In another version the objective was to guess the location of an odd or peculiarly marked stick, and in what was probably the simplest form of these "guessing" games one player would manipulate a small object and try to confuse the others as to which hand finally held it.[7] A second group of chance games were the "dice" games, in which marked stones, bones, sticks, or pieces of metal were placed in a bowl or blanket, then tossed in the air and "counted" after they had fallen.[8] Descriptions of these games of chance are so numerous that one feels safe in saying that they were the games most often played by the Natives.

Less popular than games of chance, but still very prominent, were competitions that tested strength, stamina, dexterity, or other physical skills and qualities then required of men. Foot-racing, for example, was commonplace, as was wrestling in various forms.[9] The Eskimo seemed particularly fond of rather straightforward events such as finger-pulling or high-kicking matches.[10] More prevalent among the tribes in general were contests modeled on the traditional hunting skills of throwing spears and shooting arrows. An example of this was the popular game in which arrows were shot at a rawhide netting on which concentric circles had previously been outlined, and points were awarded according to how close each arrow came to the smallest circle; in a similar game with an identical system of scoring, the objective was to throw a pole through a rolling hoop. Among several tribes a popular competition involved shooting an arrow a great distance, or planting a stake in the snow or ground, and then throwing a spear or shooting an arrow to land as close as possible to it; the scoring system was similar to our game of horseshoes. A winter variation of spear-throwing was the game in which players tried to slide a stick called a "snow-snake" through several snow barriers or, as played very often by women, attempted to slide it at such a pace as to allow it to negotiate several downhill turns within a constructed passage.[11]

The most complex of the games in which physical qualities were conspicuous were the "ball" games.[12] The balls were ordinarily animal hair covered by hide and therefore could not have had a great deal of bounce. With them the Natives played several games. Among the Northwest tribes only the Eskimo seem to have played what could be called "football."[13] A form of prisoner's base, in which the ball was tossed in the air and the person who caught it tried to run to a "base" before being caught, was probably more common.[14] Lacrosse, along with all the games in which a stick with a netted webbing or pocket was used to carry a ball was more prevalent among the tribes of eastern North America and of the Pacific coast than among those in the middle of the continent.[15] The Ojibwa, however, brought a love for this game with them as they migrated west; its popularity among the members of this tribe and the method of play is revealed in the following observations made by a North-West Company fur trader, Peter Grant:

> The "hurdle" is their favourite game; not only their young men, but men advanced in life sometimes engage in it. On this occasion they strip naked, save their breech clouts, head dress, a few silver ornaments on their arms and a belt around their waist; their faces and bodies are painted in the highest style. Each man is provided with a hurdle, an instrument made of a small stick of wood about three feet long, bended at the end to a small circle, in which a loose piece of net work is fixed, forming a cavity big enough to receive a leather ball, about the size of a man's fist.
>
> Every thing being prepared, a level plain about half a mile long is chosen, with proper barriers or goals at each end. Having previously formed into two equal parties, they assemble in the very middle of the field, and the game begins by throwing up the ball perpendicularly in the air, when, instantly, both parties form a singular group of naked men . . . [trying] to catch the ball....
>
> Whoever is so fortunate as to catch the ball in his hurdle, runs with it towards the barrier with all his might, supported by his party, while his opponents pursue him and endeavour to strike it out.
>
> He who succeeds in doing so, runs in the same manner towards the opposite barrier and is, of course, pursued in his turn. If in danger of being overtaken, he may throw it

with his hurdle towards any of his associates who may happen to be nearer the barrier than himself....

The best of three heats wins the game, and, besides the honor acquired on such occasions, a considerable prize is adjudged to the victors.[16]

More indigenous than lacrosse to the Northwest — at least to the Northwest plains — were games similar to shinny or field hockey, in which the ball was driven along the ground towards a goal by means of a curved stick. It was played as follows in front of one twentieth century observer:

[It] was played with a hide-covered ball, about five inches in diameter, stuffed with buffalo or antelope hair. Four to six players were on each side, usually composed of the followers of one chief. Each player was equipped with a curved stick, resembling a modern hockey stick, with which the ball was driven. It was not permissable to touch the ball with any part of the body. At the ends of the field, sticks were placed in the ground as goal line markers. The goals were one hundred to one hundred fifty yards apart. The game was won when one side succeeded in sending the ball across the opponent's goal line. There were no rest periods; the game continued until one side had won.[17]

The games of physical skill and chance described above were the principal ones played by the Native peoples of what became Manitoba. There were others of course; Indian youngsters, for example, enjoyed the competitions such as hide-and-seek and tag that seem to be almost universal, and as horses became more common in the eighteenth century so did horse racing.[18] The major forms of contest have been mentioned, however, and although it is extremely hazardous to offer generalizations about the behaviour of people whose ways of thinking were vastly different from our own,[19] some remarks about the motivations behind the cultural significance of the playing of these games may be made.

Probably the main reason why the Natives participated in games was that they derived so much pleasure from doing so. Peter Grant wrote of the high spirits with which the Ojibwa played lacrosse, "painted in different colors and in the most comical attitudes imaginable, gaping with their hurdles elevated in the air to catch the ball," and several whites expressed amazement at the way in which Natives could "lose" themselves, for hour upon hour, in what seemed to be rather simple games of chance.[20] It seems obvious that games provided play or fun; what is less apparent, of course, is just how or why they did so. Certainly those who favour the argument that "tension reduction" is the basis of the "play-experience" would make a great deal of what appear to have been the most prominent games played by Native women. In these societies variations of the several games were played by women, less frequently than and usually separate from the men.[21] Women were evidently particularly attracted to games played with a "ball" that was really two balls joined together by a piece of cord. Both James Isham and Andrew Graham of the Hudson's Bay Company observed women near Hudson Bay playing prisoner's base with such an object, but it was most commonly used in a game that resembled lacrosse. The ball was thrown or carried towards a goal by means of a stick, which was placed under the connecting cord; among the Plains Cree this was known as the "testicle game."[22] Suggestive as this game and the words used to describe it may be, however, the internal processes by which human beings experience or have experienced "play" cannot be traced with any certainty. All that can be affirmed here is that one reason why Natives played games was that, like most people in most cultures, they derived a great deal of "fun" from doing so.

A second motive for participation in games was no doubt the desire to gain esteem by displaying skills, attributes, or qualities of character that were valued in Native societies. To elaborate, one might point to the fact that Natives of the Northwest depended primarily upon hunting for their essentials, and that a comment made by Samuel Hearne in reference to the Chipewyan could be said to apply to all the tribes: "the value of a man among these people, is always proportioned to his abilities in hunting."[23] Games in which objects were shot or thrown at a target were structures incorporating the hunting skills on which everyone relied. It is therefore not surprising that games of this sort were very popular, especially among young males. Daniel Harmon, who spent a great deal of time among the Indians in fur trade days, reported that Assiniboine boys from the ages of four or five years to eighteen or twenty "pass nearly half their time in shooting at a mark."[24] Foot-racing and wrestling tested and inculcated speed, strength, and stamina, qualities that had less direct relevance to hunting but which were still important and highly regarded.[25] Combative games such as wrestling or "neck-pulling" seemed especially prominent among the Northern Natives; among Chipewyan youths, for example, wrestling was nearly an everyday occurrence.[26] The popularity of combative contests among the northern peoples is hardly surprising, since forms of fighting were so much a part of their cultures. Among the Chipewyan males it was customary to wrestle to defend or to gain property, ...[which in Chipewyan culture included] a wife; in Eskimo society disputes were often settled by "striking contests," in which two men alternatively hit each other but were not allowed to defend themselves against the opponent's blow.[27]

In short, among the Natives an individual could receive credit for having displayed, in a contest or game, physical skills and attributes valued in the society at large. Similarly, prestige could result from exhibiting praiseworthy attitudes and behaviour. In the ball games, for example, it was evidently "bad form" to show anger or desire for revenge as a result of the injuries that often occurred, so that the Natives accepted them with a composure that often impressed white observers.[28] Esteem could also be gained by displaying the proper behaviour once the outcome of the game had become clear. Here one must be conscious of the fact that, especially for games of chance but also for games that tested physical attributes, extremely high wagers were common. Andrew Graham reported of the Cree near Hudson Bay that

> they will stake one, two, three, even ten beaver skins at a time; and it frequently happens that he who in the morning was possessed of furs sufficient to procure at the Factory necessaries for his whole family for a twelvemonth, shall in a few hours be destitute of the means to barter a knife or an awl.[29]

The winners of the various games gained property with which they could be very generous, and gift-giving was something for which one might expect to be widely acclaimed.[30] Meanwhile the losers were expected to accept their misfortune with a stoicism that was not so much praised when present as noted disapprovingly when absent. One reason why those who had lost normally behaved as expected is suggested by Mandelbaum's work on the Plains Cree. In this tribe one could gain prestige and even wealth if one indicated transcendence of common sentiments such as sexual jealousy or regret over loss of material possessions. For example, if an offender against certain mores of the tribe dispassionately accepted the punishment administered to him — and this might include having his tepee stripped and his personal belongings taken — he could expect praise and restitution. Evidently by exhibiting indifference in the face of heavy losses, whether incurred in a game or not, the individual Native could prove to the other members of the tribe, and especially to the Spirits in control of his fortunes, that he was worthy of a better fate in the future.[31]

The Natives of the Northwest, then, competed because it was fun to do so, and because they were encouraged in their efforts by fellow members of their societies who regarded the various contests and games as conducive to the development of skills and attitudes that seemed valuable, even indispensable. This suggests that, even though native cultures were vastly different from those of the Europeans who followed them into what is now Manitoba, within the different civilizations the motivations behind the playing of games and the cultural significance of games were not dissimilar.

Notes

1. See Brian Sutton-Smith and John M. Roberts, "The Cross-Cultural and Psychological Study of Games" in *The Cross-Cultural Analysis of Sport and Games*, ed. Günther Lüschen (Champaign, Ill.: Stipes Publishing Co., 1970), 100–01. That forms of a large number of games and sports have been present in many societies can be seen in several of the articles in part 1 of Earle F. Zeigler, ed., *A History of Sport and Physical Education to 1900* (Champaign, Ill.: Stipes Publishing Co., 1973), especially in Denise Palmer and Maxwell L. Howell, "Sport and Games in Early Civilization," 21–34.

2. As Diamond Jenness has pointed out, the term "tribe" must be used cautiously, since the basic social and political unit of all the Natives discussed below was the band, or even the family. In some cases, the different bands and families were only "tribes" in the sense that they had relatively similar languages, dialects, and customs, and had common interests arising out of the need to cope with the same environments. Diamond Jenness, *The Indians of Canada*, 6th ed. (Ottawa: National Museum of Canada, 1963), especially chap. 9.

3. Ibid., especially 277–87, 308–17, 385–88, 405–22, and the accompanying map; David G. Mandelbaum, "The Plains Cree," *Anthropological Papers of the American Museum of Natural History* XXXVII, pt. 2 (1940): 165–87; Arthur J. Ray, *Indians in the Fur Trade: Their Role as Hunters, Trappers, and Middlemen in the Lands Southwest of Hudson Bay, 1660–1870* (Toronto: University of Toronto Press, 1974), 20, 22, 101–04.

4. Stewart Culin, "Games of the North American Indians," *Twenty-Fourth Annual Report of the Bureau of American Ethnology to the Smithsonian Institution, 1902–03, by W.H. Holmes, Chief* (Washington: U.S. Government, 1907), 1–846.

5. Mihaly Csikszentmihaly and Stith Bennett, "An Exploratory Model of Play," *American Anthropologist* LXXIII (1971), 47; see also Culin, "Games of the North American Indians," 34–35.

6. Mandelbaum, "The Plains Cree," 236; Culin "Games of the North American Indians," 36–43, 340–42; Wilson D. Wallis, "The Canadian Dakota," *Anthropological Papers of the American Museum of Natural History* XLI, pt. 1 (1947): 37.

7. Culin, "Games of the North American Indians," 36–43, 227, 229–30, 258–59, 270, 272, 316; Mandelbaum, "The Plains Cree," 235, 237; *A Journey from Prince of Wales Fort in Hudson's Bay to the Northern Ocean 1769–1770–1771–1772 by Samuel Hearne*, ed. Richard Glover (Toronto: Macmillan Company of Canada Ltd., 1958), 215.

8. Peter Grant, "The Sauteux Indians about 1804" in *Les Bourgeois de la Compagnie du Nord-Ouest, Recits de Voyages, Lettres et Rapports Inedits Relatifs au Nord-Ouest Canadien*, ed. L.R. Masson (New York: Antiquarian Press Ltd., 1960), 340; *Sixteen Years in the Indian Country. The Journal of Daniel Williams Harmon, 1800–1816*, ed. W. Kaye Lamb (Toronto: Macmillan Company of Canada Ltd., 1957), 225–26; *Andrew*

Graham's Observations on Hudson's Bay, 1767–91, ed. Glyndwr Williams (London: Hudson's Bay Record Society, 1969), 168; Culin, "Games of the North American Indians," 36–43, 68–69, 102–04, 185–86; Mandelbaum, "The Plains Cree," 236–37; Wallis, "The Canadian Dakota," 37.

9. James H. Howard, *The Plains-Ojibwa or Bunji Hunters and Warriors of the Northern Plains with Special Reference to the Turtle Mountain Band* (Vermilion, S.D.: Museum of South Dakota, 1965), 76; Culin, "Games of the North American Indians," 807–08; Mandelbaum, "The Plains Cree," 238; Williams, *Andrew Graham's Observations*, 168.

10. R. Gerald Glassford, "Organization of Games and Adaptive Strategies of the Canadian Eskimo" in *The Cross-Cultural Analysis of Sport and Games*, 81.

11. The games described in this paragraph were widespread among the tribes of the Northwest. See Culin, "Games of the North American Indians," 36–43, 385, 391–93, 403–04, 415–19; Glover, ed., *A Journey from Prince of Wales Fort*, 214; Howard, *The Plains-Ojibwa*, 73–74; Mandelbaum, "The Plains Cree," 234, 237–38.

12. These games are referred to as the most complex, not only because their outcomes would be determined by a wider variety of choices made by more participants, but because "strategic" decisions were probably more important in them than in other physical games or in games of chance. Culin, in his "Games of the North American Indians," 291, points out that the Natives of this continent had no games of "pure" strategy, such as chess. This is true, but Csikszentmihalyi and Bennett, in "An Exploratory Model of Play," 49, correctly criticize those who imply that the absence of games of strategy reveals a lack of the "abstract intellectual skills" required of people in more complex societies. As these two authors point out, "as far as the experience of the player is concerned," games of strategy and games of chance can only be differentiated with difficulty, and their argument would seem to be supported by remarks made by Paul Weiss in *Sport: A Philosophical Inquiry* (Carbondale: South Illinois University Press, 1969), 187–88. In any case, Native people certainly had no trouble learning games of strategy once these had been introduced to them. This is revealed by the renown achieved by some Northwest Natives as draughts players. See Lamb, ed., *Daniel Harmon's Journal*, 226, and Williams, ed., *Andrew Graham's Observations*, 168.

13. Culin, "Games of the North American Indians," 36–43, 700–01; Jenness, *Indians of Canada*, 158.

14. *James Isham's Observations on Hudson's Bay, 1743 and Observations on a Book Entitled A Voyage to Hudson Bay in the Dobbs Gallery, 1749*, ed. E.E. Rich (Toronto: The Champlain Society, 1949), 111; Williams, ed., *Andrew Graham's Observations*, 168.

15. Jenness, *Indians of Canada*, 158; Jerald C. Smith, "The Native American Ball Games" in *Sport in the Socio-Cultural Process*, ed. M. Marie Hart (Dubuque, Iowa: Wm. C. Brown Co., 1972), 351.

16. Grant, "The Sauteux Indians," 337–38. It was probably from the Ojibwa that other tribes of the Northwest learned how to play lacrosse. The suggestion that the Dakota Sioux did so is found in Culin, "Games of the North American Indians," 611. Among those Sioux who settled around Portage la Prairie after the Minnesota massacres of 1862 and 1863, the game was already familiar, as is reported by Wallis in "The Canadian Dakota," 37.

17. Mandelbaum "The Plains Cree," 237. See also Culin, "Games of the North American Indians," 636–42, and Smith, "The Native American Ball Games," 351.

18. Culin, "Games of the North American Indians," 715; Howard, *The Plains-Ojibwa*, 76–78; Jenness, *Indians of Canada*, 158; Mandelbaum, "The Plains Cree," 238.

19. On this, see A. Irving Hallowell, "Ojibwa World View" in *The North American Indians, A Sourcebook*, ed. Roger C. Owen, James J.F. Deetz, and Anthony D. Fisher (Toronto: Collier Macmillan Canada Ltd., 1967), 208–35.

20. Grant, "The Sauteux Indians," 338; Viscount Milton and W.B. Cheadle, *The North-West Passage by Land, Being the Narrative of an Expedition from the Atlantic to the Pacific, Undertaken with the View of Exploring a Route Across the Continent to British Columbia through British Territory, By One of the Northern Passes in the Rocky Mountains*, 6th ed. (Toronto: Coles Publishing Co., 1970, originally published in 1865), 150; *David Thompson's Narrative, 1784–1812*, ed. Richard Glover (Toronto: The Champlain Society, 1962), 262–63; Williams, *Andrew Graham's Observations*, 168.

21. Jenness, *Indians of Canada*, 158; Culin, "Games of the North American Indians," 31, 177, 403–4; Mandelbaum, "The Plains Cree," 23738; Howard, *The Plains-Ojibwa*, 77; Grant, "The Sauteux Indians," 339.

22. Rich, *James Isham's Observations*, 111; Williams, *Andrew Graham's Observations*, 168; Mandelbaum, "The Plains Cree," 338; Grant "The Sauteux Indians," 338–39; Howard, *The Plains-Ojibwa*, 77; Culin, "Games of the North American Indians," 650–52.

23. Glover, ed., *A Journey from Prince of Wales Fort*, 34.

24. Lamb, ed., *Sixteen Years in the Indian Country*, 225. See also the similar statement by Grant, "The Sauteux Indians," 324.

25. One's stamina on foot, for example, could have great bearing on one's success, as is indicated in Glover, ed., *A Journey from Prince of Wales Fort*, 182–83, and in Mandelbaum, "The Plains Cree," 192.

26. Glover, ibid., 67.

27. Ibid., 67–68; Glassford, "Organization of Games and Adaptive Strategies of the Canadian Eskimo," 81; Glover, *David Thompson's Narrative*, 126–27; John West, *The Substance of a Journal During a Residence at the Red River Colony, British North America; and Frequent Excursions among the North-West American Indians in the Years 1820, 1821, 1823* (Yorkshire: S.R. Publishers Ltd., 1966, orginally published in 1824), 188; Glover, ed., *A Journey from Prince of Wales Fort*, 170–71.

28. Culin, "Games of the North American Indians," 564–66; Grant, "The Sauteux Indians," 338; Howard, *The Plains-Ojibwa*, 72.

29. Williams, *Andrew Graham's Observations*, 168. See also Culin, "Games of the North American Indians," 636-37, 639, 652; Grant, "The Sauteux Indians," 338. The Chipewyan were an exception to the general pattern being described here. They seem both to have played a smaller number of games and for lower wagers than the other tribes. Samual Hearne said that they had "but few" games and that these were played for items of "inconsiderable value." This no doubt was related to the fact that, unlike other tribes, especially the ones that lived to the south of them, the Chipewyan did not regard themselves as people of plenty, and had a much greater sense of insecurity. See Glover, ed., *A Journey from Prince of Wales Fort*, 214–15; Culin, "Games of the North American Indians," 36–43; Lamb, ed., *Daniel Harmon's Journal*, 226; West, *The Substance of a Journal*, 177–78.

30. Mandelbaum, "The Plains Cree," 221, 229. Competitive gift-giving in several cultures is discussed in Johan Huizinga, *Homo Ludens: A Study of the Play-Element in Culture* (Boston: Beacon Press, 1955), 55–63.

31. Mandelbaum, "The Plains Cree," 226–27, 229, 246. The Natives were much more inclined than we are to attribute successes or failures to their relationship with the Spirit world. See Rt. Rev. Arsène Turquetil, O.M.I., "Religious Rituals and Beliefs" in *Eskimo of the Canadian Arctic*, ed. Victor F. Valentine and Frank G. Vallee (Toronto: McClelland and Stewart, 1968), especially 47; Hallowell, "Ojibwa World

View," especially 217, 233; Harold E. Driver, *Indians of North America*, 2nd rev. ed. (Chicago: University of Chicago Press, 1969), 396. The required stoicism was usually, but not always, exhibited. See Culin, "Games of the North American Indians," 174, 176; Grant, "The Sauteux Indians," 340; Milton and Cheadle, *The North-West Passage by Land*, 151.

THE BRITISH GARRISON AT HALIFAX: ITS CONTRIBUTION TO THE DEVELOPMENT OF SPORT IN THE COMMUNITY*

ROBERT D. DAY

During the colonial period, British military personnel stationed in the Maritimes were vital to the defence of the territory and the preservation of the new society. Perhaps far more important than their stalwart defensive posture was their social and economic impact on the fledgling communities in the Maritime colonies. This was especially significant in the case of Halifax. Founded by Lord Cornwallis in June, 1749, Halifax was a garrison town from the outset. Throughout the years preceding 1906, when British troops were recalled from Halifax, the British military, both army and naval forces, was a most salient feature of Haligonian life. In their study of Canadian historical geography,[1] Harris and Warkentin concluded that, "The military and government units established at Halifax after 1749 ensured that British institutions would prevail in the region." Sport too, a dominant British institution, was honourably preserved and defended.

The British garrison had a tremendous social impact on the town of Halifax. Despite periodic incidents involving military crime and disputes with civilians, relations were generally amicable. On numerous occasions the military was exalted for "their untiring efforts to conquer the devourer" — fire![2] Soldiers and sailors were lauded for their contributions to the temperance movement[3] and their support of the Naval and Military Bible Society.[4] Annual reviews of the troops in garrison provided a military spectacle to which the citizens of the town flocked. These were especially entertaining on the Queen's birthday when the entire garrison would assemble on the Common

* Barbara Schrodt, ed., *Proceedings, Fourth Canadian Symposium on the History of Sport and Physical Education* (Vancouver: University of British Columbia School of Physical Education and Recreation, 1979).

prior to engaging in a sham-fight, much to the delight of those present.[5]

Of particular interest to the "educated" community were the performances of the amateur theatrical groups in garrison. As early as 1773 the "Gentlemen of the Army and Navy" performed a play for the benefit of the poor, thereby realizing a considerable collection to be distributed to indigent families and the elderly by the ministers and church-wardens of Halifax.[6] Similar performances continued throughout much of the nineteenth century. When the 72nd Highlanders were recalled in 1851, the resident editor voiced the regret that the 72nd Amateurs were leaving without time for one last play.[7] The regimental bands too, were a constant feature of Haligonian social life. Whether the military musicians welcomed incoming troops, joined the theatricals, attended reviews and sporting events, or accompanied leisurely picnics, sleigh rides, and outings, their presence was well received. On one occasion, owing to a previous arrangement, the band could not attend a regatta. Thus, thousands of people attending the 1851 event had no military music for amusement. The editor of the *Nova Scotian* commented that:

> This is the first omission of the kind that ever occurred at a Halifax Regatta. Lacking the usual accompaniment of sweet sounds, many people, forgetful of the splendid display presented to them, voted the Regatta a bore.[8]

Nevertheless, the military maintained a high profile in the social life of Halifax, and in this sport was no exception.

As competitors, military personnel were eager to become involved in any pursuit that resembled a recreational pastime. In doing so, they often added a dimension of skill that contributed to the development and promulgation of a particular sport in the community. Whenever military personnel competed against one another, in any contest, civilians curiously regarded the attributes of the military athletes and rarely failed to be entertained. In July, 1856, the sergeants of the 76th Regiment organized a day of soldier's games and sports at the camp at Point Pleasant. Naturally, the civilian population heard of the proposed event and despite the fact that the games were held on a Thursday, a working day, a "large citizen attendance" viewed capital running, extraordinary leaping, and other sundry sport forms.[9]

Greater community interest was aroused however whenever military athletes tested their mettle against civilians. This was particularly evident on the cricket pitches. One author has even suggested that the success of the civilian cricketers against their military counterparts measured like a barometer the popularity of cricket in

Halifax.[10] Supposedly, whenever the military was defeated, cricket became very popular in the community whereas when the military elevens dominated play, the sport "was thought to be declining." Although the evidence does not completely substantiate this idea, it nevertheless serves to illustrate the potential impact of the military as competitors in community sport.

Military athletes were conspicuous in most sporting activities practised in Halifax. Peter Lindsay has maintained that the impetus given by the military regiments to the game of cricket cannot be too strongly emphasized.[11] This was certainly the case in Halifax. Despite an inauspicious beginning in the eighteenth and early nineteenth centuries, cricket was coming into vogue by 1845. In the summer of that year, the Common was seen to be occupied daily by officers of the garrison, and a formal match was reported between the Royal Rifles and the 43rd Regiment.[12] Following the Crimean War, the 62nd and 63rd Regiments were stationed in the town and helped to generate what might be called the birth of Haligonian cricket. Military matches were frequently reported in 1857 and, by the end of that season, four distinct civilian clubs were in existence.[13] The men of the 63rd were exceptionally proficient at the game and their renowned talents were frequently tested by military and civilian elevens alike. Newspaper reports of matches bore evidence that the excellence of the 63rd Regiment squad in particular encouraged the local development of the sport.

The naval presence in Halifax, which was the summer headquarters of the North American and West Indian Squadron, ensured that local aquatic sport would not be devoid of military competitors. As early as 1754, a race was rowed between a ten-oared barge belonging to H.M.S. *Shoreham* and a five-oared whale-boat, for a prize of 50 guineas.[14] By 1826, regattas were a regular event in Halifax Harbour. Military competition was, however, normally minimal. In the 1840 regatta, only two of sixteen races were specifically designed for military competitors despite the fact that the regatta was organized by the navy.[15] Prior to the 1852 regatta, the editor of the *Nova Scotian* stated that the military was evincing little interest in aquatic sports.[16] This however, proved to be of a temporary nature only. When the regatta was held in September, a level of interest similar to previous years was in evidence as races for the soldiers and sailors were included.[17] Thus, although military competitors were also present at Halifax regattas, their number was far from imposing.

Equestrian sports were similarly indulged in by military personnel. A survey of meetings prior to the demise of the sport in the late 1840s illustrates clearly that a substantial percentage of owners and riders were indeed military officers.[18] Similar participation was evident in sleighing (Tandem Club), athletics, yachting, hunting, and swimming. Only in the roarin' game, curling, was there a noticeable absence of military personages.

As competitors, the military offered a positive stimulus to the development of sport in the town of Halifax. So too, troops were periodically used to police sporting events and thereby contribute to the good order of the day. Despite a contemptuous remark elicited by the editor of the *Acadian Recorder* regarding the use of excessive force, troops patrolled the meetings of the Halifax Turf Club between 1828 and 1832.[19] When the races were resumed in the early 1860s, formal garrison orders, issued by the town major's office, ensured that detachments from each corps in garrison, numbering over two hundred men, were detailed "to be posted for the preservation of order in such a manner as the Field Officer of the Day may direct."[20] Postings such as these certainly made an indirect contribution to the development of sport in the community of Halifax.

Facility construction and maintenance were other areas in which the military contributed to the development of Haligonian sport. Unlike civilian workers whose labour was somewhat static, military fatigue parties were extremely flexible and often pursued the whims of commanding officers. These whims were periodically of a sporting nature. At other times, normally restricted military facilities were made available for spectators, and the loan of actual vessels and property was commonplace.

Horseracing provides a particularly vivid example of the military's role in establishing facilities. Halifax's first race course, constructed in the military exercising ground of the Common in 1768 by Governor Lord William Campbell, was, in the least, a para-military venture.[21] The one mile, oval track was enlarged by the military in 1831 and thereafter admirably met the annual needs of the Halifax Turf Club.[22] Because the section of the Common housing the track had originally been reserved by the military for logistical purposes, their sanction alone was imperative for the development of the race course.[23]

Similar patronage was extended in the pursuit of aquatic sports. Spectators at annual regattas were numerous and each year the Dock Yard was opened to them by the commander-in-chief.[24] Only in 1855 were the habits or movements of the spectators restricted when the vice-admiral declared that the public should confine themselves to the space from the landing to the North Boundary, abstain from smoking, and refrain from selling refreshments within the yard.[25] Furthermore, every year the receiving ship *H.M.S. Pyramus* was offered for the use of the Regatta Committee as a starting and judging platform. Barges and cutters were also loaned to facilitate the travel of committee members and their families. Naval marker buoys distinguished the course. Undoubtedly, without the assistance rendered by the military, specifically the navy, aquatic sports at Halifax would not have attained nor maintained the posture that they did during the nineteenth century.

The Halifax Common too was often maintained by military fatigue parties. Although the ground was normally neglected and remained in a poor state of repair, a city council consideration for negotiating a loan for the improvement of the site was spurred by a guarantee that garrison personnel would contribute their labour.[26] When garrison officers became enthused with cricket in 1845, they were quick to order the levelling of the ground preparatory to laying a carpet of sod.[27] In 1858, the same procedure was followed by a party of soldiers.[28]

The construction and maintenance of facilities are integral to the development of community sport. In Halifax, prior to 1860, most facilities were the result of military patronage. In several instances the military officers were perhaps solely interested in meeting their personal sporting aspirations (e.g., cricket) whereas at other times (e.g., regattas) they most certainly intended to facilitate the sporting opportunities of the citizens of the town.

By lending their prestige and expertise to sporting events, military personnel, particularly high-ranking officers, made another significant contribution to the development of sport in the community. As patrons, stewards, judges, and club officials, the military officers found a ready avenue in which to expend their leisure-time energies while in turn building a positive rapport with the community at large.

In both equestrian and aquatic sports the garrison and squadron officers often formed the backbone of the leadership corps. During the Halifax Turf Club Races of 1841 and 1842, seven of nine track stewards were military officers.[29] One might question whether this simply represented a certain respect for the uniform of the queen. Although this was undoubtedly true in part, the civilian's respect for the integrity and judgement of an officer of the Crown cannot be disputed. A similar degree of respect was surely the reason for entrusting the annual regattas in the able hands of the Royal Navy. Perhaps out of tradition, the vice-admiral commanding was named the patron of the regatta annually. But in 1856, in response to queries regarding the apparent lack of interest about the event, the editor of the *Nova Scotian* assured his anxious readers that preparations would commence when the admiral returned from a sojourn at Quebec.[30] The regatta of 1855 was characteristic of naval patronage. For the twenty race program, three of thirteen men of the Committee of Management were military officers, while one of three umpires was an officer of the Royal Navy as was the starter.[31] In 1857 and 1858, all umpires were personnel of the Royal Navy.[32] In this capacity their contribution was indeed substantial.

As competitors, peace-keepers, facility architects, groundsmen, and sports officials, the contribution of military personnel to the development of Haligonian sport was both significant and important. Despite these attributes, one final feature of their involvement was perhaps more important than all others. Often, it was the officers of the garrison who first introduced sport to the community and in many cases provided the initial impetus required to formulate clubs. Most sporting activities present in Halifax in 1860 could trace their heritage to an initial military foundation.

The first sport to be widely accepted and thereby realize a popular following was the "sport of kings," horse racing. As previously mentioned, the first race course in Halifax was built by the British governor of the province, William Campbell. The officer of the garrison subsequently organized semi-annual races until these were banned by Campbell in 1771.[33] In 1808, the military officers from the various regiments in town re-introduced the equestrian trials of speed for "Gentlemen farmers and Breeders of Horses and all amateurs of that noble animal."[34] In 1825 the Halifax Turf Club was formed by a bevy of officers. The president, secretary, and most of the members were from the ranks of the garrison.[35] Owing to the degree of military involvement in the races during subsequent years, the events were often dubbed the Garrison Races. The *Nova Scotian* concluded that "were it not for the Military and the New Brunswickers, and one or two citizens, 'sporting characters,' our Turf would be a dead letter in sporting annals."[36] Despite this patronage, the sport soon become a "dead letter" and largely remained dormant until the military equestrians again came to the fore in August, 1850.[37] The two-day garrison races were held subsequently in October and were so successful that the *Nova Scotian* proclaimed that: "The Gentlemen of the Garrison deserve great credit for the manner in which every thing was managed."[38] This success was fleeting however. During the following year the "dashing set of fellows" who commanded the 72nd Highlanders were replaced by the 97th Regiment and the proposed "contemplation" to reactivate the sports of the turf failed to materialize.[39] Once again, the sport was absent from the local scene and remained so until 1859 when the military was finally successful in reviving the once fervent pastime.[40] Despite numerous hardships, the military persevered and made horseracing one of the most popular, albeit paradoxical, sport forms in early Halifax.

Aquatic sports were equally dependent upon the enthusiasm of military sponsors. The first regattas to be staged in the town were primarily the products of the Royal Navy. In 1831, it was reported that the regatta had been organized entirely at the expense and management of the officers of the 52nd Regiment.[41] Whenever interest in the "watery sports" appeared to wane, the Royal Navy was quick in their attempt to stimulate a renewed interest. In 1850, for example, the officers of the squadron flag ship, the *H.M.S. Wellesley*, invited the garrison and the citizens of Halifax to join them in "getting up a regatta."[42] The response was overwhelming. As a result of overtures such as these, local scribes often asserted that the British Navy was inclined to promote aquatic sports solely for the amusement of the citizens of the town.[43] Indeed, the Royal Navy might well be considered the primary stimulus behind what proved to be the most popular and successful maritime sporting activity.

Similarly, the origins of curling were rooted in a large measure within military ranks. Two individuals were particularly important. One, Capt. Houston Stewart of the *H.M.S. Menai*, later the Vice-Admiral commanding the North American and West Indian Station, first oversaw the introduction of the game to Haligonians while wintering in the town about 1824.[44] Apparently, a local club was formed during that winter.[45] In 1851, the president of the Halifax Curling Club was Capt. H.M. Drummond of the 42nd Royal Highlanders. Although significant as a club officer alone, Drummond later ensured lively competition within the club. Upon returning to England in 1852, Drummond sent a pair of silver mounted curling stones to Halifax with the intention of stimulating annual interclub competition.[46] Ironically, however, other evidence of military participation in the sport is strangely absent.

Other activities too were sponsored by the garrison. Military tandem clubs were extremely active in the 1820s and although they eventually lost much of their appeal, they were reactivated by garrison officers in 1850.[47] In 1809, several officers formed a pedestrian club although the success of the venture has escaped record.[48] Aquatic sport was expanded in 1857 when the Halifax Yacht Club was formed. Many of the sixty-odd members were military officers, including both the vice-commodore and the vice-chairman.[49] In the first matches for the club's two Challenge Cups, five of sixteen entrants were military officers.[50] Whenever a new sport was introduced to the citizens of Halifax, or a new club formed, it was highly likely that members of the British armed forces would be among the primary instigators behind the scheme.

The British garrison and naval forces stationed at Halifax did make a significant contribution to the development of sport in the community. With the exception of perhaps cricket, however, military personnel at no time appeared overwhelmingly dominant as competitors. This may be explained by numbers alone. The military forces, numbering approximately 2000 to 4000, were simply dwarfed by the larger population of the town. This does not mean that they were insignificant as competitors. Conversely, they served to generate much enthusiasm among the townspeople and definitely added colour to most sporting scenes.

The impact of the garrison on facility construction and maintenance was equally significant. Without the lead taken by the troops, many sport forms may have waned while others may never have realized a popular following. Facility construction alone was integral to the development of Haligonian sport. In this the military took a strong lead.

Military officers were generally considered to be men of upright character and strong moral fibre. They were educated men and possessed the organizational abilities which endeared them to Halifax sportsmen. As a result, officers were frequently elected or appointed as stewards, judges, umpires, patrons, and club officials. Their expertise and integrity were highly respected and signalled a major contribution to Haligonian sport.

The culmination of these qualities and resultant levels of sport participation in the community were clearly illustrated by the numerous examples of sport and club formation sponsored by the military. Military personnel participated to a significant degree in nearly every sporting activity that was practised in Halifax. This alone is ample justification for surmising that, without the military patronage exhibited prior to 1860, the face of Haligonian sport would be somewhat emaciated.

Notes

1. R. Cole Harris and John Warkentin, *Canada Before Confederation* (Toronto: Oxford University Press, 1974), 184.

2. *Nova Scotian*, Aug. 17, 1846, 260.

3. Ibid., July 3, 1843, 211.

4. Ibid., Jan. 18, 1847, 21.

5. Ibid., May 29, 1848, 170.

6. *Nova Scotia Gazette*, April 20, 1773.

7. *Nova Scotian*, Sept. 15, 1851, 289.

8. Ibid., 240.

9. Ibid., July 14, 1856, 3.

10. Robert Moss, "Cricket in Nova Scotia During the Nineteenth Century," *Canadian Journal of the History of Sport and Physical Education* IX, 2 (Dec. 1978), 61–62.

11. Peter L. Lindsay, "A History of Sport in Canada, 1807–1867" (Ph.D. dissertation, University of Alberta, 1969), 90.

12. *Nova Scotian*, Aug. 4, 1845, 242.

13. Ibid., July 6, 1857, 2; July 20, 1857, 2.

14. *Nova Scotia Gazette*, July 27, 1854.

15. *Nova Scotian*, Aug. 6, 1840, 263.

16. Ibid., Sept. 13, 1852, 299.

17. Ibid., Sept. 20, 1852, 307.

18. Ibid., Aug. 31, 1825; July 23, 1840, 238; Aug. 12, 1884, 271.

19. David F. Howell, "A History of Horseracing in Halifax, Nova Scotia, 1749–1867" (M.A. thesis, Dalhousie University, 1972), 31.

20. *Halifax Garrison Orders*, Public Archives of Nova Scotia, MG 12 HQ, vol. 109: 64–65.

21. *Nova Scotian*, Aug. 23, 1758.

22. *Acadian Recorder*, Sept. 17, 1831, 3.

23. Howell, "History of Horseracing," 12.

24. *Nova Scotian*, Oct. 15, 1849, 333; Sept. 15, 1851, 290.

25. Ibid., July 30, 1855, 1.

26. Ibid., March 8, 1852, 75; *Halifax Garrison Orders*, Public Archives of Nova Scotia, MG 12 HQ, vol. 102: 187.

27. *Nova Scotian*, Ibid., Aug. 4, 1845, 242.

28. Ibid., June 7, 1858, 2.

29. Ibid., May 13, 1841, 151; June 9, 1842, 179.

30. Ibid., Aug. 11, 1856, 2.

31. Ibid., July 30, 1855, 1; Aug. 22, 1855, 2.

32. Ibid., July 27, 1857, 2; Sept. 13, 1858, 5.

33. Howell, "History of Horseracing," 4–5.

34. *Royal Gazette*, June 21, 1808, 3.

35. *Nova Scotian*, May 11, 1825, 159.

36. Ibid., Aug. 10, 1842, 251.

37. Ibid., Aug. 12, 1850, 254.

38. Ibid., Oct. 14, 1850, 321.

39. Ibid., Aug. 18, 1851, 259.

40. Howell, "History of Horseracing," 54.

41. *Nova Scotian*, Aug. 10, 1831, 248.

42. Ibid., Aug. 19, 1850, 259.

43. Ibid., Aug. 4, 1851, 242; Aug. 16, 1852, 261.

44. Ibid., Dec. 7, 1857, 3.

45. Lindsay, "A History of Sport," 24.

46. *Nova Scotian*, Dec. 15, 1851, 395; March 20, 1854, 1.

47. Ibid., Feb. 28, 1853, 65; Nov. 11, 1850, 354.

48. *Royal Gazette*, May 23, 1809.

49. *Nova Scotian*, May 11, 1857, 2; August 24, 1859, 2.

50. Ibid., Sept. 14, 1857, 2.

AMUSEMENT AND SOCIAL LIFE IN THE RURAL DISTRICTS*

EDWIN C. GUILLET

The life of the pioneer settlers in Canada was one of hardship, but the difficulties under which they lived were to some extent relieved by co-operation, not only in work but in play. The "bees" which were so characteristic of early life in Upper Canada supplied that social intercourse which is essential to a well-balanced life. Judged by modern standards some pioneer amusements were crude, leading occasionally to regrettable excesses; but there was a wholesomeness among the vast majority of the people which pervaded their social life, and frowned upon any variation from the spirit of honest fun.

In considering the pleasures of the pioneers it must first be understood that "it takes all kinds of people to make a world"; what is one person's pleasure is another's aversion. There were many who considered all worldly amusement sinful, and to be avoided at any cost. Prominent among these were the Friends or Quakers, who often took disciplinary action against members of their societies guilty of backsliding; we find, for example, that the disfavour of their co-religionists fell upon some who "had attended a noisy, unruly and unlawful assembly called a chivaree"; and likewise upon three Quakers on Yonge Street who were "guilty of assisting in tarring and carrying a woman on a rail."[1] In addition to the more serious breaches of conduct — swearing, drinking, fighting, gambling, immorality and horse-racing — other less harmful diversions, such as card-playing, music and dancing in one's home, were deprecated, and persons persisting in such practices were expelled from the society.

Though social life in a Quaker community was greatly restricted, yet most Quakers had the same sense of humour to be found among other sections of the population, even though it was usually hidden by a

* Edwin C. Guillet, *Early Life in Upper Canada* (Toronto: Ontario Publishing Co., 1933), 295–310.]

solemn face and quaint garb. In later days they sometimes had debating societies, while at all times

> their Yearly, Quarterly and Monthly meetings filled a social as well as religious need in a pioneer state of society which was very simple and had few outlets for demands of this kind. Members would travel great distances to attend these gatherings which were the occasion of lavish hospitality. Indeed these were notable social events which had a large place in the life of the early Quaker community.[2]

The early Methodists were similarly opposed to amusements of a worldly nature; in the days of the first class-meetings the violin was forbidden as a sinful musical instrument (if such a thing is possible!), chiefly because it was commonly used to supply the music for dancing. This prohibition of the one common source of music left them without any, for the accordeon and concertina were not invented until 1829, while melodeons and "pianofortes" were not common in Canada until many years later.

The scarcity of musical instruments led to greater stress being laid upon singing in the home and the church. Singing-schools were organised each winter in many neighbourhoods and provided a means of social intercourse, though the unfortunate singing-master often found it difficult to keep order among those who did not come to sing. The Methodists were particularly noted for singing in unison at their religous services, the congregational singing at the York Conference of 1831 being described as "most delightful and heavenly."[3] The Jesuit missionaries had a small organ in Quebec as early as 1661, but organs were uncommon a century ago in the churches of Upper Canada. One method of obtaining the key in which the congregation sang consisted in the striking of a tuning-fork by the leader.

While not pleasures in the usual sense of the word, the class-meeting and the camp-meeting of the Methodists often provided a "love-feast" which, despite occasional emotional excesses, may be considered as a form of higher spiritual pleasure. The services of the other denominations, while more orthodox and impersonal, were equally important in the social life of the community. Church services were early held in courthouses or other government buildings, in taverns, stores or private homes, until it was possible to erect a church building by the subscription and labour of the members.

In most denominations the service was most informal, though a sense of decorum was apparent in the custom of men and women sitting in separate sections of the room. Sometimes the men removed their coats in warm weather, and people frequently walked in and out during the course of the service; while often the week's mail was distributed at the church door at the close. There were Sunday schools for the children in connection with most churches, and in some cases they had a few books to be distributed among those whose education was sufficient to enable them to read. In fact the social life of the pioneer community centred in the church and the school, the clergyman and the teacher being not infrequently the same person. Social intercourse was extended, and education as well as amusement supplied by tea-meetings and socials, singing-schools and spelling-matches, literary and debating societies, though such organised activities were seldom found during the first years of settlement.

Many of the inhabitants of Upper Canada were not as scrupulous with regard to their pleasures as were the Quakers and early Methodists. There were many, too, who were forced by the manners and customs of the times to join upon some occasions in questionable activities which they would ordinarily have avoided. One of the worst of these customs, and the most far-reaching in its effects, was the excessive drinking of spirituous liquors, a habit which, though by no means universal, pervaded social life in all parts of the country, and was as prominent in the backwoods as in the towns. Whisky was early considered an antidote to the hardships and misfortunes of pioneer life, and a means temporarily to forget care and trouble.

At almost every gathering liquor was served in abundance, and it was considered in the thirties that he was "a moderate man who does not exceed four glasses in the day."[4] Many people attended bees, weddings, auction sales, and other social assemblies merely for the purpose of drinking; liquor was frequently taken to revival camp-meetings and consumed by those who came to scoff but did not remain to pray. Even funeral wakes were not exempt from strong drink, and on at least one occasion "so hilarious did the participants become that the corpse was offered a share of the beverage."[5] The poor quality of the drink often made its effects much worse: one writer compares the usual liquor to fire and brimstone, "made of frosty potatoes, hemlock, pumpkins and black mouldy rye."[6]

The number of inns and taverns that existed in Upper Canada in former times would surprise the present generation. Every crossroad had one or more, and the main highways supported many dozens of them. The small city of Toronto had in 1850 a total of 152 taverns and 206 beer shops to supply a population of about 30 000 and such farmers as brought their produce thither to market. Distilleries were among the first establishments in most settlements, and provided large quantities of cheap liquor, usually obtainable at 25c a gallon, or even less; and almost all taverns were maintained largely by the sale of strong drink. A traveller refers to "taverns and low drinking-houses" as the chief places of public amusement in Upper Canada;[7] while another writer[8] found "every inn, tavern, and beer shop filled at all hours with drunken, brawling fellows; and the quantity of ardent spirits consumed by them will truly astonish you." Men went from tavern to tavern treating one another all round, and the amount of liquor consumed often led to fatal accidents. Of the sudden deaths investigated by coroner's juries, excessive whisky-drinking was found to be by far the most frequent cause.

The temperance movement originated in the United States, and spread into Canada at the commencement of the second quarter of the nineteenth century. Montreal was long the temperance centre of Canada, and there the first Temperance Society was formed in 1828. A few months later a number of township societies had been formed in Upper Canada, and by 1832 there were 10 000 members of such organisations in the province. The early societies usually restricted their warfare against intoxicants to whisky, rum, and brandy, and emphasised temperance rather than prohibition; but in later years beer and wine were added to the proscribed list, and in 1835 the first of a large number of Total Abstinence societies was organised in St. Catharines. The reaction against the drinking habits of the times gathered headway down through the years, though the societies were opposed by many as a "Yankee" institution, which reason, and his own personal appetite, led Colonel Talbot to dub them "damned cold water drinking societies."[9]

Apart from the excessive use of intoxicants there were among the pioneers no very harmful habits which are not present to at least as great an extent now. The use of snuff was comparatively harmless, and both men and women were more or less fond of it in the earlier periods of settlement. The tobacco habit, while by no means universal, was quite general among all classes of the male population. Women were not usually addicted either to tobacco or intoxicants; some of the old ladies did enjoy smoking an old, blackened clay pipe, but cigarettes had not been invented, and smoking by young women in general is a very recent innovation.

Some of the girls of a century ago were not, however, averse to appearing sophisticated and risqué upon occasion. Joseph Pickering notes in his journal in 1826 that while he was stopping at Loder's Tavern on Talbot Street

> some smart lasses came in during the evening, who live just by, most of whom took a smoke with the landlord and the landlady, passing the short black pipe from one to another! Disgusting as this practise is, it is not so much so as one in common use in the eastern part of Maryland, of girls taking

> a "rubber" of snuff — that is, taking as much snuff as will lie
> on the end of the forefinger out of a box, and rubbing it
> round the inside of the mouth![10]

There were many evils traceable in a large measure to the excessive
drinking habits. Drunkenness, "the vice and curse of the country,"[11]
was generally accompanied by profanity, immorality, lawlessness
and crime. Boisterous activities and cruel habits were considered
amusing by people of low or degenerate mentality. Murder and rob-
bery were common, and while some men stole sheep, horses and cat-
tle, others repaid a grudge or satisfied a depraved desire by maiming
them. Burning barns, breaking windows, smashing store signs, and
other types of horseplay and vandalism, were of frequent occurrence,
and even in modern times such activities are occasionally carried on
where the vigilance of the police and magistrates is insufficient to
prevent them. In the first years of villages and towns there was frequently a similar disregard for the rights of property, and early
newspapers contain notices of the following type:

> Two Dollars Reward. — Whereas on Friday night last some
> evil-disposed person fired a gun at the house of the sub-
> scriber,...whereby upwards of twenty squares of glass were
> broken, and the premises otherwise injured, the above
> reward will be paid on the conviction of the offenders.[12]

Similarly in York twenty dollars reward was offered for the apprehension of the man "who is so depraved and lost to every sense of
social duty as to cut with an axe or knife the withes which bound some
of the fence round the late Chief Justice's farm on Yonge Street, and
to throw down the said fence."[13]

On many occasions the public conscience was aroused by flagrant
disregard for the principles of law and order. Mob justice was not infrequent in some parts of Upper Canada, particularly where the
regular course of law enforcement was tardy, and in instances where
a moral but not a legal crime had been committed. Prominent in this
connection was the "Old Sorrel," a species of summary justice dealt
out to those who had offended the sense of morality of the neighbor-
hood. This punishment consisted in tarring and feathering the culprit,
with the addition, at times, of "riding the fence rail"; anyone treated
in this manner was expected to leave the district immediately. Alter-
cations arising from some types of mob rule were usually ignored as
far as possible by the authorities, even where deaths resulted, though
as civilisation advanced such occurrences could not be tolerated and
have fortunately become infrequent.

A few men of low, if not perverted tastes took a savage delight in the sufferings of animals, and were to be found — as they occasionally are at the present day — carrying on such sports (?) as bull- or bear-baiting, dog-fighting and cock-fighting. Two centuries earlier these crude activities had been quite common in England, especially during the period of reaction which followed the Puritan repression of Commonwealth days; but even at that time John Evelyn considered them "butcherly sports, or, rather, barbarous cruelties,...a rude and dirty pastime";[14] while Samuel Pepys, whose interests were universal, and who was by no means fussy in his amusements, found cock-fighting "no great sport," and soon "had enough of it" and its accompaniments —"swearing, cursing and betting."[15] In Canada these so-called old English sports so offended the public sense of fair play and decency that they have been prohibited by law in modern times.

Wrestling and fighting were long popular public amusements. Gourlay stated that "the vulgar practice of pugilism, a relic of the savage state," was declining in 1817,[16] but it by no means died out. It was commonly considered that the best man was he who could knock his opponent senseless, and seldom did the rules of the Marquis of Queensbury apply to any such pugilistic encounters. Feats of strength and skill were deservedly popular at bees and other public gatherings; in fact the supremacy of a township frequently rested upon the ability of its representatives to dispose of all comers in some athletic competition. Races were less popular than wrestling or fighting for public spectacles of this kind. On one occasion the "Fifth-towners," as the inhabitants of the Township of Marysburgh were called, considered that the "Fourth-towners," across the Bay of Quinte in Adolphustown, were "too smart and stuck-up"; so they challenged them to pick out three of their best wrestlers to settle the relative "smartness" of the townships. Needless to say they were not to be "stumped," and sent Samuel Dorland, Samuel Casey and Paul Trumpour to uphold the reputation of Adolphustown against the chosen men of Marysburgh, whose names have not come down to use, perhaps because they were worsted in the encounter.

> The hour was fixed, and a nearby field was selected where hundreds were on hand "to see fair play" and help decide which township had the best men. These were all noted athletes, and they were then young and in their prime. Samuel Dorland, afterwards a colonel in the militia and a leading official in the Methodist Church, was an expert wrestler, and used to boast, even in his old days, that he seldom if ever met a man who could lay him on his back. He soon had his man down. Samuel Casey, who afterwards became

a leading military officer and a prominent justice of the peace, was one of the strongest men in the township, but not an expert wrestler. He was so powerful in the legs that his opponent, with all his skill, could not trip him up, and at last got thrown down himself. Paul Trumpour, who was the head of what is now the largest family in the township, was not so skilled in athletics; but he was a man of immense strength. He got his arms well fixed around his man and gave him such terrible "bear-hugs" that the poor fellow soon cried out "enough," to save his ribs from getting crushed in, and that settled it. The Fourth-town championship was not again disputed.[17]

There were among the pioneers many who delighted in the opportunities which Canada afforded for the field sports which they had enjoyed in the Old Land. Dr. Dunlop fills up twenty-one pages in describing — for the benefit of immigrants! — the rare hunting, gaming, hawking and fishing available in Canada.[18] But while some had leisure in which they could enjoy such pastimes, most of the early settlers were too busy to enter into them unless necessity compelled them to obtain food in that manner. Field sports cannot be described in detail here, but it is sufficient to say that fish, birds and animals now almost extinct were obtainable a century ago in a profusion which would astonish the sportsman of today.

Among the activities of this type which were sometimes a necessity was raccoon-hunting. Many a boy and his dog amused themselves in the green-corn season driving the raccoons from the fields to the woods, from which, if no other artifice availed, they were forced by felling the trees. The hunting of deer may be taken as a typical Canadian field sport. A man who frequently engaged in such amusements during the pioneer period considered that deer-hunting was

a very exciting sport; but I prefer still-hunting (or deer-stalking, as it is called in the Highlands of Scotland), to driving them into the lakes and rivers with hounds. The deer are not now [1853] nearly so numerous as they formerly were....To give my readers some idea how plentiful these wild denizens of the forest were some years since, I need only mention that a trapper with whom I was acquainted, and four of his companions, passed my house on a small raft on which lay the carcasses of thirty-two deer — the trophies of a fortnight's chase near Stoney Lake. The greater number of these were fine bucks.

I once had seventeen deer hanging up in my barn at one time — the produce of three days' sport, out of which I had the good fortune to kill seven. Parties are now made yearly every October to Stoney Lake, Deer Bay, or the River Trent. I do not know anything more pleasant than these excursions, especially if you have agreeable companions, a warm camp, and plenty to eat and drink.... This is one of the great charms of Canadian life, particularly to young sportsmen from the Mother Country, who require here neither license nor qualification to enable them to follow their game; but may rove in chase of deer or other game at will.[19]

Bird life was found in similar profusion a century ago. Joseph Pickering notes in his diary on April 8, 1826: "Pigeons, in great flocks, going out daily northward; some people with nets and decoy pigeons will catch several hundred in a day, when they sometimes take only their breasts and salt them down, and make beds of their feathers."[20] In the late summer of the same year he observed that "pigeons again made their appearance in large flocks, as also wild turkey; partridges, larger than the English breed, and quails, less than those of Europe, are also numerous."[21] The wild turkeys sometimes weighed fifteen pounds when dressed.

Fishing, which Izaak Walton so appropriately called "the contemplative man's recreation,"[22] has been a noted amusement in Canada from the earliest times. Even the Indian was inclined to look upon it as an exciting pleasure rather than a means to obtain food. Many a pioneer participated in the enjoyments of fishing in a day when even a poor fisherman could well-nigh fill his canoe in a few hours. In general the sport has changed, as the years have passed, from spearing to angling; but even if no fish are caught, the unsuccessfully angler's consolation is the same as it was three centuries ago when Robert Burton wrote: "Fishing is still and quiet; and if so be the Angler catch no Fish, yet he hath a wholesome walk to the Brookside, pleasant shade by the sweet silver streams; he hath good air, and sweet smells of fine fresh meadow flowers; he hears the melodious harmony of Birds."[23]

A sporting event early characteristic of the Candian summer was the regatta. Canoe races in which Indian and *voyageur* vied with settler aroused the greatest interest among those who lived near the waterways. John MacTaggart, writing in the eighteen-twenties, considered that there were "few finer scenes than a Canadian Regatta: fifty canoes on the smooth broad lake, *voyageurs* fancifully adorned, the song up in full chorus, blades of the paddles flashing in the sun as they rapidly lift and dip, while the watery foam-bells hurry into the hollow of the wakes."[24] The first regattas were on the St. Lawrence or the Ottawa, but as early as 1838 there were similar aquatic competitions at Fenelon Falls, and at other settlements in the "back lakes" region of the Newcastle District, which was to become in later years so popular a summer resort.

Just as characteristic of Canada were the sports of winter. Snowshoe and dog-sled had long been necessary for winter travel over Indian trail and along frozen lake and river, and they were supplemented in the days of settlement by sledge and carriole. Travel by carriole was just as pleasurable in winter as the canoe was in summer, and it was a time when travelling was but seldom pleasant. The settler's sleigh was usually home-made and its body ran very close to the ice; while that of the "gentlemen" in the towns had runners, and was often a very elaborate affair. The carriole had no covering, so travellers were well bundled up in furs. Sleighing-parties have remained a characteristic Canadian winter pleasure though the motorcar is gradually replacing horse-drawn vehicles.

Tobogganing, or, as sometimes spelled, "traboggining," was another winter sport early enjoyed by the young people. Skating, which originated in Holland, was also a favourite amusement, though it was frequently considered improper for girls to participate in such a form of pleasurable exercise. Curling commenced in Canada towards the close of the eighteenth century, when some of the officers of the garrison at Quebec became interested in the game as a means of relieving a monotonous life. In Upper Canada the game was first played at Kingston about 1820, and on the Don River at York nine years later; soon afterwards it was popular in many another settlement, particularly where the Scotch predominated. In this sport, as in many another activity, the rural settler frequently walked many miles to join his brethren in the nearest village, and all gathered at a favourite stretch of ice on river or lake.

Visiting has always been a popular diversion among all classes of people. Formal calls were made by the social set in the towns, and very informal visits in the rural districts. Births, marriages and deaths provided an excellent opportunity for the exchange of civilities, and it was usual to provide guests with food, and frequently with lodging as well; it is said that farmers thought it "nothing extraordinary to make an excursion of six or seven hundred miles in the winter in their sleighs to see their friends."[25] Sunday was the great day for local visiting, and it was generally considered that no time was so appropriate for "sparking" (courting) as Sunday evening. The improvement of roads and the invention of the motor-car have greatly facilitated travel, and might be presumed to have increased visiting; that this is not the case is the fault of the great amusement of "listening-in," not only to the radio, but also of an older variety — that major sport of many communities — listening in over the party telephone line!

Surprise parties, where ten or twelve families suddenly descended upon the home — and sometimes the larder — of mutual friends, were a popular form of visiting in the rural districts, and have survived to the present. The women obtained a considerable proportion of their pleasure in visits, for their activities were more restricted than those of the men. Many pioneer women seldom went anywhere beyond a neighbour's, the market, or the general store; their lives were often monotonous, for it was usually considered improper for females to enter into the men's activities, and there were in the country few libraries and fewer readable books. The men, on the other hand, frequently had occasion to visit the town, and their contact with the official, the merchant and the tradesman was not only diverting, but affected, even if unconsciously, their attitude towards life, and lessened the monotony of their existence. They also engaged from time to time in hunting and fishing, visited taverns, attended bees, fairs, horseraces, militia training, circuses, and elections; some also entered into curling, bandyball, lacrosse, football, quoits, and other sports.

Social intercourse among farmers was increased through the activities of Agricultural Societies and kindred organisations. There were a few societies in existence in Upper Canada before 1825, the first being at Niagara in 1793; but they did not become important throughout the province until the thirties and forties. With them came the local fairs and, later, the Provincial Exhibition, which were of value not only in developing agriculture but also in that they provided some contact with the outside world; horseracing, ploughing-matches, and, in later years, amusements more or less commercialised, were prominent at all fairs, and soon became an attraction of outstanding importance to the average citizen.

Associations among farmers' wives were not formed as early as the Agricultural Societies among the men, but in later years the Women's Institutes became increasingly important in developing social life. The Temperance Societies which became so common in rural Ontario in the forties and fifties provided many people with opportunities for advancement and pleasure similar to those afforded by the agricultural organisations, for in both cases papers were read and debates held upon subjects of popular interest.

The early settlers were too busy to indulge in amusement very often, so it was customary to crowd a great deal into one "spree," as a social gathering was often called. A bee, a wedding, or an auction sale was not always over in one day, for the participants frequently extended the jollification several days longer. This was particularly true of a wedding, which was a notable community event in the early days. A wedding procession of lumber-wagons was often a feature, and "each gallant was supposed to support his partner upon his knee, and thus economise room."[26]

While fighting was common enough at bees and other gatherings, nothing of the kind was allowed at a wedding celebration, where it was considered that everyone should be good-natured. A dance was the inevitable concomitant of a wedding; in fact to dance until daylight during several succeeding nights was not uncommon. The older people seldom attended the wedding celebration, probably feeling that their absence would be appreciated; but they usually joined in the dances.

A species of amusement once very common, and still to be found in some parts of Ontario, was the charivari or chivaree; this was, in early times, particularly connected with second marriages, or when the parties were unequal in age, or unpopular. The custom was to be found in parts of England, and in Canada it originated among the French in Quebec. Gourlay wrote early in the pioneer period concerning the usual reasons which led to the chivaree:

> I have observed no essential peculiarity in the funerals or weddings of this country; but there is a singular custom of "chereverreeing," as it is called, a newly-married couple, where the match is thought to be unequal or unseasonable; as between an old man and a young girl, or within a short period after the death of a former husband or wife. Sometimes it is in consequence of the offence so frequently caused by a neglect of invitation to the wedding.[27]

The chivaree party would steal up to the home of the newly-wedded, usually after midnight, and suddenly music (?) from tin horns, horse-bells, "bull-roarers," "horse-fiddles," tin pans, and copper kettles would burst upon the ears of those within the house. If the bridegroom did not come forth and meet the demands for refreshments, or money (to be spent at the tavern), the discordant uproar would continue the rest of the night, and often on succeeding nights. Where the marriage was considered particularly objectionable the charivari was much more serious than a serenade. The roysterers have been known to climb to the roof of the house and close up the opening of the chimney with the intention of smoking the wedding party out; fighting, and occasionally death, resulted from such proceedings. Gourlay noted that the chivaree was sometimes a subject of prosecution, but that it was generally considered best to regard it "with good humour, as a joke unworthy of serious notice."[28]

Bees were, perhaps, the most noted occasions of amusement in the rural districts in pioneer days. An early settler in the Bay of Quinté district refers to them as "great institutions in those days. Every settler was licensed to make two or three each year, provided he furnished a good 'pot pie,' and plenty of grog, and never made any objections to his guests fighting."[29] Races, gymnastics, wrestling matches, feats of strength such as putting the stone and hurling the hammer, axemanship, and skill in handling recalcitrant oxen or horses provided amusement for many of the younger people at bees. They spent the evening in dancing, while the older men and women who did not care to dance concluded the day's work by conversation about their common interests — the crops, prices, local politics, and such news as had come from the Old Land.

Paring, quilting, and the other domestic bees supplied the women with an opportunity to become acquainted; here were discussed family affairs, house furnishings, recipes, new arrivals in the neighbourhood, and the usual run of petty scandal. It has been said that these bees have never been equalled as "a clearing-house for gossip";[30] but the men learned just as much news at the tavern, the blacksmith shop, the general store and, in later days, at the barber shop, though the last-named sanctuary disappeared when bobbed hair became the fashion!

The dances or "hops" which almost invariably closed every bee were frequently held in the barn. Games and "forfeits" alternated with dancing, and were frequently accompanied by much flirtation. Such "kissing bees," like all other evils, are stated by some writers to have originated in the United States; though it may be said that in general these amusements were then considered quite innocent, whatever opinion might be held by later generations.

Notes

1. A.G. Dorland; *A History of the Society of Friends in Canada* (1927), 10.
2. Ibid.
3. Anson Green, *Life and Times* (1877), 153.
4. Letter of William Hutton in the *British Farmer's Magazine*, April, 1835, 114.
5. M.A. Garland and J.J. Talman, *Pioneer Drinking Habits and the Rise of the Temperance Agitation in Upper Canada* (Ontario Historical Society Papers and Records XXVII, 345).
6. John MacTaggart, *Three Years in Canada*, vol. 1 (1829), 199.
7. Anna Jameson, *Winter Studies and Summer Rambles in Canada*, vol. 1 (1838), 293.
8. "An Ex-Settler," *Canada in the Years 1832, 1833, and 1834* (1835), 25.
9. Speech at St. Thomas, April 23, 1832. See the *Talbot Papers*, section II, 124-6. (*Transactions* of the Royal Society of Canada, 1909).
10. Joseph Pickering, *Inquiries of an Emigrant* (1831) Nov. 2, 1826.

11. Jameson, *Winter Studies and Summer Rambles*, vol. 1, 76.

12. *Cobourg Star*, Jan. 18, 1831.

13. *Upper Canada Gazette*, July 23, 1803.

14. John Evelyn, *Diary*, June 16, 1670.

15. Samuel Pepys, *Diary*, Dec. 21, 1663, and April 6, 1668.

16. Robert Gourlay, *A Statistical Account of Upper Canada*, vol. 1 (1822), 252–54.

17. Thomas W. Casey, *Old Time Records*. Quoted in W.S. Herrington, *The History of Lennox and Addington* (1913), 137.

18. William Dunlop, *Statistical Sketches of Upper Canada* (1832), 32–52.

19. Samuel Stickland: *Twenty-seven Years in Canada West*, vol. 1 (1853), 78–79.

20. Pickering, *Inquiries of an Emigrant*, April 8, 1826.

21. Ibid., Aug. 26, 1826.

22. See the title page of the first edition of Izaak Walton, *The Compleat Angler* (1653).

23. Robert Burton, *The Anatomy of Melancholy* (1652, 1927), 478.

24. MacTaggart, *Three Years in Canada*, vol. 1, 308.

25. D'Arcy Boulton, *Sketch of His Majesty's Province of Upper Canada* (1805), 11.

26. "An old lady in Ameliasburgh" quoted in William Canniff, *History of the Settlement of Upper Canada* (1869), 239.

27. Gourlay, *A Statistical Account of Upper Canada*, vol. 1, 254.

28. Ibid.

29. "An old settler in Ameliasburgh" quoted in Canniff, *History of the Settlement of Upper Canada*, 628.

30. W.S. Herrington, *Pioneer Life on the Bay of Quinté* (Lennox and Addington Historical Society, *Papers and Records*, VI, 17).

THE SPORTS, GAMES, RECREATIONS, AND PASTIMES OF THE FUR TRADERS: LEISURE AT YORK FACTORY*

MICHAEL PAYNE

> In order to form a just estimation of the character of any particular people, it is absolutely necessary to investigate the Sports and Pastimes most generally prevalent among them. War, policy, and other contingent circumstances, may effectually place men at different times, in different points of view; but, when we follow them into their retirements, where no disguise is necessary, we are most likely to see them in their true state, and may best judge of their natural disposition.[1]

Joseph Strutt first offered this useful advice in 1801, but few social historians have followed his lead in pursuing their subjects into their retirements. The reasons for this range from a simple belief that sport and games are not "a matter to be taken seriously,"[2] to a sense that they are a "minor tributary to the mainstream of history,"[3] and that therefore, while not unimportant, they were less important than the study of subjects like "war, policy, and other contingent circumstances."

This view has been particularly strong in Canadian historiography. There have been very few attempts to write even general narrative histories of sport or leisure activity in Canada, let alone to place sport or leisure in any social, technological, or economic context.[4] As far as most text-book Canadian history is concerned, Canadians are more likely to be resolving political crises than worrying about the fortunes of the local team or playing for it themselves. Most histories of the fur

* From Michael Payne, "A Social History of York Factory, 1788–1870," Microfiche on file, Canadian Park Service, Prairie and Northern Region, Winnipeg, 1984, 75–79, 81–94, 114–124.

trade, even of fur trade society, adopt much the same point of view. Some authors do concede a certain recreational aspect to hunting or mention competition between canoe brigades,[5] and almost all comment unfavourably on the tendency to overindulge in alcohol. Rare indeed is the historian who mentions football, fireworks, or whist amongst the diversions of the fur trade.[6] The failure to consider the recreations of fur trade society means that an important part of that society is ignored. This paper will seek to redress that oversight to come extent, for York Factory at least, by pursuing York's residents "into their retirements" as Strutt suggested.

Some of the terms to be used in this paper have become subjects of heated definitional debate amongst social scientists, who for the most part have paid more attention than historians to sport and leisure. Everyone seems to agree that all cultures in all periods have included some sort of "play" activities. Indeed games, diversions, and amusements of one sort or another are one of the few universal or near universal manifestations of culture.[7] Debate arises when one attempts to define "leisure," "recreation," "sport," or "game." For example, there are those who argue that "leisure has certain traits that are characteristic only of the civilization born from the Industrial Revolution."[8] Their argument is that prior to the Industrial Revolution people had plenty of time away from work, but that work and time-off were interconnected and collectively governed. "Modern leisure" only appeared when non-work activity became a matter of individual choice or responsibility, and one's work was "set apart from...other activities."[9] "Sport," "recreation," and "game" have proved equally difficult to define in a manner agreeable to all.[10]

Historians have generally opted for less precise definitions of these terms, but ones which may be closer to what the average reader would understand by them. This chapter will follow their lead. Leisure may usefully be defined as that "time...which lies outside the demands of work, direct social obligations and the routine activities of personal and domestic maintenance."[11] Recreation or recreations are "those activities and interests that form the typical occupation of leisure time."[12] Games involve play and competition, and proceed by chance or strategy; if, however, they also require physical dexterity and activity, they are sports as well.[13]

While Canadian historians have not paid much attention to the history of recreation and leisure, some British social historians have been paying increasing attention to it in recent years. Their attempts to reconstruct "the kind of life lived by the ordinary people of the past"[14] have led them into the study of changing patterns of leisure and recreation. Two works stand out in particular as offering useful insights into the development of fur trade recreation and leisure: Robert

Malcolmson's *Popular Recreation in English Society, 1700-1850*, and Peter Bailey's *Leisure and Class in Victorian England: Rational Recreation and the Contest for Control, 1830–1885*.

Robert Malcolmson found in the pre-industrial period in England a strong popular culture of recreation based on the rural village and tied to the seasonal nature of work.[15] Not only were the amusements of the common people tied to the cycle of work, they were not clearly distinguished from that labour. Work and sociability were at least partially integrated: "non-work activity — singing, drinking, dancing, gossiping and the like — [were] guiltlessly part of the working day."[16] However, if leisure was spontaneous, easily provided, and communal, it also had a darker side. It was frequently violent or cruel, or tinged by excesses of various sorts — sexual, alcoholic, or criminal. However, the ruling elite — local gentry, justices of the peace, and clergymen — exhibited a kind of tolerant paternalism towards popular amusements, recognizing as they did "the stabilising effect of intervals of licence."[17]

The old popular recreations were not unchallenged, however. They were under attack from the eighteenth century on from a new puritanism associated with evangelical Christianity, and were disrupted by the enclosure movement, urbanization, and industrial capitalism with its new time-work discipline.[18] The first major changes to note then are the attempts to "civilize" popular recreations and to draw a tighter distinction between work and leisure.

As the old traditional village community broke down, leisure emerged, or rather re-emerged, in a new guise, forming a separated, largely self-contained sector of popular culture. Leisure time was separated from work time, and it often came to be physically separated from the workplace as well. Sports and games were played either alone or with companions who were generally not one's workmates, and many of the most popular recreations required specialized fields and equipment. To a far greater extent than had been the case before, what Peter Bailey calls the "new leisure world" of Victorian Britain was a world in which leisure activities were the product of individual choice or preference. These activities were also increasingly commercialized and institutionalized. Sports, for example, came to be played under codified systems of rules, and associations were developed to draft these regulations and to see that they were followed. Many sports were turned into professional activities. In Britain this was particularly true of football; the many local variants of this sport were eventually subsumed by rugby and "Association" football or soccer.

Obviously not all of these changes affected the recreational and leisure habits of the fur traders. Professional sports did not have any direct impact on life at fur trade posts any more than did urbanization or industrialization. However, in general terms, the leisure and recreational patterns of a post like York Factory did change over the period of this study. Peter Bailey's "new leisure world" of Victorian Britain was not exactly replicated in the North-West of the fur trade, but elements of it can be found.

When Hudson's Bay Company's employees first established their posts on the Bay they came into contact with native cultures that had already developed their own games and recreations. Indeed, aboriginal peoples around the world placed a good deal of value on leisure,[19] and the desire to be freed still further from the constraints of work and personal and domestic maintenance acted as a powerful spur to trading. European trade goods did not so much replace native-produced articles as provide labour-saving substitutes.

During the initial contact period there was extensive cultural transferral from native to European culture and vice versa, but it is interesting to note that this was not true in any great measure in the area of leisure and recreation. Indian games, sports, music, and dances remained almost exclusively the cultural property of Indians until well into the nineteenth century. Nor did they borrow much from the Europeans.[20]

The fullest study of the games of North American Indians suggests that playing cards and "nine men's morris" (a form of checkers or draughts) were "among the few games borrowed by the Indians from the whites."[21] Otherwise it was not until the late nineteenth or early twentieth centuries that North American Indians played European games or sports in any numbers....

Some Indian games or activities did eventually find favour as sports or recreations with whites. In time, activities such as lacrosse, canoeing, and snowshoeing all acquired a certain popularity. Lacrosse in fact became the national sport in Canada, and from the 1840s until the early twentieth century it was one of the most popular of Canadian sports.[22] The game was originally centred in Ontario and Quebec, particularly Montreal, and it might be worth noting that white participants only took it up when the native cultures that developed lacrosse were in decline. The same is basically true of canoeing, and snowshoeing. For example, the Montreal Snowshoe Club often referred to as the "Tuque Bleues" after the hat they adopted, traces its origins back to 1840, and as early as the mid-1840s it was organizing highly popular tramps and races.[23] It was in central Canada that the greatest cultural transfer took place between native and white in the area of sports and recreation, but only when activities like snowshoeing or canoeing had ceased to be essential to survival.[24]

The fur traders of York Factory exhibited no such tendency to turn Indian games or activities into recreations, with the possible exception of snowshoeing, which was taken up by some officers for exercise and amusement. The most frequently mentioned "sport" of the fur traders was football; indeed, John Mcdougall called it the "national game" of the North-West."[25] Mention is made of playing football as early as New Year's Day, 1734, at Prince of Wales' Fort at Churchill,[26] and the game remained a frequent part of the Christmas-New Year's holiday season at the bayside posts throughout the eighteenth and early nineteenth centuries. At York Factory it is not always mentioned as part of the festivities at Christmas-time, but up until the mid-1840s it was often noted that the men "amused themselves at football" on the plantation.[27] John Mcdougall's comment suggests that football continued as a popular sport after the post journals at York Factory stopped mentioning it. Quite probably, as it had become customary to play it at Christmas, those in charge of keeping the post journals simply stopped mentioning it.

Certainly when games occurred they were spirited affairs, but alcohol and frigid temperatures could stop even eager players. The journal entry for December 25, 1823 reads as follows:

> Ther 30 below Zero
> Stormy weather as has been the usual custom at this place part of the Men and some of the Gentlemen turned out to a game of football which was not kept up with much spirit probably from the Severity of the Weather combined with a previous too free use of the Bottle.[28]

Otherwise the games tended to be "warmly contested," as well they might be considering that on occasion prizes of substantial quantities of alcohol were offered to the victorious side.[29] Indeed, there was a close connection between football and drink at York Factory, and some commanding officers may have discouraged it in consequence. In 1845 [Chief Trader] James Hargrave indicated that he only permitted a game of football as a reward for the men's "moderate...use of spirits" that Christmas.[30]

The mention of the gentlemen, or officers, of the post joining in the games is also intriguing. It is by no means clear what rules, if any, these games were played under. The various histories of popular sport in Britain all point out that it was not until the late nineteenth century that football separated into its characteristic forms of soccer and rugby and that rules were codified. Up until that time there were almost as many versions of football as there were towns that played it. The only common characteristics were that it was played with some sort of ball, and it was a violent and dangerous pastime. In England football games were sometimes used as covers for anti-enclosure or other riots, in which the game was used as a means to tear down the mills or fences of the local landowners.[31] One French observer remarked, while watching the famous Derby football game in 1829, "that if Englishmen called this playing, it would be impossible to say what they would call fighting."[32] As a large proportion of the participants in any game at York Factory were Orkneymen, it seems fair to assume that their game would have resembled that played at Kirkwall on New Year's Day. A description of this "game" can be found in Daniel Gorrie's *Summers and Winters in The Orkneys*:

Regularly as the day [New Year's] recurs there is a gathering of the populace intent on preserving one curious and time-honoured custom from extinction. The game — which should have ended with the era of cockfighting — is virtually a trial of strength, of pushing and wrestling power between "up the street" and "down the street," the grand object of the belligerents being to propel the ball to one or the other end of town. Broad Street, where the struggle commences under the shadow of St. Magnus [Cathedral], becomes the centre of attraction about noon-tide. Sailors and porters arrive in formidable force from the purlieus of the harbour, tradesmen gather in groups, and even hoary-headed men, feeling the old glow of combative blood in their veins, hasten to the scene of anticipated contest. At one o'clock a signal pistol-shot is fired; the ball is tossed into the air from the steps of the old cross, and around it, soon as it bumps on the ground there immediately gathers from all sides a dense and surging crowd. The wrestling and struggling mass sways hither and thither, sometimes revolving like a maelstrom, and at others stationary in a grim deadlock. At intervals, the ball, as if flying for dear life, makes a spasmodic bound from the crowd; but a sudden headlong rush encloses it again, and so the struggle continues as before. For onlookers it is exciting to observe the fierce red-hot faces of the combatants, while the only appearance of good-humour displayed is a grim smile flickering fitfully across an upturned visage...Heavy knock-down blows, both foul and fair, are freely given and received. The struggle seldom lasts much longer than an hour, and when the seamen and porters win the day, they place the ball, as a trophy of conquest, on the top-mast of the largest ship in the harbour.[33]

Even if the numbers of participants were fewer at York Factory the game must have been boisterous and exciting. It may also have acted as a useful safety-valve for social tensions. The gentlemen at York were not averse to using their fists and feet to maintain discipline, and company servants had little choice but to submit. When the officers joined the football game it undoubtedly gave lowly servants a chance to get a bit of their own back in a way which did not threaten the hierarchical structure of fur trade society, for a kick in the shins in a game was not the same thing as resisting a blow in the warehouse.[34]

Other than these football games the residents at York Factory were not much inclined towards sports. Simple contests of strength, like arm wrestling or running or jumping, or of skill like throwing stones at a mark undoubtedly took place. It would be astonishing if they did not, but they were not recorded and remained spontaneous examples of play. There are infrequent mentions of races at York Factory. In the summer of 1825 a race was held between "the Govrs New Boat and Montreal light Canoe eight men each win by the former, a very near thing."[35] George Simpson McTavish mentions racing dogs with carrioles on the ice of the river at Christmas time in the 1880s.[36] These were probably not isolated cases, and dog and canoe races may very well have enlivened life at York Factory, but it would be stretching the evidence somewhat to suggest that they were a regular addition to the entertainments of the post.

Fights are more commonly mentioned in the record of York Factory, but whether or not most should be seen as athletic contests is unclear. It has been suggested that during the period of competition between the North West Company and the Hudson's Bay Company, the officers in charge of canoe brigades kept "champion prize-fighters" about, to do battle when these brigades met.[37] After the union of the companies [in 1821] these regional or brigade champions may have sought each other out to establish wider dominance when they arrived at York Factory or Norway House to deliver their furs.[38] However, virtually all the fights mentioned in fur trade records were products of the irritations of fur trade life, drink, or sheer personal antipathy. They were brawls not boxing-matches, and while spectators may have derived some entertainment from them, they probably ought not to be dignified by the term sport.[39]

Sedentary games had their devotees at York Factory....Indians were especially taken with draughts. They also integrated playing cards into their culture. Their choice of card games is never mentioned, but the Hudson's Bay Company kept plenty of playing cards in their inventory of trade goods at York Factory for either native or European purchasers.[40] Whist appears to have been popular amongst the officers at York Factory. James Hargrave was "a good player" and a willing instructor of beginners.[41] William Mactavish was not only "a great whist player," but his sister revealed that he "ponders well on every card."[42] James Hargrave also played chess, and Donald Ross at Norway House thought enough of his talents to request "a few lessons from your right reverend wisdom on the subject."[43] Checkers or draughts were also popular, and among company servants "every apartment possesse[d] its well-thumbed pack of cards, its rude cribbage-board, and sets of wooden dominoes."[44]

Gambling and games of chance, though rarely mentioned would have been a part of many of the games played by officers and servants. Company officers might criticize their native customers for gambling away their furs, but sports and recreations in Britain in the eighteenth and nineteenth centuries were often closely tied to betting.[45] Company journals contained the odd reference to gambling games like dice,[46] and according to one version Ten Shilling Creek got its name from a wager.[47] In 1836 James Hargrave wrote to Edward Smith, an officer serving in the Athabasca District, in an attempt to sort out the details of a raffle scheme. It appears that J.A. Wolfe, a resident of York Factory in the summer of 1830, tried to raffle his watch. Those interested in taking a chance on winning the watch were to have Wolfe's account at the York Factory sale shop credited with the sums they ventured. Apparently the raffle took place, and Wolfe left for Athabasca. Not all of the participants, however, had in fact transferred credits to Wolfe's account. As a result Wolfe was out of pocket, and Hargrave could do nothing for "without an authenticated list of the Debtors, together with their acknowledgement of its justice" he would not debit their accounts.[48]

The men stationed at York Factory did occasionally engage in other physical recreations that were neither sports nor games. Some appear to have found travel between posts as much a diversion as a duty.[49] Others took a certain pleasure in snowshoeing, as both exercise and a necessary adjunct to winter hunting.[50] R.M. Ballantyne's descriptions of "rambles" on snowshoes leave a strong impression of the pleasure young officers derived from this pastime.[51] Ballantyne also describes excursions in canoes.[52] In the case of snowshoeing and canoeing much of the recreational value of these activities came about as a result of their association with hunting or in some cases fishing. They were, moreover, almost exclusively the recreational property of company officers. Company servants may well have enjoyed tramping about the woods on snowshoes or carrying correspondence between posts, but for them it was merely a more enjoyable form of work than cutting wood or packing furs.

Officers also had access to other potential recreations. As long as horses were kept as draught animals at York Factory, they could also be used for riding. In 1777 Humphrey Marten, the Chief Factor at York, availed himself of this recreational resource. The late arrival of snow that fall meant that he "had a fine opportunity of riding to the Forked-tree, Four mile gulley, Sallisbury hammock, and almost to the Burnt Tent, but the old broken winded Horse did not like the Sport half so well as I did, and frequently fell on his knees probably to pray for Snow to hinder such long Journeys."[53] The eventual replacement of horses by oxen for draught purposes about 1825 undoubtedly curtailed this amusement,[54] though at inland posts horses figured prominently in fur trade recreation throughout the nineteenth century.

Company journals also include infrequent references to skating, usually with reports of injury: "One of the men fell while skating on the ice and broke his collar bone."[55] Apparently skating was only newsworthy when it resulted in an accident. It may also be that few company employees engaged in it since at the time it was a fairly dangerous activity. Until the first boot skates made their appearance in the 1860s, skates were attached to the participant's own shoes or boots by means of tight foot and ankle straps and a screw driven into the heels.[56] Since river ice was not particularly smooth, skating on it with such devices must have been risky. James Clare in a letter to William Lane offers confirmation of the difficulties faced by skaters at York Factory.

> As to skating here it is but very poor for we only had a week or so of it in the fall of the year & that was far from being good as the Ice was by no means so smooth as the polished surface of a mirr[or] so that I enjoyed but little of it.[57]

In the same vein swimming or bathing was mentioned from time to time when it resulted in some misadventure. Unlike skating, however, the accidents which took place while bathing were mortal. The post journal for 1821 recounts the unfortunate death of Haldane Snodie, "a sober, faithful, & honest young man," who "met with his untimely end by going into the river to relive himself from the extreme heat of the weather, he unfortunately gote out of his deepth, & is supposed was seized by the cramp; he immediately sunk to the bottom & appeared no more."[58] A similar accident claimed the lives of two girls in 1799:

> About noon several young Women who had been in the habbits of bathing in the River two of whom unfortunately drowned in sight of the Parents and Relations about 100 yards distant above the Factory — Every exertion was made

by our People to save them, but arrived too late to afford them any assistance. However one was picked up, about an hour afterwards and every means was used as prescribed by the Human Society for restoring to Life - but without the least Symptom of Effect.[59]

One of the girls was a daughter of George Sutherland, while the other was the daughter of "an Indian much respected by the Europeans."[60]

Hunting and fishing also came to be seen as recreational activities by the fur traders at York Factory, especially by company officers in the nineteenth century. Throughout most of the eighteenth century it is difficult to make a case for viewing hunting and fishing as recreations at fur trade posts. A good deal of the hunting for provisions was carried on by the Homeguard Cree, and fishing was considered a particularly unpleasant chore.[61] Fish were caught using nets placed under the river ice, and not usually by angling. Moreover, fish did not form a large part of the diet at York Factory until after 1822.[62] Company employees did hunt and trap in the eighteenth century, but usually for food or for furs. These furs were then traded to the company as a means of supplementing income, or kept for personal use while in the North-West.

The Hudson's Bay Company made several attempts to discourage hunting and trapping as a means of supplementing incomes, primarily because it led to "illicit" trade. In 1770 the salaries of officers in charge of posts were raised and bounties offered on the total volume of trade to discourage this illicit trade, and in 1825 most of the direct economic incentive to trap for oneself was removed when the company decreed that it would pay its employees no more for their furs than it offered Indians.[63] In addition, company servants wishing to procure furs for their own use after 1841 had to pay prices equivalent to the highest prices paid for prime furs of that sort at the London fur auctions.[64]

These alterations in company policy helped to discourage hunting and trapping as recreation for all but the officers at York Factory and they certainly made trapping less attractive as a means of supplementing earnings.[65] For the most part, hunting and fishing were always recreations of company officers. When company servants fished it was for provisions not sport, and goose, ptarmigan, and caribou hunting, even for food, came more and more to be limited to Indians and company officers.

At York Factory a competitive element was added to the spring goose hunt to encourage the native hunters. The hunter who brought in the first goose of the season was given a prize. Originally it consisted of a bottle of rum and a scarlet feather to wear as a mark of one's hunting prowess, but during the 1840s the bottle of rum was discontinued, at least officially, as part of the company's campaign to discourage alcohol consumption. Instead the hunter was to be given "2 lbs Sugar, 1 pint Molasses."[66] However, the Reverend J.P. Gardiner, a Church Missionary Society minister at York Factory, suggested that rum remained unofficially part of the prize for the first goose of the year, along with presents of pork, flour, sugar and tea.[67]

After 1821, officers at York Factory spent more and more of their work days sitting at desks keeping track of the voluminous accounts and records of the company's Northern Department. Long hours and increasingly sedentary work made many believe that officers at York needed extra leisure time for hunting and snowshoeing — less for sport or recreation than as exercise. As early as the late 1820s it appears to have been the policy of those in charge at York Factory to allow clerks to take time off from their duties at their own discretion to hunt:

> My days are past at the Desk, from 9 in the morning till 8 in the evening, tho this may be considered long hours, yet they pass over lightly. I take a turn on snowshoes for a few miles with my Gun whenever I feel inclined for a walk, besides Saturday is always a holiday, so that of the week no more than 5 days are devoted to business.[68]

For officers, hunting and associated activities were less and less a matter of securing food or valuable furs, but rather a means of ensuring good health. When ill health became prevalent "partridge" [ptarmigan] or other forms of hunting were specially encouraged to return employees to health.[69] By the 1850s the officers at York Factory were being given additional time off work for hunting, and not just as a treatment for ill-health, but as a form of preventative medicine.

> Wednesday and Saturdays are holidays for the young gentleman [sic], who generally set fox traps and visit them & hunt partridges on these occasions, principally for the sake of their health, which close confinement to the desk is calculated to injure.[70]

Concern for the effects of service at York Factory on the health of employees appears to have been limited, however. When some tradesmen requested extra time for their health, the suggestion was rejected out of hand.[71]

Health and exercise were not the only motivations for hunting and trapping of course. Some officers still enjoyed the extra money trapping could bring them, while others apparently saw it could be turned to more altruistic ends. Letitia Hargrave [James' wife] wrote that Dr. Gillespie and her brother William Mactavish had both become avid trappers sleeping out nights amongst their traps: "Willie will not trade them [his furs]. He gives them to Mr. Wilson [the officer in charge of trading at York] but he tells him to give the value to poor Indians. Not so Mr. Gillespie, he takes all he can get for his skins."[72]

Fishing is less frequently mentioned as a recreational pastime at York Factory. One reason for this might be that the diet at York after 1822 relied so heavily on fish that few had much urge to catch more. It may also have been a product of the lack of "sport" in the fish around York. According to George Simpson McTavish, Ten Shilling Creek was noted for its stocks of speckled trout. At some point in his stay at York in the 1880s he was talked into fishing with Chief Factor Fortescue who had more than an amateur interest in fishing.

> Mr. Fortescue had a beautiful imported rod, with fancy tackle, and a book of fly hooks that would have delighted an entomologist. I [McTavish] was very much afraid that I would have very little chance of catching anything against such a handicap as my outfit consisted of a small sapling cut from the woods, a stout piece of cord, a large unadorned hook, and for bait a piece of salt pork.[73]

Despite his crude equipment McTavish immediately landed three or four trout, whereupon Chief Factor Fortescue attempted to teach him how to fish properly. On his first cast with Fortescue's rod he got a bite, causing Fortescue to demonstrate how to play the fish. McTavish returned to the use of his own gear while Fortescue struggled to land the trout.

> When the time came for us to head for home, I had caught nineteen, and Mr. Fortescue one, showing that the trout, thank goodness, had not yet become civilized. They wanted no gaudy attraction to stimulate their appetites. They were after the substance of a chunk of salt pork, and despised such small allurements as a colored figment of imagination in the shape of an imported fly.[74]

In certain important aspects the games, sports, and active physical recreations of the inhabitants of York Factory differ from those enjoyed by their fellow Britons as depicted by Robert Malcolmson and Peter Bailey. Sports like cricket, boxing, bowls, and horse racing had little or no impact on leisure at York Factory despite their popularity in Britain. The reasons for this were partly practical — horses were raced at inland posts where they were available and where suitable land for racing horses could be found. Sports that required open or prepared fields like tennis, bowls, or cricket could not be played at York without a large expenditure of time and money. Boxing did not develop as a sport, perhaps because it was so frequently an impromptu part of fur trade life or because it was more an English than a Scottish sport at the time. Less simple to explain are the absence of the "blood" sports so popular in Britain in the eighteenth and early nineteenth centuries. Bull, bear, and badger-baiting, cock- and dog-fighting, setting terriers at rats, and a host of other unpleasant spectacles were an important part of the popular recreations of Britain. They had no direct equivalent in fur trade society, though there were no real practical impediments at a post like York Factory to such "sports" being developed. Perhaps fur traders got enough experience of hunting or trapping personally or vicariously to lessen the urge to torment animals as sport.[75] At any rate in this respect some of the unsavory aspects of popular recreation in Britain were avoided in the North-West.

In certain other respects, however, the parallels between sports and recreation in Britain and the North-West in the period of 1788 and 1870 are clear.[76] In both societies recreations were often communal, as in the case of football. They made use of the resources of the community, its fields, waterways, game and so on, and they were tied to the rhythms of work. They were also undergoing important changes. The commercialization of recreation so apparent in Britain was distantly echoed in Chief Factor Fortescue's specialized and expensive fishing equipment. Popular recreations in Britain were under assault from middle and upper class reformers who wished to "civilize" popular sports and recreations so as to make them less inclined towards excesses of violence or debauchery, and more controlled. In fur trade society this process may be seen in the apparent attempt to make football games a reward for good behaviour, and not an excuse for settling odd scores or excessive drinking. This urge to civilize leisure activities, and if possible turn them to more socially and personally productive ends, will be discussed in more detail [later]. The communal nature of popular recreations was also breaking down under the impact of hardening class lines and distinctions. Many sports and recreations, which in the past had drawn participants and supporters from across class lines, became increasingly classbound and often invisible to outsiders.[77] It was not always the middle and upper classes that appropriated activities for themselves and excluded other classes. The working class in England in the late nineteenth century, in effect, took over "Association" football and the music hall and made them expressions of itself. There is a direct parallel, however, between the tendency in fur trade society for hunting to become a prerogative of officers only, and a similar phenomenon in Britain which saw in the mid-nineteenth century a concerted effort to limit hunts to only aristocratic and upper-middle class participants, and to put an end to the organization of fox hunts by publicans or apprentices and working men clubbing together to keep their own packs of dogs.[78]

...Leisure at York Factory did have a darker side. Alcohol caused serious social problems at all fur trade posts, including York Factory. Problems associated with excessive consumption of alcohol affected all segments of society at York Factory, officers, servants, and Indians. This is not entirely surprising given the importance of drink to popular recreation in the eighteenth and nineteenth centuries and the quantities of alcohol consumed by all classes in British society.[79] The hard drinking traditions of Europe were brought to North America by colonists and fur traders and took root. Alcohol consumption at Hudson's Bay Company posts was high throughout the eighteenth century and remained so into the nineteenth century.[80]

Most of the attention paid to the consumption of alcohol in the fur trade has focussed on the impact of alcohol on native peoples. It was one of the few leisure activities of Europeans that was taken up by native peoples, and much has been written about its deleterious effects on Indian cultures.[81] Much less attention has been paid to the drinking habits of the fur traders.

Alcohol created a good deal of social tension at York Factory. It led to dereliction of duty by both officers and men[82] as well as to arguments and physical violence.[83] Social events were frequently marred by the affects of heavy drinking, and even innocuous activities like church services were sometimes disrupted by drunken men.[84] Worst of all, excessive alcohol consumption resulted in accidents and deaths, and on rare occasions in murder or other criminal acts.[85]

At the same time alcohol was a major item of trade. It was used extensively as a reward for dangerous or demanding work or to mark achievements such as the shooting of the first goose of the year. It was an important part of most social gatherings and its consumption was an integral part of holidays and other celebrations. While fur traders were not known for their moderation, not all celebrations degenerated into drunken revels.

A certain amount of alcohol was always shipped from England for consumption at posts, but individuals also imported their own personal stocks. Donald Ross, for example, earned the censure of Letitia Hargrave by importing ten gallons of whiskey and ordering eight more gallons of brandy from York Factory for himself and his wife.[86]

When alcohol was unavailable from England or post stocks, or for those who could not afford it, company employees showed some ingenuity in producing their own alcoholic potions. Joseph Colen showed a great deal of talent in the production of supplies of distilled spirits for the inland trade in the 1790s when war interrupted shipments from England. In fact, he appears to have produced a kind of handbook on distilling for the company.[87] In the 1880s George Simpson McTavish describes the creation of a "sugar beer" to assuage the thirsts of York Factory's residents. This beer, which was made from brown sugar, hops, and yeast was started in September after the arrival of the ship so that it would be ready for Christmas. It was not very strong "but if we could clarify it, by straining and settling, make it show a head, and taste the hops, imagination could do the rest, raising the concoction to the dignity of Bass's best."[88] Company employees also tinkered with imported spirits to suit their tastes. Something known by the evocative name of "shrub" appears to have been a particular favorite, and it was produced in great quantities at York Factory. Shrub was made with rum or some other spirit mixed with orange, lemon, or other acid fruit juice and sugar.[89] Substandard beer and spirit supplies from England were also ingeniously rendered more fit for consumption: "assisted the Coopers in starting the Bungs of the Porter Casks and putting therein some plumbs and fresh Hopes the whole of the Porter as it came from England not deserving Warehouse Room."[90]

Just as the drinking habits of British workers had produced attempts to limit their consumption of alcohol, so too were attempts made to control drinking at fur trade posts. Even before the union of the Hudson's Bay and North West Companies individuals had discussed the importance of reducing the trade in alcohol with Indians, and had recognized its baneful effects on fur traders themselves. The first concerted efforts to reduce alcohol consumption in the North-West occurred at the time of the union of the companies, and initially they were directed at the alcohol trade with Indians. The Minutes of Council for 1822 ordered that company officers reduce the amount of alcohol given to natives as gifts by one-half and that the practice of trading furs for alcohol be abolished.[91] During the 1840s these regulations were further reinforced by a total ban on the giving of alcohol to natives as gifts or in trade at the bayside posts of Churchill, Severn and York.[92] Soon after, attempts were made to extend controls on alcohol consumption to company employees. The Standing Rules and Regulations established that no individual in company service whatever his rank would be allowed to purchase more than two gallons of spirits and four gallons of wine from depot supplies in any given year.[93] In the 1850s such old company traditions as the regale of rum given to tripmen on the completion of their voyage to York Factory and on leaving the factory to return home came under attack. Despite a certain amount of resistance the regale was changed from a gift of rum to one of tea and sugar.[94] At the same time attempts to encourage voluntary temperance were gaining strength. From the 1830s post journals begin to mention that holiday celebrations were marked by moderation,[95] and the decision of men not to consume all the alcohol they were allowed was noted with approval.[96] Although in 1841 it was decided to reduce regales of rum by [50 percent] to one-half pint a day for major celebrations,[97] James Hargrave remarked with satisfaction that voluntary temperance showed even better results a year later:

> It is pleasing to observe that scarcely a single instance of intoxication was to be found among the whole party of upwards of thirty servants, and this marked improvement in their conduct has arisen from their being persuaded of the evil consequence of indulgence in regard to their healths, rather than from being restrained from purchasing. Scarcely any of them in course of the season having purchased one half of the quantity permitted them by council and the greater portion not more than one quarter.[98]

The arrival of missionaries at York Factory in 1854 provided yet another impetus to the temperance campaign. Reverend Gardiner, in particular, made special exhortations every Christmas season on the subject, apparently without much effect.[99] Gardiner's journals also suggest that the improvement in employee drinking habits that Hargrave noted was either ephemeral or wishful thinking, for by his standards the Christmas festivities at York Factory remained a drunken debauch into the 1860s.[100]

Whether or not Reverend Gardiner was correct in his portrayal of drunken excesses at York Factory, it is clear that from at least the early 1840s on the heavy drinking traditions of fur trade society were under attack. Individuals, missionaries, and the Governor and Committee of the Hudson's Bay Company all tried to alter drinking habits by regulation, example, or moral persuasion. Moreover, like their counterparts in Britain at the time, they did so for reasons ranging from practical concerns with the efficiency of a work-force to a belief in evangelical Christianity. The net effect, however, of this movement, whatever its causes, was a concerted effort to "civilize" yet another element of popular culture.

It is difficult to separate drinking from the celebrations and holidays of the fur traders, for it was a central element of both. It would be unwise, however, to ignore fur traders' capacity to find other ways of celebrating significant dates in their calendar.

It has been suggested that as much as one-third of the year was free of direct work obligations in pre-industrial England.[101] During the early nineteenth century this rather easy work rate came under attack so that

> By 1834 there were only eight statutory half-holidays in England, and the traditional calendar of religious feast days and celebrations of seasonal tasks or particular trades had been considerably pruned, both by the employers and the church.[102]

This represented the low point in the leisure time of British workers as thereafter hours of work were decreased and holidays increased. Company employees were never subject to the same restrictions on leisure time as their fellows in Britain; however, fur trade holidays were not constant over the period covered by this study. New holidays came to be celebrated, and others apparently ceased to be observed. The manner in which these holidays were marked also changed over time, as the customary diversions of each holiday developed. Nevertheless, throughout the period covered by this study something like one-third of the year would have been time off for company employees at York Factory, especially the junior officers who, as previously mentioned, were given extra holidays for their health.

The most important holiday period at fur trade posts was celebrated between Christmas Eve and New Year's Day, but other days were celebrated as well. During the 1790s Guy Fawkes Day was generally observed as a holiday. Time off was given to the men during the day, and in the evening there was a large bonfire and fireworks.[103] These amusements produced a horrifying accident in 1795:

> In the Evening the Men had a bondfire and were diverting themselves as usual when a melancholly accident befel my nephew Thomas Colen, who had indiscreetly put a number of fire Works into his breast Pockets which took fire. The consequences that ensued was dreadfull all his Cloaths were blown to pieces, and himself exhibited one of the most shocking spectacles I ever beheld, his body, hands, arms, neck, and face dreadfully mutulated — part of the bones of his fingers and Ribs are bare.[104]

Thomas Colen survived his injuries, but it seems Guy Fawkes celebrations did not, for there are no further references to bonfires and fireworks on November 5 in York Factory journals.

St. George's Day, April 23, was also celebrated at York Factory. In the 1790s the day was generally marked by the shooting of small arms at a target for prizes.[105] In 1797 the target shooting had to be abandoned due to the shortage of gunpowder, and the custom seems to have gone into decline thereafter. By the mid-nineteenth century St. George's Day was only marked by an extra allowance of rum.[106] St. Andrew's Day, November 30, was also celebrated, although this custom seems only to have begun with the influx of Scottish officers into Hudson's Bay Company service after 1821. The day was marked by an extra rum allowance and sometimes a dance in the evening, but the normal work of the post was carried on during the day.[107]

Significant events during the course of the year were also celebrated from time to time. Ship-time in addition to being a period of hard work was also a time of celebration. The departure of the ship for England was occasion for merrymaking:

> About noon that Gentleman [Captain Ball] embarked for the vessel accompanied by all the passengers, also Mr. Miles and myself who went on board to spend the day with them. After dining with them and demolishing nearly a dozen of the Old Boys wine, we bade them farewell and returned ashore with about a half dozen more bottles for amusement on the way. These, to tell the whole truth, were also near a close before we reached the Launch end; and having had a pretty strong breeze ahead on coming up the river, either that notion or the wine must still have been in our noodles when we got ashore, from the zig-zag course we made on steering up from the shore to the gate of the Fort. We however found that the gentlemen who had remained ashore were also improving the occasion as comfortably as we had been doing, — so to it we went again; and at this moment I have just made my retreat good, with just as much sober sense left me as to be able to sit down and add a few lines to my Journal.[108]

The ship's departure also came to be celebrated by balls for officers and servants which Reverend Gardiner noted with disapproval might last until 3 o'clock in the morning and which were "productive of much evil" in his eyes.[109] Even the arrival or departure of prominent company officials was used as an excuse for a dance on occasion.[110]

The Christmas holidays were the most important of the festivities at York Factory. They ran from Christmas Eve to New Year's Day, though on occasion the effects of the holidays lingered on. Indeed in 1848, Robert Wilson sprained his ankle while dancing on Christmas Day and did not reappear at the officers' mess table until February. He was still limping from his ball-room injury at the end of March.[111] Wilson's case was an extreme one, and most had recovered health and sobriety within a day or two.

The holiday season was marked by unusual indulgence in more than just alcohol. It was an occasion for football, hunting excursions, dances, over-eating, pranks and horseplay as well. The New Year's Day football games have already been discussed, as have the officers' hunting expeditions, but they played a large part in the holiday festivities. According to R.M. Ballantyne's lengthy and lively description of Christmas at York Factory, the day began in Bachelors' Hall with pillow fights, people being locked into rooms, and other such boyish amusements.[112] Games and pranks and tramps in the woods were only preliminaries to the real order of business for the day which was Christmas dinner, and then a ball. New Year's Eve appears to have been celebrated in much the same way. Extra food rations were always handed out to the men on Christmas Eve and then again at New Year's. Depending upon supplies some foodstuffs might not appear as part of these extra rations, but the list for 1829 is not untypical: "1/2 lbs. Raisins, 1/4 lb. Butter, 1/8 lbs. Tea, 2 lbs. Sugar, 2 lbs. Grease, 1 lb. Flour, 1 lb. Salt Pork, 1 1/2 lb. Fresh [Pork], 1 fresh Goose, 1 Rabbit, 1 pint Rum and 1/2 pint molasses. And the same extra allowance will likewise be delivered to them new year's day."[113] With these supplies company servants could produce a reasonable facsimile of traditional British Christmas dinners including pudding and roast goose though rabbit apparently had to serve instead of vegetables. Company officers enjoyed even more lavish fare with roast goose and beef, salt pork, partridges, and port and Madeira wine.[114]

After the dinner it was customary for a dance to be held. These dances attracted the entire community of York Factory — both officers and men and the York Factory Indians. These balls were exciting events. Music was provided by fiddlers, or in their absence any other available instruments: on one notable occasion Mr. Gladman's "beloved organ."[115] The dances were mostly Scottish reels at which the Indian women were not particularly accomplished but which they enjoyed immensely.[116] In later years other dances including some with apt local names made their appearance: the Rockaway, the Curfew Lancers, the York Factory Breakdown, the Hudson Bay Jig, and the Polar Bear Walk Around.[117]

Not everyone found equal enjoyment at them. Letitia Hargrave describes one of her infrequent visits to these balls in the following terms:

> I went and sat in a room off that in which they were dancing, for a little. It was a humbling affair. 40 squaws old and young with their hair plaited in long tails, nothing on their heads but their everlasting blankets smelling of smoke and everything obnoxious. Babies almost newly born & in their cradles were with their mothers & all nursing them in the face of everyone....I was glad to come home.[118]

If Letitia Hargrave was offended by the behaviour of Indian women, Reverend Gardiner found the alcohol consumption, sexual promiscuity, and late hours of these balls distressing. In 1858 he refused to allow his servant to go to the New Year's Eve ball. She defied him and went anyway. When he refused to have her back as a servant she went to live with the York Factory Indians across the river where, according to Gardiner, she supported herself as a "common prostitute."[119] Gardiner also worried about the pressure these balls exerted on the suggestible to slip from the path of virtue:

> Samuel Stoher one of my communicants came to me today seemingly very penitent. Poor fellow he is rather weak in his intellect & some of the officers & men have taken advantage of him He Had made a resolution that he would not attend any of the dances but he could not withstand the entreates [sic] of his work fellows...they made him very drunk. One of the officers gave him a tumbler full of Brandy & Wiskey & persuaded him that it was Brandy & water.
> To day he was crying in my house & saying there was no hope for him he said I felt your sermon last night just like a Knife cutting me up he stopped with me till after 12 o'clock fearing to go home lest the men shd. drag him to the dance.[120]

Gardiner seems, however, to have reserved a particular dislike for their impact on his sleeping and domestic arrangements:

> The festivities of the season end to day & I am really glad of it. We have not been able to sleep any night since Christmas day till about four o'clock in the morning. The dances are held in the carpenter's shop & we can hear the dancing as plain as if it was only next door: & all night long some

intoxicated persons were walking past the house, one night while we were taking supper two fell against our front door, the door burst open & the two men fell inside. It is very painful to witness so much immorality.[121]

In addition to a dance, New Year's Day was celebrated by a salute with fire arms[122] and visiting around the post all day long.

Early in the morning the clerks visit the gentlemen in charge & each gets a tumbler full of "Old man's milk" a punch made of equal parts of Brandy & milk with spices &c — the gentleman in Charge then meets all the servants in the Carpenter's shop & gives two glasses of Brandy or wine to each the servants go out & the Indians are then received first the men then the women & these also get two glasses of spirits — the servants then visit the clerks & each house in the Fort & the Clerks visit each of the men & this visiting goes on till 4 o'clock in the after noon & sometimes till late in the evening; each giving the other grog.[123]

It is clear that the dances and visiting of New Year's Day served to reinforce the communal ties of post society, and despite Reverend Gardiner's disapproval, served an important social function beyond mere diversion.

In conclusion then, if one follows the residents of York Factory "into their retirements," as Joseph Strutt suggests, the picture of fur trade society that emerges is one somewhat at odds with earlier depictions of fur trade life. It was not a life of uninterrupted toil, and fur traders enjoyed a wider variety of sporting and recreational pursuits, than has generally been suspected. While fur trade society did suffer from social tensions, sports and other leisure traditions helped to dissipate them and underlined the social cohesiveness of post communities. Nor was fur trade society static in the area of recreation and leisure. Many of these changes paralleled changes in the patterns of popular recreation in Britain which have been described as shifting from "the Roaring Boys to the Boys Brigade."[124] Indeed, development of fur trade leisure and recreation habits was primarily a reflection of the sports, recreations, and pastimes of Britain, and the changes they underwent during the eighteenth and nineteenth centuries.

Notes

1. Joseph Strutt, *The Sports and Pastimes of the People of England; Including the Rural and Domestic Recreations, May Games, Mummeries, Shows, Processions, Pageants, and Pompous Spectacles, from the Earliest Period to the Present Time* (London: William Reeves, 1830), new edition by William Hone, first published 1801, xvii-xviii.

2. See S.F. Wise, "Sport and Class Values in Old Ontario and Quebec" in *His Own Man: Essays in Honour of Reginald Marsden Lower*, ed. W.H. Heick and Roger Graham (Montreal: McGill-Queen's University Press, 1974), 94.

3. Peter Bailey, *Leisure and Class in Victorian England: Rational Recreation and the Contest for Control, 1830–1885* (London: Routledge & Kegan Paul, 1978), 1.

4. To focus on the example of sport, in addition to S.F. Wise, "Sport and Class Values" one might mention Morris Kenneth Mott, "Manly Sports and Manitobans, Settlement Days to World War One" (Ph.D. thesis, Queen's University, 1980), and Ian F. Jobling, "Sport in Nineteenth Century Canada: The Effects of Technological Changes on its Development" (Ph.D. thesis, University of Alberta, 1970) as examples of attempts to place sport in a broader historial context by relating it to social and technological change in Canada. This is less true of a number of basically narrative histories like Henry Roxborough, *One Hundred— Not Out: The Story of Nineteenth Century Canadian Sport* (Toronto: Ryerson Press, 1966); Peter Leslie Lindsay, "A History of Sport in Canada, 1807–1867" (Ph.D. thesis, University of Alberta, 1969); Alan Elton Cox, "A History of Sports in Canada, 1868–1900" (Ph.D. thesis, University of Alberta, 1969); and the better known Nancy Howell and Maxwell L. Howell, *Sports and Games in Canadian Life 1700 to the Present* (Toronto: Macmillan, 1969).

5. Campbell, *The North West Company*, (Toronto: MacMillan, 1957), 43–44, offers an exciting account of canoe brigades racing along Lake Winnipeg impelled by the sheer joy of competition and collective pride. It seems unlikely, however, that such races were common. Most North West company officers would not have allowed their men to exhaust themselves on a race so early in their travels, even if the canoemen wanted to. A canoe race would also have been a bit of a busman's holiday, and most voyageurs probably got enough paddling without races. More plausible in some respects is Morris Mott's suggestion of individual contests between brigade representatives in "Manly Sports." 43–44. It is hard to imagine that individual contests of strength or skill did not take place, and certainly fights were common. The degree to which these fights were organized as opposed to spontaneous is, however, unclear.

6. A few descriptions of the amusements of fur traders do exist: Mott, "Manly Sports" chap. 1, Payne, *Prince of Wales' Fort: A Social History 1717–1782* (Ottawa: Parks Canada, 1879) Manuscript Report Series 371, chap. IV, and most of the first-hand accounts of fur trade life: R.M. Ballantyne, Daniel Harmon, Isaac Cowie, G.S. Mctavish, Andrew Graham, etc., contain some references to what fur traders did when not at work:

7. The centrality of "play" to human existence is discussed in J. Huzinga, *Homo Ludens: A Study of the Play-Element in Culture* (London: Routledge & Kegan Paul, 1949), 1–27.

8. See Joffre Dumazedier, "Leisure" in *International Encyclopedia of Social Sciences* (Macmillan, 1968), IX: 248, and Michael Marrus, ed., *The Emergence of Leisure* (New York: Harper and Row, 1974), 6.

9. Dumazedier, "Leisure", 249.

10. For example, see Eric Dunning, ed. *The Sociology of Sport* (London: Frank Cass & Co., 1971), part 1; Donald W. Ball and John Loy, ed. *Sport and Social Order: Contributions to the Sociology of Sport* (Reading, Mass.: Addison-Wesley, 1975),

11–12; Stanley Parker, *The Sociology of Leisure* (London: George Allen & Unwin, 1976), 17–20; Jay J. Coakley, *Sport in Society: Issues and Controversies* (St. Louis: C.V. Mosby, 1978), 6–14; Marrus, ed., *Emergence of Leisure*, 1–10.

11. Bailey, *Leisure and Class*, 6.

12. Ibid., 6.

13. See Mott, "Manly Sports," 7–12.

14. Bailey, *Leisure and Class*, 1.

15. R.W. Malcolmson, *Popular Recreations in English Society 1700–1850* (Cambridge: Cambridge University Press, 1973), 5–14.

16. Marrus, ed., *Emergence of Leisure*, 6.

17. Bailey, *Leisure and Class*, 3.

18. Ibid., 3.

19. Marshall Sahlins, *Stone Age Economics* (Chicago: Aldine-Atherton, 1972), 24–30.

20. Music and dance appear to have been partial exceptions to this rule. Cree musicians around Hudson Bay learned Scottish fiddle and dance tunes, and at holiday celebrations reels were the usual dances. R.M. Ballantyne described a Christmas ball at York Factory in the 1840s for which the music was supplied by a Cree fiddler and drummer and the dances were mostly Scottish reels since they were "the only dances known by the majority of the guests." R.M. Ballantyne, *Hudson Bay, or Everday Life in the Wilds of North America* (London: Thomas Nelson, 1902), 103–5.

21. "Nine men's morris" was a game played in various forms similar to a type of draughts, according to the Oxford English Dictionary (O.E.D.). Robert Stewart Culin, *Games of the North American Indians* (New York: AMS Press, 1973), first published as the *Twenty-Fourth Annual Report of the Bureau of American Ethnology* (Washington, 1907), 32.

22. The history of lacrosse forms a large part of the previously mentioned works on Canadian sport. The first white lacrosse teams appeared in Montreal in 1842, though it was not until the 1860s that the rules of the game were codifed and the game achieved wide popularity. See Howell and Howell, *Sports and Games*, 30–33, for a brief account of the early history of the sport.

23. The "Tuque Bleues," or more correctly "Tuques Bleues," are an extremely popular subject for Canadian sports historians. Virtually all general sports histories accord them great space, and a number of articles have appeared on them. For example, Rosemary Lunerdi, "Tuque Bleue," *The Beaver*, Outfit 307: 3, (Winter 1976). See also Howell and Howell, *Sports and Games*, 26–28.

24. S.F. Wise, in "Sport and Class Values," 114, suggests that in Ontario and Quebec the development of sports like lacrosse and snowshoeing was a "fat boys," movement rather than "a rebellion of the downtrodden." They were turned into sports or recreations by an urban middle class, not by the people who had snowshoed or canoed as part of their work. A modern equivalent might be whitewater canoeing, which has been turned into a sport. Running rapids for Indians and fur traders was certainly exhilarating, and it was often attempted in a spirit of bravado, but it was not recreational.

25. John Mcdougall. *Forest, Lake and Prairie — Twenty Years of Frontier Life in Western Canada — 1842–62* (Toronto: William Briggs, 1895), 83–84.

26. Hudson's Bay Company Archives (hereinafter HBCA) B.42/a/14, fo. 17d, Jan. 1, 1734. This was probably the first game of football played in Canada.

27. HBCA, B.239/a/109, fo. 7d, Dec. 26, 1803– Jan. 1, 1804. Further references include B. 239/a/106, fo. 12d, Dec. 26, 1801; B.239/a/131, fo. 9, Dec. 25, 1822, and fo. 9d, Jan. 1, 1823; B. 239/a/132. fo. 11, Dec. 25, 1823, and fo. l1d, Jan. 1, 18?4; B.239/a/141, fo. 34, Dec. 25, 1829; B.239/a/151, fo. 19d. Jan. 1, 1839; B.239/a/163, fo. 133d, Dec. 30, 1845.

28. HBCA, B.239/a/132, fo. 11, Dec. 25, 1823.
29. Chief Factor Mactavish put up a two gallon keg of rum in 1823. HBCA: B.235/c/1, fo. 3, George Barnston to J. Hargrave, Feb. 1, 1823.
30. HBCA, B.239/a/163, fo. 133d, Dec. 30, 1845.
31. E.P. Thompson, "The Moral Economy of the English Crowd in the Eighteenth Century," *Past and Present* 50 (1971), 116.
32. Quoted in Bailey, *Leisure and Class,* 8.
33. Daniel Gorrie, *Summers and Winters in the Orkneys* (London, 1868), 82–4, quoted in *Sakatchewan Journals and Correspondance: Edmonton House 1795–1800; Chesterfield House 1800–1802,* ed. Alice M. Johnson (London: Hudson's Bay Record Society, 1967) 78–79n.
34. The role of popular recreations like football in relieving social tensions, playing out hostilities, and insulting authority with impunity is discussed in Malcolmson, *Popular Recreations,* 81–85.
35. HBCA, B.239/a/133, fo. 27d, Aug. 9, 1825. In 1840 the officers at York acquired a small pleasure boat or gig to use in the autumn after shiptime. HBCA, B.239/a/152, fos. 25-25d, March 31, 1840.
36. George Simpson McTavish, *Behind the Palisades: An Autobiography* (Victoria: Colonist Printers, 1963), 69.
37. Isaac Cowie, *The Company of Adventurers: A Narrative of Seven Years in the Service of the Hudson's Bay Company During 1867–1874* (Toronto: William Briggs, 1913), 129. Isaac Cowie's information about the pre-1821 period was at best second or third hand, and while fighting undoubtedly took place between HBC and North West Company men it is probably exaggerated to suggest officers recruited champions. What did happen was that after Andrew Wedderburn Colvile's "retrenching" scheme was put in place, the Hudson's Bay Company tried to replace relatively docile Orkneymen with more aggressive Highlanders.
38. See Mott, "Manly Sports," 43–44, and John E. Foster, "Paulet Paul: Metis or 'House Indian' Folk Hero?" *Manitoba History* 9 (Spring 1985), 3. Foster describes several near-legendary battles fought between Paulet Paul and a variety of opponents, including a huge English sailor Paulet Paul felled with a single blow. This latter battle did take place at York Factory in the 1850s, but it should be noted that neither combattant was a permanent Hudson's Bay Company employee. Paulet Paul was a Red River tripman, and the English sailor served on the York Factory supply ship. York residents were at most spectators at these fights.
39. Isaac Cowie in *The Company of Adventurers,* 129–30, describes the preliminaries to a typical "tournament of the tripmen." A challenger would parade about defying all those within earshot to fight. Usually the challenge was directed at men from other brigades, but this is hardly surprising. Group solidarity, not to mention the practical problems of paddling across half the continent with someone you had beaten unmercifully, would suggest opponents were better chosen from other brigades. Missionaries and company officers did not see much that was sporting in these encounters. See for example, Public Archives of Canada (hereinafter PAC), MG17 B2, CMS, A87, Gardiner Journal 1859-60, June 30, 1860.
40. See B.239/aa/1, p. 7; B.239/aa/5, fo. 4; B.239/aa/6, p. 319. For discerning card buyers they even stocked "Moguls," the highest quality of playing card, so named because of the picture of a Mogul on the wrapper (O.E.D.).
41. John Sebastian Helmcken, *The Reminiscences of Dr. John Sebastian Helmcken,* ed. Dorothy Blakey Smith (Vancouver: University of British Columbia Press, 1975), 94–95.
42. Letitia Hargrave, *The Letters of Letitia Hargrave,* ed. Margaret Arnett MacLeod (Toronto: Champlain Society, 1947), 90. Letitia Hargrave to Mrs. Dugald Mactavish, Dec. 1, 1840.

43. James Hargrave, *The Hargrave Correspondence 1821–1843*, ed. G.P. de T. Glazebrook (Toronto: Champlain Society, 1938), 252. Donald Ross to James Hargrave, Dec. 30, 1836.

44. H.M. Robinson, *The Great Fur Land or Sketches of Life in the Hudson's Bay Territory* (Toronto: Coles Publishing, 1972), 102.

45. "They will stake one, two, three, even ten beaver skins at a time; and it frequently happens that he who in the morning was possessed of furs sufficient...for a twelvemonth, shall in a few hours be destitute of the means to barter a knife or an awl." *Andrew Graham's Observations on Hudson's Bay, 1767–91,* ed. Glyndwr Williams (London: Hudson's Bay Record Society, 1969), 168.

46. HBCA, B.42/a/44, fo. 15, for example.

47. HBCA, B.239/a/121, fos. 4-4d, Oct. 12, 1814.

48. HBCA, B.239/b/92, fo. 44d, J. Hargrave to Edward Smith, May 18, 1836. Another raffle scheme tried in 1848 also went awry. An officer tried to raffle his gun as a money-making ploy but the contest was prohibited by James Hargrave. Hargrave seems to have objected less to the raffle than to the idea that an officer would stoop to such an ungentlemanly form of commerce. See PAC, MG19 A21, Hargrave Family Papers, reel C84, Letitia Hargrave to Mrs. Dugald Mactavish, April 1, 1848.

49. HBCA, B.239/a/111, fo. 8, Jan. 28–Feb. 3, 1805.

50. See chapter on "Accident, Disease, and Medicine at York Factory" in Michael Payne, *A Social History of York,* for a discussion of the value of snowshoeing as exercise.

51. Robert Michael Ballantyne, *The Young Fur Traders: A Tale of the Far North* (London: Ward, Lock & Co., 1904), 212–19, and *Hudson Bay or Everyday Life in the Wilds of North America During Six Years Residence in the Territories of the Hon. Hudson Bay Company* (London: Thomas Nelson, 1902), 94–97. Much of the enjoyment of their jaunts came from the accidents which befell beginners.

52. Ballantyne, *Hudson Bay,* 108–12.

53. HBCA, B.42/a/94, fo. 14, Humphrey Marten to Samuel Hearne, Jan. 4, 1777.

54. Bruce Donaldson, *York Factory: A Land-Use History* (Ottawa: Parks Canada, 1981),193.

55. HBCA, B.239/a/135, fo. 7, Dec. 28, 1826. A similar accident occurred at York Factory in 1777, see HBCA, B.42/a/94, fo. 21, Feb. 23, 1777.

56. Lindsay, "History of Sport," 49-50.

57. Public Archives of Manitoba (hereinafter PAM), MG1 D11. William Lane Correspondence, James Clare to William Lane, Feb. 15, 1847. Elsewhere in Canada skating only became generally popular after prepared ice surfaces appeared in the 1850s and the boot skate was introduced. Lindsay, "History of Sport," 51–52.

58. HBCA, B.239/a/128, fo. 25, July 27, 1821.

59. HBCA, B.239/a/101, fo. 98, July 25, 1799. Unfortunately the method used to try to revive the girl is unknown, other than it was prescribed by the Human or Humane Society.

60. Ibid.

61. *Andrew Graham's Observations,* 294–95.

62. See "The Standard of Living at York Factory" in Payne, *Social History of York Factory.*

63. HBCA, B.239/k/1, fo. 71d, Minutes of Council, resolve #88, 1825.

64. Minutes of Council 1841, resolve #71. See E.M. Oliver, *The Canadian North-West: Its Early Development and Legislative Records* (Ottawa: Government Printing Bureau, 1915), II: 827.

65. George Simpson McTavish in *Behind the Palisades,* 60, does mention that for junior clerks, for whom expenses were high and pay relatively low, the few pounds they could earn trapping were welcome additions to their financial

resources. Company servants did continue to trap furs during their hours off work, some with great success, but their numbers at York Factory were in decline. HBCA, B.239/a/148, fos. 33-33d, Jan. 16, 1835, for example.

66. HBCA, B.239/a/155, fo. 40, April 28, 1842.

67. PAC, MG17 B2, CMS, A87, Gardiner Journal 1860-61, May 6, 1861.

68. PAC, MG19 D23, Unfinished Journal of a Clerk, 10, March 1, 1829.

69. HBCA, B.239/a/141, fo. 40, Feb. 7, 1830.

70. PAC, MG17 B2, CMS, A94, William Mason Journal 1855, Nov. 14, 1855.

71. Hargrave, *Letters*, 132. Letitia Hargrave to Mrs. Dugald Mactavish, Dec. 2, 1842.

72. Ibid., 180. Letitia Hargrave to Mrs. Dugald Mactavish, March 30, 1844.

73. McTavish, *Behind the Palisades*, 95.

74. Ibid., 95. Fortescue was not alone in the purchase of elaborate fishing gear, William Mactavish also was a well-equipped fisherman. In 1842 he wrote to his father asking for "a good strong Hickory fishing Rod 18 feet long in four pieces to screw together, with Reel, Line, & two spare top pieces also a fly Book and a good assortment of flies some trout small flies, sea trout flies with tinsel on the bodies and a few Salmon flies." PAC, MG19 A21, C83, Hargrave Family Papers, 287, William Mactavish to Dugald Mactavish Senior, Aug. 31, 1842.

75. This would certainly seem to be the case with George Barnston who, after joining a group of Indians on a beaver hunt, wrote: "I seized an ice chisel struck it into the ice, but paused — and thought what am I about to do? to assist in depriving an animal of life known to be surpassed only by man in foresight and sagacity, and fit to serve him as an example in pursuing the path of peaceful industry and social innocence — This Consideration stopt my arm and damped my eagerness for the pursuit of the prey — As became a Fur Trader however, I assisted the Indians a little, and at the end of the 2nd Day they killed two Beaver." HBCA, B.239/c/1, fo. 113, George Barnston to James Hargrave, June 22, 1823.

76. These parallels would in all likelihood also exist between the North-West and eastern Canada if more were known about recreational patterns in Ontario, Quebec, and the Maritimes.

77. Hugh Cunningham, *Leisure and the Industrial Revolution c. 1780–1880* (London: Croom Helm, 1980), 186.

78. Ibid., 133. Cunningham traces this "challenge" to popular participation in hunts back to about 1840. Of course game and property laws had always meant that labouring men had had to poach if they wanted to hunt, or tagged along with their social superiors in fox hunts, etc. If Cunningham is correct in placing the beginning of the attempt to exclude the working class from hunts at about 1840, this may be one case in which fur trade society to some extent anticipates events in Britain. The relationship between class and leisure is, however, an ambiguous one. At the same time as many sports and activities were becoming class specific, attempts were being made to use sport to bridge class barriers. Over the nineteenth century cricket, for example, lost much of its classlessness; yet in the mid-nineteenth century some cricketers took to wearing a belt with the motto "The Prince and the peasant by cricket are united." Ibid., 119.

79. Per capita alcohol consumption in Britain rose through the nineteenth century to a peak in the mid-1870s. Thereafter it declined somewhat as attempts to encourage temperance, limit the numbers of licensed liquor outlets, etc., began to take effect. Bailey, *Leisure and Class*, 88.

80. Payne, *Prince of Wales' Fort*, 36–38. Care should be taken not to overstate the problem caused by alcohol at ports like York Factory. Between 1714 and 1801 a study of mortality figures at York Factory indicates only two deaths in which alcohol was the primary cause. See William B. Ewart, "Causes of Mortality in a Subarctic Settlement (York Factory, Man.), 1714–1946," *Canadian Medical Association*

Journal CXXIX, 6 (Sept. 15, 1983), 572. Actual consumption of alcohol may not have been much higher than current Canadian levels of about 12 litres of absolute alcohol per adult per year. What was different was how eighteenth and nineteenth century people tended to drink. With few social inhibitions against drunkenness, when they drank it was likely to be to excess followed often by lengthy periods when no alcohol or little alcohol was consumed. See for example, *The Canadian Encyclopedia* (Edmonton: Hurtig, 1985) vol. 1, 44, s.v. "Alcoholism."

81. A full review of the material produced on this contentious issue is probably impossible. A good review of the major historical works on this subject up to 1971 can be found in James W. St. G. Walker, "The Indian in Canadian Historical Writing," *Historical Papers/Communications historiques* Canadian Historical Association (1971): 21–51. Much has been written since that attempts to answer his criticisms of the treatment of natives in Canadian historiography, but his assessments of the dominant trends in native history retain some value. A fascinating treatment of this problem can be found in Andre Vachon, "L'Eau-de-vie dans la société indienne," Canadian Historical Association *Report* (1960): 22-32.

82. See for example, HBCA, B.239/a/95, fo. 42d, or B.239/a/123, fo. 20, March 29, 1816.

83. See for example, HBCA, B.235/c/1, fo. 3, George Barnston to James Hargrave, Feb. 1, 1823.

84. PAC, MG17 B2, CMS, A87, J.P. Gardiner Journal 1861–62, Oct. 20, 1861.

85. See for example, HBCA, B.239/b/81, fos. 8d–9d, William Hemmings Cook to Mr. Sinclair, June 8, 1811, or B.239/b/50, fos. 18d–19, John Thomas to Joseph Colen, July 6, 1789. The latter is a lengthy account of the murder of William Appleby at Hannah Bay. Appleby, while in a "drunken distracted condition," was "importunate" with an Indian's wife. In a fit of "rage and jealousy" the Indian shot Appleby and his associate John Horn. Appleby was killed and Horn wounded.

86. Hargrave, *Letters*, 158, Letitia Hargrave to Mrs. Dugald Mactavish, Sept. 10, 1843.

87. HBCA, A.64/2, Miscellaneous Notebook 1791. The rather interesting notebook, which includes plans for the distillery at York Factory, seems to have been the work of Colen.

88. McTavish, *Behind the Palisades*, 68.

89. For example, 168 3/4 gallons of this mixture were made in 1827. HBCA: B.239/a/135, fo. 17, June 15, 1827.

90. HBCA, B.239/a/105, fo. 8, Oct. 25, 1800.

91. HBCA, B.239/k/1, fo. 16d, Minutes of Council 1822, resolve #97.

92. HBCA, B.239/k/1, fo. 120, Minutes of Council 1841, resolve #94.

93. HBCA, B.239/k/2, fo. 156d, Standing Rules and Regulations 1844, resolve #59.

94. HBCA, B.239/b/104, b fos. 32d–33, William Mactavish to Sir George Simpson, Sept. 9, 1853.

95. For example, HBCA, B.239/a/148, fo. 30d, Jan. 1, 1835.

96. HBCA, B.239/a/151, fo. 18d, Dec. 25, 1838.

97. HBCA, B.239/a/154, fo. 25, Jan. 1, 1841.

98. HBCA, B.239/a/155, fo. 20, Jan. 1, 1842.

99. PAC, MG17 B2, CMS, A87, J.P. Gardiner Journal 1860–1, Dec. 29, 1860.

100. Ibid. Gardiner's disapproval of the drinking habits of his parishioners may have clouded his judgement in this area, however.

101. Marrus, *Emergence of Leisure*, 5.

102. Bailey, *Leisure and Class*, 12.

103. HBCA, B.239/a/91, fo. 8, Nov. 5, 1790, B.239/a/97, fo. 6, Nov. 5, 1794, B.239/a/99, fo. 3d, Nov. 5, 1795.

104. HBCA, B.239/a/99, fo. 3d, Nov. 5, 1795.

105. For example, HBCA, B.239/a/99, fo. 12, April 23, 1796.

106. HBCA, B.239/a/168, fo. 31d, April 23, 1848.

107. HBCA, B.239/a/141, fo. 31, Nov. 30, 1829; B.239/a/148, fo. 24d, Nov. 29, 1834; B.239/a/151, fo. 14, Nov. 29, 1838.

108. PAC, MG19 D23, Unfinished Journal of a Clerk, 6, Sept. 20, 1828.

109. PAC, MG17 B2, CMS, A87, J.P. Gardiner Journal 1859–60, Sept. 30, 1859; Gardiner Journal 1860–61, Sept. 20, 1860; and Gardiner Journal 1861–62, Sept. 14, 1861.

110. HBCA, B.239/a/132, fo. 30, Aug. 14, 1824.

111. Hargrave, *Letters*, 182, Letitia Hargrave to Mrs. Dugald Mactavish, March 30, 1844.

112. Ballantyne's books suggest pranks, practical jokes, and horseplay formed a large part of the pleasures of life in Batchelors' Hall, or its equivalent at other posts. His description of Christmas at York Factory is much quoted and accords well with other sources, accounts of what occurred at York at Christmas-time. *Hudson Bay*, 100–06.

113. HBCA, B.239/a/141, fo. 34, Dec. 24, 1829.

114. Ballantyne, *Hudson Bay*, 102.

115. Hargrave, *Letters*, 110, Letitia Hargrave to Mrs. Dugald Mactavish, May 14, 1842.

116. Ballantyne, *Hudson Bay*, 105.

117. These dances are mentioned as being part of the festivities in the 1880s. *Winnipeg Daily Times*, April 13, 1883, 5, quoted in Michael Cross, ed., *The Workingman in the Nineteenth Century* (Toronto: Oxford University Press, 1974), 60.

118. Hargrave, *Letters*, 94–95, Letitia Hargrave to Mrs. Dugald Mactavish, Feb. 20, 1841.

119. PAC, MG17 B2, CMS, A87, J.P. Gardiner Journal 1858–59, Dec. 31, 1858, and Jan. 29, 1859.

120. PAC, MG17 B2, CMS, A87, J.P. Gardiner Journal 1860–61, Dec. 31, 1860.

121. PAC, MG17 B2, CMS, A87, J.P. Gardiner Journal 1861–62, Jan. 1, 1862. Gardiner gives the following breakdown of the alcohol consumed that Christmas season by approximately 50 men:

Sold to Officers and Servants	Brandy	16		3/8 galls.
"	Wiskey	17		"
"	Port Wine	5	3/8	"
"	Rum	33	7/8	"
Regales for Servants	Rum	10	1/4	"
For the Company's Ball	Rum	3		"
"	Shrub	1		"
"	Port Wine	1		"
"	Brandy	1		"
"	Whiskey	1		"
Given for Visiting New	Shrub	4	1/2	"
Year's day	Brandy	2	1/2	"
"	Port Wine	3		"
		104	7/8	"

He also states that 8-10 gallons of alcohol were given to Indians as well. Ibid.

122. HBCA, B.239/a/133, fo. 10d, Jan. 1, 1825.

123. PAC, MG17 B2, CMS, A87, J.P. Gardiner Journal 1861-62, Jan. 1, 1862.

124. Geoffrey Gorer, *Exploring English Character* (London, 1955), 13, quoted in Bailey, *Lesiure and Class*, 174.

SECTION 2

THE VICTORIAN TRANSITION, 1850–1890

From the mid- to late-nineteenth century, a transition in sports occurred throughout the English-speaking world and in much of Western Europe. Ball games became far more popular than they had been; in urban areas in particular, formal organizations became prominent means of organizing and facilitating sports; rules of play became standardized across large geographic areas; and an impressive and convincing ideology or philosophy of sports was developed. These and other less important aspects of the Victorian transition in sports in Canada are discussed in the three items in this section.

In the first article, Gerald Redmond notes that many of the "modern" features of twentieth-century organized sport actually appeared in the nineteenth century. They first became visible in the earliest industrial nation, Great Britain. Because Canada was mainly a British country, and because Canada itself underwent a process of industrialization after 1850, developments in Canadian sport tended to resemble those that occurred slightly earlier in the United Kingdom.

In two ways in particular did Canadians follow the lead of the British. First, they adopted and then embellished the "games-buildcharacter" ideas that were developed especially by British clergymen and educators. Second, Canadians, like the British, became immensely attracted to ball games. This is not to say that the appeal of other sports necessarily declined, because in fact for a time in both Britain and Canada rowing reached the height of its popularity. However, from the mid- to late-nineteenth century British and Canadian people took up rugby, soccer, cricket, tennis, curling, bowling, and golf to a degree that earlier generations in both countries would have found incredible. Canadians also embraced baseball, an altered form of cricket that was in the process of becoming the national game of the United States. Moreover, Canadians "invented" two new ball games of their own: lacrosse and hockey.

Actually, it was Montrealers who "invented" lacrosse and hockey, and early in the 1890s James Naismith, a former Montrealer living in Springfield, Massachusetts, "invented" basketball. These are only three of the reasons Montreal has been singled out by Redmond and others as a birthplace of modern world sport and especially as the cradle of Canadian sport.[1] Redmond also mentions the ways in which urbanization contributed to "the 'club' system" of organizing sports, the importance of railways in generating regular competitions between athletes from different town and cities, and the limited but gradually increasing role of women in sports.

The "rise of organized sport in Canada" in the last forty years of the nineteenth century is the subject of the second article in this section. In his usual attractive style, S.F. Wise notes the differing athletic traditions of certain ethnic groups, and goes on to identify the sports that can be associated with various classes. He mentions the popularity of team games and the important role played by people from Montreal in developing some of these activities. Finally, he emphasizes the influence of the "solidly respectable business middle class and its allies in the professions, the universities, and the military" in promoting sports. Sometimes they did so in peculiarly Canadian ways for particularly Canadian reasons.

Alan Metcalfe's article on the evolution of organized physical recreation in Montreal addresses many of the same themes and developments as the selections by Redmond and Wise. After 1870, Metcalfe says, industrialization and rapid population growth "began to make a significant impact on the patterns of physical recreation." Sports clubs grew rapidly in number. Leaders in religion and education began to promote sports because they felt the qualities inculcated by these activities were desirable. New means of creating facilities for sports were utilized as the population increased and land values rose; public money even began to be used on occasion for this purpose. By the 1890s organized sports were an important feature of life among Montreal's middle- and upper-class citizens of British background. They were beginning to appeal also to members of other ethnic groups and to the working class. Members of the working class, however, liked their sports packaged in different ways than the middle and upper classes. Moreover, working-class individuals were attracted to prize fighting and to the animal blood sports, which the "better" people despised by this time.[2]

Taken together, these three articles reveal the transformation of Canadian sports that occurred in the four decades after 1850. They also identify origins of some of the important developments that would occur in the hundred years after 1890.

Notes

1. See S. F. Wise and Douglas Fisher, *Canada's Sporting Heroes, Their Lives and Times* (Don Mills, Ont.: General Publishing Company and Canada's Sports Hall of Fame, 1974), chap. 2.

2. See Peter DeLottinville, "Joe Beef of Montreal: Working-Class Culture and the Tavern, 1869–1889," *Labour/Le Travailleur* 8/9 (Autumn/Spring 1981/82): 9–40.

Canada as elsewhere, this relationship should be investigated with benefit to all who are interested in the social significance of both these aspects of culture.

The academic study of leisure and sport, and the related area of recreation, has rapidly increased in recent years, gaining respect and influence, so that there are now national and international associations and societies devoted to such aspects as their history, philosophy, and sociology, replete with their associated professional journals and texts, conferences and congresses, and supported by an increasing number of related courses in academic institutions. Within the vast literature being generated, there are signs of a growing awareness of the interdependence alluded to at the beginning, such as in the "sport content" of recent leisure texts.[4] In one analysis of "the leisure industry" it is stated that[5] "the development of organizations functioning specifically to cater for people's leisure interests is a feature of the twentieth-century western world."

A major purpose of this article is to demonstrate that, as far as organized sport is concerned, the roots of this "leisure industry" can actually be traced back to the nineteenth century. Although sport has an enduring pedigree even to the earliest civilizations, it can be fairly argued that the phenomenon of "modern sport," like the modern world, was born of the Industrial Revolution and developed over approximately the past two hundred years. At the beginning of the nineteenth century, sport was emerging from medieval inhibitions, still mainly local and rural in nature, generally informal and unstructured, lacking codification or mass direction, and usually rigidly based upon class distinctions. It was largely during the Victorian era, however, that sport became international and urban, closely allied to technology, a highly organized and complex social force.

During this period, too, the traditional ascetic attitude of the Church was gradually transformed into a largely athletic one, as most religious institutions quickly became patrons of sport and found moral benefit in its practice (a convenient stance to say the least, since by 1900, many clergy and their congregations were sport participants, or spectators, or both). At the same time, sport was embraced in similar fashion by the educational institutions, and inserted into the curricula of schools and colleges of the western world on an ever-increasing scale. These changes were more obvious on a greater scale in Great Britain and the United States during the nineteenth century. But even in Canada, with its much smaller population spread over a more vast area, this transition in the nature of sport occurred. Perhaps it is not surprising, however, since so much of Canadian history has been moulded from American and British influence. Nevertheless, the expansion of sport in nineteenth-century Canada reflected significant aspects of its cultural development. In the preface of his classic work on medieval sport, *The Sports and Pastimes of the People of England*, published in 1801, Joseph Strutt maintained that "in order to form a just estimation of the character of any particular people it is absolutely necessary to investigate the Sports and Pastimes most generally prevalent among them."[6] Since then, events and other writers have confirmed the validity of Strutt's thesis many times over. Another assertion of this paper, therefore, is that a pre- and post-Confederation examination of *sport* is necessary for "a just estimation of the character" of the Canadian people. A comprehensive examination is of course impossible in the space available but it is hoped that a brief analysis of selected factors — such as British influence; Montreal as "a cradle of Canadian sport"; urbanization and transportation; political patronage; women's participation; Sunday leisure time; school and college sport — will sustain conviction that organized sport by the year 1900 was characterized by many of the features usually identified with "the leisure industry" of this century.

The British Influence

If one were obliged to select but a single factor as the most significant in the history of sport in Canada during the nineteenth century, it would be British influence. This is not to deny or disparage other ethno-cultural contributions — such as the earlier and long-standing French presence, the indigenous activities of the Indians, the American import of baseball, or the participation of the other European ethnic groups in the latter part of the century — or to maintain that the British effect in this respect was always beneficial, superior or welcome. But it was paramount. Strutt's work already referred to, revealed the English as a sports-loving people for centuries before 1800; and this in turn provided the model for a similar account of the sporting traditions of the neighbouring Scottish people.[7] And if, as it has been maintained here, modern sport is largely a product of the Industrial Revolution, then the United Kingdom as its birthplace seems a logical starting point. In fact, many authorities have acknowledged Britain as "the mother of modern sport." Arlott and Daley have pointed out "there is a tendency to suggest that England invented a number of games but that is not strictly true....England's contribution to sports is that it developed many of them to a high standard and formulated them so that they might be played competitively in orderly fashion."[8]

According to the late H.A. Harris, consideration of the place of sport in modern society need begin only at the point where games become national, which depended upon agreement throughout the country on a code of rules for each game, and in his view: "In this develop-ment, Britain led the World."[9] P.C. McIntosh has agreed with these sentiments earlier but stressed the export factor: "the panorama of World Sport in the middle of the twentieth century shows games and sports from many different countries of origin....Nevertheless, the majority of sports in current practice, and the very great majority of the more popular, were exported from Britain."[10]

British influence in sport then, was seen as unparallelled during the nineteenth century with respect to the transformation to orderliness, the development of organizations, and export to other lands. Al-though it may be inaccurate, therefore, to describe Britain as the cradle of sport, it may be described as the main crucible in which modern sport was forged for mass production and consumption and later dis-tributed on a world basis through the international network of the Em-pire (now Commonwealth).

Sports are diffused by people, and in the evolution of modern sport, explorers preceded the colonists and made the first social contacts in the new lands ("the first recorded international football match" was between British seamen seeking a North-West passage, and Green-land Eskimos, in 1586).[11] After settlement, these territories were often maintained or expanded by military means, and soldiers joined mer-chants, missionaries, and other settlers in leisure-time pursuits. The off-duty British garrison and its environs in British North America, as in other countries,[12] often became the social center where indigenous pastimes were enjoyed and developed or British sports maintained.[13] As Lindsay maintained in his analysis of "The Influence of the Military Garrisons" prior to Confederation:

> While the parts played by individuals and institutions in the development of sport in Canada were major ones, there can be no doubting that the sporting example set by the British army garrisons gave impetus to that development. At a time when commissions in the army were bought, the of-ficers would have been products of the English Public Schools system, and its attendant sporting traditions....Not only did they provide funds for trophies and awards in many different sports, but they also provided the necessary organization and leadership.[14]

Lindsay is the most comprehensive historian of Canadian sport be-tween 1807 and 1867 (the year 1807 was selected as the starting point since in that year, the Montreal Curling Club, "the first regularly or-ganized sporting club in Canada," was formed), and his well-documented, prodigious account of the growth of approximately 40 pre-Confederation sports indicates the paramount British influence at work throughout. A major recommendation in his conclusion, in fact, is for further investigations into "whether British influence has hindered or spurred the development of indigenous sports in other countries which were once early British colonies."[15] The contemporary comment of a traveller around 1860 is also revealing. "The Canadians," he said, "are thoroughly a people for amusement, and enjoy all kinds of recreation exceedingly. They follow out the customs of the English to a great extent, and participate freely in the games so loved in the old country."[16] In a vastly different climate and terrain, it seems that the leisure-time pursuits of the British in British North America, as far as sport was concerned, still largely resembled those of the mother country in many respects.

The same comment applies in the post-1867 Dominion of Canada, where the British-born or their descendants were in the forefront of the phenomenal "rise of sport" which occurred in the latter half of the nineteenth-century.[17] They naturally predominated in the development of traditional British sports such as association or rugby football, cricket, curling or golf; but also in the creation and promotion of "new Canadian" sports like ice-hockey or lacrosse.[18] This is perhaps not surprising in view of the fact that in 1871, out of a total Dominion population of nearly three and a half million people, "British Isles origins" accounted for no less than 2 110 502 in number; and thirty years later in 1901, this figure had increased to more than three million of British stock out of a total population figure of 5 371 315.[19] To be sure, the numbers of immigrants from "other European origins," notably Dutch, German, Italian, Russian, and Scandinavian, was now increasing significantly, and these were appearing on the sporting scene as well. But organized sport still largely reflected the fact that this was a British Dominion in social character. Even in the middle of the Prairies in south-east Saskatchewan during the 1880s and 1890s one could find "an exotic experiment of English colonization" in the form of Cannington Manor.[20] Here the activities of the transplanted upper-class pioneers included tennis, cricket, football, horseraces (including steeplechase), fox-hunting, shooting, sailing on Cannington Lake (as well as painting, reading and discussion groups, amateur theatricals and a Choral Society).[21] Also in the west at this time, it was the men of the North-West Mounted Police, most of whom were British, who were the most active in the formation of first clubs and competition in many similar sports. And the NWMP post, like its predecessor in the East, the British military garrison, also became the social centre of several pioneer communities.[22]

Montreal, the Cradle of Canadian Sport

Prior to its westward expansion, however, the "cradle of Canadian sport"[23] was the city of Montreal. Here was the centre of a vast commercial empire, the headquarters of the fur trade, banking and shipping enterprises, and canals and railways construction projects. Its sporting status was achieved initially by a group of dynamic businessmen and entrepreneurs, as well as professional men and military officers, who represented the confident civic elite. Such people had leisure and wealth enough to enjoy themselves in various kinds of recreation from an early period. Gradually, an increasing number of colleagues and employees were able to participate as well as their leisure time also increased, until sport in many forms was available to all by the close of the nineteenth century. The unique growth of sport in Montreal was a social reflection of the city's general significance in Canadian history.[24]

Most of the first clubs in numerous sports in Canada, in fact, were formed during the nineteenth century in Montreal, such as: Montreal Curling Club (1807); Montreal Snowshoe Club (1840); Montreal Olympic Club (1842/43); Montreal Lacrosse Club (1856); Montreal Football Club (1868); Montreal Golf Club (1873); Montreal Toboggan Club (ca. 1880); and the Montreal Aquatics Polo Club (1887). It is also probable that the following were the first of their kind: Montreal Fox Hunt (1829); Montreal Racquets Club (1840); Montreal Skating Club (1859); Montreal Pedestrian Club (1873); Point St. Charles Canoe Club of Montreal (1875); Montreal Swimming Club (1876); and the Montreal Bicycle Club (1878). A further treasure hunt for "sporting firsts" (trivia?) would also reveal, for example, that as early as 1802 the first billiards table "owned and operated by public license" was registered at Montreal;[25] whilst in 1836 the first racquets court was built there at the corner of Craig and St. Peter streets;[26] and the "first snowshoe races" were said to have taken place around Montreal in 1843.[27]

The sport of ice-hockey has been described as the national religion of Canada, the Dominion's "dance of life" and "the Canadian metaphor";[28] and even so serious a scholar as William Kilbourn has suggested Toronto's Maple Leaf Gardens as "the most important religious building in Canada."[29] No other sport has so affected the athletic conscience or nationalistic soul of this nation.[30] For this reason considerable prestige accrues from pioneering associations with this Canadian invention, and the debate concerning the origins and evolution of ice-hockey here has been long-standing and unresolved. Nevertheless, the codification necessary for it to be regarded as an organized and new sport, most resembling the ice-hockey of today, occurred in Montreal between 1875 when "the first true game of organized hockey was played in the Victoria Rink" and 1877 with "the printing in full of hockey's first rules."[31]

A similar claim is justified with regard to the development of lacrosse, also. Before ice-hockey became so popular that it qualified as "Canada's national game" in so many respects, lacrosse was described in those terms in the title of a book published by a Montreal dentist, Dr. George Beers, in 1869.[32] Thought to have derived from the North American Indian game of baggataway, lacrosse was first played by whites at various athletic meetings in Montreal during the 1840s, sponsored by the Olympic Club and the Caledonian Society.[33] The Montreal Lacrosse Club, formed in 1856, was probably the first lacrosse club ever organized. In 1867 a National Lacrosse Association was formed, which by November of that year could claim no less than 80 member clubs and 2 000 registered players.[34] Earlier, in July of Confederation year: "Mr. Johnson of Montreal took 18 Caughnawaga Indians to England for several exhibition games, and Mr. L. Weir of the Montreal Lacrosse Club organized a club in Glasgow, Scotland."[35]

Later the indefatigable Dr. Beers arranged two more successful tours of the British Isles, the first in 1876 and again in 1883, selecting players from the Montreal Club and the Caughnawaga Indians. Before these overseas promotions, "the first international match" in lacrosse was played at Montreal between the Mohawks of Troy, New York, and the Montreal Lacrosse Club, in 1868. Seventeen years afterwards, when a North of Ireland lacrosse team visited Canada, it was naturally the guest of the Montreal club.[36]

Beers was also a leading proponent of the Montreal Amateur Athletic Association (M.A.A.A.), the formation of which has been called "a landmark event in Canadian sporting history" and "undoubtedly the most important single development in the history of Canadian sport." The M.A.A.A. was incorporated in 1881 through the amalgamation of many clubs and became Canada's first comprehensive sport and social club, with literally thousands of members. From its ranks came leaders who in turn formed subsequent national sport associations.[37] The verdict of Metcalfe, in his valuable and detailed analysis of "Organized Sport and Social Stratification in Montreal, 1840-1901", supports the thesis of British Influence:

> The predominant position of the British, white collar middle class, *first as participants and always as organizers is striking*....It was the upper middle class who acted as the stimulus to the growth and development of sport, both on a local, provincial and national level and it was the men with organizational and commercial background who had the

Table 1

Growth and Development of Selected Sports in Nineteenth-Century Canada

SPORT	FIRST CLUB(S)	FIRST INTERNATIONAL COMPETITION(S)	NATIONAL ASSOCIATION(S) FORMED
Baseball	Burlington; Hamilton; Barton; Toronto (1854)	a) 3 Canadian teams competed at Detroit Tournament, U.S.A. (1867) b) First Canada vs. U.S.A. series (1878)	Canadian Baseball Association (1864, then 1876)
Basketball	Montreal; St. Stephens, N.B. (1892)	Montreal Y.M.C.A. vs. Vermont, U.S.A. team (1893)	*Canadian Basketball Association (1923)*
Canoeing	Point St. Charles (1875)	T. Wallace of Cobourg, Ont., won international race at Lake George, U.S.A. (1880)	*Canadian Canoe Association (1900)*
Cricket	St. John's, Newfoundland (1828)	a) Toronto vs. St. George's, U.S.A. b) Canada vs. U.S.A. (1844)	Canadian Cricket Association (1892)
Curling	Montreal (1807)	Toronto vs. Buffalo, N.Y. (1864 and 1865)	"Canadian Branch" of the Royal Caledonian Curling Club (1852)
Cycling	Montreal; Halifax (1876)	National Track Cycling Championships, entries from Canada and U.S.A., in Ontario (1890)	a) Canadian Wheelmen's Association (1882) b) *Canadian Cyclists Association (1900)*

Table 1 (continued)

SPORT	FIRST CLUB(S)	FIRST INTERNATIONAL COMPETITION(S)	NATIONAL ASSOCIATION(S) FORMED
Golf	Montreal (1873)	Niagara vs. Chicago (1876)	Royal Canadian Golf Association (1894)
Gymnastics	Montreal (1843, then 1860)	(Lou Seivert of Toronto competed in 1904 Olympic Games)	Canadian Gymnastic Association (1899)
Harness Racing	Quebec (1864)	Canadian Circuit of the U.S. National Trotting Association formed, in Ontario and Quebec (1884)	a) National Trotting Association (1889) b) Canadian Trotting Association (1914)
Horse Racing	Quebec (1789, then 1817)	(American horses competed in various races in British North America, then Dominion of Canada)	Canadian Jockey Club (1895)
Ice-Hockey	Montreal (1877)	American College team toured Ontario and Quebec (1894)	a) Amateur Hockey Association (1886) b) Canadian Junior Amateur Hockey Association (1887)
Lacrosse	Montreal (1842, then 1856)	a) Caughnawaga Indian team toured Britain (1867) b) Several contests between American and Canadian Clubs (1868)	a) National Lacrosse Association (1882) b) National Amateur Lacrosse Association (1892) c) Canadian Lacrosse Association (1887)

Table 1 (continued)

SPORT	FIRST CLUB(S)	FIRST INTERNATIONAL COMPETITION(S)	NATIONAL ASSOCIATION(S) FORMED
Lawn Tennis	Toronto (1876)	a) J.F. Hellmuth of Ontario in Finals of U.S. Championship (1880) b) U.S. players competed in Canadian Championships at Toronto (1883)	Canadian Lawn Tennis Associations (1890)
Rowing	Bytown (1839)	A crew from St. John, N.B. defeated an American crew at Boston (1855)	Canadian Association of Amateur Oarsmen (1880)
Rugby	Montreal (1868); Halifax (1870)	McGill University vs. Howard (1874)	Canadian Intercollegiate Rugby Football Union (1897) *Rugby Union of Canada* (1929)
Shooting	Montreal (1850); Quebec (1862)	Ontario Rifle Association Team competed in England (1871/1872)	Dominion of Canada Rifle Association (1869)
Skating	Montreal (1850)	a) Montreal Skating Club sponsored a "world" championship (1867) b) Louis Rubenstein of Montreal acclaimed as "world figure skating champion" (1883)	Amateur Skating Association of Canada (1888)
Snowshoeing	Montreal (1840, then 1843)	150 members of Montreal Snowshoe Club competed at Carnival in Vermont U.S.A. (1886)	*Canadian Snowshoe Union* (1907)

Table 1 (continued)

SPORT	FIRST CLUB(S)	FIRST INTERNATIONAL COMPETITION(S)	NATIONAL ASSOCIATION(S) FORMED
Soccer	Montreal (1865)	a) Central Association of Ontario vs. St. Louis, U.S.A. (1884) b) Reciprocal tours by Canadian and U.S. teams (1885–1887) c) Canadian team toured United Kingdom (1888)	Dominion Football Association (1878)
Swimming	Montreal (1850, then 1876); Toronto (1875)	a) An American won first "Canadian Championship" race in Montreal (1889) b) Americans won every event at first official Canadian Championships in Ottawa (1898)	*Canadian Amateur Swimming Association* (1909)
Yachting	Kingston (1826)	The Annie Cuthbert from Hamilton Yacht Club defeated American Yacht to win Goodwin Cup (1874)	*Canadian Yachting Association* (1931)

expertise necessary for the long-term development of an organization who provided the leadership....Increasingly these were the men who first as participants and later as organizers provided the necessary guidance for the growth and institutionalization of sport....Sport in Montreal during the nineteenth century was the history of the English, Irish, and Scottish Canadians. French involvement came late and was never a powerful influence on the development of organized games.[38]

One of the earliest instances of political patronage of sport occurred in Montreal in 1844 when the first "Olympic Games" in North America were held there. Obviously these were not a part of de Coubertin's modern festival (begun in 1896, and celebrated at Montreal in 1976), but it certainly was an auspicious two-day occasion, with as many as twenty-nine events, including five lacrosse matches. These Games were given the unprecedented support of the Governor-General, Sir Charles Metcalfe, and the City Corporation. Wise and Fisher were certainly not reticent in their evaluation of the significance of these Montreal Olympic Games of 1844:

Neither in Britain nor in the United States had anything quite like these Games yet been held. Toronto, a few years earlier, had held a number of field days; so had some American cities. But in their size, organization, variety, and social and cultural diversity, Montreal's Olympics were unique — *on the basis of them Montreal has a strong claim to be considered one of the birthplaces of modern organized sport* [author's italics].[39]

It would appear that the colonial British sporting pioneers in Canada were even ahead of their countrymen at home in certain respects.

The Political Patronage of Sport

The Vice-Regal patronage of sport in the Dominion which occurred in the nineteenth century after 1867 was unique and a significant factor in the development of Canadian sport. Various governors-general, prestigious figures whose leisure activities tended to be followed with interest throughout the nation, participated in and promoted many sports. The official residence at Rideau Hall in Ottawa became a social centre at which winter sports were particularly enjoyed. Lord Dufferin, governor-general from 1872–1878, had a curling rink built there at his own expense, formed a Vice-Regal club, and promoted curling widely, instituting the Governor-General's prize for the popular sport. This impetus was maintained by the next two holders of the office, the Marquis of Lorne and the Marquis of Lansdowne.[40] Their successor Lord Stanley (1888-93) inhabited Rideau Hall when "sport figured more prominently than ever before"[41] and as the donor of the Stanley Cup — "the holy grail of hockey" — his place in Canadian history is assured. Lord Aberdeen (1893-98) was another keen curler; but the next Scot in office, the Earl of Minto, was more keen on skating and founded the Minto Skating Club (from which there later emerged a Canadian World Champion, Barbara Ann Scott), and established the Minto Cup trophy for lacrosse. During his tenure it was maintained yet again that "sport now played a more prominent part in the life of Rideau Hall than before."[42] Although direct government involvement in organized sport in terms of actual financing through the public purse was really a feature of the next century, prior to 1900 Canadian sport certainly enjoyed the increasing patronage of political figures as not only governors-general, but others such as Sir John A. Macdonald and Donald A. Smith (later Lord Strathcona), actively supported the organized leisure-time pursuits of the citizens.[43]

The Process of Urbanization

Apart from Ottawa and Montreal, of course, the city of Toronto also soon became a contender for the centre of organized sport in Canada. Before 1900 Toronto boasted some fifty athletic and sporting clubs and was the home of many Dominion and Ontario sport associations.[44] The distinguished Canadian historian A.R.M. Lower, seeking to show that "the growth of organized sports is therefore a good indicator of the turn from rural values to urban, from grave to gay, from puritan to pagan," used several examples of leisure-time pursuits in Toronto during the 1880s to support his argument, indicating the city's importance in this respect during this period.[45] Ottawa as the capital city would always have a certain snob appeal surrounding its sports, and Montreal's status as the "cradle" was unique as stated, but by the late Victorian period Toronto rivalled and perhaps surpassed them both as a home of organized sport.[46] This is certainly not surprising since the process of urbanization was an integral feature in the growth of organized sport.

Cities have existed for thousands of years, of course, but only in the modern world have they accommodated a significant proportion of the world's population. In 1800, when this amounted to less than 900 million people, urban dwellers in cities of 20 000 or more made up only 2.4 percent of the world total; by 1950, with a world population approaching 4 *billion*, this percentage had increased ninefold. This change has been particularly dramatic in Western Societies, again as an inescapable facet of the Industrial Revolution. For example, today no less than three-quarters of Americans are estimated to live in environments officially designated as "urban."[47] To a very large extent, therefore, modern sport is urban sport. The city has become the natural nerve centre of the international sport complex, home of the masses of participants and spectators, and the site of huge stadia and other facilities. This process was well established in the previous century, by the close of which *Homo Ludens* was mainly an urban species.[48]

The population of the new Dominion of Canada in 1867 was approximately three and a half million people, of which by 1871 less than 20 percent lived in either cities or towns.[49] By 1901, 35 percent of the population could be labelled as urban. The 1871 census indicated that there were 20 cities or towns with more than 5 000 inhabitants, with the largest being Montreal (115 000), Quebec (59 699), Toronto (59 000), St. John (41 325), and Halifax (29 582). Other urban areas of note (i.e., over 10 000 in population) were: Hamilton (26 880), Ottawa (24 141), London (18 000), and Kingston (12 407). In 1901, not only had the number of cities and towns with more than 5 000 residents increased to 62 in number, but now no less than 24 of them had a population of more than 10 000.[50]

The origins of many games and pastimes were located in rural environments, but the "club" system which typified organized sport was mainly a product of urbanization and it superseded the traditional rural approach to recreation. Urban living imposed new restrictions on individuals, yet it also offered more opportunities for groups with a common interest in a particular activity to organize regular competition under established rules. Thus many sports were codified and played according to quite stringent regulations and within a specified duration of time. The sport of lacrosse provides one interesting example of this development. In 1867, the rules of lacrosse stipulated that "a match will be decided by winning three games out of five" and a "game" occurred each time a goal was scored. Consequently, the actual duration of a game could have been short, to the annoyance of the spectators. In 1880 Toronto was defeated by the Montreal Shamrocks who scored the mandatory three goals in only 6 minutes 25 seconds![51] — Or the game might have to be postponed because of darkness. In 1888, the National Amateur Lacrosse Association (N.A.L.A.) fixed a time limit for matches; and six years later, the N.A.L.A. changed all association matches to the majority of games in two hours. Such accommodations became one of the outstanding features of organized sport in post-Confederation Canada of the nineteenth century, as the number of local clubs in towns and cities increased, and regional, provincial, and national associations began to emerge and govern sport.[52]

The Impact of the Railways

An important aspect in the development of organized sport in urban areas was transportation, both within and between the cities and towns.[53] Although transport along rivers and lakes predominated in Canada, the spread of railways which began after 1850 had the greatest impact in this respect. Up to that year less than 100 miles of track had been laid, but by the time of Confederation a varied network of over 2 000 miles of rail linked the major centres of Ontario in particular, Québec, and the Maritimes. Some railways also went across the international border. The most famous of these iron roads, the trans-continental Canadian Pacific Railway (C.P.R.) was completed in British Columbia in 1885. By the turn of the century there were nearly 18 000 miles of railways across Canada, from the Atlantic to the Pacific. From the beginning these railways facilitated greater social contact and mobility and contributed greatly to the increase in sports clubs and competition. Railway companies soon offered cheaper excursion fares and special rates (or "generous concessions") to sports bodies, and numerous associations and teams were equally quick to take regular advantage of them. Apparently the C.P.R. had a special interest in the Montreal Baseball Club and granted full exemption for its team managers as well as special half-fare rates for its opponents. The Canadian Wheelmen's Association frequently benefited from similar largess, too, and even had the use of special trains to all parts of the Dominion for its meetings. Matches between members of the National Lacrosse Association (N.L.A.) league involved considerable railway traveling, thus in 1889 the practice of deducting traveling expenses from the gate receipts for the visiting team was introduced. Railway companies were confident of rower Edward (Ned) Hanlan's ability to draw the crowds and paid a commission from their revenue to the Hanlan Club. Employees of several railway companies also formed their own sports clubs and teams, such as at The Great Western Railway Club or the Montreal Grand Trunk Boat Club.[54] The *Globe* of Toronto reported in 1898 (December 20): "At a meeting which was held in the Railway Y.M.C.A. last evening a basketball league was organized composed of the following shops: machine, blacksmith, car, and erecting shops."

Table 2

Multi-Sport Governing Bodies in Nineteenth-Century Canada

Organization	Year of Formation	Brief Description
Montreal Amateur Athletic Association (M.A.A.A.)	1881	Formation described as "undoubtedly the most important single development in the history of Canadian sport... Canada's first substantial sporting and social club." Established by the confluence of several clubs — (Montreal) Snowshoe, Lacrosse, Bicycle, Football clubs, and Tuque Bleue Toboggan Club — into one Association (incorporated under Quebec Act). Possessed excellent indoor and outdoor facilities for several sports; soon joined by chess, debating, drama, hockey, music and skating clubs as well. Several national associations in Canadian sport (see table 1) evolved from the "energies and organizational expertise" of the M.A.A.A., including the A.A.A. of Canada (1884).
Amateur Athletic Association of Canada	1884	Organized to regulate "such athletic sports as are not under control of other Associations [and] ... mainly to regulate amateur competitions on the cinder path" (i.e., track and field). In particular, it was the authoritative body on the question of *amateur status*, which became a serious problem with the increase of professional sport. Later it was re-named the Canadian Amateur Athletic Union (1898).
La Société canadienne pour l'avancement du sport	1899	Formed by prominent members of the French-speaking community in Montreal for the purpose of establishing a "Golden Book of Honour" for outstanding athletes, a sporting archives and library, and a scientific approach toward coaching and training. Despite the patronage of the Governor-General, the Mayor of Montreal, and M. Dandurand, promotor of "Queens Parc" a complex of lacrosse, cycling and horseracing, the society only lasted a year or so.

In short, the impact of the railways on the social activities of urban residents in the nineteenth century was considerable, especially with respect to the growth of organized sport.[55] Whilst it is mainly the jet-engine airplane which renders the schedules of the North American sports leagues of today possible, the foundation for such consistent and wide-ranging competition and interaction was largely laid on the ground by the railways of the nineteenth century.

From Religious Asceticism to Athleticism

Mention of the "Railway Y.M.C.A." reminds us of the remarkable growth of this institution in the previous century. Begun in 1841 in a back-street of London, England, where tea and bible readings were offered to young men as an antidote to the vices of the city, the Young Men's Christian Association rapidly expanded across North America and quickly assumed the appearance of an *athletic* association. It had built hundreds of gymnasia, appointed directors of physical education, and even promoted its own sports, before the turn of the century. In many ways, the Y.M.C.A. epitomized the new emphasis being given to physical activities by the Church and its related bodies.[56]

Again, in Canada the transformation from religious asceticism to athleticism was less pronounced and slower than in Britain or the United States, but the trend was obvious in the nineteenth century. Because of laws which severely restricted physical recreation on Sundays (such as the Lord's Day Act of 1845) early sport competitions in the urban centres of Canada were largely confined to weekdays, thereby usually precluding participation by the working class. When early closing on Saturdays became more widespread from the 1850s onward, however, working men were able to participate more.[57] Yet for many, Sunday remained the only really free day from work, and therefore Sunday sport became an issue. Sabbatarianism, "the doctrine of strict observance of the Sabbath" (i.e., no sport on Sundays), seemed out of step with the industrial society which was being created in the nineteenth century; and violations of Sunday sport ordinances became more frequent as traditional attitudes were challenged. While the Mayor of Toronto ordered the arrest of a group of young boys (aged 13 to 16) for playing shinty on a Sunday in 1863 (a crime for which George Brown, the famous editor of the *Globe*, felt that 24 hours in the jail cells would be a suitable deterrent),[58] thirty-two years later a Toronto High Court judge reversed a judgement in an appeal case involving four golfers fined for playing on Sunday, stating that "this game of golf is not a game within the meaning of the law. It is not noisy. It attracts no crowds. It is not gambling. It is on a parallel, it seems to me, with a gentleman going out for a walk on Sunday, and as he walks, switching off the heads of weeds with his walking stick."[59]

As Schrodt has pointed out in her analysis of sabbatarianism and sport in Canadian society: "This rather lenient attitude was to become more prevalent as the nineteenth century drew to a close, but at the same time it aroused strong opposition from the Lord's Day Alliance." This Alliance was formed in 1899 to protect the Sabbath as day of rest and worship, and since its birth it has campaigned vigorously but vainly against Sunday sport.[60]

If any one factor was mainly responsible for the failure of the Lord's Day Alliance to restrict Sunday sport, it was the triumph of nineteenth-century "muscular Christianity" — a glib phrase invented during the 1850s to describe sentiments which were most successfully espoused in the novels of Charles Kingsley (*Westward Ho!*, 1855; *Two Years Ago*, 1857), and Thomas Hughes (*Tom Brown's Schooldays*, 1857). Briefly, the essential elements of this timely gospel were that sports (especially team games) contributed significantly towards the development of moral character, fostered a desirable patriotism, and that such participation and its ensuing virtues were transferable to other situations and/or to later life, i.e., from the playground-or-playing field to the battlefield.[61] Indeed, many have seen muscular Christianity as a major factor in the growth of the British Empire, and even the Western world. Here was an attempt to reconcile the centuries-old Christian faith with the new realties of the modern world to the apparent satisfaction of Victorian and Edwardian consciences. The "games-build-character" theory was obviously a convenient and seductive one, which was avidly adopted by the Church in its various denominations, as well as by private religious associations, all struggling to meet the unique social challenges of an industrial society, particularly in the second-half of the nineteenth century. As Helen Meller so aptly described it in England:

> A new development came to their rescue, which was to solve all their problems, then and in the foreseeable future. It was, in a word, sport. The evolution of organized sport at the public schools unleashed one of the greatest forces considered to be on the side of the angels in the late nineteenth century....It could obviously be argued that physical exercise was vital for those brought up in the un-natural conditions of an urban environment and destined to spend much of their life in sedentary occupations, and that a healthy body and a sense of well-being were

legitimate objectives for any Christian. Further, sport absorbed energies and thought which idleness might otherwise lead astray to evil outlets, and finally team games and innocent competition were ideal methods of social training in codes of desirable social conduct.[62]

Inevitably, with such moral justifications, traditional "holy days" became simply "holidays," and the Sabbath was gradually assimilated into the sporting calendar. Church leagues in various sports arose on either side of the Atlantic. Despite its intelligent and vocal critics — from Wilkie Collins and later Rudyard Kipling to George Orwell, among others, who saw it rather as a form of "Athletic Paganism" — the doctrine of muscular Christianity was embraced comprehensively both in the United States[63] and in Canada[64] during the nineteenth century. And, of course, it was a major motivation behind de Coubertin's eventual founding of the modern Olympic Games, the largest international multi-sports festival of all times, during the 1890s.[65]

The cult of athleticism which characterized the public schools and universities of Victorian England (and Scotland, in such schools as Fettes and Loretto) was replicated to a large extent in the educational institutions of Canada as well, where the tenets of muscular Christianity became firmly entrenched during the nineteenth century.[66] Lindsay documented this foundation in British North America prior to 1867, in his chapter on "Sport in Schools and Colleges";[67] and Cox continued the analysis in the Dominion until 1900, under the heading of "The Influence of Schools and Universities," which he described as "abundant and long lasting." He pointed out that "many of the schools and universities were staffed by Englishmen steeped in the traditional English love of sports."[68] As in England, the students of these Canadian institutions were unique pioneers in the organization of amateur sports — particularly such team games as association and rugby football, cricket, and ice-hockey — and the extension of competition in these sports throughout the nineteenth century. Here again British influence is seen as paramount; and once more the significance of Montreal is indicated, since the students of McGill University were especially active in this regard. But one could go on to recognize the interdependence of the other factors briefly mentioned here, also, for most of the schools and colleges involved were located in cities (again, the educational establishments of Toronto in particular rivalled Montreal for sporting supremacy) and benefitted from the urbanization trend; and improved transportation, especially railways, enabled intercollegiate sport to thrive.

The Participation of Women

One other factor needs to be mentioned in this brief survey, i.e., the participation of women in organized sport in Canada during the previous century. Hall maintained that the history of women's sport in Canada prior to 1914 could be conveniently divided into four major time periods; (1) the absence of sport (1600–1860); (2) the beginning of participation (1860–1880); (3) the "new woman" and athleticism (1880–1900); (4) the increasing involvement in sport (1900–1914).[69] Obviously, categories 2 and 3 mainly concern us here; but many of the gentle women of British North America, of course, did participate in many recreational pastimes such as canoeing, croquet, dancing, fox hunting, horseback riding, tobogganning, and the like. However, their non-participatory but admiring presence was more usual and welcome:

> Female attendance at horse races, regattas, cricket matches, and other such spectator sports was obviously encouraged, as most early nineteenth-century newspaper reports of these events carried verbose tributes to the ladies present, often to the exclusion of any mention of the results of the contests themselves. On reading these old newspapers, one receives the distinct impression that the whole success of the organized sports meeting depended entirely upon the number of ladies who could be encouraged to decorate the scene with their gay ensembles.[70]

Ladies "wrapped in furs as cuddlesome companions" and known as "muffins" were also considered as essential accoutrements to the officer owners of expensive carrioles during their leisure-time winter excursions.[71]

It was in the second half of the nineteenth century that many well-to-do women in Canada began to break away from their traditional roles as admiring spectators of male sport or as non-competitive participants in more genteel activities. They now became involved in other sports such as baseball, basketball, bicycling, curling, field hockey, golf, ice-hockey, and pedestrianism, either through becoming a part of men's sports clubs, or by forming their own. Naturally their athletic emancipation was also greatly affected by some of the factors already mentioned — British influence; urbanization; patronage by the powerful and the sanction of the Church; and the growing respect for athleticism in academic circles — but in addition women had two unique barriers to overcome before they were a significant force in organized sport. One was the deeply-ingrained attitude in the society of the time that not only was female participation in certain sports (especially team games involving body contact) considered to be "unfeminine" or "unladylike," but that also it could actually be unhealthy or even dangerous to their more delicate frames and constitutions. Some of the pioneering endeavors by female sportswomen, therefore, were constantly subject to criticism (mostly, but not always, by males) along these lines. However, there was support as well from several quarters and definite progress. Much of that progress was obtained by sportswomen challenging contemporary fashions in clothing and daring to wear controversial sporting attire which was more revealing but much more suitable for various physical activities. (The fashionable crinoline was one major impediment to active participation.) The most dramatic example was provided by the famous "bloomers" worn by many bicycle riders; or by their "bicycle skirt" with a "daring but practical split." By the twentieth century the Canadian sportswoman "had come of age" with "a costume for everything" whether it be "the hideous black middies she wore for basketball," the ankle-length calico skirts used for tennis, or the "hand-made homespun from the Highlands" golf suit.[72] As Lindsay summarized:

> Despite being continually urged throughout the nineteenth century, to remain ladylike, decorative, and static, by 1900 women had experienced independence from the dictates of fashion and prescribed activities. No longer choosing to be encased and hobbled in sweeping skirts, no longer restricted to gentle games deemed by over-protective males as suitable to the delicate female constitution, no longer rebuked by society for seeking pleasure in physical exercise, the woman of the new century bicycled towards the goal of individual freedom, and emancipation from cultural taboos.[73]

Although women's sport is an area which still has its fair share of controversies today, no one would deny that the sportswomen of the previous century were initially responsible for gaining a significant measure of female athletic emancipation. Their contribution was yet another manifestation of the transformation which organized sport had brought in the leisure habits of Canadians.

Conclusion

Hopefully, leisure researchers of the future may be persuaded to investigate the phenomenon of organized sport in the previous century

Table 3

Women's Participation in Canadian Sport in the Nineteenth Century

Sport	First-or-early participation and association(s)
Archery	Montreal Ladies' Club (1858)
Baseball	Girls reported playing in Newcastle and Chatham, N.B. (1890); ladies' club formed in Nanaimo, B.C. (1890).
Basketball	Ladies playing at Toronto and Whitby, Ont. (1895).
Bicycling	Many lady members in clubs during 1880s and 1890s from 1894, ladies formed own clubs: ladies' half-mile race at Goderich, Ontario (1895).
Curling	First ladies' club, at Montreal (1894).
Equestrian Sports	First Dominion Championships for Women in (1895)
Fencing	Toronto Club catered for women members (1895); University College, Toronto, formed a women's club (1895).
Field Hockey	First ladies' club, at Vancouver (1896).
Figure Skating	60 ladies demonstrated "Fancy Skating" at Halifax (1863); ladies of Rideau Club, Ottawa, held a Figure Skating Competition (1890)

Fox Hunting	Ladies participating at Montreal (1873).
Golf	In the 1890s clubs at Hamilton, Montreal, Niagara, Oshawa, Ottawa, Quebec, Sherbrooke, Toronto, Winnipeg and Victoria all had female members; first ladies' interclub match, Toronto vs. Rosedale (1896); first ladies' interprovincial match, Toronto vs. Montreal and Quebec (1897).
Ice-Hockey	Ladies' team organized in Barrie, Ontario (1892); female students at McGill University, Montreal, hold interclass games (1894).
Lawn Tennis	Tournaments for women organized at Ottawa (1881) and Montreal (1881); first Dominion Championships for Women at Toronto Club (1883).
Racquets	First Dominion Championships for women at Ottawa (1881).
Rowing	Many regattas during 1870s included events for ladies; one-mile girls' single-sculling race in Grand Trunk Regatta, at Montreal (1880).
Snowshoeing	Ladies' Prince of Wales Club formed at Montreal (1861).
Swimming	Ladies granted privileges at Montreal club on 3 days a week (1889).
Tobogganing	First competitions of Tuque Bleue Club in Montreal included a "combined lady-and-gentleman" race (1885).

more fully, perhaps as a foundation for the more comprehensive and complex leisure industry of today. The factors outlined briefly here certainly need more examination and other aspects need to be explored. Anyone interested in the temperance movement, for example, should find an analysis of its relationship to the growth of organized sport to be a worthwhile project. Similarly, there is a productive area of investigation into nineteenth-century sport awaiting the researcher who is interested in the economics of leisure, and the related areas of amateurism and professionalism. Whatever paths are followed, it is already clear that organized sport in Canada before 1900 revealed the development of many organizations which functioned "specifically to cater for people's leisure interests"; and it could be argued that this was a feature of the nineteenth-century Western world.

Notes

1. C. Diem, *Weltgeschichte des Sports und der Leibeserziehung* (Stuttgart: J.G. Cotta'sche Buchhandlung Nach F, 1960); J. Arlott, and A. Daley, *Pageantry of Sport: From the Age of Chivalry to the Age of Victoria* (New York: Hawthorn Books, 1968).

2. J.R. Betts, *America's Sporting Heritage: 1850–1950* (Reading, Mass.: Addison-Wesley, 1974); K. Dunstan, *Sports* (Australia: Cassell, 1973); H.A. Harris, *Sport in Britain: Its Origins and Development* (London: Stanley Paul, 1975); M.L. Howell and N. Howell, *Sports and Games in Canadian Life: 1700 to the Present* (Toronto: Macmillan, 1969).

3. C.R. Blackburn, "The Development of Sports in Alberta, 1900–1918" (M.A. thesis, University of Alberta, 1974); R.D. Day, "Impulse to Addiction: A Narrative History of Sport in Chatham, Ontario, 1790–1895" (M.A. thesis, University of Western Ontario, 1977).

4. See, for example, T.L. Burton, *Making Man's Environment: Leisure* (Toronto: Van Nostrand Reinhold, 1976); S. Parker, *The Sociology of Leisure* (London: George Allen and Unwin, 1976); K. Roberts, *Leisure* (London: Longman, 1970); and R.W. Vickerman, *The Economics of Leisure and Recreation* (London: Macmillan, 1975).

5. Roberts, *Leisure*, 63.

6. J. Strutt, *The Sports and Pastimes of the People of England* (London: Thomas Tegg, 1801), 2.

7. R.S. Fittis, *Sports and Pastimes of Scotland* (Paisley: Alexander Gardner, 1891).

8. Arlott and Daley, *Pageantry of Sport*, 13.

9. H. Uberhorst, ed., *Geschichte der Leibesubunger*, vol. 4 (n.p.: Berleg Bartels und Wernitz K.G., 1972), 136.

10. P.C. McIntosh, *Sport in Society* (London: C.A. Watts, 1963), 80.

11. S.E. Morison, *The European Discovery of America* (New York: Oxford University Press, 1971), 597.

12. See, for example, the counterpart in India described in L. Collins and D. Lapierre, *Freedom at Midnight* (New York: Simon and Schuster, 1975).

13. M. Atwood, "Days of the Rebels, 1815–1840" in *Canada's Illustrated Heritage* (Toronto: Natural Science of Canada, 1977), 117; L.F. Hannon, *Forts of Canada* (Toronto: McClelland and Stewart, 1969), 155–59.

14. P.L. Lindsay, "A History of Sport in Canada, 1807–1867" (Ph.D. dissertation, University of Alberta, 1969), 351.

15. Ibid., 398.

16. G.M. Craig, ed., *Early Travellers in the Canadas, 1791–1867* (Toronto: Macmillan, 1955), 252.

17. Howell and Howell, *Sports and Games in Canadian Life*, 59–136.

18. A.E. Cox, "A History of Sports in Canada, 1868–1900" (Ph.D. dissertation, University of Alberta, 1969); G. Redmond, "The Scots and Sport in Nineteenth-Century Canada" (Ph.D. dissertation, University of Alberta, 1972); H. Roxborough, *One Hundred Not Out: The Story of Nineteenth-Century Canadian Sport* (Toronto: Ryerson Press, 1966).

19. *The Canadian Pocket Encyclopedia*, 31st annual ed., 1976–1977 (Toronto: Quick Canadian Facts, 1977), 23.

20. A.E.M. Hewlett, "England on the Prairies," *The Beaver* (Dec. 1952): 20–25.

21. J. Batten, "Canada Moves Westward, 1880–1890" in *Canada's Illustrated Heritage* (Toronto: Natural Science of Canada, 1977), 51–57.

22. P.D. Routledge, "The North-West Mounted Police and their Influence on the Sporting and Social Life of the North-West Territories, 1870–1904" (M.A. thesis, University of Alberta, 1978).

23. S.F. Wise and D. Fisher, *Canada's Sporting Heroes* (Don Mills, Ont.: General Publishing, 1974), 21.

24. G. Redmond, "The Olympic City of 1844 and 1976: Reflections upon Montreal in the History of Canadian Sport'" *CAHPER Journal* 42, 4 (March–April 1976): 43–51.

25. Roxborough, *One Hundred Not Out*, 92–93.

26. Howell and Howell, *Sports and Games in Canadian Life*, 41.

27. H.W. Becket, *The Montreal Snow-Shoe Club* (Montreal: Becket Brothers, 1882), 9–11.

28. B. Kidd and J. Macfarlane, *The Death of Hockey* (Toronto: New Press, 1972), 4.

29. W. Kilbourn, *Religion in Canada: The Spiritual Development of a Nation* (Toronto: McClelland and Stewart, 1968), 6.

30. See the prologue in Wise and Fisher, *Canada's Sporting Heroes*, xi.

31. Ibid., 44–46.

32. W.G. Beers, *Lacrosse: The National Game of Canada* (Montreal: Dawson Brothers, 1869).

33. F.E. Leonard and G.B. Affleck, *A Guide to the History of Physical Education* (Philadelphia: Lea and Febiger, 1947), 401; Montreal *Gazette*, Aug. 29, 1844.

34. Lindsay, "A History of Sport in Canada," 117–32.

35. Leonard and Affleck, *A Guide to the History of Physical Education*, 402.

36. T.G. Vellathotham, "A History of Lacrosse in Canada Prior to 1914" (M.A. thesis, University of Alberta, 1968); A.M. Weyand and M.R. Roberts, *The Lacrosse Story* (Baltimore: H. and A. Herman, 1965), 40–51.

37. Wise and Fisher, *Canada's Sporting Heroes*, 19–20.

38. A. Metcalfe, "Organized Sport and Social Stratification in Montreal, 1840–1901" in *Canadian Sport: Sociological Profiles*, ed. R.S. Gruneau and J.G. Albinson (Don Mills, Ont.: Addison-Wesley, 1976), 96–97. Italics in the original.

39. Wise and Fisher, *Canada's Sporting Heroes*, 13. Italics added.

40. Redmond, "The Scots and Sport in Nineteenth-Century Canada," 161–62.

41. R.H. Hubbard, *Rideau Hall — An Illustrated History of Government House, Ottawa* (Ottawa: Queen's Printer, n.d.), 33.

42. Ibid., 102.

43. Howell and Howell, *Sports and Games in Canadian Life*, 59–136.

44. *Athletic Life*, (March 1895), 150.

45. A.R.M. Lower, *Canadians in the Making: A Social History of Canada* (Toronto: Longmans, 1958), 321–26.

46. J. Weiler, "The Idea of Sport in Late Victorian Canada: Sport and Athletic Institutions in Toronto, 1880–1900" (paper supplied to the author by Mr. T. West, curator of Canada's Sports Hall of Fame, Toronto, n.d.).

47. M.L. De Fleur, W.V. D'Antonio, and L.B. Le Fleur, *Sociology: Human Society* (Glenview, Ill.: Scott, Foresman, 1973), 279.

48. J. Huizinga, *Homo Ludens: A Study of the Play Element in Culture* (Boston: Beacon Press, 1955).

49. L.O. Stone, *Urban Development in Canada: An Introduction to Demographic Aspects* (Ottawa: Dominion Bureau of Statistics, 1967), 29.

50. *Census of Canada,* 1901, 18–22.

51. Howell and Howell, *Sports and Games in Canadian Life,* 72.

52. Cox, "A History of Sports in Canada"; I.F. Jobling, "Sport in Nineteenth-Century Canada: The Effects of Technological Changes on its Development" (Ph.D. dissertation, University of Alberta, 1970).

53. G.P. de T. Glazebrook, *A History of Transportation in Canada,* vol. 2 (Toronto: McClelland and Stewart, 1964).

54. Cox, "A History of Sports in Canada,"; Jobling, "Sport in Nineteenth-Century Canada."

55. See J.R. Betts, "Organized Sport in Industrial America" (Ph.D. dissertation, University of Michigan, 1951).

56. C.H. Hopkins, *History of the Y.M.C.A. in North America* (New York: Association Press, 1951); Leonard and Affleck, *A Guide to the History of Physical Education,* 515–28.

57. Lindsay, "A History of Sport in Canada," 9–10.

58. Ibid., 45.

59. Cox, "A History of Sports in Canada," 134–35.

60. B. Schrodt, "Sabbatarisnism and Sport in Canadian Society," *Journal of Sport History* (Spring 1977), 22–23.

61. McIntosh, *Sport in Society,* 69–79; G. Redmond, "The First Tom Brown's Schooldays and Others: Origins of Muscular Christianity in Children's Literature, 1762–1855," *Quest* 30 (Summer 1978): 4-18.

62. H.E. Meller, *Leisure and the Changing City, 1870–1914* (London: Routledge and Kegan Paul, 1977).

63. G. Lewis, "The Muscular Christianity Movement," *Journal of Health, Physical Education and Recreation* (May 1966): 27–30.

64. F.H. Armstrong, H.A. Stevenson and J.D. Wilson, *Aspects of Nineteenth-Century Ontario* (Toronto: University of Toronto Press, 1974); A. Metcalfe, "Some Background Influences on Nineteenth-Century Canadian Sport and Physical Education," *Canadian Journal of History of Sport and Physical Education* (May 1974): 62–73.

65. J.M. Leiper, "The International Olympic Committee: The Pursuit of Olympism, 1894–1970" (Ph.D. dissertation, University of Alberta, 1976).

66. G.G. Watson, "Sports and Games in Ontario Private Schools: 1830–1930" (M.A. thesis, University of Alberta, 1970).

67. Lindsay, "A History of Sport in Canada," 335–50.

68. Cox, "A History of Sports in Canada," 391–406.

69. M.A. Hall, "A History of Women's Sport in Canada Prior to World War I" (M.A. thesis, University of Alberta, 1968).

70. P.L. Lindsay, "Women's Place in Nineteenth-Century Sport," *CAHPER Journal* (Sept.–Oct. 1970): 25–28.

71. Hannon, *Forts of Canada,* 153; Atwood, "Days of the Rebels," 117.

72. Hall, "A History of Women's Sport in Canada."

73. Lindsay, "Women's Place in Nineteenth-Century Sport," 28.

Although it was in 1896, the same year that portentous "fair hall" was built, that Jake Gaudaur of Orillia won the world's professional rowing championship from James Stanbury of Australia on the Thames in England, he had been a local hero — at least to Orillians — for many years. In 1875, on Lake Couchiching, racing in one of those doubled-ended lapstreak skiffs mentioned so affectionately in *Unconventional Voyages*, Gaudaur won his first race, defeating Hughie Wise of Toronto over four miles. And there, and on Lake Simcoe at Kempenfeldt Bay, Gaudaur rowed for the next quarter of a century against the world's best: Australians, Englishmen, Americans, the mighty Ned Hanlan himself. In this period, an age just reaching its end when Arthur Lower began to attack the family woodpile, Lake Simcoe and Lake Ontario, the Kennebecasis and Bedford Basin, were nearly as important to the world of international rowing as the Thames itself, and certainly ranked with the Schuylkill and the Hudson.

The likelihood is that most inhabitants of Barrie were quite conscious of the prowess of Gaudaur, and of a good deal more that was going on besides in the way of organized sport. As early as 1846, Barrie, then a village of some 500 people, had its own curling club, one of the first such organizations in Canada West.[2] It appears, too, that the people of Barrie were quite familiar with the casual professionalism typical of track and field sports in the post–1867 period. In 1875, for example, a match race for stakes of $100 a side was held at Barrie "for the championship of Canada" between Dobson, the local pride, and a Galt flash named McCall. McCall won by fifteen feet over the 150-yard distance; "the result disappointed many here as Dobson was considered the faster runner, having beaten his rival on two former occasions." Interestingly, the match race was held "at the race-course," suggesting that yet another organized sport had reached Barrie some time before.[3] In 1891, when Ottawa turned down an opportunity to act as host for the annual regatta of the Canadian Association of Amateur Oarsmen, Barrie put in a bid; so did its rival Orillia.[4]

Probably Arthur Lower was aware of these local activities; but if so, he chose not to recall them. When we were colleagues at Queen's he more than once reproved me (with a directness and a kindness that were both characteristic) for wasting time indulging my interest in sport. For him, sport was not a matter to be taken seriously, and he dismissed it from his mind. Not that he shared the revulsion against physical activity that the classicist M.I. Finley once called "perhaps the most remarkable of all existing academic taboos"; his love of the outdoors, of the challenge of our lakes, rivers, and Shield country has been the devotion of a lifetime. It was rather that games and pastimes had nothing of moment to contribute to the higher earnestness of the historian's calling or to the understanding of a people's past, when compared to pursuits — political, religious, economic — of real significance.

Yet there was more than this. In *Canadians in the Making* he describes our North American descent into barbarism "from the stern Puritanism, self-sacrifice and sense of duty of our grandfathers," to "the gay insouciance, the craving for cheap excitement, of the city mob," a process that has pushed us from the seventeenth century point our development had reached back to the second or third century of the Roman Empire. "In no surer way does our present period mark this turn — this historical retrocession...than in the emphasis it begins to place on sports." Instead of "the zeal and vehemence that went into the life of the nineteenth century — especially in such areas as politics and religion," today "every ordinary man in the country is glued to his television set watching baseball or hockey." Sport, however, not only symbolizes the process of retrocession, it is an agent in that process. It relates "to the lighter side of life," sapping its dignity and reality. Scarcely had we won through to a degree of civic cultivation, than "the irresponsibles of society," the gay blades of the elite and the sordid many at the bottom, deflected our development from rural to urban values, from "Puritan to pagan."[5]

So sport, one gathers, is taken seriously by the historian after all. Arthur Lower, in fact, has given more attention to sport, and assigned to it a greater significance than any previous Canadian historian, even though one may not agree with his assessment of its adverse role in Canadian social development. Sports and games had never been absent from Canadian life, not even from the small town of Barrie, and were certainly not an exclusively urban preoccupation, although the role of the city in their rapid evolution in the late nineteenth century was vital. "The Canadians," a traveller commented about 1860, "are thoroughly a people for amusement, and enjoy all kinds of recreation exceedingly. They follow out the customs of the English to a great extent, and participate freely in the games so loved in the old country."[6] Not only the English, but every people making up the Canadian population had its distinct tradition of athletics, a tradition usually closely related to the social position and outlook of the group.

Among French Canadians feats of strength and endurance connected to the occupations of a rural people were prized. E.Z. Massicotte, who published his *Athlètes canadien-français* in 1909, subtitled it "Recueil des exploits de force, d'endurance, d'agilité, des athlètes et des sportsmen de notre race, depuis le XVIIIe siècle," and concentrated his attention upon strongmen and rough-and-tumble fighters, beginning with the legendary Grenon, *l'Hercule du nord*, whose massive strength amazed and cowed Wolfe's redcoats. There was Joseph Montferrand, hero of the French-Canadian lumbermen of the Ottawa Valley, who at eighteen defeated the best boxers from the English garrison in Montreal, and later "le champion de la marine anglaise" in a seventeen-second encounter at Queen's Quay, Quebec. Indeed most of the stories about Montferrand, like those about other early French-Canadian hero-figures, have to do with his conquests of English or Irish, as when, ambushed by Orangemen on a bridge between Hull and Bytown, he threw his assailants right and left into the river, while "calling upon the Holy Virgin and making the sign of the cross." In Massicotte's tales about the giants of the past, from Grenon to Louis Cyr, there run two threads: a veneration for power, muscularity, and amazing feats of endurance, and a depiction of the characteristic *Canadien* folk-hero, who by demonstrations of immense strength or by the terror of his wrath (though calm, dignified, and slow to anger) abashes and dismays the bullies of another race, thus testifying to the virtue and hardihood of his people. It is hardly surprising, given such values, that French Canadians (who have of course distinguished themselves in such Canadian team sports as hockey and lacrosse) should have excelled in weightlifting, gymnastics, wrestling, boxing, and marathon running, but it is surely evident as well that the values of fortitude, toughness, and endurance so central to the traditional popular culture of French Canada have a significance — and merit an investigation — transcending the humble realm of sport.

Similarly, the Canadian Scots had an athletic tradition already old by the late nineteenth century. Their sport of curling, so perfectly suited both to our climate and to Scottish gregariousness, had been played in Canada since the eighteenth century. One day someone — perhaps an historian who is also a curler — will explain the cultural meaning of this game, and why a sport so peculiarly Scottish should have reached a level of general popularity and a level of performance so high, that by the 1960s Canadian curlers (of all manner of national origins and chiefly from the West) should have been acknowledged as the world's best. Certainly in its origins the game was exclusively Scottish and middle-class in nature; the first formal curling club was that of Montreal (later the Royal Montreal), where twenty merchants met at Gillis' Coffee House on January 22, 1807 to lay down the rules for the club.[7] After 1820, when clubs were organized in Quebec and in Kingston, curling spread throughout Upper Canada, Nova Scotia, and New Brunswick. Bonspiels, attracting rinks from all over Upper Canada, were held as early as 1859 (on Toronto Bay); in 1865, on Lake Erie near Black Rock, an international bonspiel between Canadian and American curlers, twenty-seven rinks a side, was held.[8] By Confederation, it was evident that the game had spread beyond its Scottish devotees; in New Brunswick, for instance, the St. Stephens club had "several Chipmans" among its members, another Loyalist family, the Streets, were prominent among the curlers of Newcastle, while in 1860 one James Milligan of the St. Andrew's Club of Saint John, is recorded as having scored an eight end.[9] By the 1890s there were curling clubs at Port Arthur, Rat Portage, Winnipeg, Portage La Prairie, Regina, and Calgary; in 1892 "J.D. Flavelle's rink of cracks from Lindsay, Ont. was beaten by Harstone of the Winnipeg Granites," an event of sufficient interest to warrant three columns in the Toronto *Globe*.[10] Covered rinks with "made" ice began to appear in Ontario in the 1880s; Toronto had six such large buildings, including that of the Granite Club, and there were others in Ottawa, London, Peterborough, Guelph, and Brantford.

The men who curled were hardly "the irresponsibles of society," whether from above or below. Curling in the late nineteenth century was a middle-class game, for respectable citizens, too, have their diversions. Certainly curling related to "the lighter side of life," but of course it always had, even among dour Calvinists. There were at least some signs, however, that decorum was entering the game. The 1876 annual of the Ontario Curling Association has an engraving of the famous Toronto Red Jackets playing on Toronto Bay, with a basket of whiskey bottles at one end of the rink. The 1879 annual carried the same engraving, but a black cloth was modestly draped over the basket. Curlers themselves scarcely thought they were taking a hand in the downfall of Ontario civilization; they thought they were building character. The game was supposed to be about "good humour and kindly feeling under all circumstances and provocations"; that quality, "in combination...with manly strength and cool judgement cannot fail to make men who will do equal honor to the land of their forefathers and the country of their adoption."[11]

In curling, as in other sports of the time, competition broadened out from that of local clubs to the rivalry of communities, regions, and provinces. The railway was a major factor in that process, greatly assisting the spread of the competitive network in curling as in other sports. In the late nineteenth century it was commonplace for railways to run curling specials at cut-rate fares. As a result, the hundred or more clubs in Ontario exchanged visits during the season and participated by district group in playdowns for the provincial championship. Each group sent two rinks to Toronto annually to compete for the Ontario Tankard.[12] In the Maritimes, special trains were laid on for the Interprovincial Tournament; in 1876 this tournament featured "a grand Bonspiel, Nova Scotia against New Brunswick," then "Scotch-born players against all comers," and finally the club matches, with the St. Andrews rink of Saint John meeting the Caledonian Club of Picton, the Thistles of Saint John against Halifax, New Glasgow against Chatham, and Pictou against Fredericton.[13] In Ontario, as in the Maritimes, curling was a pastime for small communities as well as large: the sport pages of the Montreal *Gazette* in the 1870s and 1880s show that curlers in Lucknow, Simcoe, Ayr, Wingham, Port Hope, Lindsay, and Milton were quite as active as their fellows in Toronto, London, Hamilton, Ottawa, and Chatham.

More than any other national group, the Scots, through their Caledonian games, stimulated interest in track and field sports. One of Canada's greatest all-rounders, the Scottish-Canadian Walter Knox, was the product of the long-standing Scottish interest in such sports; a near-contemporary of Arthur Lower, he grew up in Orillia. By the 1870s Caledonian games were being held at many points in Canada, and were becoming less exclusively Scottish in character. When the Montreal Caledonian Society held the twentieth renewal of its games in 1875, more than three thousand people attended, including competitors from sister societies in Ontario and in the neighbouring states. The Scottish flavour remained; pipe bands, sword dancers, and the inevitable tots dancing the Highland Fling competed alongside the runners, jumpers, and caber and hammer tossers. So, however, did Indians from the local reserves; one of them won the high hurdles.[14] It is important to note, however, that the Scots were by no means alone in their love for such sports. Throughout Ontario, parts of Quebec and the Maritimes, hundreds of social, ethnic, and religious organizations held athletic events during their annual picnics. At about the same time the Caledonians were having their games in 1875, another Montreal group, the Catholic Young Men's society, held its picnic on St. Helen's Island. The sports included not only races from 100 yards up to an open mile (the boys' race of 200 yards offered a $2 prize to the winner), but aquatic competitions "open to amateur members of Irish Catholic Societies."[15] Such sports were as normal and natural a part of popular social life as were the dancing, singing, games, and speech-making which also went on at picnics. John A.'s political picnics were adroit devices for capturing popular attention; most of the time, despite our historians, most Canadians were not thinking about the Pacific Scandal or the National Policy. Church and Sunday School picnics, the annual games of the firemen and the police, the outings of employees of the Grand Trunk and of various banks all featured sports competitions. McGill, Queen's, and Toronto universities held their own athletic competitions, and university "cracks" looking for wider worlds to conquer competed in open events at meets in Ontario and Quebec.

In sum, and taking track and field only as a single example, Canadians were extraordinarily active in athletics in the decades immediately following Confederation. This wealth of physical

stemmed not from some sinister collaboration between the elite and the plebs, but out of the national athletic traditions of the people themselves, and from conditions of life in which physical accomplishment and "manliness" were accorded value. Organization of track and field sports came because the very intensity of competition demanded it: the need to eliminate the "ringers" and hidden professionals, to regulate the rivalry between communities, to dispense with bizarre competitions (like three-legged races), to bring some uniformity to a confused situation. By the early 1880s, the Montreal Amateur Athletic Association began to sponsor an annual field day, and claimed that the winners of its events were Canadian champions. These meets were dominated by American athletes, mainly from the athletic clubs of New York City, although the Scots of Glengarry took their share of medals. "Do we not discourage, instead of encourage young Canadian athletes, and hinder, instead of foster, the development of Canadian athletic sports, by assembling our home talent, year after year, only to march in the triumphal procession of their Yankee conquerors," asked the *Spirit of the Times* of Toronto. It was thwarted nationalism that prompted the formation of the Canadian Amateur Athletic Association in 1884 for the explicit purpose of holding the Canadian championships; the first were scheduled for precisely the same day on which the New York clubs held theirs.[16]

Certain general propositions about sport in Canada in the late nineteenth century can be put forward, even though, within the present narrow compass, it is impossible to illustrate them adequately. The last forty years of the nineteenth century, and not just the decade of the 1890s, was the era of the rise of organized sport in Canada. Social historians must inevitably examine this sporting revolution; when they do, they will discover that it was not a divergence from the main lines of our social development but part and parcel of that development. Organized sport may possibly have arisen because older, more austere outlooks were weakening, although that interpretation is at least open to question, but certainly its rise is connected to that of a society becoming more urban, more differentiated, and, at the same time, more integrated. During these decades Canadians, on the evidence of their newspapers and periodicals, were among the most sports-minded people in the western world. They pursued physical activity with the same dedication they brought to politics and religion, and with a joy, exuberance, and inventiveness not usually typical of their approach to public affairs. Certainly the generation that found a political solution to the problems besetting British North America in the 1860s was a creative one; our historians have satisfied us on that score. But it was at least remarkable that the same generation, and the next following, should have created or refined such sports as lacrosse, hockey, football, and basketball. In their adept organization of athletic leagues and federations to bridge gaps between communities and provinces, the Canadians of this era demonstrated the same capacity for skilful corporate leadership as they had in confronting the challenges of a vast country in commerce, industry, and transportation. Since the people who were leaders in public and business affairs were frequently the leaders in athletics and recreation as well, the attitudes they displayed towards sport, far from being signs of moral decay, were those also valued in society at large.

Sport was not really dominated in this period by the effete or ir-responsible sections of society. It is true that remnants of the colonial elites and their imitators continued to indulge in sports thought to be genuinely British in character, but having little relevance to the cir-cumstances of Canadian life. It does not seem true that the mass of Canadians, whether farmers, small shopkeepers, clerks, or labourers, had much leisure for sports, except as spectators, at the time of Con-federation. Only rarely, as in the case of Ned Hanlan, could a son of the people turn his athletic potential to professional advantage, though the steady movement towards shorter hours and Saturday half-holidays was to democratize sport before the end of the century. The real innovators, organizers, and enthusiasts in the field of sport were neither the aristocratic few nor the labouring many, but the solid-ly respectable business middle class and its allies in the professions, the universities, and the military. Unless a sport commanded the in-terest and involved the energies of members of these groups, it was unlikely to become either organized or popular.

Boxing, at least in its professional form of bare-knuckle prizefight-ing, was a sport reprobated by the respectable classes. It was con-sidered a lower-class form of entertainment, at about the same level as cock-fighting. As early as 1860, the police magistrate of Montreal sent a posse to break up a prize fight between "two low disreputable bullies named Jules Rivet and Essal LaPointe."[17] In 1881, participa-tion in or connection with a prizefight was made an offense under the Criminal Code; according to the member for Annapolis, it was well known that those who attended such brutal spectacles were "of the most degraded description, men of vicious propensities and accus-tomed to sensual indulgence of almost every kind."[18] Such judge-ments partook not only of moral revulsion but of class bias. Pugilists came almost entirely from the lower classes, were usually Irish, American, or French-Canadian in origin, and were backed by gamblers, tavern keepers, and hotel owners. Their following was composed of labourers and urban "riff-raff," and their fights were fre-quently accompanied by disorders and a variety of petty criminal acts.

There is some evidence that the police forces in the cities shared the taste of the unregenerate; at any rate, their reluctance to prosecute under the Act of 1881 was notorious. Following a prizefight at Albert Hall in Toronto, the crown attorney urged the police to bring charges; "they, however, think as he took the initiative in prosecuting the lotteries, he should also move in this matter."[19] Some countenance was given, however, to what were termed "scientific sparring exhibitions," when gloves were used and the Queensberry rules (introduced in 1867) followed. Thus in 1877 "a very large audience, and wonderfully respectable in its composition," watched such an exhibition in Nordheimer Hall, Montreal, between "Professor Richardson" and "Professor Wood" of the Montreal Gymnasium.[20] Similarly, in Toronto's Adelaide Street Rink in 1885, some 1500 people, "including Lieutenant Governor Robinson and many prominent citizens" attended a sparring match between the American Charles Mitchell and John F. Scholes of Toronto.[21] Despite these exceptions, boxing did not really win an audience among the business and professional elites who patronized other sports; as a result, it was relatively late in achieving a degree of national organization. Not until 1897 were the first Canadian amateur championships held. The sport achieved some marginal respectability only when the Y.M.C.A. encouraged it, after the turn of the century, as an appropriate form of physical exercise.

Much the same fate, oddly enough, was accorded the inoffensive sport of competitive walking, or pedestrianism. Throughout the period it was regarded as a "hippodrome" entertainment for the vulgar. In 1879, for example, Miss L.A. Warren, a "famous lady pedestrian" from Philadelphia, challenged all (female) comers in Montreal, and was bested over 25 miles on an indoor track by a strapping Montreal girl, Jessie Anderson. According to the *Gazette's* reporter, the atmosphere in the arena was abominable, "what with the wretched ventilation of the hall, the closeness caused by the crowd, and the amount of smoking and expectorating going on." When the American eventually fainted, "some unfeeling cads present had the bad taste to attempt an exultant cheer"; the reporter thought it particularly disgraceful that the crowd had helped the Canadian girl by "attempting to trip and standing in the path of the American."[22]

If such essentially spectator sports as boxing and pedestrianism were left almost exclusively to the urban labouring class, there were other sports, in which the emphasis was upon participation, that were confined to higher levels of society. Though cricket had been assiduously played for many years before Confederation, chiefly through the example provided by officers in garrison towns and by the entourages of provincial lieutenant-governors, it remained the sport of a minority, fostered by the private schools. Sir John

Colborne's "prepare-a-Tory" foundation, Upper Canada College, played cricket from its inception in 1830; the social connotations the game has had in Canada are conveyed by a match between U.C.C. and "the gentlemen of Toronto" in 1836. The list of participants is a roll-call of the colonial elite; it included two Robinsons, two Keefers, a Phillpott, a Boulton, Rowsell (the government printer), William Henry Draper, and the inimitable Sir Francis Bond Head himself.[23] Periodically, in the post-Confederation era, brave statements about the health and future prospects of cricket were made:

> The game of cricket in Canada is without doubt waking up and this year we look to its being a most prominent feature in the line of sports. The winning of the international match by the Canadians last summer was a thing which went in no small way to make the sport popular and the activity of the officers of the existing clubs has given a hold to the game which...will establish cricket as a sport second to none in the Dominion. Toronto and the west generally has had a big share of the cricket and we do not see why Montreal as the bigger city should not have a large slice.[24]

Efforts were made to organize the game in the same way in which other successful Canadian sports had been. An Ontario Cricket Association was formed in 1880 with the Marquis of Lorne as president and William Hamilton Merritt as secretary, but its attempts to create public interest through a series of matches for a trophy, in emulation of sports like lacrosse, ended in failure. The O.C.A. gave up the ghost in 1891, to be replaced by the equally unsuccessful Canadian Cricket Association. Native Montrealers did not take to the game; uprooted Englishmen and the occasional enthusiast from Bishop's College School at Lennoxville formed the nucleus of what cricket was played.[25] One of the sport's staunchest advocates, G.G.S. Lindsey, thought that the lack of a monied and leisured class told against cricket. He put his faith for the future of the game in the graduates of U.C.C. and Trinity College School, Port Hope, who could go forth to social leadership in Ontario, "schooled in the game, trained to command [and] learned in the art of handling an eleven." Perhaps the University of Toronto might help, as well, since boys from the private schools usually went on to it; "we believe," he wrote, "the game is not played at Queen's."[26]

Yet though the central provinces might lack a monied and leisured class in the English sense, their growing towns and cities were producing a prosperous business and professional middle class with strong interests in sports. Well before Confederation, respectable

Montrealers might be seen in the winter months scaling their mountain on snowshoes; the Montreal Snow Shoe Club was founded in 1843, and others were to follow. At first such clubs were purely social in character, members taking part in weekly tramps culminating in convivial evenings. Organized competition over measured courses with established rules had come by 1867, with annual fixtures between clubs. The love Montrealers had for snowshoeing (and for the winter carnival the snowshoers were foremost in organizing) aroused only bafflement in other centres; in 1885 the *Gazette* editorially abused a Toronto newspaper for its failure to grasp the beauty of snowshoeing. "Montreal," it declared, "contains more genuine sport to the square inch than any other city in the Dominion, Toronto included."[27] Snowshoeing, at least as practised by the English-speaking clubs (which seem to have had little to do with such clubs as *Le Canadien* and *Le Trappeur*), was an elaborate and self-conscious synthesis of a number of cultural traditions. Members of the St. George's Club were proud of their "picturesque costumes of blanket coat and knickerbockers, red sash, scarlet stockings and *tuque bleue*." Picturesqueness did not mean indiscipline, however; "at the word of command from the President we fall in line and in Indian file begin the ascent of the mountain at a stiff and steady pace." Once within sight of Prendergast's or some other favourite inn, "the leader cries 'tally ho!' and all are off at full speed, each anxious to be first in." Snowshoers saw themselves as engaged in a manly pastime that was distinctively Canadian. "No Greeks of Hellas were more proud than we," said John Reade at the annual St. George's Club dinner in 1881:

> What firmer bulwarks can a nation have,
> Than sons thus trained in eye, in foot, in hand,
> In quick resource, in temper and in skill?
> And he who has not felt his blood grow warm
> As through the frozen woods he makes his way,
> O'er the deep snow which crisps beneath his feet
> Has missed no common joy, and little knows
> The bliss our northern winter can bestow.

Although snowshoeing was to flag as a winter pastime for respectable Montrealers in the later years of the nineteenth century, younger men being drawn off by hockey, the snowshoe clubs left a considerable legacy. The Montreal Snow Shoe Club was one of the founding organizations of the Montreal Amateur Athletic Association, that bastion of middle-class involvement in sport. The high-mindedness of the snowshoers, the earnestness with which they approached their chosen pastime, imbued the Montreal conception of amateur athleticism.[28]

Another sport which never spread beyond narrow class lines was the hunt. Montreal, Ottawa, Quebec, and Toronto all had their hunt clubs; these cities' newspapers deferentially referred to "the fine old English manly sport of fox hunting." The Montreal *Gazette's* accounts of this supreme form of colonial mimesis do not differ in any substantial way from what a Zena Cherry might write in today's Toronto *Globe and Mail* of the doings of Toronto's pink-coated gentry out King and Kleinburg way. There were the mandatory lists of "those of our leading citizens" in attendance, studded with "Hons.," "Ladies," "Colonels," and the odd upwardly mobile "Doctor"; there was casual mention of country estates, hunt breakfasts, *recherché* luncheons and "Miss Marion Lewis's capital seat." Horsiness as the road to ultimate respectability was not confined to the Allans, the Willgresses, the Dawes', the Richardsons, and other merchants, financiers, bankers, and distillers; among them there were also the Baumgartens and, indeed, the Taschereaus and the Galarneaus.[29]

Though the fantasy world of the hunt was a tiny one, it was directly connected, at least in the larger centres, with one of the most organized and popular sports of the period, horse-racing. Active participation was of course confined to little men and large animals, but in an era when most of the population fancied its judgement of horseflesh, thoroughbred racing was enormously popular. By 1867 there were few towns of any size not boasting of a race track and at least one race meeting a year. Montreal had its Province of Quebec Turf Club and its Blue Bonnets course; Toronto had the Woodbine and the Ontario Jockey Club. In both cities the track stewards included some of the wealthy families who also patronized the hunt. The OJC, organized in 1881 with Col. Gzowski as its first chairman, had directors from Hamilton, St. Catharines, Brantford, Niagara Falls, Peterborough, and Chatham as well as Toronto.[30] Race meetings were occasions on which the elite mingled, though not too closely, with the democracy, and were social events as well as sporting occasions. As described in the press, the scene was always a brilliant one, with mandatory references to the beautiful contrasts provided by the dresses and sunshades of "the fair sex," the flags, banners, and racing colours. Racing crowds were invariably happy and light-minded:

> The assemblage yesterday afternoon was a very large and fashionable one, amongst those present on the grand stand and in the carriages around the enclosure being many of Montreal's leading society people. Conspicuous among the vehicles around the course was a genuine tally-ho coach, on

the top of which were seated a number of ladies and gentlemen. Lieutenant Colonel Whitehead drove the coach out in splendid style, and several gentlemen of the Hunt did the honors and dispensed the hospitalities (on ice) in truly royal style.[31]

While "the wealth and fashion of the Queen City all flocked to the Woodbine," so did thousands of their humbler fellow citizens; at the spring meeting in 1891, for example, there was an attendance of 15 000 on the first day and nearly 20 000 on the second.[32] Here, perhaps, does Arthur Lower's conception of the social dimensions of sport most nearly apply.

The patronage of the rich was not, however, extended to trotting, a form of racing that was prevalent in the rural areas of both Ontario and Quebec. Farmers and the inhabitants of small towns and villages were the chief devotees of this sport; Western Ontario particularly was a hotbed of it. It was frequently alleged in the press that trotting was a thoroughly corrupt form of racing; "for years the patron of the trotting track has been classified with the gambler and the blackleg, for honesty dwelt not there."[33] Lacking support, both financial and administrative, from the kind of people who patronized thoroughbred racing in Canada, the trotting horsemen proved incapable of organizing to protect themselves from "the predatory horde of outlaws" drawn to their tracks, and eventually trotting became one of the very few Canadian sports to seek shelter within an American organization. The first Canadian trotting circuit was organized in 1884, under the auspices of the National Trotting Association of the United States.[34]

Above all other sports, Canadians of this period were interested both as players and spectators in team games. With three of them, lacrosse, hockey, and football, the business, professional, military, and university communities of Montreal had direct associations, and with a fourth, the latecomer basketball, the connection was close. Field lacrosse was the brainchild of a prosperous Montreal dentist, W.G. Beers. As a child, and possibly too while a student at Lower Canada College, Beers had played the ancient Indian game of baggataway. Montreal interest in lacrosse had arisen from a demonstration by Indians from Caughnawaga at the St. Pierre race course as early as 1834. The first recorded match between whites and Indians was held in 1844, under the auspices of the Olympic Athletic Club; the first organized team was that of the Montreal Lacrosse Club, formed in 1856 and composed of players from Montreal's upper crust, including such names as Christie, Blackwood, Redpath, and Coffin. During these years a number of changes were made in the Indian game, especially to the form of the stick and through greater emphasis upon passing and teamwork, but it remained for Beers to give real symmetry to the sport.[35] It was Beers who fixed the size of the field and the nature of the goals, determined the number of players and the names of the positions, laid down the rules governing illegal play, and gave a match its duration (best three of five "games" or goals). Through his initiative, a convention of fifty-two delegates representing twenty-nine lacrosse clubs in Ontario and Quebec met at the Sons of Temperance Hall in Kingston on September 26, 1867 to form the Canadian National Lacrosse Association, and to adopt the rules he had first formulated in 1860.[36] Beers, much prouder of this accomplishment than of his founding of the *Canadian Journal of Dental Science*, published in 1869 the first definitive book on the sport, *Lacrosse: The National Game of Canada*. He believed that his refinement of the rough and formless Indian game was "as much superior to the original as civilization is to barbarism." Not only did lacrosse have the virtue of rapidly converting spectators into players through the excitement and admiration its skills aroused, but it had physical and moral benefits as well:

> Lacrosse stimulates nutrition, invigorates and equalizes the circulation, quickens and frees the function of respiration, strengthens the appetite and digestion, and purifies the blood. Its sociability calls forth a nervous stimulus which acts enticingly on the muscles....Lacrosse knocks timidity and nonsense out of a young man, training him to temperance, confidence and pluck....It shames grumpiness out of him, schools his vanity and makes him a man.

Perhaps wisely, he offered no professional opinion about its effect upon the teeth.

In the years after Confederation, lacrosse was truly the national game of Canada, or at least of the central provinces and British Columbia, where it rapidly took hold. The early teams were dominated by the sons of the well-to-do, but as W.K. McNaught pointed out, lacrosse was "the cheapest of all games." It needed no expensive equipment; "a single lacrosse stick and simple running gear is all that is required for action."[37] Soon young men from town and countryside alike took up the game, clubs proliferated, intense local rivalries grew up, and inter-city leagues at several levels of competition appeared. Not only did lacrosse become the first mass participation sport, but it attracted large crowds of spectators as well. The speed, physical challenge, and patterned flow of the game were exciting enough, but there was also the heady brew of national pride in a sport that was uniquely Canadian, as this Montreal *Gazette* headline indicates: "The Great

Game for the Championship of the World: Shamrocks of Montreal, Q., against Torontos of Toronto, Ont.: A Beautiful Day and an Exciting Match: Several Thousand Spectators Witness a Well Contested Match: The Longest Championship Game on Record."[38]

Hockey followed much the same evolution as lacrosse. Its precise place of origin is in dispute, but Montreal nurtured it. It too was first the game of the military, university men, and the athletic enthusiasts of middle-class Montreal, and though its rise was not so rapid as lacrosse's, it too was eventually invaded by players from all levels of society. Hockey rules did not spring from the mind of a single man, but were certainly much influenced by lacrosse; the game underwent considerable experimentation and change during the 1870s and 1880s before the pattern familiar today began to emerge and the great age of the sport to dawn.

Hockey's history is familiar enough; that of Canadian football is perhaps less well-known. Young gentlemen in Montreal were playing something they called football as early as the mid-1860s, although there seems to have been no consistency in the numbers of players, the scoring rules, or the precise object of the game.[39] It was at about this period that in England a clear division was being made between association football (soccer), then emerging as the game of the working class, and rugby football as the game of the public schools and of gentlemen amateurs. Both forms were played in Canada, with Montreal as the cradle of rugby and Toronto of soccer. American college football evolved directly from the well-known incident of May 15, 1874, when a visiting McGill team played Harvard according to Canadian rules. Not so familiar, however, is the fact that Harvard continued to play McGill and other Montreal clubs into the 1880s, in a period when the American game was developing quite different rules. Under pressure both from American universities and from native advocates of English rugby pure and undefiled, Canadian footballers stubbornly refused to alter the game they had created. As late as 1882, the Montreal Football Club played Harvard, but its chief local rival, the Britannia club, which "for several years had had annual matches with Harvard, this year [has] made no attempt to arrange one, declining to recognize the American innovations in Rugby Union, and considering it inadvisable to attempt any compromise with them."[40]

Meanwhile, the Montreal game pushed its way steadily into Ontario, spreading first to Ottawa and to Royal Military College in Kingston, then to private schools like Trinity College and U.C.C. and eventually to strongholds of soccer like the University of Toronto and Queen's. It was in 1883 that Queen's (having been converted to the game by R.M.C.), rather inauspiciously inaugurated its brilliant winning record in Canadian football by winning the "Central Association

Championship" — a better term might have been the Calvinist Cup — over Knox College "by one goal for Queen's and one (under protest) for Knox."[41] In 1884 the newly-formed Ontario Rugby Football Union was scheduling matches not only among the colleges already mentioned, but with Ontario Agricultural College at Guelph, and teams from Peterborough, Hamilton, and London,[42] and by 1885 an interprovincial game was played between selects from Ontario and Quebec.[43]

Despite its violence, and the prevalence of gore and serious injury, characteristics allegedly dear to the "mob," football was to remain for many years a class sport, played before small crowds of the knowledgeable. Although as then played it had its moments of swift, open movement, for the most part it resembled a primitive phalangial combat, much more enthralling to players than to bystanders. The nature of football gives special point to the question prompted by the general enthusiasm of the urban elite of this era for playing and promoting sports: why should members of highly conventional middle-class communities, the repositories of civic respectability, have been so drawn to athletics in general, and to so violent a sport as football in particular? It is not an answer to say that young men from favoured backgrounds have a natural propensity for frivolity, lightmindedness, and social irresponsibility. No one who reads accounts of early football games — Ralph Connor's description in *Glengarry School Days* (1902) is a relatively late example — can fail to be impressed by the strength of the contemporary conviction that football was a test of the capacity for leadership in the everyday world, and that players were expected to exhibit qualities of manliness, courage, and gentlemanly behaviour under the most trying conditions.

The institution that above all others expressed the involvement of the middle class in sport was the Montreal Amateur Athletic Association. The M.A.A.A. was essentially a federation of five clubs, the Montreal Lacrosse Club, the Montreal Snow Shoe Club, the Montreal Bicycle Club, the Tuque Bleue Toboggan Club, and the Montreal Football Club. It was operated by a board of directors drawn from each club; the board was charged with responsibility for property management, the scheduling of events in the many sports in which the association took part and many other matters, including the busy social round for which the association's main building was the centre. In the late nineteenth century, the M.A.A.A. was unquestionably the most powerful sporting body in Canada, with a decisive influence upon the development of most sports that Canadians engaged in. Its membership, including members from associated organizations, was over two thousand; membership cost the by no means negligible sum of ten dollars a year. In 1882 the M.A.A.A. acquired Barnjum's Gymnasium for $12 300, issuing bonds to pay for the purchase. By 1888, its playing fields and buildings were valued at more than $30 000, its annual revenue from dues was nearly that amount, and it had a healthy bank surplus. In addition to its constituent bodies, the association sponsored hockey, baseball, chess, fencing, and dramatic clubs, and ran a reading room and a library.[44] Affiliation also existed between the M.A.A.A. and a number of other upper middle-class sporting clubs, including the Montreal Yacht Club, the Montreal Hunt Club, and the St. Louis Canoe Club.[45]

The ideals animating the members of the M.A.A.A. were those of the social milieu from which they came, that is, those of the upright, honourable, and puritanical Canadian gentleman:

> The moral influences of the M.A.A.A. are very considerable. Honour and fair play are inculcated, gambling or strong drink not tolerated on its premises or grounds; to prevent any chance of the former, cards were prohibited, its founders considering there were enough means of amusement elsewhere. Pure amateur sport of all kinds is encouraged, and anything tending to professionalism or hippodroming strongly opposed. A loyal feeling for everything Canadian and national is engendered, and in fact, no more healthy and strong moral organization exists for young men anywhere.[46]

Typical of the membership of the M.A.A.A., and also very much swayed by its moral athleticism was Dr. James Naismith. Born near Almonte, Canada West in 1861, Naismith grew up in a Calvinist community in which the Scottish emphasis upon hard work, "manly" sports and the value of education exerted a powerful influence upon the young. Determined to follow the ministry "in order to help my fellow beings," Naismith went to McGill on a scholarship in 1883, and graduated in theology in 1890. At the same time he became an outstanding athlete, playing centre at football for McGill and excelling in lacrosse, wrestling, and gymnastics. Upon graduation, he felt called to that special combination of Christian living and athletic endeavour that was the Y.M.C.A. ideal. While studying at the Y.M.C.A. training school at Springfield, Massachusetts, in 1891, Naismith made the final contribution of a remarkably creative phase in Canadian social history by inventing the game of basketball. The new sport was the outcome of pure logic suffused by the athletic ideals of the Montreal milieu. Naismith sought a sport in which physical contact would be reduced to a minimum, in which play would be as free-flowing as in lacrosse or hockey, and in which technical skill would have unfettered opportunity to determine the result. As he said in introducing the game to its first players, "if men will not be gentlemanly in their play, it is our place to encourage them to games that may be played by gentlemen in a manly way, and show them that science is superior to brute force with a disregard for the feelings of others."[47]

Naismith's objects in inventing what rapidly became a world sport lay bare a central irony in the role of the Canadian urban elite as pioneers in the organizing and popularizing of sport: they were overwhelmed by their very success. The common man, increasingly free to engage in leisure-time physical recreation, invaded games supposedly the preserve of society's leaders, and brought to them attitudes that had little to do with the gentlemanly code.[48] In one sense, the stand of the M.A.A.A. and bodies like it for amateurism as against professionalism was an attempt to draw class lines in sport. Increasingly, the respectable patrons of sport complained of professionalism and rough play, especially in lacrosse. After a particularly rough game between Montreal and Cornwall in 1890, one Montreal journal considered that "the sooner the national game is handed over to the keeping of the professionals the better, for gentlemen cannot afford to have anything to do with it." Increasingly, Canadian nature itself was evoked as an escape from the Goths:

> There is something primitive and poetical about the canoe, and canoeing is one of the few pastimes which has not yet degenerated like many of its fellows. A writer some time ago put it aptly when he said: "All gentlemen are not canoeists, but all canoeists are gentlemen." It is, perhaps, due to this fact more than to any other that a canoe camp is invariably a delightful place, where all meet on terms of equality...[and] jolly good fellowship.[49]

By the 1890s, the exodus was under way, though its extent within particular sports must await investigation. More and more, the urban elites turned to sports which they could pursue "on terms of equality and jolly good fellowship," insulated from the mass of their countrymen. Golf, for example, had been played in Canada at least since Confederation; the Montreal Golf Club, founded in 1873, was the first club organized for play in North America.[50] In the 1890s, golf clubs sprang up not only around Montreal but in the vicinity of many Ontario cities and towns, with attendant labour forces of hired professionals, greenskeepers, and clubhouse flunkies. The clubhouses themselves, sprawling frame edifices reminiscent of Saratoga Springs hotels, were not merely pleasure palaces: they were social fortresses. Tennis, too, won a new popularity among the respectable classes. The Canadian Lawn Tennis Association, founded in the 1890s, "welded the game together and gave it a certain *prestige*." Soon tennis clubs, often in association with golf and country clubs, appeared, even in such communities as Uxbridge, Woodstock, Meaford, Wingham, Elora, Lindsay, and Owen Sound.[51] Yacht clubs, too, attracted the well-to-do. In Toronto, "everybody who is anybody either owns or has an interest in some kind of sailing craft"; the Royal Canadian Yacht Club, boasting such members as Aemilius Jarvis and George Gooderham, built a palatial club house on the Island, a town club house as well, and purchased a steam yacht to ferry their members between the two.[52] In Montreal, H.M. Molson and the great Canadian engineer George Herrick Duggan, men "generous of their time and wealth," built up the St. Lawrence Yacht Club during the 1890s.[53]

Cycling offers a case study of this social process. The penny-farthing bicycle, called, oddly enough, the "ordinary," cost as much as $300, much too expensive for most young men. The first cycling clubs to be organized in North America (in 1878) were in Boston and — inevitably — in Montreal. Within four years the Canadian Wheelman's Association had been formed to organize racing meets among the many clubs in Ontario and Quebec, and "to secure improvement of the public roads and highways." In 1883 the C.W.A. declared a Canadian champion, W.B. Ross of Montreal; his brother, P.D. Ross, an outstanding McGill athlete who was to become the proprietor of the Ottawa *Journal*, was vice-president of the Toronto club.[54] In 1889 the invention of pneumatic tires and the inner tube by John Dunlop made detachable wheels and substantial production economies possible; the subsequent invention of the coaster brake made the bicycle a less dangerous vehicle. The consequence of the mass-produced, inexpensive "safety bicycle" was a minor transportation revolution; it was also, in a sporting sense, a social one. The bicycle craze meant that now, in the words of a cycling pioneer, "patrician and peasant" rode and raced together.[55] This situation did not long remain. As cyclists from lower down the social scale challenged the dominance of the "patricians" in the sport, the latter turned to a new and more exclusive interest.[56] The career of Dr. Perry Doolittle is probably representative. A Trinity College man and a wealthy Toronto physician, Doolittle had been one of the founders of the C.W.A. and a successful racer. By the end of the nineties, he had shifted his attention to the horseless carriage, helped found the Ontario Motor League, was an executive of the Canadian Good Roads Association and of the Toronto Automobile Club, and from 1920 until his death in 1933 was president of the Canadian Automobile Association.

The relationship of sport to national athletic traditions, to social class and to certain dominant ideas centring upon the code of the gentleman and the concept of manliness seems plain enough, although each of these matters warrants further investigation. It is by no means as clear why middle-class Canadians, especially in Quebec and Ontario, should have turned so wholeheartedly to sport in the late nineteenth century. It is true, of course, that other countries, such as Britain, France, and the United States, were undergoing a similar experience, and therefore the Canadian case might be considered simply another example of what was a general movement. It is not at all certain, however, that the Canadian pattern runs parallel to those in other countries. Eugen Weber has recently offered a socio-economic explanation for the rise of sport in France which appears to suggest some fruitful lines of inquiry. He argues that since the economic slumps of the eighties and nineties meant higher relative incomes for the upper and middle classes, especially for members of the professions, it was possible for "a higher proportion of the leisured young" to wait a relatively long time "before turning to money-earning activities." He couples this suggestion (it is no more than that) with the hypothesis that the leisured young chose sport, as an alternative to the colonies or to artistic ventures, as a reaction against the drudgery and stagnation of contemporary French life. "Action, liberation, adventure and the heroic life were what the colonies seemed to promise. So did sports."[57]

While one can follow Weber in viewing the rise of sport in Canada as "a fat boy's" movement rather than "a rebellion of the downtrodden," his explanation is pitched too firmly in terms of the young to fit the Canadian case. Had it not been for the enthusiasm, ability, and money of men already securely established in the community, Canadian sport would hardly have made the headway it did. Moreover, the nature of the post-Confederation sports movement bears a stamp that is quintessentially Canadian.

Virtually all sport, at its first level, is an expression of the purely physical and of the joy of play. Anyone who has pursued athletics beyond this level knows that these attributes must be overlaid by mental and moral discipline; serious athletic competition is a test of body, brain, and will. In this sense sport is universal, and in the late nineteenth century Canada produced a large number of superior athletes. But Canadians were not content with playing a game well. They had an ineradicable itch for order. In nearly every sport in which middle-class Canadians were deeply involved, they sought to rationalize it, to reduce it to its fundamentals, to eliminate confusions, to make it conform to rules and regulations. Not only did this obtain with respect to the process of play itself, but the environment surrounding play must also be tidy and respectable. Sport was not a rebellion against established verities. It was their very lust for order and pattern that made Canadians innovators. Anything savouring of hippodromes, bread and circuses was to be rejected; sport was to be integrated into the rhythms of Canadian life.

In another way, too, the Canadian approach to sport had a special character. Nowhere else, and certainly not in the chaotic United States, was the movement for the organization of national competition so pronounced. Scarcely had a sport been received, refined, invented, or taken up than clubs were formed and competition ensured within communitities or localities, then broadened swiftly to the provincial and even to the national level. Canadians wanted national champions, partly out of community pride, partly out of the strong belief that their games were their own and that they played them superlatively well. It was no accident that among the first passengers to be carried east on the newly-completed C.P.R. was a British Columbia lacrosse team, challenging for the national championship.

Middle-class Canadians of city and town still thought of themselves as a rugged northern people. In a society becoming more and more urban, sport was a surrogate for direct contact with the challenging vastnesses of our great land. In struggling against its forests, its water, and its climate a hardy and venturesome people had been formed; athletic endeavor was proof that these qualities still remained. And, when opportunity offered, more and more respectable Canadians turned back to nature and, like Arthur Lower, rediscovered older realities in pitting themselves against the northern land.

Notes

1. A.R.M. Lower, *My First Seventy-five Years* (Toronto: Macmillan, 1967), 12.

2. Alan Metcalfe, "Tentative hypotheses related to the form and function of physical activity in Canada during the 19th century" (paper delivered to the Symposium on the History of Sport and Physical Education, Edmonton, 1970, University of Alberta Library), 3.

3. Montreal *Gazette*, Nov. 25, 1875.

4. *Dominion Illustrated Monthly* 6, 149 (May 9, 1891), 455.

5. A.R.M. Lower, *Canadians in the Making: a Social History of Canada* (Toronto: Longmans, 1958), 320–21 and passim.

6. G.M. Craig, ed., *Early Travellers in the Canadas, 1791–1867* (Toronto: Macmillan, 1955), 252.

7. "One Hundred and Fifty Years of Curling," *Canadian Sport Monthly* 33, 11 (March 1957), 14.

8. James Hedley, "The Game of Curling," *Outing Magazine* 22 (Dec. 1889), 210.

9. James Hedley, "Curling in Canada," *Dominion Illustrated Monthly* 1, 3 (April 1892), 177.

10. Toronto *Globe*, March 3, 1892.

11. Hedley, "The Game of Curling," 211.

12. Hedley, "Curling in Canada," 173."

13. Montreal *Gazette*, Jan. 18, 1876.

14. Ibid., Aug. 24, 1875.

15. Ibid., Aug. 20, 1875.

16. Ibid., April 22, 1884.

17. Ibid., Oct. 24, 1860.

18. Canada, Parliament, *Debates of the House of Commons*, Feb. 11, 1881, 938.

19. Montreal *Gazette*, March 30, 1883. See also ibid., Feb. 28 and March 25, 1884.

20. Ibid., Jan. 23, 1877. Wood was in fact the American professional Billy Madden. Ibid., March 30, 1885.

21. Ibid., Feb. 24, 1885.

22. Ibid., Feb. 24, 1879.

23. G.G.S. Lindsey, "Cricket in Canada," pt. 4, *Dominion Illustrated Monthly* 2, 3 (April 1893), 160.

24. Montreal *Gazette*, April 20, 1885.

25. Lindsey, "Cricket in Canada," pt. 3 (Nov. 1892), 619.

26. Ibid., pt. 4 (April 1893), 163, 167.

27. Montreal *Gazette*, Feb. 24, 1885.

28. Snowshoers are still very much with us, of course; but the nearest modern counterparts in spirit to the early snowshoers are the cross-country skiers, who have the same northern virtues, outlandish garb, and technical mystique possessed by the nineteenth-century Montrealer as he communed with his sub-arctic land.

29. Montreal *Gazette*, Oct. 3, 1881, Oct. 9, 1882, Oct. 8, 1883, Oct. 26, 1885, Nov. 2, 1885.

30. Ibid., Aug. 17, 1881.

31. Ibid., June 22, 1883.

32. *Dominion Illustrated Monthly* 6, 152 (May 30, 1891), 526.

33. Ibid., 5, 111 (Aug. 16, 1890), 102.

34. Montreal *Gazette*, April 22, 1884.

35. A.M. Weyand and M.R. Roberts, *The Lacrosse Story* (Baltimore, 1965), 13–16.

36. Ibid., 18.

37. "Cricket, Lacrosse or Baseball," *Bystander* (Aug. 1880), quoted in Ottawa *Citizen*, Jan. 25, 1967. McNaught was then secretary of the National Lacrosse Association. See also his *Lacrosse and How To Play It* (Toronto, 1873).

38. July 31, 1876. The Shamrocks were recruited from the Irish working class of Montreal.

39. Even so, the Canadian term "rouge" was already being used for a kick in goal. See D.M. Fisher, "It's Time To Set Football's History Straight," *Sports Canada* 1, 1 (Aug. 1969), 22.

40. Montreal *Gazette*, Oct. 9, 1882.

41. Ibid., Dec. 10, 1883.

42. Ibid., March 26, 1884.

43. Ibid., Oct. 25, 1885.

44. *Dominion Illustrated Monthly* 2, 27 (Jan. 5, 1889), 6–7; Montreal *Gazette*, April 17, 1882.

45. *Dominion Illustrated Monthly* 2, 27 (Jan. 5, 1889), 6–7.

46. Ibid.

47. Canadian Sports Hall of Fame, Toronto, Biographical File, Dr. James Naismith.

48. Undoubtedly the movement from country to town during the period was important in the democratizing of sport; so too was the shorter hours movement.

See Ian F. Jobling, "Urbanization and Sport in Canada, 1867–1900" (paper presented to the Symposium on the History of Sport and Physical Education, Edmonton, 1970, University of Alberta Library, 1–10).

49. *Dominion Illustrated Monthly* 5, 110 (Aug. 9, 1890), 87.

50. In 1885 it acquired the title "Royal," a token that served "to show the kindly interest Her Majesty takes in her subjects, however remote they may be." Montreal *Gazette*, July 4, 1885.

51. Scott Griffin, "A Chat about Lawn Tennis," *Massey's Magazine* 2 (July–Dec. 1896), 58–60.

52. *Dominion Illustrated Monthly* 5, 111 (Aug. 16, 1890), 103.

53. Ibid., 6, 145 (April 11, 1891), 354.

54. Montreal *Gazette*, May 19, 1884.

55. P.E. Doolittle, "Cycling of Today," *Massey's Magazine* 1 (Jan.–June 1896), 406–7.

56. Eugen Weber, in his "Gymnastics and Sports in *Fin-de-siècle* France: Opium of the Classes," *American Historical Review* 76, 1 (Feb. 1971): 70–98, has pointed to a similar social phenomenon in France. See especially 80–82. What, one wonders, was the social position of the J. McKee from Arthur Lower's Barrie who won the Dunlop road race in Toronto in 1903? See *History of the Dunlop Road Race, 1894–1921* (Toronto, 1922), 5.

57. Weber, "Gymnastics and Sports," 96, 98.

THE EVOLUTION OF ORGANIZED PHYSICAL RECREATION IN MONTREAL, 1840–1895[1]*

ALAN METCALFE

Any cursory examination of today's newspapers, T.V. coverage, patterns of consumer spending, and salaries of professional athletic entertainers indicates that sport and physical recreation play an important role in the lives of large numbers of Canadians, yet little analysis of their growth, development, and role in life has been undertaken by Canadian historians.[2] The basic ideology, patterns of behaviour and sports which formed the foundations of urban recreation emerged in the second half of the nineteenth century when Canada first felt the impact of urbanization and industrialization. These changes occurred in the 1870s and 1880s, the formative era in the evolution of organized physical recreation.

The choice of Montreal, 1840–95 [as a city in which to trace these changes] was not fortuitous; it presents an ideal case study of Canadian sport and society. In the first place, Montreal was the first city in Canada to feel the brunt of industrialization. Secondly, the growth of organized sport in Canada was closely associated with the city of Montreal.[3] Finally, the period 1840–95 was chosen because it encompasses the change from pre-industrial forms of recreation to the beginnings of the era of mass sport.

1840–1870

Before 1840 organized physical recreation was the exclusive preserve of a small, select segment of Montreal society. The first organized club, the Montreal Curling Club (1807), was formed by a group of Scottish merchants while the Hunt (1829), Cricket (1829), Tandem (c. 1837),

* *Histoire sociale/Social History* 11, 21 (May 1978): 144–66.

and Racquet Clubs (c. 1839) owed their existence, in part, to the officers of the Montreal Garrison and the social elite of Montreal society.[4] In each instance great emphasis was placed upon the social significance of the activities; dances, social gatherings and the demonstration of desirable social behaviour were as important as the playing of the game.

During the winter of 1840, a group of Montrealers gathered on a regular basis for the purpose of tramping on snowshoes around the environs of Montreal. These informal gatherings led to the formation of the prestigious Montreal Snow Shoe Club in 1843. At the same time, the Olympic Athletic Club (1842) was formed, which, for a brief period during the 1840s, sponsored intra- and inter-city cricket, track and field, rowing, and the 1844 Montreal Olympic Games. The membership of these early clubs was drawn from the highest strata of Montreal society; crossing ethnic lines, it included future judges, Members of Parliament, lawyers, doctors, government officials, businessmen and garrison officers.[5] The infrequent gatherings were social occasions attracting the cream of Montreal society. These sporting activities along with the Hunt and Tandem Clubs were part of a social milieu which to a degree mirrored the life of the English aristocracy. The activities themselves reflected their origin in the traditional sports of Scotland and England.

This flurry of athletic activity in the early 1840s produced the first evidence of public concern over the availability of recreational facilities. On August 20, 1844 the editor of the *Montreal Transcript* wrote:

> There ought to be a piece of ground set apart in the neighbourhood of every city for the practice of manly sports — for cricket, and all other kinds of sports. Montreal, unfortunately, possesses no such place, nor is there a single public walk or garden in which those who compose the humbler classes can go either for exercise or recreation.[6]

Apart from the Racquet Club, the Garrison Cricket Grounds on Sherbrooke Street and the river for curling in winter, there were no public or private facilities for sporting recreational activities. This pattern of private facilities for the wealthy and a dearth of grounds for the public was to remain throughout the nineteenth century.

It would be erroneous to suggest that there were any regular patterns of recreation. For the most part regattas, track and field, hunting and tandem rides were infrequent occurrences. Only three activities — curling, snowshoeing, and cricket — could lay any claim to regularity. Cricket was played every summer by the officers of the garrison. Throughout the winters, six to ten members of the Snow Shoe Club tramped across the Mountain on Tuesday evenings and the countryside on Saturday afternoons, in each instance ending up at Dolly's Chop House for a "convivial" evening. Weekly curling matches on the river rinks frequently concluded with the two rinks adjourning to a local hostelry where the loser paid for the dinner. It was in curling that the basic patterns of organized sport first developed. The Montreal Club was joined by the Thistle Club (1842) and Caledonian Club (1850) which resulted in regular inter-club competition. Their matches were played on the river rinks until 1848 when the Montreal Club moved into indoor sheds and the first relatively permanent sporting club facilities were opened. The increased interest in recreation that the curling clubs reflected was also illustrated in the first provision of commercial sporting facilities; a floating bath (60' x 25' with a saloon and 60 dressing rooms) opened in June 1849 opposite Bonsecours Market.[7] Later in the same year, a fencing school was opened for the officers of the garrison and the gentlemen of Montreal. These clubs and commercial ventures reflected a growing interest of Montrealers in recreation.

The year 1856 witnessed the formation of the Montreal Lacrosse Club and an increased interest in sport. Within four years, the city boasted ten snowshoe, six cricket and nine lacrosse clubs.[8] The proliferation of clubs was accompanied by the growth of specialized athletic facilities: the Montreal Cricket Grounds, McGill College Grounds, Montreal Lacrosse Grounds, and...a new commercial venture — the Victoria Skating Rink (1862). These developments were neither general nor widespread — all the clubs, private grounds and commercial facilities were located in the predominantly English-speaking St. Antoine's Ward, a pattern that remained constant until the early 1890s.

The early 1860s also witnessed an increase in the number of inter-club competitions in cricket, lacrosse and snowshoeing. However, the competitions were still held infrequently and no pattern of regular competition could be observed. There was an observable difference between the socially oriented sporting clubs and those whose focus was turning towards competition. The Montreal Tandem and Hunt Clubs, the exclusive preserve of the social elite, tended to be for lifetime sports in which age and physical prowess were not as important as social status. The youth-oriented active sports clubs attracted their membership from a wider, but still limited segment of society. The young Molsons and Allans were on the playing fields, joined by bank clerks, engineers and university students. Organized physical recreation was in an embryonic state and limited to a select segment of Montreal society.

Figure 1: Density of Buildings in the Wards of Montreal, 1861–1891

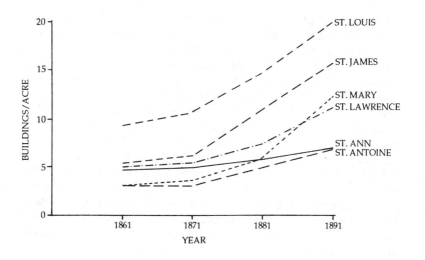

Figure 2: Number of Sporting Clubs in Montreal, 1840–1894.

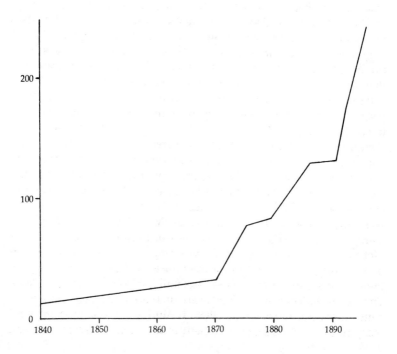

1870–1890

It is difficult to pinpoint the moment when organized sport entered its major development era, but there is evidence to suggest that changes were afoot in the 1860s. A short-lived Mechanics Lacrosse Club (1861), the Erina Snow Shoe Club (1860s), a Grand Trunk Railway Snow Shoe Club (1863) and high school teams signified the involvement of different segments of society. By 1869 the Montreal Snow Shoe Club Races were graced by "a crowd of the great unwashed of the city."[9] Not only were the participants and spectators changing, but the focus of competition also. In 1866 the first championship of Canada lacrosse game was played; by 1869 the Montreal S.S.C. published their first record of victories gained during the racing season.[10] The outcome of the contest was becoming increasingly important. These changes were to accelerate during the 1870s and 1880s, an era which witnessed the growth of new sports, the creation of basic organizational structures, basic patterns of land utilization, and the development of public attitudes towards recreation which were to influence patterns of recreation well into the twentieth century.

These changes were directly related to the processes of urbanization and industrialization which, by the 1870s, were beginning to have a marked effect upon all aspects of life and living. Increased density of population and housing (see figure 1) especially in the predominantly French wards to the east of St. Lawrence Main created pressure on public and private facilities and helped promote the movement into the suburbs of Cote St. Antoine, St. Jean Baptiste, Hochelaga, Point St. Charles, and St. Henri.[11] At the same time various groups campaigned for a decrease in the working hours, usually with limited and temporary success. In 1872, the Saturday Half Holiday and Nine Hours Labour League gained temporary reductions in work hours which, for the most part, returned to their original hours by the late 1870s. Dry Goods Store Clerks supported the Early Closing Movements of 1882 and 1888, while the Saturday Half Holiday Movement reappeared in 1885.[12] Notwithstanding the temporary nature of their success, it is probable that during the 1870s and 1880s, increasing numbers of Montrealers gained a decrease in working hours.

The period 1870 to 1887 witnessed a significant increase in the number of sporting clubs (42 to 141) (see figure 2). This growth took place largely in the team sports of lacrosse, (15 to 45); baseball, (6 to 21); and hockey, (0 to 18) (see table 1).[13] At the same time, new sports were emerging: the Montreal Golf Club (1874), Montreal Swimming Club (1876), Montreal Bicycle Club (1878), the Lawn Tennis and Yacht Clubs in the late 1870s and hockey in 1875. Not only did the number of clubs change, but the nature of the competition also — time boundaries, officials, and championship competition all appeared. The history of lacrosse illustrates clearly the changes taking place. In the early 1870s, games were played spasmodically throughout the summer; by the late 1870s, this pattern had given way to regular exhibition and infrequent championship games. In 1885 the five major lacrosse teams, including two from Montreal, established a series system of play for the championship. This was actually a league with a schedule of games throughout the summer— sport had become a regularized pattern of behaviour. At the same time, there was increasing pressure to change the method of determining a winner from the best three games out of five to a defined time period. Finally, this proliferation of sporting clubs in Montreal and Canada led to the formation of local, provincial and national organizations to codify rules, control behaviour, and integrate competition.

Table 1: Number of Sport Clubs in Montreal, 1840–1894

Club	1840	1861	1871	1877	1881	1887	1891	1892	1893	1894
Curling	1	3	3	3	4	3	5	5	5	5
Hunt	1	1	1	1	1	1	1	1	2	1
Snowshoe	1	10	7	15	20	16	17	17	16	22
Cricket	1	6	6	6	3	8	13	14	16	21
Lacrosse	—	9	15	31	25	45	36	53	56	49
Skating	—	1	1	1		1	2	2		1
Football	—	—	1	9	8	5	12	16	15	15
Baseball	—	—	6	14	14	21	11	14	19	10
Rowing	—	—	1	—	4	7	1	8	11	7
Hockey	—	—	—	4	2	18	23	19	28	46
Bicycle	—	—	—	—	1	1	2	2	4	4
Lawn Tennis	—	—	—	—	1		3	6	3	5
Quoits	—	—	—	—	1	3	3	3	5	7
Soccer	—	—	—	—	—	4	9	19	30	29
Others	3	2	1	1	4	8	7	10	12	23
No. of Sports	7	8	10	10	16	17	19	21	21	23
Total Clubs	7	32	42	85	88	142	145	189	222	245

Among the active participants there was a clear differentiation between social and competitive sports although the boundaries were sometimes blurred. The yacht, racquet and golf clubs joined the hunt and tandem clubs as elite life time sports where youth was more often a hindrance than a help. These social sports focused as much on the private club house as on the competition itself. The same was true to some extent for the snowshoe and curling clubs although their base of support was somewhat wider. it was these exclusive sporting clubs that were central to the social life of the upper segments of Montreal society.

If there was any democratization in sport during this era, it was in the competitive sport clubs. However, even in this instance, there were inter-sport differences. Certain sports witnessed no significant growth during the period 1870–1887; football (1 to 5), cricket (6 to 8), and bicycling (0 to 1) were played nearly exclusively by the anglophones of St. Antoine's Ward, drawing heavily from high school students, bank employees, university students and graduates, and the younger Molsons, Redpaths, and Allans. They were of course exclusive English-speaking clubs.

Lacrosse (15 to 45), baseball (6 to 21), and hockey (0 to 18) witnessed significant growth during the 1870s and 1880s. Hockey rightfully belongs with the first group as no evidence can be found of any teams existing outside of St. Antoine's Ward. Lacrosse and baseball were played throughout a far wider area of the city (see table 2). Although they were still located in the predominantly anglo wards of St. Antoine, St. Lawrence, St. Anne and Point St. Charles, clubs were beginning to emerge in the east end of the city.[14] The most important change was the emergence of clubs in the working class areas of St. Anne, St. Henri and Point St. Charles. In fact, it is likely that baseball appealed to a different section of the population.

Table 2: Locations of Lacrosse and Baseball Games
Played in Montreal, 1878–1887

	St. Antoine Ward	St. Lawrence Ward	Pt. St. Charles Cote St. Henri St. Anne Ward	St. James St. Louis St. Mary
Lacrosse	189	25	13	4
	(82%)	(11%)	(6%)	(1%)
Baseball	4	2	22	3
	(13%)	(6%)	(71%)	(10%)
Total	193	27	35	7
	(73%)	(10%)	(13%)	(4%)

The number of clubs masks a factor critical to the growth of recreation in Montreal — the permanency of the clubs. Table 3 illustrates that few clubs outside the predominantly social clubs could be considered to have any degree of permanency.[15] However, it was those permanent clubs that significantly influenced the long-term development of sport. The casual teams, on the other hand, reflected a growing interest in organized recreation on the part of an increasing number of Montrealers.

Table 3: Permanence of Lacrosse and Baseball Clubs
in Montreal, 1870–1889

		Over whole period	Over five years	2–4 years	1 year
Lacrosse	120	5	12	12	91
		(4%)	(10%)	(10%)	(76%)
Baseball	63	1	6	9	47
		(2%)	(9%)	(14%)	(75%)
Total		6	18	21	138
		(3%)	(10%)	(12%)	(75%)

All the permanent clubs exhibited similar characteristics: a private club house, grounds, non-playing members, and a strong social component. For the most part, they were located in St. Antoine's Ward, drawing their membership from the English-speaking business and financial community. There is evidence of new groups becoming involved in the formation of permanent clubs which reflected a widening base of participants. Perhaps the most interesting of these was the Shamrock Lacrosse Club which, on the playing field, was working class. The Shamrocks provide an interesting case study of the way in which working men gained entrance to the exclusive amateur sport fields. Formed in 1868 by a group of Irish Roman Catholics, the Shamrocks became the most successful lacrosse team in Canada between 1868–1886. The working class origins of this team are unquestionable.[16] However, the working class nature of the Shamrocks can be overstated. From the outset, they depended upon the active support of prominent Irish Canadians: James McShane, Mayor of Montreal, C.J. Doherty, Q.C., and many other leading Irish Montrealers. [17] Financial support and administrative expertise were given to the club by the upper segments of society. All the administrative posts were held by businessmen and clerks; only at the committee level were any mechanics included in the administrative structure. Although the evidence is scanty, the majority of active players appeared to be mechanics and clerks; there is no evidence of labourers, bricklayers, carpenters, or any of the traditional trades. The men involved in the new industrial establishments were the players. The Shamrock Lacrosse Club was, therefore, working class only on the playing field — the leadership and organizational expertise was provided by the middle class and those workers with clerical training.

The second group of relatively permanent clubs whose players were drawn from a different segment of society were those that bore the name of the Grand Trunk Railway (G.T.R.). As early as 1863, there was a Grand Trunk Snow Shoe Club but this ceased to exist in the mid-60s. In fact, only one club could claim a continuous existence, the G.T.

Boating Club (1876). Predating this club by two years was the Cricket Club which existed spasmodically into the twentieth century. A football club was started in 1875 but died soon afterward and was resurrected in 1885 as the G.T.R.F.C. Although having a degree of continuity, the G.T.R. clubs exerted no influence on provincial and national organizations but were most important in the growth of sport in Montreal and specifically in working class Point St. Charles. These clubs all exhibited the same basic growth patterns: initiated by the clerical staff in the various offices and played by the clerks. The mechanics, machinists, and shop workers were conspicuous by their absence except for periodic challenge matches. The type of person involved was classically illustrated in 1892 when the war canoe, Minne-Wa-Wa, capsized drowning six members of the G.T.B.C.[18] Five of the six were clerks and one a machinist; all were Sunday School teachers, and three were active in the Y.M.C.A. They epitomized the upwardly mobile working class who accepted the basic Victorian ethic — true "muscular Christians."

The 1870s also witnessed the first evidence of French Canadian participation in organized sport. However the only clubs with any degree of permanency were Le Canadien (1878) and Le Trappeur (1884) snowshoe clubs.[19] These were essentially social clubs whose membership was drawn from the professional segment of the French community.

By far the greatest number of clubs existed for one season and then disappeared (see table 3). Groups of young men banded together to challenge each other in lacrosse, baseball, and cricket, and to form snow shoe clubs. During the 1870s these were drawn from banks, retail and wholesale dry goods stores, telegraph offices, and the various offices of the G.T.R. There is also evidence of French Canadian baseball and lacrosse teams. Finally, mechanics in the G.T.R. works and other factories formed teams to play infrequent lacrosse and baseball games. The existence of these "fly-by-night" clubs reflected the increasing importance of recreational activities to a widening but still limited segment of Montreal society. Recreation had not yet become a regularized pattern of behaviour nor had it spread much beyond the white collar anglophone workers. However, it was beginning to permeate down into the working class via the factory workers.

Although an increase in participation is an accurate indication of the growing importance of organized recreation, the nature of its growth, the codification of rules, the development of attitudes towards recreation and the behaviour associated with it, lay in the hands of a small group of organizers and administrators. All of this group, whether associated with permanent or temporary clubs, were drawn from white collar workers. Within this select group, the most powerful were from the Montreal Amateur Athletic Association (M.A.A.A.) formed in 1881 by the amalgamation of the Montreal Lacrosse, Snow-shoe and Bicycle Clubs.[20] It was the leaders of these clubs and par-ticularly the M.A.A.A. who were instrumental in creating local, national, and provincial organizations, codifying the rules, estab-lishing codes of behaviour, and generally organizing amateur sport. Montrealers were instrumental in the formation of the National Lacrosse Association (1867), the Canadian Football Association (1873), Canadian Wheelmans Association (1883), Canadian Amateur Athletic Association (1884) and the Canadian Amateur Skating Association (1888). More important still was the underlying value system which has been the foundation stone of the rationalization of organized sport in modern Canadian life. This value system drawn, for the most part, from English ideas, was institutionalized in the ideal of athleticism and permeated amateur sport.[21] Simply stated, sport must be a means to an end and not an end in itself. The playing field was to be a place for the demonstration of desireable social attributes and the develop-ment of character. Therefore, it was the way the game was played rather than the outcome that was important. This ideal was nurtured in the high school and university and transmitted to many of the white collar workers. Therefore, from the outset these recreational activities were perceived to be a valuable instrument for the demonstration of desirable social attributes. The approach to recreation is illustrated most clearly in a speech given by Lord Lansdowne at the Montreal Winter Carnival in 1884.

> But gentlemen, it seems to me that we may be quite mis-taken if we regard these national sports and amusements which you have promoted with so much success as destined to provide amusement and attract visitors, and nothing more. They have their serious place in our national as in our individual life. Neither the individual nor the nation can exist without recreation. Amid the strain and pressure of life, whether our habitual vocation calls us to the field or to the city, to the desk or to the bar, to the legislature or to the study, the recreation which shall give strength to the intel-lectual fibre, which vary the monotony of our daily exist-ence, which shall give refreshment to the jaded body and overwrought mind, which shall render our youth manly and active and our maturity vigorous and robust is as neces-sary to us as the air we breathe.[22]

The importance of this set of ideas and the need to justify recreation is illustrated in the increasingly important role of various social institutions in meeting the needs of people in a developing urban industrial society. Institutions such as the church and school underwent a reappraisal of their fundamental assumptions and slowly redefined their objectives to meet new social needs. Among the means used to attain the new objectives were a variety of organized sporting activities. However, the promotion of these activities was not indiscriminate; in all instances they were means to an end and never ends in themselves. Sport was used to inculcate desirable social qualities such as teamwork, perseverance, honesty and discipline — true "muscular Christianity."

Perhaps the most important institution was the church. Various denominations were concerned with the provision of recreational activities from early in the 1870s. St. Anne's Roman Catholic Church located in the heart of Griffintown was the site of many meetings of the Shamrock Lacrosse Club from 1870 on. In fact, this church was central to the whole life of this district. The Protestant churches did not supply facilities for this type of social activity until a much later date, although indications of a change in attitude towards the provision of recreational opportunities was evident as early as 1872. At the laying of the cornerstone of the new Y.M.C.A. building, the Rev. Dr. Burns of the Canada Presbyterian Church stated:

> Much less was their association a mere literary club, although it served for literary purposes. He had respect for the whole man — like the churches, which ruled that the body as well as the spirit should be cared for. To look after the body was proper, and if baths, gymnasiums, and places of innocent recreation could not be provided elsewhere than by Christian Associations, these ought to look after them.[23]

This was a revolutionary statement at that time yet there is no evidence that this advice was heeded until much later in the century. During the 1870s there were spasmodic efforts to provide sporting activities, most likely for middle class youth. In September, 1872, the St. James South West Methodist Sunday School held a picnic with athletic sports at Beloeil.[24] Mr. Osborne's Bible Class organized an "Olympic Athletic Club" in 1876.[25] However, it was not until the mid 1880s that churches began to sponsor relatively permanent sporting clubs. Between 1884 and 1890 at least eight churches, all west of St. Lawrence Main, initiated lacrosse, snowshoe, soccer, baseball, cricket or athletic associations. Perhaps more significant is the fact that three of the churches were located in St. Anne's Ward and Point St. Charles, in the areas with the highest density of blue collar workers.[26] By the end of the

1880s, it appears that some churches were beginning to provide physical recreational opportunities for certain segments of the workers.

Both the Y.M.C.A. and high schools included physical recreation in their programs during the late 1870s. Early in the 1880s the Y.M.C.A. provided classes for businessmen and others and sponsored snowshoe, football, lacrosse and aquatic polo clubs. It was not until 1891 that the first Physical Director was appointed. High school sport was extracurricular and was in evidence from the mid-1870s. However, both these institutions were middle class both in membership and ideology and therefore their impact was limited to a small segment of Montreal society.

Fragmentary though this evidence is, certain tentative conclusions can be drawn as to the role of these institutions in the provision of recreational activities. By 1895, they were just beginning to overcome the inertia of conservative leaders who found it difficult to accept physical recreation as part of the work of the church, youth association or schools. When it was offered, it was to the middle class and those workers who accepted their value system. The sport that was played fell very clearly within the boundaries of the amateur code and the values associated with it. It was not until the era of mass sport that these institutions would play an important role in the provision of recreational activities.

Facilities

Physical recreation is predicated upon the existence of facilities. As the century progressed and Montreal's population and physical size expanded, land value increased while availability of vacant land within the city decreased. This decreased availability of land was paralleled by an increased demand for facilities. Therefore, the availability and provision of facilities became one of the most important factors determining the nature and extent of the development of organized physical recreation. The 1870s witnessed increased pressure on private facilities and vacant land, and an expression of public concern over the provision of "breathing spaces," parks, baths, and athletic grounds. Since permanent private and public facilities were the sole locations for organized sport, the individuals who controlled their development assumed an importance out of all proportion to their numbers.[27] These were drawn exclusively from the business, commercial, and professional segments of the community, a small elite. This same group controlled the Town Council and thus determined the acquisition and use of public land, the establishment of priorities, and the creation of laws to control life in the urban environment. This powerful group believed in the innate goodness of free enterprise and resisted public intervention in private affairs. Their attitudes to the question of public recreational facilities can easily be imagined and are clearly revealed in the growth of public parks and swimming baths.

There was little public concern over parks until the 1870s. Before this time, parts of Mount Royal (Fletcher's Field), Logan's Farm and St. Helen's Island were used by the public for picnics and athletic sports. These areas were all acquired by the city as public parks during the 1870s. Their acquisition gives a clear picture of the attitudes of the Town Council. St. Helen's Island (1873) and Logan's Farm (c. 1875) were acquired by the city as gifts from the federal government at no cost to the city of Montreal. On May 24, 1876, Mount Royal Park was officially opened to the public after fourteen years of council indecision, public apathy, and private greed had skyrocketed the cost from $350 000 to over $1 million.[28] In fact, Mount Royal was public in name only, as a working man, whose predictions proved correct, wrote to the *Star* on July 25, 1871: "It would only be for the rich who could reach it in their carriages."[29] The acquisition of Mount Royal was the sum of Council efforts to provide public parks. On occasion in 1870, 1871, 1873, 1879, and 1890, individuals raised the question of public parks in the poor districts of the east and west, but all to no avail.[30] More urgent questions of sanitation, transportation, and education served to ensure that public parks occupied a low position on the agenda of the Council.

The Council evinced little interest in the provision of athletic facilities; parks were regarded as ornamental gardens for evening strolls or breathing spaces for the growing city. However, the organized athletic clubs, finding it increasingly difficult to afford facilities of their own, petitioned the Council for grounds in the parks. In 1876 the Cricket Club requested a ground in Mountain Park, which was followed by a joint petition from the Lacrosse and Football Clubs for the same.[31] This resulted in grounds for "cricket, lacrosse, and other athletic games" being laid aside for that year. Further petitions in 1877 and 1878 by various groups indicated that the success of 1876 was short lived.[32] Throughout the ensuing 16 years, periodic petitions for parks, recreation grounds, children's playgrounds and athletic grounds were greeted with lukewarm enthusiasm. The temporary nature of any success is clearly illustrated in 1894 in Ald. Stevenson's reiteration of a motion first introduced in 1877 "that Fletcher's Field be laid out for cricket, lacrosse, baseball."[33] The only relatively permanent success was the award to the socially prestigious Montreal Golf Club of an eight year lease to a portion of Mount

Royal.[34] However, Fletcher's Field, Logan's Farm and St. Helen's continued to be used for athletic sports but at no cost to the Council.

Athletic facilities and public parks catered to a small segment of the population; public baths, on the other hand were created for the masses. The history of the free public baths reveals clearly the public apathy towards recreation (or health) facilities for the masses, and the popularity of physical recreation among a segment of Montreal society who were strangers to the fields of amateur sport. As early as 1862, John G. Dinning submitted a prospectus to City Council for the construction of a public swimming bath. This plea was rejected as were others in 1870, 1871, 1879, 1881, and 1882. In each instance, the question focused on the need for a swimming bath in the densely populated St. Anne's Ward; on each occasion, the Council referred the matter to a Committee, after which no action was taken. The Council, in 1877, attempted to get permission from Ottawa to open public baths on the river but was refused. However, in 1883 Council gave permission for the construction of a public bath at a cost of $1 000 in the waste weir of the Lachine Canal between Wellington Street and Grand Trunk bridges. On June 18, 1883, the (26' x 160') bath was opened to men and boys, from 5:00 a.m. to 8:00 p.m. six days a week, and was inundated with customers: no less than 3 296 in the first four days! It proved to be so popular that rules had to be drawn up restricting the bathing time to twenty minutes. The different value system of the clientele was graphically illustrated at the end of the first week when the Council felt it necessary to pass a resolution requiring "frequenters of public baths to wear bath trunks."[35] Even though the swimming bath used water from the Canal which was contaminated by sewage, it retained its initial popularity throughout the period. In 1884, a new public bath was opened on St. Helen's Island but its distance from working class areas detracted from its popularity. On August 1, 1890, the first public bath built specifically as a bath was opened at Desery St., Hochelaga.[36] The inhabitants of the east end greeted it with the same enthusiasm as did their brethren in the west. Once again it was restricted to men and boys. The success of the public ventures indicates very clearly the interest of the working man in some form of physical recreation. It also illustrates their dependence on middle class sponsorship and support in terms of the creation of recreational facilities. They were to a large extent victims of the conditions in which they lived and over which they had little control.

The paucity of public facilities placed increased pressure upon private and commercial grounds and vacant lots. As a result of increased population within the city, vacant land disappeared and land values increased to such a degree that it became impractical for clubs to retain their athletic grounds. The nature of this problem was demonstrated in 1876 by the increased taxes on the Montreal Lacrosse Grounds, $2 500 a year.[37] This was the first evidence that clubs were finding it difficult to find the financial resources to support their operations. However, the response of clubs was immediate — movement to the suburbs where land was cheaper. In 1878 the Shamrock Lacrosse Club, beset by rising costs, moved to a portion of the old Priests' Farm just outside the western city limits on St. Catherine Street. By 1891 the club was forced to move again to new grounds in north east Montreal. St. George Cricket Club disbanded in 1880 due to the loss of grounds through road construction. By 1886 the Montreal Lacrosse Grounds and the Montreal Cricket Grounds, the centre of sporting activities in Montreal, were under pressure from real estate demands. In July, "The Phillips estate management had ordered their property (Montreal Lacrosse Grounds) on Sherbrooke and St. Catherine Street surveyed into building lots."[38] Within a year both the lacrosse and cricket grounds had been lost to real estate developers and in 1889 the M.A.A.A. (lacrosse) opened their new grounds in the western suburb of Cote St. Antoine.

Movement to the suburbs was one response to the financial problems that beset clubs; another was amalgamation into Amateur Athletic Associations (A.A.A.). In 1877 the Montreal Lacrosse and Snow Shoe Clubs amalgamated to rent club rooms in the Montreal Gymnasium.[39] This informal amalgamation was legalized in 1881 with the formation of the M.A.A.A. with its own grounds and a gymnasium. Even this powerful group found it difficult to resist the demands for land and was forced to move to Cote St. Antoine in 1889. Other groups attempted to amalgamate with varying degrees of success. In the east side on grounds at the corner of St. Catherine and Delorimer the St. Lawrence A.A.A. (1887) was followed by the Crescent A.A.A. (1892) and the Gordon A.A.A. (1893), the first two succumbing to financial disaster. Cote St. Antoine A.A.A. was formed in 1890 and the Shamrock A.A.A., an amalgamation of three lacrosse teams, held its inaugural meeting on its new grounds in 1892. It would appear that movement to the outskirts and amalgamation were the only answers to the increase in land values.

These grounds were not the only facilities available for recreation. The 1870s and 1880s witnessed the emergence of a number of clubs catering to the wealthy; in every case elaborate club houses and facilities were created at considerable expense to the members. The Handball Club (1880) was the first to renovate old facilities. A new club house was built for the Montreal Golf Club in 1881.[40] Also in 1881, the Pointe Claire Boat Club opened a new club house.[41] The West End Lawn Tennis Club opened in 1881 and the Montreal Yacht Club extended its premises to include a tennis court and a new club house in 1886. The 120 members of the new Racquet Club (1889) spent $12 000 to build their courts while the Cote St. Antoine Tennis Club boasted four courts and a club house in 1891.[42] The early 1890s witnessed the Park Toboggan Club, St. Lawrence Curling Club, Grand Trunk Boating Club, and St. Lawrence Yacht Club adding to their facilities. Organized physical recreation had arrived for a select segment of Montreal society. Without exception they followed the example of the older Hunt and Curling Clubs in emphasizing the social aspects of club life.

There was a further group of facilities created for the use of a select social group; these [were erected by] semi-commercial joint stock companies whose investors, for the most part, were members of the clubs. The first of these was the Victoria Skating Club (1862). Various gymnasiums were opened in the 1860s and 1870s: Montreal (1867), Union (1870), and Barnjums (1876). Kilgallan's Floating Bath graced the waterfront from 1870 until it burned to the waterline in 1885.[43] Perhaps the most interesting of all was the Athletic Club House (1885) on Cote Des Neiges Road. A joint stock company formed by snowshoers for the use of snowshoers, it lived a precarious existence throughout the early 1890s and was the focal point of the snowshoe tramps of the various clubs.[44]

All the previously mentioned facilities were fostered by the participants themselves. There were, however,...further facilities that were sponsored by entrepreneurs for financial gain. The first [ones] were ostensibly built as race courses but became multi-purpose locations for amateur and professional athletic activities. The [initial one] was Fashion Race Course (Blue Bonnets) in the west end (1870). Within two years Decker Park (1872) had opened at Mile End and Lepine Park (1872) in Hochelaga. The last was a joint stock company which built the Montreal Driving Park (1883) in Point St. Charles. In each instance, the courses were located on the periphery of the city.

As early as the 1850s entrepreneurs staked out areas on the St. Lawrence River, cleared off the snow, and charged people for the use of the area for skating. In the late 1850s and early 1860s, two covered indoor rinks were built in St. Antoine's Ward; however, it was not until the late 1870s that a large number of open air rinks sprang up on vacant sites throughout the city. The 1880s were the high point of the impermanent open-air ice rink; they developed on spare pieces of land within the areas of densest population, and disappeared as the land was used to build houses, factories, or offices. The distribution (see figure 3) of ice rinks reveals their availability to all segments of the community, the majority being located in the areas of mixed blue and white collar workers.[45] What these rinks do indicate is an increased base of participants interested in recreational activities. It is impossible to determine who used these rinks, but since an entrance fee was charged, it is logical to assume that for the workers living on a marginal subsistence level, even these ice rinks lay beyond their reach on a regular basis. Therefore, it was probably the more solid and affluent segments of the working community who were the mainstay of these rinks.

There is little doubt that even though increased land prices caused many clubs to lose their grounds there was a significant increase in the number of facilities during the period after 1870. By the late 1880s at least 36 permanent athletic facilities existed in Montreal. Their location illustrates some basic characteristics about organized physical recreation. Nearly without exception the grounds, private clubs, and semi-commercial facilities were located in the predominantly English-speaking wards. In fact, there was a heavy concentration in the select St. Antoine's Ward and the English suburb of Cote St. Antoine. The only exception to this rule was the shift towards the north east in the 1890s, to Logan's Farm and St. Helen's Island — public parks, and to the more commercially-oriented race tracks which served all parts of Montreal. It would, therefore, be difficult to avoid the conclusion that organized physical recreation to 1890 was created by the English, for the English and played by the English Canadians.

Figure 3: Private and Commercial Athletic Facilities Montreal, 1860–95

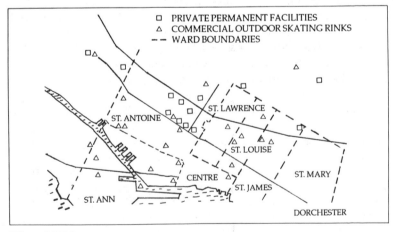

The 1890s

The consolidation of the anglophone, white collar power in determining the form, organizational structure and ideology of sport continued in the 1890s, but, in fact, sport was entering a new era, the era of mass sports. An examination of figure 1 indicates a phenomenal growth in the number of clubs in the three-year period 1891–94 — over 100 clubs. Although there was some increase in the select sports of lawn tennis and yachting, the greatest increase was in team sports: lacrosse (36 to 49), hockey (23 to 46), cricket (13 to 21), the emerging sport of soccer (9 to 29), and the newly invented sport of basketball (1891) (0 to 11). Even more important was the establishment of regular schedules which signalled the arrival of sport as an integral part of the recreational activities of Montrealers. As has been mentioned the first league was formed in lacrosse in 1885. However, it was not until the 1890s that leagues became the basic structure for sporting competition. By 1894 there were 24 leagues operating in Montreal in seven sports. This proliferation of teams and leagues was due to the widening base of participants. Juveniles (under 15) were organized into leagues in soccer and lacrosse. More indicative of the incipient democratization of sport was the spread of clubs throughout the whole city and away from the dominant St. Antoine's Ward. A comparison between tables 2 and 4[46] indicates clearly that in the case of lacrosse there had been a significant shift from St. Antoine's Ward (82 to 30 percent) to the rest of Montreal, particularly to the working-class area of St. Anne's and St. Gabriel's and to the area east of St. Lawrence Main. For the most part, the new groups entering organized physical recreation were drawn from the English-speaking community; only in lacrosse and snow-shoeing could any evidence of significant French Canadian involvement be found. Clearly organized sport was no longer the exclusive preserve of a social elite.

Table 4: Location of Lacrosse and Soccer Clubs in Montreal, 1891–94

	St. Antoine	St. Lawrence	St. Cunegonde St. Anne St. Gabriel	St. Louis St. James St. Mary	Others
Lacrosse	23	13	18	18	4
	(30)	(17)	(24)	(24)	(5)
Baseball	4	4	9	7	2
	(15)	(15)	(35)	(27)	(8)
Total	27	17	27	25	6
	(26)	(17)	(26)	(25)	(6)

Commerical Recreation

In an emerging industrial society the provision of entertainment for the masses takes a low priority. By definition, pleasure and present-oriented activities catered to a different segment of society from those who adhered to the gospel of work, dedication and self-denial.

However, it would be erroneous to place a class connotation on this group; individuals from all walks of life espoused this present-oriented philosophy with its rejection of work as the only meaning of life. Entrepreneurial commercial sporting spectacles epitomized these values, sponsored for material gain, providing a vehicle for gambling — they were popular throughout the period 1870–95 and there is little doubt that the so-called working class provided a significant segment of the audience who watched these events and drank and gambled at them.

The gradual increase in the number of spectator-oriented promotions during the period after 1870 is concrete evidence of the interest of segments of the population in recreational activities. Some, such as horse racing, boxing exhibitions, and wrestling, while frowned upon by the churches and upholders of public morals, were never declared illegal. Other activities, such as Sunday entertainments, faced persistent harassment and some sports, prize fighting and cockfighting, were actually illegal. What is indisputable is that there was commercial entertainment involving physical activities which appealed to a group different from those who played amateur sport.

Perhaps the most popular of all spectator sports was horse racing which had been practised in Quebec for many years. Frequent references to challenge matches, spring and summer flat races, trotting during the summer and winter, and annual steeplechases attest to the variety of races and their widespread support. Prior to 1870, the only regularly scheduled races were the annual Montreal Hunt Club Steeplechases. These traditionally English pastimes were exclusive in every sense, the participants being members of the club, the location a farm belonging to a member, and the spectators drawn from the social elite of Montreal. In 1870, two steps were taken that influenced horse racing. First, some leading Montreal citizens formed Turf and Trotting Clubs to regulate summer and winter racing.[47] From that time on regular spring, summer, fall and winter meets were run under the auspices of these groups. In 1881 they expanded their influence with the establishment of the Province of Quebec Turf Club. Thus the organization and control of horse racing was in the hands of the social elite and only incidentally provided spectacles for a different segment of society.

Far more important to the growth of horse racing as a spectacle was the establishment of three relatively permanent race tracks. Fashion Race Course on the west side, Decker Park at Mile End, and Lepine Park in the east end were opened in 1870 and 1871 by three tavern owners, Joe Emonde, Mr. Decker of the Albion Hotel and Mr. Lepine. It was at these locations that the prestigious Hunt, Trotting and Turf Clubs held their annual meets. However, more important to the mass of racing enthusiasts were the numerous challenge matches — flat races, ten mile buggy races, twenty mile races, trotting matches, handicap events, four days of races and a variety of others — which proliferated through the period 1870 to 1895. Gentlemen, councillors, butchers, farmers and others raced their horses against time and each other. References to the composition of the crowd indicated that the horse racing fraternity crossed class boundaries embracing all segments of the community.

Illustrative of human preoccupation with the unusual was the popularity of sporting "fads" which spread across North America, achieved instant popularity, and then died. These fads attracted as many as 5 000 spectators at one location for a number of weeks or months and then disappeared as quickly as they had come. Between 1869 and 1871 velocipede racing...attracted large crowds to Guilbault Gardens and other locations throughout the city. Newspapers and ministers railed against the drinking, gambling and immorality associated with these dens of vice. After the death of velocipede racing in 1871 there were no popular fads until 1879 with the emergence of the professional walking matches in Perry's Hall and Gilmore Gardens. Pedestrians who walked for purses of up to $10 000 had all but disappeared by 1880 and were not replaced until 1888 with the professional and amateur six day races at the Victoria Rink. What all these "fads" had in common was mass appeal and an association with gambling.

Other commercial sporting ventures included "sparring exhibitions," world championship wrestling bouts, and various strength demonstrations which attracted spectators at infrequent intervals throughout the second half of the nineteenth century; these contests attracted a clientele different from that attending the amateur sporting competitions. Perhaps even more important is the fact that commercial athletic entertainments became more popular as the century progressed providing entertainment for increasing numbers of the working class.

A six-day work week effectively excluded large numbers of people from attending the weekday and Saturday entertainment. This left Sunday as the one day generally available for rest and recreation. Despite persistent complaints about "Sabbath desecration," Sunday was the day of recreation for many Montrealers.[48] Although the spectators were drawn from all segments of society, the events were located, without exception, in the predominantly working class areas of the city and thus the majority of the supporters were drawn from this class. At the same time, they crossed ethnic boundaries and provide one of the few instances in which French- and English-speaking Canadians attended the same events.

These sporting entertainments were the antithesis of the amateur sports popular amongst the middle class of St. Antoine's Ward. Often violent, involving bloodletting and pain, these "games" were practised for financial gain and immediate pleasure and not for the demonstration of desirable social qualities. Invariably involving gambling and drinking, "debauched spectacles" focussed on the working-class areas of St. Cunegonde, St. Jean Baptiste, and St. Mary's Ward or just outside the city boundaries, which placed them beyond the jurisdiction of the Montreal City Council and in the purview of apparently more amenable councils. The periodic railings against "Sabbath desecration" provide a fascinating insight into the nature of this Sunday subculture and the popularity of these entertainments. The summer of 1870 was the high point of the velocipeding craze which aroused the ire of the editor of the *Montreal Star* who expressed frustration at being unable to control the Sunday activities taking place at Mile End, just beyond the city limits.[49] On Sunday, May 22, 1870, nearly 5 000 spectators gathered to watch the velocipede champions Pacquette and Alard. Swearing, drinking and betting accompanied this three heat race.[50] During the same year, crowds of up to 4 000 attended velocipede races, acrobats, prize fights, cockfighting, and clog dancing in St. Henri, St. Jean Baptiste and in Guilbault's Gardens within the city boundaries. The problem became so acute that the City Council held a special meeting to consider steps to be taken to prevent desecration of the Sabbath and the excessive drinking associated with it. No action was taken![51] In the ensuing twenty years the Sabbath question was raised on several occasions, in 1871 over prize fighting and velocipede racing in St. Henri and Rond St. Jacques, and Sunday entertainments in Viger Garden.[52] The City Council, in November, 1873, passed a motion "That power should be obtained to pass by-laws for the better observance of the Sabbath."[53] By 1878 complaints were being made about the "unruly mobs congregating on Sunday in the Villages of St. Henri and St. Jean Baptiste in connection with sports openly carried out in both villages."[54] Crowds of over 3 000 attended these regular Sunday afternoon athletic sports. Large crowds also watched three Sunday horse races on the Lachine Canal in Cote St. Paul in 1880.[55] In 1884 saloons, billiard rooms and skating rinks were doing a thriving business, and in the early 1890s attention turned to the skating rinks and the increasingly popular game of hockey.[56] All these examples illustrate the existence of a thriving Sunday entertainment industry which catered, to a large extent, to the working class. Significant segments of this group were not overcome by their hours of work and living and working conditions but rather with their one free day a week found momentary pleasure and an escape from reality in these spectator events where they could swear, gamble, drink and enjoy the companionship of other like-minded individuals. Surely a vivid and telling rejection of the value system of the work-oriented middle class!

One further activity which represents values antithetical to those espoused by the middle class amateur athletes was the illegal sport of cockfighting. Throughout the second half of the century, cockfighting faced an active campaign by the R.S.P.C.A. [Royal Society for the Prevention of Cruelty toward Animals] to suppress it — yet it continued to exist. It is through the prosecutions initiated by the R.S.P.C.A. that we are able to gain a glimpse of this sub-culture. The twenty-two fights prosecuted between 1860 and 1895 were located without exception in working class areas: near the Lachine Canal in Point St. Charles, by the tanneries in St. Henri, and on the border of St. James and St. Mary's Ward.[57] Twenty-nine of the forty-three participants prosecuted were blue collar workers. Although the majority of fights were organized by particular ethnic groups, there was some interaction between the French and the English, certainly more than in middle-class amateur sport.

Whereas organized sport was restricted to those groups that adhered to the amateur ideal, commercial and Sunday sport drew its support from all segments of the community. Contrary to gloomy verdicts on urban life, the evidence of a widespread net of Sunday entertainment suggests that the submerged mass of the population did not accept the puritanical influence of the church and the work ethic, but actively sought pleasure and enjoyment. The provision of commercial spectator sport throughout the working-class areas is concrete evidence of the existence of a present- and pleasure-oriented philosophy among significant segments of Montreal society.

Conclusions

The years 1840 to 1895 witnessed a change in organized physical recreation from infrequent socially oriented activities for a select social group to the spectator-oriented mass sports. However, it was not until 1870–1890 that urbanization and industrialization began to make a significant impact on the patterns of physical recreation. This era witnessed a major increase in the number of clubs, the introduction of new sports, the development of organizational structures, the introduction of public parks and swimming baths, and the building of private and commercial facilities. All of these events established patterns of urban physical recreation that have remained little changed to the modern day. Within this era of change, certain factors emerged that were central to the growth of recreation: the dominance of the

English-speaking white collar segment of St. Antoine's Ward, the incipient democratization in certain team sports, the growth of commercial recreation based on a different value system than that which dominated amateur sport, and finally the establishment of patterns of urban land utilization upon which modern systems are predicated.

Perhaps the dominant factor was the centrality of the anglophones of St. Antoine's Ward. Organized physical recreation was conceived and nurtured by this group who maintained their exclusiveness throughout by creating a number of select social sporting clubs, with private facilities and club houses, and by liberal use of the blackball to keep out unwanted intruders. As club sport developed, they placed upon it their own imprint in the guise of the amateur code. This code which gave meaning to sport beyond mere victory and enjoyment, permeated all organized club sport throughout the nineteenth century. Their imprint was made even stronger by their control of the administrative structure of amateur sport and through the dominant role in the promotion of sport of the university, high school, Y.M.C.A., and churches.

If there was any real democratization in amateur sport, it was in the team sports of lacrosse, baseball, and soccer. Even in these instances, the sports permeated down from the elite clubs to the white collar workers in various retail and wholesale establishments and then to the offices of the G.T.R. The first workers to become involved were the mechanics in the newly created factories in the English-speaking St. Anne's Ward and Point St. Charles. This movement was facilitated by the increasing involvement of churches located in working-class areas in promoting sport in the late 1880s. Therefore, the segment of the working class who first became involved in sport was that group that was most sympathetic to the middle-class values of work and thrift.

Whereas amateur sport was organized and played by a small segment of Montreal society, commercial entertainment catered to all segments of the population. The evidence suggests that there was growing commercial involvement in the provision of sport both for participants and spectators. The existence of a widespread network of Sunday entertainment is suggestive of the involvement of segments of the population different from the group participating in organized amateur sport.

Perhaps the most important single factor was the emergence of distinct patterns of land utilization which were to influence urban recreation patterns well into the twentieth century. Central to these patterns was the dominant role played by the middle classes whose values determined the patterns of land utilization and attitudes to recreation. Unfettered individualism and a belief in restricted public interference in public or private affairs led to a limited involvement in the creation of public parks. The availability of Mount Royal, Logan's Farm, and St. Helen's Island, in fact, ensured that there would be no city recreational policy and thus few sporting facilities created by the city. Sport, a frivolous activity to these Victorians, was a private concern; therefore, the creation of facilities was left in private hands. Thus, the people who had access to sporting facilities were those who could afford it — the wealthy. Even in these instances, the value of land in an expanding city was such that athletic clubs were forced into the suburbs in the search for grounds at a reasonable price. In the absence of public involvement in the construction and maintenance of facilities this meant a decreasing availability of facilities in areas of densest population. The only evidence that facilities and opportunities were being provided for the masses is seen in the development of commercial recreation and in the increasing involvement of social institutions such as the church and Y.M.C.A. in the provision of recreation.

In conclusion, it would appear that although for people in power recreation was, for the most part, a frivolous diversion from the real meaning of life — work, recreation did, in fact, become increasingly important as the century progressed. Despite public apathy it is evident that for many people recreation was an important element of life in the emerging industrial society. The patterns created during the 1870s and 1880s formed the foundation stone upon which the growth of mass recreation in the 1890s and the twentieth century was based and thus assume an importance out of all proportion to their contemporary significance.

Notes

1. A criticism that could be levelled at this paper is that the material is for the most part taken from English newspapers and thus ignores the majority of the population of Montreal. In terms of organized sporting clubs, there is no evidence of significant French participation. A survey of *La Minerve* in 1865, 1875, 1885, and 1895 indicates that sport reporting was nearly non-existent. In 1865 and 1875, the few references to sport were never more than one line. By 1885, the reporting was limited to an occasional two or three line statement. The references throughout were similar to those found in the *Star* and *Gazette*. Throughout the four years, horse racing was most important. There were occasional references to billiards and fishing. The only references to sport clubs were to those French clubs that are identified in the main body of the essay — snowshoeing in the 1870s and 1880s with the advent of Le Canadien and Le Trappeur Snowshoe Clubs; swimming in the 1880s with the success of the bilingual Montreal Swimming Club. The first reference to lacrosse was in 1895 with the inauguration of Le National Lacrosse Club.

2. In fact, there have been no serious studies of sport and physical recreation by Canadian historians. The only substantial work is the book written for popular consumption by S. Wise and D. Fisher, *Canada's Sporting Heroes* (Toronto, 1975).

3. Ibid., 13–26.

4. P. Lindsay, "The Impact of the Military Garrisons on Sport," *Canadian Journal of History of Sport and Physical Education* 1, 1 (May 1970): 33–44.

5. A. Metcalfe, "Organized Sport and Social Stratification in Montreal, 1840–1901" in *Canadian Sport Sociological Perspectives*, ed. R. Gruneau and J. Albinson (Toronto, 1976), 77–101.

6. *Montreal Transcript*, Aug. 20, 1844.

7. Ibid., June 25, 1849.

8. These figures were taken from a Scrapbook of the M.A.A.A. Obviously they are speculative in nature, but can be taken to represent a significant increase in the number of clubs.

9. *Minutes of Montreal Snow Shoe Club*, 1869.

10. Ibid.

11. The data for figure 1 were taken from Census 1861, 1871, 1881, 1891.

12. Material from the *Montreal Star*, 1870–1895.

13. The figures for 1840 and 1861 were gleaned from *Scrapbook of the M.A.A.A.* for 1870–95, the *Montreal Star*.

14. These figures were obtained from the *Montreal Daily Star*, 1878–87. They represent all lacrosse and baseball games for which locations were given.

15. The existence of the lacrosse and baseball teams was determined from the *Montreal Daily Star*, 1870–89. The clubs that existed for over ten years number 17; 2 lacrosse, 4 snow shoe, 1 cricket, 3 football, 3 curling, 3 hockey and 1 baseball. See: A. Metcalfe, "Organized Sport," 87.

16. Evidence of the working-class nature of the team can be found in *Montreal Star*, Oct. 9, 1874; H.W. Becket, *Scrapbook of the M.A.A.A.* (1877–80), 315–24.

17. This was clearly demonstrated when the Shamrocks raised $12 000 for their new ground. The subscription list read like a "Who's Who" of Irish Montrealers.

18. *Montreal Star*, July 4, 1892.

19. There was a French-Canadian baseball club in 1872 but there was no evidence of it existing for more than a few months.

20. The Montreal Amateur Athletic Association (M.A.A.A.) was central to the growth of organized sport in Montreal and Canada. For a fuller discussion of their role, see Metcalfe, "Organized Sport."

21. The amateur ideal has affected organized sport throughout the twentieth century and is central to an understanding of sport in modern society.

22. *Montreal Star*, Feb. 5, 1884.

23. Ibid., Sept. 9, 1872.

24. *Montreal Gazette*, Sept. 7, 1872.

25. Ibid., April 26, 1876.

26. Grace Church, Corner of Wellington St. and Fortune; Point St. Charles Methodist, Wellington and Charron; St. Stephens, College and Inspector.

27. Their influence can be seen in the punitive municipal laws enacted by the Town Council that effectively prevented use of roads and public highways for other than transportation.

28. Council reversed their position on several occasions. Public meetings to discuss the park were greeted by public apathy. The appropriation costs doubled when several rich Montrealers successfully doubled their prices for some marginal scrub land.

29. *Montreal Star*, July 25, 1871.

30. Ibid., Dec. 9, 1879; Dec. 20, 1870; May 11, 1871; June 25, 1873; Aug. 25, 1887; March 14, 1890.

31. *Montreal Gazette,* May 10, 1876.

32. Ibid., April 23, 1877, April 25, 1877; *Montreal Star,* June 8, 1878.

33. *Montreal Star,* May 1894.

34. Ibid.

35. The material on the opening of the public bath was taken from the *Montreal Star,* June 16–23, 1883.

36. *Montreal Star,* Aug. 1–2, 1890.

37. *Montreal Gazette,* Feb. 14, 1876.

38. *Montreal Star,* July 28, 1886.

39. *Montreal Gazette,* March 27, 1877.

40. *Montreal Star,* Oct. 6, 1881.

41. Ibid., June 17, 1881.

42. Ibid., Dec. 17, 1891.

43. Ibid., Sept. 21, 1885.

44. The Athletic Club House was created by snowshoers to be used as the rendezvous for over the mountain tramps. The accounts of the indoor football and men waltzing together, dispel some of the more puritan views of these Montrealers. Many of these young men rose to the most responsible positions in the commercial, financial and educational world of Montreal.

45. The material was gained from the M.A.A.A. files in the National Archives and the *Montreal Star.* The majority of the open-air ice rinks were identified to exist between 1875 and 1884.

46. Lacrosse and soccer locations were gleaned from the *Montreal Star,* 1891–94.

47. *Montreal Star,* Dec. 10, 1870.

48. "Sabbath desecration" was the subject of editorial comment in the *Star* on 35 occasions between 1870 and 1894.

49. *Montreal Star,* Aug. 15, 1869.

50. Ibid., May, 25, 1870.

51. Ibid., Oct. 15, 1870.

52. Ibid., March 27, 1871; April 10, 1871; June 19, 1871.

53. Ibid., Nov. 18, 1875.

54. Ibid., May 15, 1878.

55. Ibid., Jan. 12, 1880.

56. Ibid., March 19, 1891; March 17, 1892.

57. Material from the *Montreal Gazette* and *Montreal Star.*

SECTION 3

THE PAST HUNDRED YEARS, 1890–1989

In the decades after 1890, sports became more popular and influential than ever, and by the 1980s few Canadians did not participate or take an interest in some of them. The items in this section deal with important themes and developments in Canadian sports during the past hundred years.

One reason sports had grown in popularity in the Victorian years was improved equipment and facilities. This was also a reason for the increasing appeal of these activities after the 1890s, and the illustrations that begin this section have been selected to reveal this fact. Better facilities made conditions of play progressively safer and more predictable. They also made playing or watching games more attractive. At the same time better equipment made the body in motion more and more efficient and more and more beautiful.

Adjustments in rules and styles of play accompanied and to some degree followed from changes in equipment and facilities. The alterations in rules and tactics made over the years in Canadian hockey, outlined in the second item in this section, were related, as Ken Dryden suggests, to a series of improvements in the skates, sticks, protective equipment, and ice surfaces available. Dryden has been justifiably praised for the skill with which he educates his readers through *The Game* on the realities of professional hockey. He deserves credit as well for providing some eloquent passages on the usefulness of historical knowledge.[1]

At the end of the Victorian era, women were just beginning to take part in sports in significant numbers. As Helen Lenskyj points out in her article, women in Ontario (and across the country) became far more active in the early twentieth century. However, they were still expected to place "femininity first." They were not to worry about the outcomes of their games, and they were supposed to exhibit grace, skill, and (feminine) beauty rather than strength, speed, or toughness. These ideas were effectively challenged only in the 1960s, and they still influence both the kinds of sports women are encouraged to play and the manner in which they play them.[2]

If a professional athlete is one who is paid or provided with an allowance for performing, then professional competitors have been around for thousands of years. In Britain during the Victorian era, some upper-class sportsmen developed the ideal of the "amateur" — the person who plays for love of the game, not for the material rewards. These sportsmen even reinterpreted and largely falsified ancient Greek sports history in order to give their idea a pedigree.[3] Canadians soon followed their example and established clubs, leagues, associations, and championship events from which professionals were excluded.

In most sports only wealthy people could compete at a high level while living up to strict amateur principles. By early in the twentieth century "shamateurism" was rampant. As Don Morrow reveals in his article on the athletic war of 1906-08, the members of the Montreal Amateur Athletic Association recognized this fact and suggested a compromise with professionalism. This compromise would have reduced the difficulties administrators had in deciding upon who was eligible for events. Several British organizations had adopted it already: they allowed amateurs to compete with or against professionals without thereby becoming professionals themselves. The officers of the Canadian Amateur Athletic Union rejected this idea. For various reasons the Montreal Association's ensuing challenge to the national organization and its philosophy was unsuccessful. After 1909 strict principles continued to be applied in most amateur competitions. This was one reason shamateurism remained a prominent feature of Canadian sports until after World War II, and still exists today.

Some of the most dedicated adherents of strict amateur principles were clergymen. As the articles by Redmond and Metcalfe in section 2 indicated, Protestant clergymen became more receptive to sports in the Victorian era than they had been previously. After the 1890s, clergymen were enthusiastic about the character-building potential of sports — if the activities were organized and supervised by the right people. This was true in particular of clergymen in the denominations that embraced the social gospel. As David Howell and Peter Lindsay suggest, leaders in the major Protestant denominations tried to use sports to gain contact with and the confidence of young men, especially those who lived in Canada's rapidly growing cities.

Probably the most zealous promoters of sports in Canada in the late-nineteenth and early twentieth centuries were educators in the nation's private boys' schools. The selection from Jean Barman's book on private schools in British Columbia supports this statement.[4] The headmasters and teachers at these schools frequently were British emigrants who had attended private (what were called "public") schools in the United Kingdom. If they hadn't done so, they believed they knew what life at a private school should be like because they had read Thomas Hughes's extremely influential novel *Tom Brown's Schooldays*. Private schools were supposed to develop character. Character was fostered by sports, especially the team ball games, which to educators and other influential citizens seemed the most praiseworthy sports of all.

Clergymen and educators knew that a sense of community not only could be reinforced but sometimes could be created through sports. Leaders of working-class organizations knew this too. As Bruce Kidd reveals, in the interwar years the leaders of the Young Communist League used sports blatantly and militantly to foster class loyalty. Probably they would have achieved better results had they promoted or facilitated sports in a more relaxed, less aggressive fashion.[5]

John Herd Thompson and Allen Seager address a subject that has received much attention from journalists, sociologists, and historians. This is the (supposed) gradual Americanization of Canada's sports culture. Thompson and Seager argue that there is plenty of evidence to show that Canadian sports become more Americanized during the interwar years. They also identify some facts that suggest that, at the same time, sports became a more "effective national unifying influence" than they had been. Their statements remind us that it is always difficult to distinguish just which influences or trends emanate from the United States, and seldom appropriate to say that particular influences or trends can be associated with all sports.

Academics too seldom acknowledge that people engage in sport partly because doing so enables them to talk with, share stories with, laugh with, in short socialize with their friends. This is as true of professional athletes as it is of recreational ones.[6] The social attractions of participating in sports are emphasized in Enrico Cumbo in "Recreational Activity at the Hamilton Venetian Club." Cumbo mentions the popularity of bocce at the Club, and says the appeal of this sport lies partly in the "stops and breaks" built into the game that allow for "drink and conversation."[7] This article suggests also the ways in which sports have helped to foster and maintain a sense of community among ethnic groups in Canada.

Scores of articles and books have been written on Canada's great athletes of the twentieth century. Few of these publications provide satisfying discussions of the relationship between the athletic hero or heroine and his or her supporters and followers. From the few pages printed here from Peter Gzowski's *The Game of Our Lives*, we gain an appreciation of the manner in which Maurice Richard "connected" with French Canadians in the 1940s and 1950s. In both his style of play and his battles of his English "bosses" he seemed to represent *les Canadiens*. Richard did not consciously attempt to do this of course. He just tried to score goals and help his team win. But sometimes he unintentionally communicated important messages.

The journalist Jim Coleman has said that "the most significant victory in the history of Canadian sports" came in the eighth game of the Canada-Russia hockey series of 1972.[8] The final item in this section was published a few weeks after that incredible series. Douglas Fisher contend, that Alan Eagleson, the organizer of the series (and subsequently of many others), best "symbolized ...the spirit and attitude of the Canadian team." In doing so he revealed some of the attractive and unattractive traits that international followers of sports associate with Canadians.

Canadians and Russians would not have been competing against each other had not technological innovations made international travel cheap and convenient. They also would not have been competing against each other had not continental Europeans and people around the world become sports-crazy in the twentieth century. Like Canadians, they discovered enjoyment, beauty, and a sense of pride through playing or watching competitive, physically demanding games.

Notes

1. Rick Salutin makes some interesting observations on this in "Ken Dryden and the Recovery of History" in *Marginal Notes: Challenges to the Mainstream* (Toronto: Lester and Orpen Dennys, 1984).

2. See Jean Cochrane, Abby Hoffman, and Pat Kincaid, *Women in Canadian Sports* (Toronto: Fitzhenry and Whiteside, 1977), chap. 7f.

3. David C. Young, *The Olympic Myth of Greek Amateur Athletics* (Chicago: Ares Publishers, 1974), especially chap. 2–4.

4. See also David Brown, "Sport Darwinsim and Canadian Private Schooling to 1918," *Canadian Journal of History of Sport/Revue Canadienne de l'histoire des sports* 16, 1 (May 1985): 27–37, and Brown, "Militarism and Canadian Private Education: Ideal and Practice, 1861–1918," *Canadian Journal of History of Sport/Revue Canadienne de l'histoire des sports* 17, 1 (May 1986): 46–59.

5. See Bryan Palmer, *Working-Class Experience: The Rise and Reconstitution of Canadian Labour, 1800–1980* (Toronto: Butterworth, 1983), 78–81.

6. George Plimpton's books often reveal this.

7. See the similar remarks on the similar games of curling and horseshoes by Paul Voisey and Bil Gilbert, respectively, in *Vulcan: The Making fo a Prairie Community* (Toronto: University of Toronto Press, 1988), 165, and "Pitchin' Shoes," *Sports Illustrated*, Sept. 24, 1984, 69–70. An excellent chapter on Sport and Sociability" can be found in Richard Holt, *Sport and Society in Modern France* (London: Macmillan, 1981).

8. Jim Coleman, *Hockey Is Our Game* (Toronto: Key Porter Books, 1987), 16.

ILLUSTRATIONS

Late in the nineteenth or early in the twentieth century, in order to enjoy swimming races, ski-jumping contests, hockey games, or other events, spectators frequently had to put up with a blazing sun, a biting wind, or a cold bench located dangerously close to the athletes. Over the years spectator facilities became safer, more comfortable, more attractive in a number of ways (see photos 1–7).

1. Swimming races at English Bay, Vancouver, 1906. (Western Canada Pictorial Index, University of Winnipeg, 283-9111)

2. A swimming competition at the Pan-Am Pool, Winnipeg, 1968. (Western Canada Pictorial Index, University of Winnipeg, 1043-31270)

3. The Calgary ski jump on the east side of the grandstand at the exhibition grounds, 1921. Chinook winds made jumping difficult. (Glenbow, Archives, Calgary, NB-16-504)

4. Ski jump at Canada Olympic Park near Calgary, used at the 1988 Winter Olympic Games.

5. Edmonton's Thistle Rink, c. 1900. (Provincial Archives of Alberta, B6528)

6. Edmonton Exhibition Stock Pavilion, built in 1913. Later became Edmonton Gardens. (Provincial Archives of Alberta, B8855)

7. Northlands Coliseum in Edmonton, (Alberta Government, Audio
   Visual Services, Edmonton, 7905717)

G.H. "Whitey" Merritt was the goaltender on the 1892–93 Winnipeg
Victorias team (photo 8). Like other goalies of his time, he did not
wear pads. The shots he handled didn't hurt very much: the short,
bandy-style hockey sticks used in the 1890s were not efficient tools for
shooting. The skate blades were straight and thin, and did not foster
agility.

By late in the 1920s most hockey players used rockered tube skates
that enabled them to stop or turn much more efficiently than did the
skates available thirty years earlier. By the 1920s, too, players had been
utilizing chest-high hockey sticks for a quarter century, and had
learned to shoot a puck with power. Goaltenders had adopted thick
pads. Still, the goalie on the Renfrew team (photo 9) was not very worried about being hit in the face. By the 1960s, goalies needed masks
in order to contend with the far harder, less predictable shots that had
been developed.

8. Winnipeg Victorias Hockey Team, 1892–93. Merritt is front row centre. (National Archives of Canada, C79304)

9. Hockey team from Renfrew, Ontario, 1929. (National Archives of Canada, C79384)

In the 1880s, members of Toronto's Parkdale Baseball Club (photo 10) played their game without gloves or cleated shoes. By the turn of the century, teams still used everyday footwear, but had gloves that offered some protection to their hands. The Neilburg, Saskatchewan, All-Stars of 1935 (photo 11) used cleated baseball shoes and they had thickly padded gloves to contend with the relatively new, lively, cork-centred baseballs that jumped quickly off the bat. In the 1930s, gloves were available that had the fingers tied to each other by string or cord and that had webbing between the thumb and index finger. Still, these gloves were not very flexible and balls easily popped out of them because the pockets were not large. Spectacular one-hand catches in the outfield or back-hand stabs of sharp grounders in the infield became common only after World War II, with gloves that had huge webbing and built-up heels and that almost swallowed the ball on contact.

10. Parkdale Baseball Club, Toronto, 1888. (National Archives of Canada, PA60605)

11. Neilburg, Saskatchewan, All-Stars, 1935. (Saskatchewan Baseball Hall of Fame and Museum Association Incorporated)

Early in the twentieth century, when women chose clothes for curling they did not place a high priority on athletic efficiency, and they wore long, cumbersome dresses (photo 12). Still, even if they had worn pants and sweaters like contemporary men, they would have played with ordinary house brooms and everyday shoes. By the 1960s women were encouraged to wear clothes that allowed them to move freely (photo 13). Furthermore, like men, women had been using special curling brooms for several decades, and had just begun to adopt either "slip-over" teflon sliders or curling shoes that contributed to both a smooth delivery and rhythmic sweeping.

12. Lady curlers, c. 1906. (Provincial Archives of Manitoba, N1875, photograph by Foote)

13. Mabel Mitchell of Brandon, Manitoba, delivering a rock, late 1970s. (*The Brandon Sun*)

CANADIAN HOCKEY*

KEN DRYDEN

When I was at Cornell, I was a history major, but I managed to graduate with little sense of history. With most of my courses organized by century or epoch or personality, focussing on political, diplomatic, or military events, I got little hint of the social currents underlying each, which affected each so profoundly. It wasn't until I began uncovering some of the roots of hockey that I discovered my own best metaphor for what history and culture can mean.

For me, it began a few years ago. I was in a friend's house in Ottawa and while he was called to the phone, I picked up a book lying on a table in front of me and began to browse through it. It was called *The Hockey Book.* It had been written in 1953 by a journalist named Bill Roche, who had covered professional hockey from the mid-1920s until 1940. During that time, he had begun collecting stories and reminiscences of players, coaches, managers, and referees from the past, finally putting them together in a book. It was the recurring themes that startled me most: hockey as big business, the decline in interest in the United States, the NHL's pandering to the American fan, the increase in fighting and brawling — all were themes we had been led to believe had begun with our generation. Even more fascinating were references to different styles of play.

Until then, I hadn't known that hockey was once an onside game (where back passing was permitted but forward passing was not), that hockey had been played by seven players a side, that the forward pass was something introduced late to the game, or that there could be any connection between the forward pass and stickhandling, between stickhandling and body-checking. The "dump and chase," for me, had been a feature of expansion, but here it was being vilified in the 1950s in almost the same words as we vilify it today. Later I would realize that anything in one time can be linked to anything in another, that

* *The Game: A Thoughtful and Provocative Look at a Life in Hockey* (Toronto: Macmillan, 1983), 211–28.

there is always someone who took a slap shot in 1910 or built a car in 1880, even if the recollection is exaggerated and the connection artificial. More important now was the discovery that hockey before my time was more than just tales of "Cyclone" Taylor's goal while skating backwards, George Hainsworth's twenty-two shutouts in forty-four games, Howie Morenz's death from a broken leg and his subsequent funeral in the Montreal Forum. And if there was a connection between the forward pass and stickhandling, maybe there were other connections as well. There suddenly seemed to me a story I had never heard, a link between present and past that might tell us why we play as we do. So I went back to the beginning to find out.

In the early 1870s, a group of Montreal lacrosse players were looking for a winter game. At first, they simply put on skates and tried to adapt lacrosse to ice, but quickly they found that unsatisfactory. One of their group, J.G.A. Creighton, suggested that they use shinny sticks and a ball instead (shinny, an ancient stick-and-ball game, was something like today's field hockey). The experiment proved more successful. But with lacrosse discarded, they would need a new model for their game. As many of them were rugby players as well, they decided to make it English rugby. So a scrum became a "bully" or a faceoff; and hockey became an "onside" game (with no forward passing). Its "first 'public' exhibition" was held on March 3, 1875, in Montreal. The *Gazette* previewed it this way:

> A game of hockey will be played at the Victoria Skating Rink this evening between two nines from among the members. Good fun may be expected, as some of the players are reputed to be exceedingly expert at the game. Some fears have been expressed on the part of the intending spectators that accidents were likely to occur through the ball flying about in a too lively manner, to the imminent danger of lookers-on, but we understand that the game will be played with a flat, circular piece of wood, thus preventing all danger of its leaving the surface of the ice.

Though hockey-like games had been played for centuries, this was the sport's true departure point. Rules were drawn up, and with rules came organization, and with it a continuity and structure that in time would draw to it and gather up all other ad hoc variations.

It was a far different game from any we now know, yet present in it were principles that would affect how we play a century later. Perhaps most obvious was its ponderous, slow pace. There were nine men to a side, later seven, finally six by 1911, and, importantly, no substitutions were permitted except for injury. It was the accepted sporting tradition of the time. Sports were character-building exercise, it was argued, so games were a "test," and suffering, more than efficiency, their noblest characteristic. Football players played "both ways," hockey players all the time at an all-the-time pace, the patterns and skills of the game, the nature of the contest, held back and limited. (Later, when rosters increased and non-injury substitutions were permitted, hockey used all of its available players, rotating them in greater numbers of lines and defense pairs. Other sports kept most substitutes in reserve as injury replacements or "special team" players. It meant that only in hockey would an injury require a team to play undermanned. As a result, the ethic of playing with injury, often painful, dramatic injury, although disappearing from other sports, has remained.)

But there were other reasons for the disappointing pace. Early skates had long, heavy, unrockered blades, like those of today's goalie skates, making turning awkward and difficult. Games were played in thirty-minute halves, the ice, unflooded at intermissions, gradually becoming slow and snowbound. But most important, hockey was an *onside game*. To sportsmen of the time, there seemed something vaguely unethical about a puck (or a ball) being passed forward, as if territory gained this way was somehow unearned, so a forward pass was whistled down as offside. The puck could be advanced only by the puck carrier, invariably the centreman, his wingers left and right and slightly behind, mere secondary figures, watching him, reacting to him, waiting. The defence was out of the offensive play entirely.

It meant a game that moved at the pace of the puck carrier, dependent always on him for its initiative and creativity. Since his options were limited, defenders could defend [against] him in large numbers with little risk. They could skate slowly in front of him to slow his pace, or funnel him helplessly towards their salivating teammates. It was usually with no other play to make, and nearing the blueline, that his wingers came into play: a back pass, a lateral pass left or right, often ahead and offside, more often the puck just taken away.

Yet it was out of this slow and static style that the priority skills of our game emerged, and in many ways have never changed. Offensively, it was skating and stickhandling; defensively, body-checking. Body-checking had not been a feature of the original game, but made its appearance soon after. I have found no explanation for it, yet using other circumstantial evidence, a reasonable hypothesis emerges. It had to do with an often small ice surface (though the Victoria Rink was of contemporary North American dimensions, 200' x 85', many early rinks were a curling-size, 112' x 58'), cluttered with eighteen players, then fourteen, many of them out-of-season rugby players used to body contact, their hockey skills new and primitive, their equipment clumsy; the unavoidable result would be frequent if inadvertent collisions. But, inadvertent or not, early players soon discovered that in a puck carrier's game, collisions were effective deterrents. So from accidents emerged our basic defensive strategy. As for skating and stickhandling, with no forward pass there was no other way to advance the puck. Skating was the fundamental skill, of course, but speed (which itself might take a player around or between opponents) was not yet a consistent tactic. Instead, it was by stickhandling that scoring chances were earned.

It took more than fifty years for the forward pass to be introduced. In that time, the tiny, curling-size rinks that had more than doubled in size to a nearly contemporary 185' x 86', nine-man sides had diminished to six-man sides, rosters growing to twelve, then to fifteen, as non-injury substitutions were permitted; and many of the game's myths and attitudes had become firmly entrenched: its straight-ahead, straight-line playing patterns, body-checking and body contact, the puck carrier as focus and creative man, and the consequent slow, congested attitude of the game. The game was tied up in lines and rules and ice surfaces, and it had never been allowed the freedom of open ice. (By contrast, Soviet hockey emerged out of soccer and "bandy" — a game something like field hockey on ice — each with large playing surfaces, giving it an open-ice attitude that remains.)

The forward pass should have changed all that. Borrowed from basketball, more recently from football, it was brought in to restore hockey's offence–defence balance, and give it a much-needed aesthetic boost. For defence had taken over the game. NHL teams had averaged nearly five goals a game in 1920. Five years later, it was three, in 1929 fewer than two (Canadiens goalie George Hainsworth recorded twenty-two shutouts in forty-four games that season, and seven of the league's other nine goalies had ten shutouts or more; Ace Bailey of the Leafs won the scoring title with thirty-two points), a figure dangerously low for a league trying to sell itself to a new American audience. The rule was introduced in stages, was tinkered with for a few years, and was finally settled into place for the 1931 season. With no centreline (it was not introduced until the 1943–44 season), two bluelines divided a rink into three parts roughly equal in size — the offensive, defensive, and neutral zones. Under the new rule, the puck could be passed forward in each of the three zones, but not across either blueline. It should have revolutionized the game, but it didn't.

Offensively, it opened up the immense possibilities of team play. Before, the game had been tied to the puck carrier for its pace and initiative, for its creativity. Now the focus could change. It could be on the others, darting ahead into open spaces without the puck, creating the play, pushing the pace of a game to the sprint speed of a pass. Moreover, defencemen could now join in on offence. In the past, playing at the rear had meant a permanent defensive exile for them, as those ahead were offside to any pass. It meant infrequent forward "runs" by the even more rare defenceman who took them, or most commonly, lofting the puck high down the ice while teammates, as if covering a punt, raced beneath it. But with the forward pass, a defenceman could set the game in motion from behind, then move up, adding support, quarterbacking a five-man attack inside the offensive zone.

It should have meant a whole new set of basic skills, for the defenceman and everyone else. Passing, of course, and skating should have become critical, and so too the creative mind that made both work. Stickhandling would no longer be important. A slow, intricate art, like dribbling in basketball or soccer, it was an artistic self-indulgence, out of touch with the themes of speed and team play that had emerged with the new rules.

On the other side, as the offence changed, so too would the defence. The change of focus from the puck carrier to the rest that would give the game its new variety and pace — and take away the stickhandler — should have taken away the body-check. Needing a slow, static, predictable game to be effective, a body-check should have worked no longer.

This is, of course, what should have happened, but it didn't and it never really has. Fifty years of history, fifty years of habit and tradition, intervened. There was no revolution, no conquest of styles, no abrupt change, no player suddenly obsolete and extinct. The forward pass became simply part of the game, part of an ancient game played on an ancient grid that was unsuited to it. And because change did come, because more goals were scored and the game was speeded up, it seemed a success, and few wondered what other possible changes were missed. This was the turning point. The limits of the forward pass were never explored. The limits to our game were set. It was from this moment that other nations, with other styles, got their chance.

Why did we not foresee the possibilities of the forward pass as others later would? It was what Clarence Campbell called the "snow-bankers" tradition of our game. The boy becomes a man; the player a coach, a manager, a scout, a father; a game is passed like tribal history, one voice, one mind. There was no bigger picture, no history in like games, in soccer or basketball, no parallel traditions in schools or universities, no critical mind, no oblique other eye to break the relentless continuum; there was simply no other way to play. Our writers and journalists, those outside the game, were experts with no vision, or with vision, no audience. And without external competition, without incentive, there was no chance that this would change. So, locked in our rooms with nothing but our own navels to look at, we saw nothing, and missed our chance.

Since then, for nearly fifty years, the story of hockey has been speed. It was the forward pass that gave speed its chance; later it was the centre red line, better ice conditions, better equipment, better training and conditioning of players, and shorter shifts that accelerated its impact. But it was speed unaccommodated, never allowed to work, because the playing patterns, skills, and attitudes of our game were never changed to make it work. As a result, the major developments in our hockey — forechecking, the dump and chase, escalating violence, the slap shot, tactical intimidation, the adrenaline attitude of the game — are all logical implications in a pyramid of implications with unharnessed, undirected speed as their root.

But this is a view in panorama. The story of a game moves much more slowly, one step at a time.

In the 1930s, forechecking appeared. In response to the forward pass, defences began packing five men together near the defensive blueline, making passing and puck control more difficult, poised to strike in counterattack. Offences continued to pass ritually into their midst, usually without success, but the new forward momentum of the game carried the players into the offensive zone, often into the vicinity of unclaimed pucks. It was the beginning of forechecking. Nothing so relentless and systematic as that which would come later, yet greatly troublesome for defenders unused to its pressure, and obliged by the rules to *carry* the puck across the blueline, not to pass it. Moreover, forechecking represented an important discovery: offence could be played without the puck. Until then, checking had seemed a strictly defensive skill. But if offence was in part territorial, then checking in the offensive zone — forechecking — could have an offensive purpose. And if speed (without any other accommodations for it) made a puck more difficult to control, then forcing bad plays (turnovers) might become more important than making good ones yourself.

As usual, defences readjusted, easing their pressure by lofting the puck the length of the ice. As usual, the pendulum returned. This time, the league intervened. To silence fans annoyed by this negative tactic, it brought in an icing rule. And the defensive pressure returned. But out of it had come a new development — from the forward pass and the game's new speed, new skills and styles of play were emerging geared to an out-of-possession game.

In the early 1940s, the offence–defence–aesthetic balance proved unable to right itself, and the league intervened again. Many players had been lost to the war, and those who replaced them had found the styles and tactics they inherited too difficult to play. So teams simplified them. Less skilled passers, unable to penetrate a packed defense, made no pretense of passing, instead shooting the puck ahead of them to the corners, and chasing after it. It was what we later came to disparage as the dump-and-chase style, and it was in these early war years that it had its systematic beginnings. But more troublesome were the problems the defence faced. They were in a box. The rules prevented them from passing the puck over the blueline. Yet the alternative, shooting it out, meant only that it would be shot back in for the struggle to begin again. And it was a struggle. For the attacking team had the blueline behind it as a safety barrier, and could harass with five men unworried by consequences. The defence simply needed help. And help it got.

Frank Boucher, a former great player and coach with the Rangers, then assistant to league president Red Dutton, was asked to recommend changes to the game. He suggested a centre red line, and a rule that would permit passing over the blueline as far as the centreline. He wanted a way to force attacking defencemen out of the offensive zone, to break the defensive logjam and make the game faster and more interesting. In fact, his rule worked, though not in the way he intended. The defence got its needed breaks, the game got faster, but, its patterns unchanged, the lowest-common-denominator dump-and-chase style, explainable by the times, persisted, even as the war ended and the top-class players returned to make it less explainable.

Moreover, an attitude was untouched. For more than seventy years, offence and defence had been kept apart — by traditions, by rules, by the styles and tactics that had emerged from each. There was an offensive zone, a defensive zone, a neutral zone between. In the defensive zone, a team played defence. In the offensive zone, offence. And with no forward passing, or passing over bluelines, there was no way to join them. Boucher's rule should have been the link. It should have brought offence and defence together for the first time. It should have created more open ice, and with it more passing, more speed, more open-ice skills, more attackers and defenders outdistanced from the play, less eleven-man congestion from the bluelines to the nets. It should have turned offence and defence into all-ice-activities, each the transition of the other. But old habits and traditions die slowly. The game speeded up; the schizophrenia remained. Offence was still offence; defence, defence.

(At this moment, after the war, after the forward pass and the centre red line, after nearly seventy years of tradition had hardened the arteries of our game, Soviet hockey was beginning.)

With the new centreline, the dump-and-chase style only intensified. In a 1947 story, *Time* described it as "high-pressure 'shinny'." *Saturday Night*, under the headline "It Isn't Hockey," disagreed, certain it could be neither shinny, nor tag, nor wrestling, nor jiujitsu, in the end unsure just what it was. Journalist Bill Roche knew only that he didn't like it. "...[W]hen an entire forward line gets a breakaway against a defence pair," he wrote in *The Hockey Book*, "and the puck-carrier, instead of skating over the blue-line and setting up a clean play for his mates, merely heaves the rubber in a corner to start a free-for-all scramble — well, I feel like walking out of the rink and often do." The dump and chase had come to dramatize all that had changed in hockey, all that was wrong with it, according to many: the absence of great stickhandlers and body-checkers, the great individual players whose skills could be seen and appreciated, the intricate teamwork of the Cooks and Boucher of the Rangers and others like them, the *colour* of the game. All gone. Replaced by a shot, a chase, a congested crush of bodies, and speed. But whose bodies, and doing what? Not passing or stickhandling — they were not needed in this game. And how could a defenceman, chasing to the boards for a puck, deliver a body-check? Goals? Mostly they were from ganging attacks, from a strategic clutter of legs and bodies, and blinded goalies behind them. The "screened shot" became a popular phrase at the time, and for fans came its logical companion, the "screened goal."

"On half the goals scored nowadays not ten percent of the fans know who scored," Boucher complained to journalist Trent Frayne in 1953. How then did the fans recognise a goal? "By watching for the ... glare of the red light," according to Frayne. (Twenty-five years later, syndicated columnist Jim Murray, claiming to have watched hockey for thirty years without seeing a goal, asked the question, "...what does a goal look like? What colour is it? What does it sound like? Is it bigger than a breadbox?") But the dump-and-chase style survived. It was a team game everyone could play. It required no real finesse, just good legs and a willing mind. And as perhaps our first real venture into team play, involving all five men, it showed us how effective five players, working together, can be. As a rueful Boucher admitted, "Any club that doesn't use it will have its brains beaten out." To those who felt the game limited and uninteresting, there were no apologies. This was the modern game. Like everything else in the postwar world, it was based on speed — "speed in cars, speed in sports, speed in ladies," *Saturday Night* wrote in 1951. But it was speed for what purpose, and to what end?

What happens to a game when it speeds up? What happens to its patterns and skills and to those who play it? I once read an article on senility in which the writer said that what many regard in the elderly as a hopeless inability to function is often nothing of the kind. Instead it has to do with the shattering impact of pace. When people age, their minds and bodies slow down, and require more time to do the same things. An old man can walk to the store, he just needs longer to get there. But for most daily functions, we are not allowed additional time. A certain unforgiving pace is expected. It is at this pace, a normal living pace, that the elderly must function. Yet when they try, their minds and bodies get muddled; they appear senile. It is what each of us feels at every age when things move too fast. On a squash court with someone my equal, I play comfortably, the scope of play well-matched to what I can do. But against someone who is clearly superior, my mind and body seize up, and I lose the co-ordination I had at the slower pace.

It is no different for a game when it speeds up. Simply, it becomes harder to play. Offence, defence, team skills, individual skills; with less time for each, each must be done more quickly: by practising skills to perform them faster, by using different skills that take less time, by changing the way skills are used — or, as the games goes faster, probably by all three. And if we don't find enough time, if the game moves too fast for its patterns and skills, it loses its co-ordination and breaks down. It becomes overmatched, overwhelmed by speed. For speed, like the forward pass and the centreline, like the non-injury substitution, changes the way a game can be played. It gives a game new skills, and takes away others. It requires direction and control.

Yet we have made no accommodation to it. Instead, we have allowed it to dictate our style of play. Speed makes passing more difficult, so we pass less, and do something easier that takes less time. We have not changed our ancient straight-ahead, straight-line patterns, though they were only appropriate to the onside game. To accommodate speed, but also to make passing possible, we could move on diagonals across the ice, to give a better target, to find open ice, to use its width unharassed by offside lines. But we do not. We dump and chase, or shoot from a distance, and the faster the game gets, the less chance there is that we can do anything else. Gradually, speed had created a whole range of new and necessary skills, and a new approach to the game, but after the war, after forechecking and the dump and chase, speed also had another effect.

Hockey was a rough game, and had been very nearly from its start. Its speed, its confined, congested playing areas, had almost guaranteed it, and made body-checking accepted defence strategy. But the forward pass, and later the centreline, made body-checking immensely more difficult. Never abandoned, as it might have been, it evolved in part into something else after the war. The sequence was not surprising, for what does a defenceman do when a game speeds up and changes direction on him? When locked in tradition, he continues to do what his coach and his instincts have taught him to do. He body-checks. But more often than not, given the increased speed of the skaters, he misses, but not completely. For just as a well-avoided hip turns into a knee, so a shoulder becomes a high-stick, or a hook, and a punishing ride to the boards.

This was something new. The stick and the boards had never been used so systematically in this way before. But, stuck in old traditions, it was how the defence responded to the game's new speed. And the league allowed it. To the finesse player, it was one more crushing blow. What good was it to skate and stickhandle to gain an advantage so easily wrestled away? Why not just dump and chase like the rest? It was from this simmering frustration that violence emerged. Brawling and stick-swinging became more frequent and vicious than before. Not grim and calculated, goon against goon, as it was decades later; this was human nature boiling over. Often it was the game's biggest stars, Maurice Richard, Gordie Howe, Ted Lindsay, [Bernie] Geoffrion, hooked and high-sticked until they would take no more. The league intervened with fines and suspensions for the worst abuses, but did nothing to penalize its insidious causes, in the end more damaging to the game.

The effect has been profound. The game was pushed far more completely down the dump-and-chase road, its various alternatives plainly discouraged. The game was made more violent. The hockey stick had been allowed a new use. Not just as a tool of offence and defence, but as a weapon as well, a legal weapon to impede and punish. Those with memories of the 1920s of 1930s, or before, will insist there were more serious incidents of violence in other times. Perhaps so. But it was in the later 1940s that a pattern of violence entered the game. For the first time, it became part of the regular play. And when it wasn't removed, it only meant it would get worse. The nature of violence, the emerging style of play, guaranteed it.

The 1950s and 1960s brought other changes, yet the direction of the game never varied. Recently, I watched some kinescopes of games of that time. It was hockey's "golden age" as I remembered it: six teams, the Rocket, Howe, Hull, Beliveau, all seen through my childhood eyes. I had wanted to see how we compared, the Canadiens then and now, the best of this time and the best of that. I had grown suspicious of middle-aged recollections and highlight packages that showed Richard always scoring, Beliveau always elegant, Doug Harvey always in quarterback command. I wanted to watch complete games, games at random, season games, with good teams and bad, for it would tell me far better about the hockey of the time.

I was disappointed. To those used to the 1930s and 1940s, the game may have seemed dizzyingly fast, but to eyes used to the present, it appeared slow. Shifts were two minutes or longer (down from five minutes in the 1930s), the leisurely pace of the game geared to it. Players dumped the puck ahead often enough that Jacques Plante innovated out-of-crease play for goalies, but chased after it less rigorously than they would a decade later. It was a possession game, of sorts (like the Soviets, I had been told), but it involved little passing: the puck brought to centre by a centreman or a defenceman, wingers spread suitably wide right and left (how often as a child I heard Foster Hewitt say, "The Leafs are at centre, three abreast"), the defence stacked up, waiting, the patterns of the game still rigidly intact. To me, it looked like an ancient siege. An army on one side charging, an army on the other waiting; each taking turns.

By the early 1960s, shifts were shorter by thirty seconds or more, the game was faster, the level of skill consistently higher. The slap shot was new, and wonderfully exciting until everyone had one, then badly overused. Goalies rushed for their masks, moved out to cut angles, and gradually got bigger. Yet the slap shot marked no fundamental change to the game. It was in fact only a variation of the dump-and-chase style, born of the same root problem — the inability to penetrate a defence. A player could shoot for the corners of a rink, or take a distant shot on net. The traditional wrist shot, intended for in-close attempts, lost power from a distance, and was of little use. The slap shot took its place. It produced glamorous new stars, most especially Bobby Hull and Frank Mahovlich, and a glamorous new image. This was the league's competitive and commercial zenith. And if the style of play remained basically unchanged, it was clearly well-played. Indeed, watching it, I felt I was seeing players who had taken it about as far as it could go.

The 1967 expansion changed everything. Shading and subtlety left the game; trends, unseen, ignored for many years, were suddenly unmistakable. The stereotypes had come true. There were one hundred and twenty new players, one hundred and twenty old. New teams, old teams, teams in the same league bore little resemblance one to another; and side by side, teammates and linemates the same. It was massive dilution, and produced massive disparity. The march towards the dump-and-chase style, towards stickwork and violence, slowed by the skills of the 1960s, accelerated.

The game was caught in a familiar spiral. Shifts got shorter, the game speeded up; the faster it got, the more difficult to play, the fewer alternative styles of play, the more systematic the style, the more time without the puck, the shorter the shifts, the faster it got. And the faster it got, the more players on the puck, the more crashing and bumping, the more violent it got — like punting for field position, trying for a turnover. It was offence based on a defensive skill, forechecking: over centre, into the corners, and chase, again, again, again. Goalies passed the puck; defences banged it around the boards and out; defences rushed up to keep it in. It was all a matter of who got there first, with how many, and how much punishment you could take.

The game became an immense physical struggle. In corners, along the boards, in front of nets, the puck would be the centre of two or three or more players constantly fighting for it. It made for a new range of skills, for players who were bigger, stronger, tougher, by skill and power better able to manoeuver in the clutter and emerge with the puck, by temperament loving to hit and be hit; it made for centres better trained for the more frequent faceoffs (in the 1950s, there was an average of about sixty faceoffs a game; today's average is nearly eighty); it made for penalty-killers and power-play specialists, the quid pro quo.

The game had become rougher. If speed and confined space had guaranteed collisions in the first place, more speed, more congested space, and this style of play would guarantee more. If collisions were unavoidable, they would be made calculated: a hit now, a message for the next time, and there would be a next time. The style of play made it so. It was intimidation, an effective tactic in an overexpanded league. Great disparity wouldn't allow competition on the same level, yet teams had to compete. So, if it wasn't with artistry or finesse, it would be with *character* — hard work, discipline, courage — and no little intimidation. Teams could find character even among the lesser players available to them; intimidation was to make a good player worse. And it worked. The league circled and jabbed at the worst abuses; the Flyers won two straight Stanley Cups. Violence had been allowed to make sense.

It had come down to this, one final development many years coming, the Flyers its visible iceberg tip. For what happens to a game when it picks up speed and never learns to use it, when its balance of speed and finesse is disturbed, when finesse turns to power? It becomes a game of energy — an *adrenaline game*. Listen to its language. Listen to a coach talk about a game. He talks of "emotion," of being "up" or "not up"; of "pressure," two men on the puck, defence "pinching" on the boards, "hits," turnovers, shots, all in exquisite volumes; and especially of "momentum," head-shaking, hand-shrugging "turning points" and the irreversible destinies that flow from them. Adrenaline *is* important to a game, but like the batter who chokes a bat too tight, not all the time. It is important to sharpen senses, not to overcome them; to enhance skills, to push them to their high-pitched best, but not to replace them. We have lost the *attitude* of finesse necessary to a game, and now we pay a double price. For adrenalin has its dark side. Fouled or resisted, it turns to anger, frustration, retaliation. And inside a pattern of violence allowed many years before, it sends violence spiralling higher.

It is a hundred years since the original Montreal rules, almost fifty years since the forward pass. For us, it has been like a journey through a maze, one path, then many, and finally coming to where we can go no further, and realizing that we missed a turn along the way. Yet had the Soviets not held up a mirror to our game, first in 1972, and again this year, much of what happened might have gone unnoticed. We had been the best, we had always been the best. So, however we played, it was the best way. And there could be no other way to play. That the Soviets played differently was well known to us by 1972. That their style would work against the world's best players was not. Nor was it seriously considered. They had taken up hockey only twenty-six years before, in 1946. But playing more months of the year, more hours of the day, they had short-cut time: world champions in eight years, Olympic champions in ten; their long domination of amateur hockey beginning less than a decade later.

Indeed, their tardy start for them would prove fortuitous. For 1946 was after hockey's great upheavals, after the forward pass, after the centre red line, leaving the Soviets no accumulation of obsolete thinking to burden their future. They had, as well, a long tradition in hockey-like games such as soccer and bandy. Soccer, played by most of the world's countries, was much more advanced in strategies and techniques than hockey. To its off-season players, the first coaches and players of Soviet hockey, the common principles of the games were quickly evident. This was of no small importance. It would give the Soviets the necessary confidence and will to develop their own school of hockey, quite distinct from the Canadian game.

In the 1972 series, we dominated those parts of the game to which our style had moved—the corners, the boards, the fronts of both nets, body play, stick play, faceoffs, intimidation, distance shooting, emotion. In the end, it was enough. But disturbingly, the Soviets had been better in the traditional skills—passing, open-ice play, team play, quickness, finishing around the net—skills we had developed, that seemed to us the essence of hockey, but that we had abandoned as incompatible with the modern game. The Soviets had showed us otherwise. It would be unfair, perhaps incorrect, to say that nothing had come of it. Yet little has. What we didn't understand, what we don't understand now, is that body play, stick play, faceoffs, intimidation, distance shooting, and the rest have become the fundamentals of our game; that the fundamentals of any game are the basic skills needed to play it, and our present game requires those. To a dump-and-chase game, passing and team play are not fundamental. We may practise them rigorously, we may intend to use them in a game. But unless they fit in a style of play, and are rewarded, it will come to nothing. To change the fundamentals of a game, a style of play must change; to change a style of play, the attitudes and patterns that underlie it must change first.

Yet still there was room for illusion. The pendulum that was swinging away from us seemed to stop for years. They won, we won; they changed a little, so did we. And the more we played, the more their bewildering patterns seemed not bewildering at all. What had seemed to us so unpredictable — the crisscrossing patterns, the breakaway pass through center, the goalmouth pass to an unseen defenceman — was really just surprising. And when it stopped being surprising, it began to seem predictable; and less successful.

The Soviets needed open ice for their open-ice patterns and skills. They wanted a high-tempo game, 4-on-3, 3-on-2, 2-on-1, always outnumbering an opponent, fast-shrinking numbers on a fast-shrinking ice surface. It was this way that their skills worked best. It was up to us to see that it didn't happen. We forechecked when we were sure of not being trapped; peeled back when we weren't. We jammed the middle to interrupt their first pass, which set their game in motion, which created the tempo and the numerical advantage they needed. We checked hard in the centre zone, and retreated when we couldn't always be certain of at least three defenders to clutter the defensive zone. On power plays we waited more patiently, watching for the offside defenceman and the offside winger we had ignored before. And it worked, more often than it should have worked against a team of their calibre.

In their intricate, patterned game, there seemed a fatal flaw. A few years ago, a friend working at the Canadian embassy in Moscow told me he had seen the Soviet soccer team play several times. What had amazed him, he said, were its obvious similarities to the Soviet hockey team, in style and patterns of play, in its very *look*. Yet, on a world scale, it was decidedly mediocre, and the hockey team was not. Why? he wondered.

Later, I asked an international soccer coach the same question. He described the Soviet team much as we might the hockey team — well-conditioned, highly skilled, highly disciplined and organized, its style based on speed and passing. Yet in this patterned style was a basic weakness. For when a team knows what it will do next, soon an opponent knows too, and can defend against it. The Soviet style was *too* patterned, *too* predictable, he said, and in the large, cozy world of soccer, there could be no greater sin. Offence, by its nature, must be unpredictable. It may evolve out of earlier pattern and understanding, but its ultimate act is individual creation. No team can depend on weaving rink-long textbook patterns. They are too easily interrupted and broken. And, as with a memorized speech, when it happens you lose your place and must start again to find it. Except that then everyone is waiting.

It was what I was beginning to feel about the Soviet hockey team. There was also something else. The Soviets were remarkably ineffective as one-on-one players. Since they were quick skaters and excellent puck-handlers, it was a game they should have excelled at, but they didn't. They always needed the extra man. It was basic to their game. Find the open man, and use him. But nearing a net often there is no open man. A puck-carrier must do it himself. He must use his skills to create an advantage, his will to do the rest. But the Soviets seemed never to make that commitment — looking, always waiting for the open man until the chance was lost. It was a burden from *their* past, on their game, one they seemed no better at handling than we did ours. Problems remained for us, of course (facing Goose Gossage, a batter may know what's coming, but he still has to hit it). Still, it was something. And if instinctively I knew the Soviets had found the right direction, if not quite, I hoped, maybe believed, that our high-pressure, high-energy style could interrupt theirs, could break it down and simplify it, just as it had broken down our own; that in our game we possessed the permanent antidote to theirs.

Then came the Challenge Cup [of February 1979]. I don't know when it happened. I don't know how. I don't know even if I understand it the same way the Soviets understand it. I am convinced only that it happened — that the Soviets fundamentally changed their approach to the game, that they understand finally that hockey is not a *possession game*, nor can it ever be. Possession was what they were supposed to be about: passing, team play, always searching for the open man, regrouping to start again if their possession seemed threatened. But a puck cannot be physically carried up the ice like a football; and a hockey player is not protected from physical battering as a basketball player is. He can be overpowered, the puck can be wrested from his stick by one or two or more opponents, with little recourse except to pass it on to someone else soon harassed the same way. A possession game is hyperbole. The puck changes teams more than 6 times a minute, more than 120 times a period, more than 400 time a game, and little can be done to prevent it. And when it is not changing possession, the puck is often out of possession, fought after, in no one's control. It is the nature of the game, North American or European. There is sustained possession at other times only when a team regroups to its own zone to set up a play. If possession is team style, it will be frustrated. Worse, if it is attempted, it will make a game cautious and predictable.

Instead, hockey is a *transition game*: offence to defence, defence to offence, one team to another. Hundreds of tiny fragments of action, some leading somewhere, most going nowhere. Only one thing is clear. A fragmented game must be played in fragments. Grand designs do not work. Offences regrouping, setting up, meet defences which have done the same, and lose. But before offence turns to defence, or defence to offence, there is a moment of disequilibrium when a defence is vulnerable, when a game's sudden, unexpected swings can be turned to advantage. It is what you do at this moment, when possession changes, that makes the difference. How fast you can set up. How fast you strike. What instant patterns you can create. How you turn simple advantage into something permanent. It is this the Soviets have learned to do, and the balance has been swung.

In the Challenge Cup, for the first time the Soviets joined in the game. They had always stayed a little separate from it, not adjusting and readjusting opponent by opponent, moment by moment. It was as if they feared that the compromises of a particular game and a particular opponent would distract them from a course they believed in; certain that eventually they would raise the level of their game to whatever was needed so that it wouldn't matter anyway. Then, [during the Challenge Cup series], they entered our game, found its weaknesses, and exploited them. They chased the puck in the offensive zone and the neutral zone, turning the tables and using the smaller ice surface to *their* advantage. They got the puck, with forty feet of ice, or fifty, or eighty, with two teammates or three, and created something with it; no regrouping, no setting up, a teammate in motion, the defence off-balance, a pass, a 3-on-2, a 2-on-1 — instantly. It was all-ice commitment, but always under control. It was *our* game played *their* way, a game exactly suited to their skills. Their smaller bodies were strong enough, tough enough, to stand up to the game, to wrestle for the puck, to get it and move it, if rarely to punish. Their short, chopping, wide-gaited stride was quicker to start up, quicker to change direction, quicker to gain advantage and keep it. And finally they had an opportunist's touch, a model transition game.

It worked spectacularly. It offered no patterns to interrupt, no time for us to organize and prepare. It made the unpredictability of the game seem theirs. We had the puck, then they did, and it was too late. By pressuring us, they took pressure off themselves. And without pressure, our offence couldn't work. So we turned up the adrenaline game higher. Only this time it couldn't go high enough. We couldn't move our bodies fast enough, long enough. The Soviets were too quick. We exhorted and yelled; the robot-like Soviets, annoyingly dispassionate to our eyes, played with no less commitment, but with control. Too often the puck moved past us just as we arrived. Usually it was late in periods, or late in games, when we tired slightly. Then, when we were committed and out of position, the trouble got worse. It was like throwing haymakers at a counterpuncher: the harder we threw, the worse it got. In 1972, the Soviets had seemed intimidated by our frightening will; now they turned it against us. Yet the essence of their style of game did not change. It was the final irony. In countering our game, they discovered they could play theirs more effectively.

So where do we stand? There can be no more illusion now. We have followed the path of our game to its end. We have discovered its limits. They are undeniable. More and better of the same will not work. The Soviets have found the answer to our game and taken it apart. We are left only with wishful thinking. We must go back and find another way.

We have paid an enormous price as originators and developers, as custodians and keepers, as unchallenged champions of the sport. That others coming later, unbound, would take greater, more creative steps is understandable. That we should fail to fight back is not. Yet there is a fatalism about Canadians that extends beyond hockey. To a child of celebrated parents (England and France's progeny), raised in the shadow of a southern colossus (America's neighbour), others had always seemed to do things bigger and better; others always would. So, never precocious, never rebellious, reasonably content, we ride their coattails and do *pretty* well. In hockey, now that we've been caught from behind, we wonder why it took so long.

Except that in sports, it doesn't have to happen that way. The biggest, or richest, or most scientific does not always win. The Yugoslavs beat the Soviets in basketball; for Argentines, the Dutch, and others do the same in soccer. For us, the first and biggest problem is not the Soviets, it is ourselves. If we can do little about our national state of mind, we can do a lot about rethinking our national game. Most of our traditions date back fifty years. Since then, there have been two major rule changes, a revolution in all things *speed*, and the emergence of a new hockey model. But the league never carried through the logical consequences of its own changes, and others got their chance. Now we forget what those consequences were. We must go back and find them, ask ourselves if traditions and myths that once made sense make sense any longer.

Mostly, the answer is no. But the value in tracing a game to its roots is to find out why it is no; to realize that once there were reasons, often good reasons, for why things were as they were; to realize that in time good reasons can become obsolete; to watch those same reasons take

FEMININITY FIRST: SPORT AND PHYSICAL EDUCATION FOR ONTARIO GIRLS, 1890–1930*

HELEN LENSKYJ

Physical education was formally established in the school curriculum in Ontario at a time when educators, social reformers and medical professionals were growing increasingly concerned at the effects of rapid social change upon the next generation. Many women, they believed, had abandoned their "proper sphere," thus abdicating the responsibility to teach their daughters appropriate "feminine" behaviour. The formalization of physical education instruction, and the parallel developments in domestic science instruction at the turn of the century, were two official responses to the perceived problem, signifying the public takeover of aspects of gender-role socialization formerly entrusted to the private family, and the entrenchment of a sex-differentiated curriculum.

Developments in physical education for girls in the period 1890–1930 need to be examined in the context of prevailing attitudes towards women's health, and societal forces which restricted women's participation in sporting and recreational activities. The tendency to define physical activity in exclusively male terms was widespread at the turn of the century. Inspectors' reports in the 1890s, for example, consistently cited "manliness" as an important outcome of physical education, but corresponding references to its value for girls' character training were conspicuously absent.[1] The definition of a "feminine woman" did not encompass competence in sports and physical activities beyond a level necessary for health, or more specifically, for reproductive health.[2] Medical and pseudomedical opinion provided fuel for the debate over girls' sport, as medical "experts" assumed the role of "moral physiologists."[3] By the turn of the century,

* *Canadian Journal of History of Sport/Revue canadienne de l'histoire des sports* 13, 2 (Dec. 1982): 4–17.

doctors were warning against excessive *inactivity* on the part of females, since a moderate amount of exercise was believed to be conducive to health and fertility. Changing views of human sexuality were partly responsible for the new position. As Vertinsky has pointed out in her study of parallel trends in the U.S.A., behind the drive to promote organized sport, physical education and guided recreation for children and youth was "masturbation phobia": educators and social workers, campaigning to produce strong and healthy (hence, "pure") mothers of the next generation, realized that the methods which served "as a means of refrigerating the passions and creating spartan habits" among boys must surely be of value to girls, too.[4] This view of the value of sport and recreation was emerging in Canadian educational circles by the turn of the century.

With this basis in medical opinion shaped by social convention, it is not surprising that contemporary researchers find it difficult to identify all the criteria on which authorities of this period based their judgements. Gerber identified certain common features of "acceptable" sports and activities: they could be performed gracefully, without sweating, and were primarily the domain of upper-class women with leisure time and access to private facilities.[5] A more sophisticated schema was developed by Metheny, who identified principles which determined the acceptability of certain activities for women. Those considered inappropriate included activities requiring women to overcome the resistance of the opponent by bodily contact, or the resistance of a heavy object by direct application of bodily force. Activities requiring movement over a long distance or for a long period of time were also viewed as undesirable. Modified versions were sometimes acceptable: for example, the use of objects of light or moderate weight, races of moderate length or duration, activities producing aesthetically pleasing movement, those using a manufactured device to increase speed (such as in skating), and games where a spatial barrier, such as a net, prevents bodily contact.[6] It will be seen that developments in physical education for girls in Ontario generally conformed to these standards.

The school experiences of girls in Ontario prior to 1900 did little to promote physical fitness or athletic competence. Despite various department of education regulations allotting class time for drill, gymnastics and calisthenics, only 57 percent of all students engaged in these activities in 1894.[7] An instructional manual written in 1866 was used in normal schools until 1893, but, like other publications of this time, it appears to have concentrated on the instruction of boys. An 1893 textbook, Public School Physiology and Temperance, included a twenty-page chapter on exercise. It stated that beneficial exercise depended upon the age, health, sex, and occupation of the individual, and proceeded to warn against an excess of competitiveness: "the satisfaction of defeating an opponent at lawn tennis ... may goad a young girl or an ambitious youth to physical harm."[8] Thirty-two exercises in a program of light gymnastics, based on the German and Swedish systems, were included in the chapter. These were obviously intended for girls, since all the illustrations depicted a female figure, wearing a dress reaching her ankles and a tight-fitted jacket and belt.[9] This kind of attire perhaps necessitated the direction to stop exercising if dizziness or discomfort resulted. Using bending, stepping, and arm-swinging motions, these exercises involved the use of dumb-bells (which, the reader was advised, should be "too light" rather than "too heavy"), wands, and small rings. Other manuals added bean bags and indian clubs to this list of light objects which were to be held, or waved, but never thrown. The development of "grace and freedom of movement," and the correction of "false position and habits of sitting, standing and walking" were the stated aims of this "physical culture" program. There was, perhaps advisedly, no suggestion in the text that girls would find this program enjoyable, or that competence in such activities would bring any extrinsic rewards. It did point out, however, that physical culture constituted mental as well as physical exercise, by requiring quick responses to commands or signals.

Organizations like the Young Women's Christian Association (YWCA) viewed physical culture as a way of promoting the spiritual and social welfare of "working girls." The London YWCA, for example, organized two clubs in factories in 1902, holding lunch-hour meetings with singing and physical culture. An article in the 1900 *YWCA Gazette*, despite its tone of amazement that young women were capable of performing "very difficult" exercises, stressed the fact that the participants were capable of both serious effort and actual enjoyment during physical training.[10] Two prominent American educators, Gertrude Dudley and Frances Kellor, made more sweeping claims for the value of athletic training in a 1909 publication:

> aside from this health value ... [athletics] develop on the mental side keen perceptions and complex thought processes; on the esthetic side, good personal habits and improved appearance; and on the social side, group consciousness, with its many varying expressions of graciousness and power.[11]

Prescriptive literature of the "health and beauty" variety was beginning to stress the association between mental health, physical wellbeing, and the maintenance of a harmonious marital relationship. A 1904 publication, *My Lady Beautiful*, presenting exercises for developing "a beautiful, wellrounded bust", reminded the reader, "It is essential to refrain from indulgence in anger, grief, worry, jealousy, etc. if you desire the best results from this or any other exercise."[12] A comparison of these exercises with those in the physiology textbook suggests that "bust development" was one of the goals of the physical culture program, too.

Warnings against tight clothing and uncomfortable shoes were given in several health manuals of this period, including the textbook, *Public School Hygiene*, first published in 1910. Loose and light clothing was recommended, especially in the area of the chest and abdomen, and the "narrowed waist" was cited as "the forerunner of indigestion, weakness, nervous debility and consumption."[13] It is not coincidental that medical authorities predicted these same consequences, and others more dire, for those who engaged in "the secret indulgence." A chapter on masturbation in *The Science of a New Life*, a book aimed at adult, married readers, carried this warning:

> The wearing of corsets — whether worn tight or not — or constrictions of any kind around the body, prevent a free circulation of the blood, and also operate against its purification, confining it in abnormal quantities in the pelvic portion of the body, and so irritating and creating a desire in the sexual department of the woman.[14]

So pervasive was the "masturbation phobia" of this author, John Cowan, M.D., that even hairstyles "covering that part of the brain in which amativeness is located" were condemned for their part in promoting "sexual excess" in women.[15]

It is clear that a warning against masturbation was implicit in the Ontario hygiene textbook, but, like the earlier physiology text, it avoided explicit treatment of topics related to human sexuality. In view of the delicate manner in which books for adult readers addressed these topics, this tendency is hardly surprising. In contrast, a topic which had little immediate relevance for public school age children — temperance — was treated in considerable detail: five chapters on alcohol in the hygiene text, and a section on the effects of alcohol and tobacco in each of eleven chapters of the physiology text.[16]

Physical culture clearly met the requirements of graceful movement involving light objects and requiring little exertion. Decorum was ensured by the conduct of such classes out of public view. In 1895, however, there was a report of a performance of "calisthenic entertainment" by female students from the department of physical education at McGill University. Praising the students' marching, the reporter, using the usual methods of comparison with male performance, claimed that their precision "would have done credit to a veteran infantry corps." Predictably, too, the performers were commended for their gracefulness: "the grace with which the gayly beribboned hoops were manipulated, now making a frame for the face, now slowly circling around ... as the body swayed to one side or the other, was simply charming."[17]

Opportunities for university women, and for the more privileged sector of society, were expanding by the turn of the century. Tennis, basketball, croquet, golf, fencing, field and ice hockey, and the ubiquitous physical culture, were among the activities for female students at the University of Toronto and at McGill, both of which had diploma courses in physical education for women by 1908. Private clubs, some of which were established by and for women, facilitated the participation of middle-class women in activities such as bicycling, tennis and swimming. More often, women had to share the facilities with men, using them on designated "Ladies' days." Although the YWCA was offering swimming as an important part of its physical culture program by about 1914, the women's facilities at this time rarely included pools, and some even lacked gymnasiums. Women, consequently, used the facilities of the Young Men's Association (YMCA).[18]

Women's participation in sports like basketball and ice hockey appears incompatible with prevailing notions of a "feminine woman." An examination of the "feminine version" of these sports, however, reveals that, in most cases, the usual criteria were met. A very effective method of keeping the nature and pace of women's sport "ladylike" was to require participants to wear voluminous and constrictive clothing: corsets, stockings, long skirts, tight bodices and belts, and, for outdoor activities like bicycling, hat and gloves. Despite Amelia Bloomer's innovation of the 1850s — "bifurcated" skirts which permitted greater freedom of movement — it was not until the introduction of the bicycle to Canada in 1885 that women adopted this "unconventional" mode of dress in large numbers. A more common solution to the problem of restrictive female clothing, and the one usually advocated by men, was the introduction of a "foreshortened version" of the sport for women.[19] Examples of this trend are numerous: the 1899 Spalding official basketball rules for girls and women, lighter stones in curling, shorter courses for golf. Even when no formal modifications were made, women's dress often compelled a minimum of movement: tennis, for example, was played "standing still," according to Gerber's account, and a male swimming instructor in 1899 claimed that "a swim of one hundred yards (in a woman's bathing suit) proved as difficult as a mile in my own suit."[20]

Early events in women's ice hockey illustrate how standards of "feminine" behaviour were incorporated into activities generally viewed as "masculine." Ice hockey was well established at the University of Toronto by 1902, and intercollege (later, interfaculty) competition was common; as well, Jarvis and Harbord Collegiate teams played Victoria College. The university teams initially adopted the men's intercollege rules, but this soon developed into a major issue. At a 1910 meeting, a motion was passed to "eliminate bodychecking, which means that no shoving of a person into the boards by using bodily strength would be permitted." A 1961 publication of the women's athletic association of the university observed that "a similar meeting has been called almost every year, and fifty years later this problem is still with us."[21] The element of body contact in hockey had to be controlled, if it were to remain as "approved" activity for high school and university women. Predictably, it did not achieve the popularity of basketball, which, when played under the rules for women, was a relatively slow-paced, "non-interference game."

The introduction of lines, and the rules against snatching the ball and close guarding ensured a minimum of body contact or rough play. Women's attire for these and most other physical activities remained bulky, but "ladylike": skirts or bloomers were worn, and the legs were concealed by black stockings. Dudley and Kellor drew attention to players' clothing in their discussion of teaching methods for basketball: "It is difficult to avoid holding and catching clothing because of the loose, baggy suits, and *special training is needed to avoid such plays.*"[22] It is significant that they did not recommend more practical attire for players, but instead required that girls and women adapt to the clothing.

Improvements in facilities came about gradually. A department of education regulation in 1909 required a gymnasium to be built in all collegiates within two years, or collegiate status would be forfeited. By 1929, all collegiates and half the high schools had gymnasiums. Segregation of boys' and girls' facilities was common. For example, there was often a large "boys' gym" and a small "girls' gym," a schoolyard divided by a line to separate the sexes, even a "boys' entrance" and a "girls' entrance." At Jarvis collegiate, one tennis court was provided for girls, three for boys.[23]

In 1911, physical education programs across Canada received impetus through the Strathcona Trust Fund. The relatively small amounts of financial support were used to purchase equipment and texts, but, more importantly, in order to qualify, schools were required to conform to a system of physical education set forth by the fund's administrators. Since 50 percent of the amount had to be used for military drill and rifle shooting, the benefits to girls' physical education were halved at the outset.[24] Patriotic fervour during the war years contributed to the tendency to equate physical education to military drill, and the resulting approach to teaching was of limited value to either girls or boys. Another stipulation of the fund was that the British system (which in turn was based on the Swedish, Swiss, and other European methods) be adopted. Commonly referred to as Swedish exercises or Swedish gymnastics, this system stressed precision and uniformity of movement, in response to commands. Thus, for girls' physical education, the Strathcona System served merely to entrench sex-differentiated programs and a militaristic approach to physical training. It is doubtful that the component which has been shown to have an impact on adult involvement in sport — enjoyment of school physical education — was ever present while this system held sway. Some educators, however, were opposed to the militarism of this approach, and their numbers grew as attitudes changed in the postwar period, with the result that the physical education curriculum was extended in 1921 to include games. By the end of the 1920s, the "Swedish system" had been replaced by the "Danish system."[25] The speed with which this new system was adopted, following North American tours by Danish gymnasts demonstrating these exercises in the 1920s, suggests that girls' physical education curriculum was subject to ad hoc changes rather than rational planning to meet educational priorities and goals. There was, however, one aspect of female involvement in sport about which teachers, doctors, philosophers, and even the Pope felt compelled to voice their concern — competition.

By the 1920s, women were participating in increasing numbers in competitive sports, despite the conservative approach of many physical educators at the public and high school levels. Most Ontario high schools, by this time, had girls' athletic associations which played a key role in the organization of intramural competition; in addition, interschool competition in basketball, track and field, and softball, which began in 1918, continued to expand until 1931.[26] Competition was well established at universities: McGill, for example, had intramural and/or intercollegiate tournaments in archery, badminton, basketball, ice hockey, swimming and tennis by the early 1930s.[27] Although university education was only accessible to a limited number of middle-class women, the proportion of female students was increasing significantly at this time, from 13.9 percent, in 1919–20, to 23.9 percent in 1929–30; over 25 percent of graduate students were female.[28] Several, but not all, of the successful athletes in the twenties and thirties benefitted from the opportunities which university offered. There were, however, other avenues for female athletes to train competitively, as the number of sports clubs and organizations for women increased, especially in the Toronto area. Corporate and individual sponsors contributed to the development of women's athletic clubs at this time, removing some of the financial constraints which, until this time, had restricted working-class women's participation. A prominent example was Bobbie Rosenfeld, 1928 Olympic women's silver medalist in the 100 metre sprint and member of the women's relay team which won a gold medal. Rosenfeld worked at a chocolate factory in Toronto, and competed for a club funded by the company, the Patterson Athletic Club. Another gold medallist, in the high jump, Ethel Catherwood, was sponsored by the mining millionaire, Teddy Oke, who was also responsible for founding the Parkdale Ladies' Athletic Club.[29]

Women's participation in track and field events in the 1928 Olympics was an issue which mobilized the opposition in the continuing debate over women's "proper place" in sport. It was this kind of competition, particularly the proposed 800 metre run, that prompted Pope Pius XI to condemn women's participation in track event. (The 800 metre run was dropped until 1960, leaving the longest race for women the 200 metre, an "appropriate" distance for females.)[30]

In the U.S.A., the argument over competition had been partly resolved six years earlier, when the national athletic union, a male organization, took control over women's athletics and virtually abolished competitive sport for young women.[31] In Canada, a similar fate seemed imminent in 1924, when the Amateur Athletic Union of Canada (AAU) formed a standing "women's committee" with a male chair and female secretary. By 1926, however, this had become the Women's Amateur Athletic Federation, with a female executive, affiliated with the AAU but virtually autonomous.[32] Unfortunately, physical educators in Ontario tended to follow the American example, discontinuing almost all interschool competition by the mid-1930s, but, outside of the school system, opportunities for participation through clubs, leagues, YWCA's, etc. continued to grow at this time, and Canadian women's remarkable progress in sport was reflected in their numerous successes in international competition, a high level of spectator interest, and extensive newspaper reporting of women's sport.[33] The authorities, however, continued to agonize over the dangers of physical activity for women's health; specifically, their participation in competitive sporting events during menstruation was considered to be a serious threat to their physical and mental well-being. Although earlier attitudes towards menstruation had been somewhat modified by the 1920s, with compulsory rest no longer viewed as either necessary or beneficial, doctors continued to warn against "excessive exercise" and activities requiring jumping or tumbling. Physical education textbooks (for teacher-training) at this time dealt with this issue in remarkable detail, some giving arguments pro and con, and others selectively citing the research which supported the restrictive position. Agnes Wayman's book, *Education through Physical Education*, is typical of the latter kind. The conclusion of a Dr. E. Arnold, following "experiments" at his normal school, cited by Wayman, deserve to be reproduced here to do justice to the "logic" of the argument:

> Whenever economic efficiency is the deciding factor, restriction of menstruation is profitable; whenever fertility is of importance, it is undesirable. This would seem to interdict a regimen of exercise which will diminish the menstrual function for that period in a woman's life when she would be fertile.... What is needed is restriction in quantity of competition in any form. What is further needed is to diminish the quality of competition by taking the intensiveness of competition out of women's athletic efforts. The exploitation of oncoming womanhood by national or international competition is a menace to womanhood, the magnitude of which one can only contemplate with a shudder.[34]

This type of argument was used as a rationale for the elimination of interschool competition for adolescent girls. It is significant that a physical education professor of Wayman's stature, and many of her female colleagues throughout the U.S.A., accepted this kind of alarmist pseudo-medical pronouncement so uncritically. Wayman even added her own unsupported generalizations to the debate: "physicians state that the hospitals and sanitaria are increasingly full of girls and women who will never be able to become mothers — girls with misplaced organs, 'nervous diseases and other ailments' caused by participation in 'the wrong kind of sports'."[35] Clearly, interschool competition fell in this category, but intramural was permissible, when conducted "under the leadership of properly trained women instructors, who have the educational value of the game in mind rather than winning." Among the alleged dangers of interschool competition were the out-of-town travel and cheering audiences which threatened the already "unstable" emotional makeup of the adolescent girl.[36] The notion of the "dictatorship of the ovaries" which had dominated medical thinking before the turn of the century continued to colour the thinking of doctors and educators.[37] The comments of a Dr. Lindsley, cited by another prominent figure in women's athletics, Florence Somers in *Principles of Women's Athletics*, typify the view that the various systems in the adolescent girl's body are competing for a finite supply of available resources, with the developing reproductive system obviously first in its demands:

> The entire endocrine balance is being established and the
> adolescent girl who is subjected to highly emotional situa-
> tions is but sowing the seed for a nervous breakdown later
> on by putting undue stress on these glands of internal secre-
> tion, which are trying to adjust themselves to the
> physiological changes taking place at that time, and are real-
> ly having all they can do.[38]

The preoccupation with the reproductive health of adolescent girls
is evident in Somers' bibliography, where she listed 60 references to
journal articles related to the topic of menstruation and physical activity. At a time when the predominantly male medical profession
had assumed responsibility for the "normal" functioning of women's
reproductive cycles, it is perhaps not surprising that they viewed any
variation as an *abnormality* which they must correct. Canadian doctors
were strongly influenced by the views of their American colleagues:
medical textbooks and journals originated, for the most part, in the
U.S.A., and American "experts" were invited to the Canadian athletic
and medical conferences and cited at length in Canadian literature.[39]
Dr. A.S. Lamb, head of McGill's physical education department, led
the attack on women's competitive athletics during the Olympic
debate, employing the arguments by which his American counterparts had successfully swayed public opinion several years earlier.
The debate over female sport activity continued into the thirties. Even
then, the questions remained unchanged: did sport jeopardize
women's reproductive health? Did physical activity enhance
women's health and, therefore, make them better wives and mothers?
Did female athletes experience less difficulty in child-bearing? No
one asked: Did sport promote confidence and self-esteem in women?
Did women enjoy the challenge of competition, the joy of movement
and the satisfaction of personal progress in athletic activities? These
questions were not asked because the answers were not considered
important; the "wife and mother" issue was paramount. Not all of the
official pronouncements, however, stemmed from concern for the
next generation of mothers. The actions of the medical profession, in
particular, were motivated by self-interest: the goal was to maintain
the predominantly male monopoly over women's reproductive
health which had been achieved through the promotion of hospital
births and the outlawing of midwifery.[40] In addition to the financial
benefits of maintaining the status quo, the male-dominated medical
profession enjoyed its role as an authority on moral issues, especially
those related to female morality. Like other conservative sectors of
the male business community, it had a vested interest in maintaining

a social system in which women's position remained subordinate. Thus, it was undesirable, purely in economic terms, to promote a spirit of competition in women, in the field of sport, which might have implications for their participation in fields like education and business — and threaten the comfortable status quo. A physical education instructor cited by Dudley and Kellor expressed this fear regarding interschool competition: "There is a great danger of sacrificing some of the finer traits [of girls] for the peculiar boldness which outside contests bring out."[41] Similarly, Wayman claimed:

> There is ... no real reason why girls should participate in the same games and sports as boys. The girl does not need to have her combative instincts developed. She is not or should not be interested primarily in making or breaking records. She should be interested in events and types of activities which make for grace, poise, suppleness, quickness, agility, dexterity, beauty, general strength and endurance ... events where form and skill is emphasized, rather than in events requiring great strength and speed.[42]

In other words, sport for girls should enhance what were viewed as their "natural" physical traits — grace and beauty. Girls do not need to compete, to fight, to achieve, to excel because such behaviour lies in the male domain.

It must be recognized, as this point, that the rationale for these restrictive attitudes did not stem solely from the prevailing ideology of woman's frailty and her subordinate position in society. From the medical perspective, contemporary sports medicine research has substantiated some of the claims related to menstrual variations. A recent study found delayed menarche among female athletes of up to two years.[43] Menstrual irregularity and amenorrhea (cessation of menstrual periods) has been found to occur among athletes more than in the general population, but the primary cause is loss of weight or body fat, not exercise per se. Similarly, in the case of delayed menarche, there is no clear causal relationship: body fat, again, is an important factor, and it has been suggested that the thin, late-maturing athletes are the ones who continue to train strenuously, thus maintaining the conditions which delay menarche. The "myth of the misplaced uterus" has been debunked, although it is acknowledged that women who already have prolapse of the uterus may experience more symptoms during vigorous exercise. The role of exercise in either reducing or increasing menstrual cramps remains undetermined, but it is encouraging to note that contemporary medical attitudes towards this and other issues in sports gynecology appear to be more positive towards female athletes than in the past. Popular literature on this topic frequently makes the observation that fear for the safety of the female's reproductive organs, and not the male's, is somewhat curious, in the light of their respective locations in the human body.[44]

From the ideological perspective, the "separate but equal" philosophy of some of the pioneers in women's sports would find support among some contemporary feminists, but it is generally agreed that boys and girls should play and compete together until puberty, when the different growth spurts give an unfair advantage, first to girls and ultimately to boys, in terms of weight and height. Pedagogically, the claim that competition serves only the talented, and deprives less competent students of the opportunity to improve, was valid, but the fact that its early proponents viewed the inter/intramural debate as an either/or situation resulted in talented girls being deprived of the opportunity to excel, merely because excellence in sport was not considered necessary or desirable for a girl — "she is not, or should not be interested in making or breaking records." Significantly, there seems to have been little agonizing over the plight of boys who lacked the talent for interschool competition, perhaps because the budget for boys' sport was sufficient to provide facilities and instruction for both levels.

The historical materials presented here illustrate the significance of socialization determinants for women's involvement in physical activity at the beginning of the century. There was clearly a conflict between the notion of "feminine woman" and "athletic woman," particularly after the reproductive health of active girls came under scrutiny; the pseudo-medical claims that sport jeopardized girls' child-bearing capability were virtual proof of the ancient fear that sport masculinizes females. Traditionalists were alarmed to observe, too, that situations such as sporting contests brought out "masculine" traits in girls, hence, those who preferred to deny that girls enjoyed physical challenge, excitement, the struggle to win and to achieve excellence, took the necessary steps to repress such traits, by abolishing competition.

Sport was viewed as a means of developing feminine beauty and grace. Only for boys was the goal to build physical and mental endurance, and control over one's body. For boys, this kind of learning was functional in the "world of men," as was illustrated by the old saying that wars were fought on the playing fields of Eton. The so-called male bonding which took place on the fields could be observed by women, as spectators, but never emulated by them.

Notes

1. See, for example, *Ontario Department of Education Report, 1895* (Toronto: Warwick, 1896). As part of their 1895 reports, inspectors were required to respond to questions about the physical health of staff and pupils, and sanitary conditions in the schools under their jurisdiction.

2. The definition, of course, was class-bound. There was little concern that working-class women would lose their "femininity" by engaging in the kind of strenuous physical activity — labour, not leisure — which was necessary for their survival.

3. The term "moral physiologists" was used by Patricia Vertinsky in "The Effect of Changing Attitudes Towards Sexual Morality Upon the Promotion of Physical Education for Women in Nineteenth-Century America," *Canadian Journal of History of Sport and Physical Education* 7, 2 (1976): 26–38.

4. Ibid.

5. Ellen Gerber, "The Changing Female Image," *Journal of Health, Physical Education and Recreation* (Oct. 1971), 59.

6. Eleanor Metheny, *Connotations of Movement in Sport and Dance* (Dubuque, Iowa: Brown, 1965), 48–52.

7. Department of Education inspectors' reports, cited by Helen Bryans, "Secondary School Curriculum for Girls" in *Physical Education in Canada*, ed. M. Van Vliet (Toronto: Prentice-Hall, 1965), 126.

8. William Nattress, *Public School Physiology and Temperance* (Toronto: Briggs, 1893), 178.

9. Ibid., 100–01.

10. Cited by Josephine Shaw, *When Women Work Together* (Toronto: YWCA, 1966), 130–31.

11. Gertrude Dudley and Frances Kellor, *Athletic Games in the Education of Women* (New York: Holt, 1909), 26–27.

12. Alice Long, *My Lady Beautiful* (Chicago: Progress, 1908), 167.

13. A.P. Knight, *The Ontario Public School Hygiene* (Toronto: Copp Clark, 1919), 106.

14. John Cowan, *The Science of a New Life* (New York: Ogilvie, 1919), 366.

15. Ibid.

16. *Public School Hygiene.*

17. A Montreal newspaper report cited by Jesse Herriott in "The Department of Physical Education for Women," *McGill News* (Autumn 1935), 36.

18. Ibid., 37–38; Jean Cochrane et al., *Women in Canadian Life: Sports* (Toronto: Fitzhenry and Whiteside, 1977), 24–33; Shaw, *When Women Work Together*, 131.

19. The view that women are "truncated males" who can only engage in "foreshortened versions" of men's sports, was presented as recently as 1969, by Paul Weiss in *Sport, A Philosophic Inquiry* (Urbana, Ill.: Southern Illinois University Press). His "philosophy" was popular with some physical educators, but has been attacked by feminist scholars, including Thomas Boslooper and Marcia Hayes in *The Femininity Game* (New York: Stein and Day, 1973), and Jan Felshin in *The American Woman in Sport*, ed. Ellen Gerber et al. (Reading, Mass.: Addison-Wesley, 1974).

20. Gerber, "The Changing Female Image," 59; Edwin Sandys, Swimming Instructor, 1899, cited by Marjorie Loggia, "On the Playing Fields of History," *Ms Magazine* (July 1973), 63; Canadian developments at this time are described by

Lindsay, "Women's Place in Nineteenth-Century Canadian Sport," *Canadian Woman's Studies* 1, 4 (Summer 1979): 22–24, and by Alison Griffiths, "They Who Risked Their Delicate Organs," *Branching Out* 5, 4 (1978): 10–13.

21. A.E. Parkes, *The Development of Women's Athletics at the University of Toronto* (Toronto: University of Toronto Press, 1961), 5–6.

22. Dudley and Kellor, *Athletic Games in the Education of Women*, 179–80, 194. My emphasis.

23. *Girls' Sport, A Century of Progress* (Ontario: OFSAA, 1979), 23–24.

24. Frank Cosentino and Maxwell Howell, *A History of Physical Education in Canada* (Toronto: General Publishing, 1971), 27–29.

25. Ibid., 44.

26. *Girls' Sport*, 10.

27. Herriott, "Department of Physical Education," 37–38.

28. DBS Statistics cited by Mary Vipond, "The Image of Women in Mass Circulation Magazines" in *The Neglected Majority*, ed. Susan Trofimenkoff and Alison Prentice (Toronto: McClelland and Stewart, 1977), 118.

29. Donald McDonald, "Twenties and Thirties Were the Golden Age," *Champion* (March 1981), 4–6.

30. Frank Cosentino and Glenn Leyshon, *Olympic Gold* (Toronto: Holt, Rinehart and Winston, 1975), 81–82; McDonald, ibid., 5.

31. Boslooper and Hayes, *The Femininity Game*, 98.

32. Nancy Howell and Maxwell Howell, *Sports and Games in Canadian Life* (Toronto: Macmillan, 1969), 155.

33. Cochrane, *Women in Canadian Life*, 37–43.

34. E. Arnold, cited by Agnes Wayman, *Education Through Physical Education* (Philadelphia: Lee and Febiger, 1934), 200.

35. Ibid., 127.

36. Florence Somers, *Principles of Women's Athletics* (New York: Barnes, 1930), 37–42.

37. Barbara Ehrenreich and Diedre English used the term "dictatorship of the ovaries" in their discussion of medical attitudes of female health, in *For Her Own Good* (Garden City, N.Y.: Anchor, 1979).

38. Dr. Lindsley, cited by Somers, *Principles of Women's Athletics*, 44.

39. See Wendy Mitchinson, "Historical Attitudes Towards Women and Childbirth," *Atlantis* 4, 2, Part II (Spring 1979).

40. Susan Buckley, "Ladies or Midwives" in *A Not Unreasonable Claim*, ed. Linda Kealey (Toronto: Women's Press, 1979), 131–49.

41. Cited by Dudley and Kellor, *Athletic Games in the Education of Women*, 151.

42. Wayman, *Education through Physical Education*, 128–29.

43. W.D. Ross and R. Ward, "Growth Patterns, Menarche and Maturation in Physically Active Girls" (Proceedings of the Conference on the Female Athlete, Institute of Human Performance, Simon Fraser University, 1980), 63–71.

44. Ibid., 69; Mona Shangold, "Sports Gynecology," *The Runner* (June 1981), 35–38; Gary Selden, "Frailty, Thy Name's Been Changed," *Ms Magazine* (July 1981), 51–53, 95.

A CASE STUDY IN AMATEUR CONFLICT: THE ATHLETIC WAR IN CANADA, 1906–08*

DON MORROW

The major objective of this article is to examine the issues prominent in Canada's amateur "athletic war." Officially, the schism boiled down to a disagreement between two groups over whether or not amateurs could be allowed to participate with and/or against professionals in team sports while still retaining their amateur standing. The two warring factions were the Canadian Amateur Athletic Union (CAAU) and the Amateur Athletic Federation of Canada (AAFC); in reality it was an ideological power struggle between the emerging centre of sport in twentieth-century Canada, Toronto, and the revered hub of organized sport in nineteenth-century Canada, Montreal. The struggle lasted from February 1, 1907 to September 6, 1909, or just over two and a half years.

By comparison, Canada's athletic war was enacted structurally along parallel lines to the amateur conflict in the United States between 1886 and 1889. This schism resulted in the formation of the Amateur Athletic Union in the United States in 1889.[1] A similar controversy took place in Great Britain in 1895 when the Rugby Football Union split into two groups with the Northern Union adopting the concept of "broken time" payments.[2] All three countries, Great Britain, the United States and Canada, underwent bitter struggles to preserve the *ideal* of amateurism. The protection of an ideal — amateurism — was the issue, even though the three countries approached the problem from different directions:

> To comprehend the principles which underlie the development of the amateur ideal in Great Britain, and especially England, it must be clearly understood that British

* *The British Journal of Sports History* 3, 2 (Sept. 1986): 173–90.

amateurism has always been much more the concern of the representative bodies governing and legislating for individual sports than of any one central organization.[3]

Centrality of management was a key factor in the amateur conflicts of both the United States and Canada.

The critical period in defining amateur status dates from 1879 when the Henley Stewards "promulgated their very strict definition of an oarsman"[4] which prohibited competitive sport entrants who were mechanics, labourers, artisans and in general anyone who worked with his hands for a daily wage. The issue of amateur exclusivity became more acute during the 1880s and 1890s in rugby football and rowing, respectively, as payments to athletes rather than social status became the significant amateur criterion in Britain.[5] The extension or development of amateurism erupted so strongly in British association football during 1907–08 that the very existence of the sport was threatened.[6] Both Savage and Guttman interpret the amateur rule in late nineteenth-century Britain as an "instrument of class warfare"[7] that had its roots and meaning in an "individual consciousness" concept of pure sport among British sportsmen imbued with the persistent traditions of the British public school.[8]

In the United States, the early amateur definitions emanated from the National Association of Amateur Oarsmen (1872) and were more "legalistic" than the earliest British amateur distinctions. The 1879 amateur definition of the NAAA of America was:

An amateur is any person who has never competed in an open contest, or for a stake, or for public money, or for gate money, or under a false name, or with a professional for a prize, or where gate money is charged; nor has ever at any period of his life taught or pursued athletic exercises as a means of livelihood.[9]

This definition is couched in negative phrasing; it is really a definition of a non-amateur in that it particularizes the circumstances in which an amateur becomes a professional. By implication, amateurism was the absence of professionalism. This negative concept of the amateur permeated all attempts to define amateur status over the next thirty to forty years in both the United States[10] and Canada. More significantly, these negative definitions invited obeying the letter but not the spirit of the amateur law[11] and were more the source than the cure for amateur abuses.

The first amateur definition in Canada was thought to be that listed by the Canadian Association of Amateur Oarsmen in 1880:

> An amateur is one who has never assisted in the pursuit of athletics exercises as a means of livelihood, who rows for pleasure and recreation only during his leisure hours, and does not abandon or neglect his usual business or occupation for the purpose of training for more than two weeks during the season.[12]

More negative than positive or affirmative, the exclusivity of this supposedly first Canadian Amateur definition was softer than one framed by the Montreal Pedestrian Club in 1873:

> [An amateur is] one who has never competed in any open competition or for public money, or for admission money, or with professionals for a prize, public money or admission money, nor has ever, at any period of his life taught or assisted in the pursuit of Athletic exercises as a means of livelihood *or is a laborer or an Indian.*[13]

This 1873 amateur definition is a perfect *ménage à trois* of American legalistic or negative stricture, of the British social criterion for amateurism and of the Canadian ethnic twist pertaining to Indians. Decidedly, the definition is of a non-amateur and is a negative and more characteristic of the flow of amateur distinctions leading up to the athletic war than the 1880 Canadian Association of Amateur Oarsmen definition. The exclusion of Indians was derived from their superior skill in lacrosse, snowshoe racing and, to a certain extent, in footraces as well as their perceived inferior social status.[14]

The first parent-body or custodian of the amateur ideal in Canada was the Amateur Athletic Association of Canada (AAAC) formed in 1884 at the instigation of the Montreal Amateur Athletic Association.[15] The increasingly powerful MAAA had been affiliated with the American National Association of Amateur Athletes but the Montreal group was seeking unified regulation for track and field. Delegates from cricket, rugby, lacrosse and cycling who attended the formative meetings of the Amateur Athletic Association of Canada in 1884 did so "under the misapprehension that the Association was to cover all sports."[16] There was a void of leadership in Canadian sport that was waiting to be filled; by accident, then, a track and field control group assumed governing dominance of Canadian sport. Instead of encouraging or promoting or fostering the development of sport, the AAA of Canada was a regulator, a *custodian* of the amateur principle which it defined in 1884, in parallel fashion to the American 1879 NAAA:

> An amateur is one who has never competed for a money prize or staked bet, or with or against any professional for any prize, or who has never taught, pursued or assisted in the practice of athletic exercises as a means of obtaining of livelihood. This rule does not interfere with the right of any club to refuse an entry to its own sports.[17]

Obviously, the definition is of a non-amateur, is negative and legalistic and noteworthy for the touch of absolute right of exclusivity of the last line which gives the definition a patented British-Canadian flavour.

The prevailing concept of the professional athlete in Canada during the 1880s and 1890s was equated with prostitution;[18] the term professional was used to characterize an athlete who would sell his athletic talent to the highest bidder, fix the outcome of contests and generally dupe the public for personal profit. A commercial basis for sport had been developed in baseball due to American influences. Lacrosse followed suit in order to attract fans who learned quickly to enjoy good baseball over poor lacrosse. Rowing was openly professionalized and respected in Canada because of the phenomenal success of the world champion, Edward Hanlan; however, baseball, lacrosse, rugby football and ice hockey (in the 1890s) were semi-professional or covertly professional.[19] Popular individual sports such as bicycle racing and speedskating contained distinct, open categories for professionals and for amateurs, but no mixed races of the two classes or categories were sanctioned by the AAAC.

As senior leagues in team sports became more competitive, with greater and greater emphasis on winning championships, the more concentrated and numerous were the efforts to build quality teams while pretending to adhere to the amateur strictures of the national governing body. Charges of professionalism were rampant in the 1890s in team sports; even paid referees were banned from playing amateur sport of any kind and were fixed instead with the professional label.[20] Jobs or placements, sponsorship, end-of-season performance bonuses and outright payments to athletes were made under the disguise of amateurism; two-year residence rules were agreed among leagues in a pre–reserve clause era. The AAAC was monopolized with the arduous and complex tasks of investigating charges of professionalism, suspending proven violators of the amateur definition (or, in perverted jurisprudence, suspending athletes whose only guilt was that they could not prove their amateur innocence) and reinstating athletes who had been suspended but were ready to repent and were willing to follow the lines of simon-pure amateurism.

Because of the trend towards international competition and because of the importance placed on US competition for Canadian athletes and even more because the MAAA recognized the crowd-drawing features of American athletes competing in Canadian track and field championships, the AAAC formed an alliance with the AAU of the United States in 1898 and became the Canadian Amateur Athletic Union (CAAU).[21] In so doing, the CAAU claimed "jurisdiction" over some 17 sports inclusive of the increasingly commercial and popular team sports. Jurisdiction implied the assumed custodial role of control in applying the letter of the amateur law.[22] Even though the CAAU sought national control in amateur sport, most affiliations were from sports clubs as compared with national sport governing bodies.[23] While the CAAU preached ironclad opposition to professionalism, team sport clubs paid lip-service adherence only to the idea. Prestigious trophies such as the Stanley Cup in hockey and the Minto Cup in lacrosse were controlled by trustees outside the realm of the CAAU. Despite all kinds of suspensions and regulations in the name of amateurism, professional or non-amateur, commercial lacrosse, hockey and to a lesser extent, rugby football,[24] were flourishing by 1905. The situation in these sports (and in the administration or policing of the amateur concept) was ludicrous. The preservation of the amateur ideal reached the proportions of mummification. Further, its application was inconsistent and at times, catch-as-catch-can. Trends and pressures towards commercial sport created an athletic bubble waiting to be burst.

Between 1901 and 1905, the Executive Committee of the CAAU, its board of governors, dealt almost exclusively with allegations, suspensions and questions concerning the issue of amateur athletes playing with or against professionals and not losing their amateur status.[25] In lacrosse, team members accused of professionalism were forced to file affidavits of innocence as bona fide amateurs before a judge[26] or be suspended. The National Amateur Lacrosse Union made a formal request to the CAAU in 1903 to allow amateurs to compete with or against professionals.[27] The CAAU's response at first was unalterably negative, but one year later, the organization voted unanimously to permit any athletic union in Canada to become a subscribing member of the CAAU within the next six months in return for the concession that all athletes suspended as professionals in these unions would be automatically reinstated as amateurs if the unions agreed to abide in future by the CAAU amateur definition.[28] The CAAU was quite conscious of what its representatives termed the "present unsettled condition of athletics in Canada"[29] yet its solution of reinstatement with affiliation was band-aid in effect, treating only the symptom, not the causes, of the problem. In 1905, the NALU forced the CAAU to make a direct decision on the issue of amateurs competing with or against professionals. In a lengthy and heated meeting amid threats of resignation from CAAU executives including the president, the CAAU voted "not to enforce the penalties provided for in the event of amateurs competing with or against professionals"[30] in the sport of lacrosse only.

This concession for the good of the "national" sport[31] was relatively radical and quite unconstitutional. At the next annual meeting of the CAAU in September 1905, President Gorman attempted to rescind the concession but he was not supported by the delegates.[32] One year later, at the 1906 annual meeting, the CAAU members voted overwhelmingly to annul the concession to lacrosse.[33] Unless the CAAU disbanded or changed its role and constitution completely, it was the only possible method available to manage the problem. Meanwhile, that bastion of amateur ideals and prime mover in the organization of Canadian sport, the MAAA, was caught in the continuing dilemma. Net gate receipts for its lacrosse team had reached $5 000 by 1904 while travelling costs, accident insurance rates and facility maintenance costs were increasing rapidly.[34] Its arch rival, the Shamrock Lacrosse Club, was in the Minto Cup in 1904 while playing with and against known professional athletes, and the Ontario-based Canadian Lacrosse Association was siphoning off the best players in open professional lacrosse.[35] Trembling on the precipice of professionalism, the MAAA, hailed by Toronto organizations as the Montreal *Almost* Amateur Athletic Association, retrenched momentarily at its semi-annual meeting in November 1905 to reaffirm its position in support of the principle of pure amateurism in the face of the 1905 CAAU concession to the NALU to allow amateurs to remain amateurs while competing with or against professionals. Unanimously the membership of the MAAA declared "unreserved adhesion to the letter and spirit of the amateur law embodied in the MAAA constitution."[36] But the lure of lacrosse victory and attendant benefits were too great. Exactly five months later,[37] the Directors passed a motion to allow amateurs to play with or against professionals without jeopardizing their amateur status. The motion was ratified by the membership in a 250–12 vote.[38] It was a significant change from the single most powerful sporting agency in Canada at the time. The Montreal press gushed its admiration with headlines such as: "The M.A.A.A. to Cut the Gordian Knot."

The prevailing rationalization from the MAAA was something like: it is better to have the professional element openly recognized than to continue under various disguises as has been the practice over the past three years. A veritable parade of MAAA founders rose to the stage before the press to support the new motion arguing that the disguised professional athlete was the "road-agent of sport because his work is in the dark and in hiding" and that the professional evil must be faced courageously or else the "canker [would] flourish beneath the surface." [39] The only vocal opponent among MAAA members quoted scripture to the audience and proclaimed that calamities like the Johnstown flood and the San Francisco earthquake would be visited upon Montreal if the amendment was adopted. [40] Adopted it was and the MAAA was committed. Before the end of the same month, April, 1906, the NALU followed the lead of the MAAA by adopting the same resolution and changing its name to the NLU. [41]

With the combined powers of the NLU and the MAAA directed towards a practice that was openly touted as commonplace in cricket and football in the mother country, [42] royal sanction and divine blessing seemed imminent. By August 1906, the public press published betting information: "in one well known restaurant on St. James Street, there has been 3 000 dollars lying about since yesterday afternoon for Montreal supporters to cover. Last night the betting was even, this morning the Shamrocks were willing to give ten to eight." [43] By the autumn, sentiment prevailed to follow the same course in rugby football and ice hockey. [44] Non-Montreal, non-team sport, devout amateur idealist executives of the CAAU recognized the delicacy of the situation and dragged their heels through the month of September, the normal annual meeting time of the CAAU. It was just too much cognitive dissonance for amateur idealists. Finally, the CAAU met on October 27, 1906, and passed the motion (in an almost perfect Toronto sport versus Montreal sport vote) to annul its year-old motion to support the innovation of amateurs playing with or against professionals in lacrosse. The course of the amateur sport river had been successfully redirected and was not blocked by a CAAU dam, at least as far as team sports, in particular lacrosse, and the MAAA were concerned.

For years, the MAAA had dominated the CAAU. An MAAA member had been CAAU president for half of its 23 years of existence and the annual meetings of the CAAU were held traditionally in the Windsor Hotel, Montreal. On several occasions, MAAA members filibustered or block-voted to get their way in the CAAU. There was a decided Montreal sport nepotism led by the MAAA, and the CAAU annulment of the concession to allow amateurs to play with and against professionals was a bold, locked-horns position between Toronto and Montreal. Ironically, the new president of the CAAU amateur policing body was the Toronto police force deputy-chief,

Stark. The MAAA did not back down and withdraw its new constitutional position; the CAAU posture officially was to allow the MAAA to re-think its position and "if they are determined to embrace professionalism," let the association resign honourably.[45] Stark concisely encapsulated the CAAU's perspective on the MAAA situation: "If they find that they cannot change the laws of the Union to suit their view, and if they intend to follow those views in defiance of the Union's laws, then they should withdraw voluntarily."[46] The *Toronto Globe* was convinced that the MAAA would be expelled from the CAAU and that no more "shilly shallying" of the earlier days of the CAAU would take place.[47] Finally, after many "secret" meetings, the Montreal press blurted the news:

> Revolution in Canadian Athletics
> M.A.A.A. Burns Its Bridges

An open letter to the Montreal public announced the MAAA's withdrawal from the CAAU over the amateur playing with or against professionals issue.[48]

Logically, the Montreal press praised the courage and foresight of the MAAA while Toronto papers proclaimed that the MAAA was merely avoiding a professional investigation by the CAAU[49] and that its action showed that gate receipts and championships were being put ahead of the amateur principle on the road to the ultimate extermination of amateur sport.[50] The CAAU's first action against the MAAA was to discredit the races of the Amateur Skating Association of Canada by writing to the National Amateur Skating Association in the US to warn them to decline competition or risk suspension as professionals,[51] and by advertising speedskating races in Toronto on the same day as the Montreal championships. This move backfired when the two American skating associations and the Canadian one defied their respective national amateur governing bodies to form the International Skating Union in 1907.[52] It was the first in a long series of labyrinth manoeuvres on the part of athletes, sports clubs and sporting organizations to weave their way through the barriers of amateurism. It was also a catalyst that stimulated the MAAA to call a meeting, via mail, to form a new governing body of sports in Canada. Along with the letter went a copy of the proposed constitution and by-laws which followed those of the CAAU except for the with and/or against professionals clause. Characteristic of the MAAA, the letter must have been distributed only locally since the only representatives to attend the meeting were sports clubs in Montreal.[53] Yet, when the new Amateur Athletic Federation of Canada was formed on February

1, 1907 the constitution read: "This union recognizes and claims jurisdiction over all athletes and all athletic sports in Canada."[54]

It was a mistake, ultimately, to remain localized and the
presumptuous jurisdictional claim provided ammunition for the
Toronto press to state that the "Funny Federation" was a burlesque of
professional promotion, "making about the 23rd bubble of the kind
that the Montreal jokers have passed off in the last 3 to 4 years."[55] The
"athletic war"[56] had begun officially, with the formation of the AAFC.

It is significant that the AAFC by its actions was not merely breaking
away from the CAAU; it was in fact a usurper,[57] an earnest pretender
to the Canadian sport governing crown in the same manner as the
NYAC-stimulated AUU of the United States had been in 1888. The
battleground between AAFC and the CAAU was sport, the quest was
national control of amateur sport and the persons who suffered most
during the two and half years war were the athletes. The athletic war
itself was a battle of wills and obstinacy on both sides. Each faction
actively campaigned and recruited prospective members. The AAFC
issued circulars to explain its aims and objectives that were directed
towards eliminating the nonsense of "thinly veiled professionalism."[58] "It is the aim of the Federation to have affiliated with it
all clubs, leagues, unions and associations devoted to the promotion
of clean sports and the maintenance of the amateur spirit." [59] Claiming national scope, the Federation remained a circle of wagons around
Montreal throughout most of the athletic war years. Some provincial
sport associations, such as the Maritime Provinces Amateur Athletic
Association, at first pledged allegiance to the new sport governing
body[60] but the CAAU intervened with a crushing and unsuspected
coup; the prestigious Canadian track and field championships were
awarded by the CAAU to Halifax in 1908 thereby breaking the 23-year
tradition of selecting Montreal as the site of the games and instead,
currying the favour of the Maritimes Association to keep those provinces in the CAAU.[61] The circle of wagons tightened around Montreal.

Accusations of shady practices in the conduct of amateur sport flew
back and forth between Toronto and Montreal during the spring and
early summer of 1907. The AAFC would recognise CAAU athletes in
their sports but the reverse could not be tolerated by the CAAU, for
to do so would be conceding to play amateurs with and against professionals. The *Toronto Globe* kept publishing what the Federation perceived as "malicious rumours" that the AAFC was the home and
central promotional agency for professional sport.[62] Similarly, the
Toronto papers implied indirectly and delightfully that the Federation was doomed since the Michigan- and northern Ontario-based
professional hockey teams all lost money in 1906–07.[63] The AAFC

tried to dispel the myth of alleged professional athlete jurisdiction by publicly stating: "We simply look upon them as paid employees. If they misbehave themselves, however, we will prevent them from playing with or against our amateurs."[64] If the CAAU stood to benefit by Montreal-based athletes competing in their events, it simply compelled the athletes to compete under a different club name,[65] but only at the Union's discretion.

The AAFC, led by the MAAA, believed it was just a matter of playing a waiting game. At its first annual meeting in 1907, the MAAA president, Victor Buchanan, was elected president of the AAFC. He strongly recommended that the AAFC move quickly to establish representatives in each province to acquire national status. No action was taken; instead the collective and arrogant perspective of the Federation members was that sport clubs across the country were "occupying a neutral stand, pending only the necessary display of strength on our part to induce them to come in."[66] Ottawa athletic executives recognized the AAFC weakness and advised the Federation to "wake up and start a vigorous campaign in support of its principles.... There must be work and plenty of it to put the Federation in proper perspective."[67] The public press in Montreal called the CAAU a "mollycoddle" organization that was at complete fault in setting "brothers against brothers, and friends against friends in an athletic war that would if permitted to go on destroy the entire usefulness of athletics in Canada."[68] Far from being dormant, the CAAU campaigned actively in all provinces and upheld its strict amateur principles whenever it deemed necessary. To the CAAU's credit, it faced the AAUUS head-on in withdrawing sanction to the NYAC in a matched track race featuring Toronto runners in Madison Square Gardens in March 1907.[69] Once bitten, twice shy, the American AAU retaliated in July when the Federation attempted a smooth manoeuvre at the Ottawa summer sports festival. MAAA athletes were sent to the game carrying amateur registration cards of the AAUUS but wearing MAAA colours. If the CAAU accepted the cards, it would mean acceptance of the AAFC athletes in a CAAU-sanctioned meting. The AAUUS cards were not recognized.[70] The next day, July 31, 1907, the *Montreal Star* announced that the "dread athletic war is over"[71] since the AAUUS pledged immediate affiliation with the Federation and would no longer recognize the CAAU. Leslie Boyd of the MAAA and James E. Sullivan of the AAUUS had engineered the Federation/AAUUS agreement in Jamestown, Virginia; the Ottawa fiasco served to speed up the process.[72] The Boyd–Sullivan entente was significant to the future of the athletic war machinations. The Federation claimed victory but announced magnanimous generosity to the wayward sports clubs in the CAAU in reaping the spoils of war; it would accept them with open arms rather than follow the "dog-in-the-manger policy of the CAAU."[73]

The Federation really did expect that if it held up the banner of AAUUS support, athletes and clubs across Canada would march eagerly under its umbrella. But the CAAU was unruffled by the vaunted power of the AAUUS:

> We will try standing alone....Surely we are strong enough to stand alone now when we have been standing for many years with such support as the AAU has proven. Twas a broken reed we were leaning upon. What sort of cowardly work is this anyway? Here we have an ally in fair weather, in foul, just when we might need him, he deserts to the enemy.[74]

The weak link in the AAUUS/Federation chain, was that all AAFC athletes had to observe the amateur definition of the AAUUS which did not permit amateurs playing with or against professionals.[75] On the contrary, the CAAU had 16 organizations representing 16 sporting clubs; by September 1907, it boasted the continued strong affiliation of 37 organizations representing 479 clubs.[76] One year later, in 1908, the CAAU embraced 900 sporting clubs and an athletic membership of some 60 000 athletes representing every province in the Dominion.[77] The key to the success of the CAAU was directly attributable to its hard work in dividing the whole country into provincial, self-governing amateur bodies, all allied to the central agency;[78] the CAAU actively and persistently recruited[79] while the Federation retreated to its special circle of wagons with US reinforcements at the ready.

The war did not rage but dragged on. The Montreal press recognized the futility of the situation and pleaded for cessation for the good of the sporting public and the athletes.[80] Neither governing body relented. Looming on the athletic horizon was the spectre of the 1908 Olympic Games in London. The Olympics were the very symbol of unification and purification in international amateur sport. For the good of the Games in the mother country and for the good of Canadian Olympic athletes, a temporary truce in the war was effected by Colonel Hanbury-Williams representing the British Olympic Committee in Canada. He called a meeting of the CAAU and AAFC representatives in the Governor General's office in Ottawa for November 30, 1907.[81] An eight-item truce was drawn up with two major features: any disputes over amateur status of potential or actual Olympic athletes were to be left to the Canadian Olympic Committee whose membership would contain CAAU and AAFC representatives; secondly, in all athletic competitions bearing on the Games, the two bodies would "mutually withdraw and abstain from all disqualifications, rulings and penalties enacted in consequence of or depending upon the difference between the two associations."[82] It was a guarded hands-off-the-Olympics-policy. As if to underscore their good will, both organizations published Christmas greetings to all amateur athletes in the Montreal and Toronto press beginning in 1907[83] and continued to do so each year of the athletic war as peace gestures befitting the season.

Both sides observed the truce within reasonable bounds until ten days before the Olympic marathon in July 1908. The feud intensified when Leslie Boyd, president of the MAAA and a representative of the Canadian Olympic Committee in London, lodged a protest on behalf of the AAFC against the CAAU-sanctioned marathon runner, Tom Longboat, an Onandaga Indian whose fame was international in scope since his victory in the 1907 Boston marathon.[84] The AAUUS attempted to have Longboat declared a professional as early as one week after that achievement.[85] In effect, Longboat became a political pawn in the Canadian athletic war, but not necessarily its victim.

As the story unfolded, it was revealed that Boyd spent most of his time at the Olympics with the American contingent, particularly with Mr. James E. Sullivan. The latter registered a protest against Longboat on behalf of the AAUUS.[86] The CAAU received advanced warning of the protests pending and worked to block their success by publishing a lengthy document explaining the CAAU's intensive investigation of Longboat's amateur status before the Olympics and outlining, often in bold type almost dripping with venom, the reasons why the US was determined to prevent Longboat from running.[87] The letter was given to the associated press and circulated to all the main newspapers of the world by the CAAU.[88] Upon publication of this document, the protests were denied by the AAFC and the AAUUS for the next ten days.[89] When the protest was made public, the CAAU screamed treachery and the *Ottawa Journal* labelled Boyd's action as nationally disloyal and dishonourable.[90] The point was that the precise terms of the Canadian Olympic truce had been directly violated by Boyd.

The protests were overruled by the British Olympic Committee after assurance of Longboat's amateurism from the other two Canadian Olympic representatives.[91] Ultimately, Longboat collapsed at the 20-mile mark, [92] the Italian Dorando Pietri was disqualified and the American, Hayes, was proclaimed the Olympic marathon victor. As for the athletic war in Canada, Boyd's actions in protest broke the Federation's circle of wagons. It was the beginning of the end, the major tactical error of the AAFC. The MAAA published its support for Boyd's actions[93] but neither Montreal nor Toronto was buying the arguments of the MAAA due to its obvious vested interest in its own president. Even Canadian athletes such as Bobby Kerr, the 1908 Olympic gold medallist in the 200 metres, referred to Boyd as a "cat's paw for Sullivan,"[94] and the *Toronto Globe* ran an article under the huge headline: "Mr. Boyd's United States Chums and Associates."[95] The Toronto theory was that US coach Murphy and Sullivan were known to love to "sow a few seeds of disruption [and] ... irritation" to upset Longboat and throw him off before the race.[96] Even the *Montreal Star* expressed its shame at Boyd's perceived collaboration with Murphy and Sullivan.[97] Boyd's "weak-kneed" excuse was that he was protecting Federation athletes from possible professionalization, but the *Toronto Daily Star* noted that there were ten other Canadian athletes in the exact same status as Longboat at the Olympics: "Why didn't Boyd protest them all? Why make fish or one and flesh of the other? To protect his men? Fudge! Longboat had a grand chance, and Sullivan simply used Boyd as a puppet to try and lay Longboat in his athletic grave."[98] By late August 1908, the same Montreal press that one year earlier had breathed a heavy sigh of athletic war relief with AAUUS affiliation, was making pleas for peace on the strength of splitting off from the AAUUS.[99] To quote a founding member of the MAAA, A.W. Stevenson, in 1908: "they have been scallowagging around too much with these Americans and just as long as they have anything to do with these people they are going to have trouble. They are a bumptious lot running a crowd of professional athletes."[100] The CAAU taunted the fractured Federation with: "[The AAFC] has a legitimate sphere laid out for itself in governing the professional sports which they called into being."[101] Peace, to the CAAU, was only possible if the Federation dropped the amateurs competing with/or against professionals' concession.

In September 1908 the Canadian Olympic Committee denounced Boyd's actions and the AAFC's support for Boyd based on the 1907 Olympic truce agreement.[102] A press cartoon encapsulated perfectly, with hyperbolic licence, the athletic war situation.[103] The Federation tried one last ploy to gain public support. Together with the AAUUS, they plotted to discredit Longboat in the public view by attempting to get him to accept a material reward for a six-mile race in Williamstown in October 1908, but the trap failed[104] and Longboat openly turned professional a short time later.[105] On April 20, 1909, after six months of retrenchment, the AAFC, represented by MAAA delegates, came to Toronto to appeal for athletic peace. The Toronto papers chided the MAAA delegates as the only ones who would be entertained by the CAAU since the AAFC was "Marathon

Anathema"[106] to the CAAU. Negotiations were protracted right through the summer because the MAAA stubbornly refused compromise of its major amateur concession,[107] even though the AAFC reinstated many transgressors at its third annual meeting that year.[108] In late August, both groups sanctioned a track meet in Montreal where CAAU and AAFC athletes competed against each other.[109] This was the first jointly-approved athletic competition since the start of the war and a major gesture of goodwill by the powerful CAAU.

Finally, after a lengthy national peace conference over the Labour Day weekend in Ottawa, the athletic war was ended:

> The Barriers Are Now Raised — Athletic Peace Comes At Last
>
> The A.A.U. of Canada was formed here yesterday by the amalgamation of the A.A.F. of C. and the C.A.A.U. The hatchet was buried forever and neither side claims a victory, both declaring that they have acted for the betterment of Canadian athletics only.[110]

With a touch of political elegance, Sullivan published a large congratulatory letter on behalf of the AAUUS in the Canadian press.[111] The CAAU ratified the peace and the new governing body at its last annual meeting on November 27, 1909,[112] and the AAFC officially disbanded one month later.[113]

The basis for peace was rooted in the newly-adopted definition of an amateur by the AAUC and in administrative, constitutional and voting systems comparable with the federal-provincial government structure in Canada (i.e. provincial, autonomous amateur associations under the AAUC umbrella). All athletic members were pledged to the strict enforcement of the amateur ideal with a general sense of having 'rescued' sport from professionalism. The new AAUC remounted the pedestal of nineteenth-century amateurism with some minor alterations exemplary in its 1909 A-B-C amateur definitions:

> Class A amateur — one who has never competed for a wager, taught or competed for a livelihood, received lost time payment, sold or pledged prizes, promoted an athletic competition for personal gain. "Any athlete guilty of the above can never be reinstated."
>
> Class B — an athlete who has competed with or against a professional for a prize or where gate money is being charged, or has entered in any competition under a name

other than his own, shall be ineligible for registration and competition as an amateur.

Class C — "All others shall be considered eligible for registration in the C.A.A.U. and its affiliated bodies."[114]

Class A was, clearly, a giant throwback to the blanket, non-amateur, negative definition of the 1870s and 1880s and was, once again, the focal point of the national amateur governing body. Class B was the "guilty by touch" category of non-amateurism, and Class C was for all those who dropped through the fine mesh of the new amateur sieve, the vast majority, it was hoped, of clean-living, simon-pure athletes. Guilty non-amateurs were not labelled with a professional tag; they were merely categorized. Significantly, there were three corollaries to Class C: one to allow amateur athletes to retain their amateur status in the face of competing with or against professionals in cricket, golf or indoor bowling; the other two concessions must have been appeasement for the AAFC, since National Lacrosse Union athletes were granted the right to petition the AAUC to be permitted to play with or against professionals "until such time as the Board of Governors shall unanimously decide that strict amateurism can be satisfactorily established in the senior series of that game,"[115] and the Interprovincial Amateur Hockey League was granted the same privilege for one year. The trophies of those two professional-like sports, the Stanley Cup in hockey and the Minto Cup in lacrosse, were regarded "money-making mediums for groups of mercenary promoters."[116] New amateur trophies, the Allan Cup and Mann Cup respectively, were donated, with the AAUC solicitation, within a year of the formation of the new Canadian amateur governing body. The theory was that the trophies would be AAUC-controlled and would provide incentives to wean the wayward sports back to the fold. Hockey entrepreneurs seized the moment to create the National Hockey Association, a declared professional hockey body and the forerunner of the National Hockey League.

The athletic war in Canada was a very significant conflict in the history of Canadian sport because the war so firmly re-established the pure amateur ideal in Canadian sport. Unlike the NYAC/AAUUS situation, the usurping pretender to the amateur crown, the MAAA, did not bring significant change. The resolution of the war merely served to embalm and enshrine an outmoded amateur ideal. Amateurism was being pushed uphill against the twentieth-century direction of sport in general. The issue brought to a head by the MAAA was one of peaceful co-existence with professionalism; had the MAAA and the AAFC elected to govern professional sport instead of tolerating it, the evolution of Canadian sport truly might have been altered. The 1908 Longboat protest issue brought the warring factions together by default; the AAFC lost all credibility by Boyd's actions. Yet, because the Federation remained close-knit in Montreal, the result of the war was inevitable. The CAAU was masterful in its quest for national support. Adherents of the old amateur ideology re-sold its virtues and were supported by a parallel Olympic ideology. None of the problems in Canadian sport was solved by resolution — the victory was Pyrrhic. Great Britain, the United States and Canada each confronted, wrestled with and embraced the idea of amateurism between 1870 and 1910. In Canada, the athletic war was a significant conflict that brought sport to the brink of development beyond nineteenth-century ideals.

Notes

1. See, Arnold W. Flath, "A History of Relations Between the National Collegiate Athletic Association and the Amateur Athletic Union of the United States (1905–1963)" (unpublished Ph.D. dissertation, University of Michigan, 1963), 26–35.

2. Howard J. Savage, *Games and Sports in British Schools and Universities* (New York, 1928), 195.

3. Howard J. Savage, *American College Athletics* (New York, 1929), 46.

4. Ibid.

5. Savage, *Games and Sports in British Schools and Universities*, 194–96.

6. Ibid., 196.

7. Allen Guttman, *From Ritual to Record: The Nature of Modern Sports* (New York, 1978), 31.

8. Ibid., 31–32, and Savage, *Games and Sports in British Schools and Universities*, 198.

9. Savage, *American College Athletics*, 37.

10. Ibid.

11. This point is amplified in ibid., 49.

12. Cited in Keith L. Lansley, "The Amateur Athletic Union of Canada and Changing Concepts of Amateurism" (unpublished Ph.D. dissertation, University of Alberta, 1971), 17.

13. Constitution and By-Laws of the Montreal Pedestrian Club, (Montreal, 1873), 8, brackets and emphasis mine.

14. See Frank Cosentino, "A History of the Concept of Professionalism in Canadian Sport" (unpublished Ph.D. dissertation, University of Alberta, 1973), 28–36, for a full discussion of ethnic amateur exclusion in Canadian sport.

15. Lansley, "The Amateur Athletic Union of Canada," 26–29.

16. *Toronto Mail*, April 12, 1884, cited in Consentino, "The Concept of Professionalism," 120.

17. Lansley, "The Amateur Athletic Union of Canada," 30–31.

18. Cosentino, "The Concept of Professionalism," 134–35.

19. Ibid., 146–75.

20. Ibid., 176.

21. Lansley, "The Amateur Athletic Union of Canada," 57.

22. Ibid., 62–64.

23. There were eleven national sport governing bodies in 1901, only two of which, the Amateur Skating Association of Canada and the National Amateur Lacrosse Union, were affiliated with the CAAU.

24. Respective trophies for these sports were the Stanley Cup, donated in 1893, the Minto Cup, donated in 1901, and the Grey Cup, donated in 1909.

25. Minutes of the Meetings of the Board of Governors of the CAAU, 1901–05.

26. Ibid., May 6, 1904, 124–25.

27. Ibid., Aug. 13, 1903, 116–17.

28. Ibid., Sept. 3, 1904, 141–44. The concession would have been attractive just on a short-term basis since athletes requesting reinstatement were required to pay the CAAU expenses in reinstatement investigation. Ibid., 127.

29. Ibid., 141.

30. Ibid., June 26, 1905, 149–52.

31. The reasons for the concession were aligned with costs, public interest, professional precedents in Ontario and the desire to be competitive with Ontario teams. Ibid.

32. Minutes of the Annual Meeting of the CAAU, Montreal, Sept. 16, 1905, 40–43.

33. Ibid., Montreal, Oct. 27, 1906, 3.

34. Minutes of the Meetings of the Directors of the Montreal Amateur Athletic Association, Minute Book Number 7, Nov. 21, 1904, 17–18.

35. The Canadian Lacrosse Association declared its professionals and was not affiliated with the CAAU.

36. MAAA Minutes of the Semi-Annual Meeting, Nov. 20, 1905, 133.

37. MAAA Minutes of the Meetings of the Directors, April 20, 1906, 193.

38. President Buchanan even pressured, without success, the 12 dissenters to alter their vote in order to be able to publish the decision as unanimous. *Montreal Daily Star (MDS)*, April 30, 1906, 2.

39. *MDS*, April 21, 1906, 22.

40. Ibid., April 30, 1906, 2.

41. Ibid., April 27, 1906, 2.

42. Ibid., April 21, 1906, 2.

43. Ibid., Aug. 4, 1906, n.p. Single wagers of 75 dollars were covered on bets pertaining to whether or not a certain player, such as Howard or Hoobin, would be ruled off during the match.

44. *MDS*, Sept. 8, 11, 12 and 14, 1906. The Sept. 14, 1906 article is filled with arguments concerning the perceived benefits of the concept of amateurs playing with and against professionals.

45. Ibid., Oct. 31, 1906, 2. A motion to expel the MAAA was put on the floor of the Oct. 27, 1906 annual CAAU meeting, but no seconder was found. Ibid., Oct. 29, 1906, 2.

46. Ibid., Nov. 1, 1906, 2.

47. *Toronto Globe*, Nov. 5, 1906, 8.

48. *MDS*, Nov. 6, 1906, 10. The MAAA was careful to point out the concession to allow amateurs to compete with or against professionals without losing their amateur status was the only change to the CAAU amateur definition and that professional athletes playing for the MAAA would be paid for their services, but would never be entitled to club membership or MAAA privileges.

49. *Toronto Globe* Nov. 10, 1906.

50. Ibid., Nov. 16, 1906.

51. *MDS*, Jan. 8, 1907, 6.

52. Ibid., Feb. 2, 1907, 12. Both the Toronto and Montreal races were held on the same day. The Toronto races paled in comparison while those in Montreal attracted US amateur and professional skaters. Ibid., Feb. 4, 1907, 6.

53. Ibid., Jan. 28, 1907, 3.

54. Ibid., Feb. 1, 1907, 3.

55. *Toronto Globe*, Feb. 4, 1907, 3.

56. The term "athletic war" was used frequently in the primary sources.

57. Lansley, "The Amateur Athletic Union of Canada," 68.

58. *MDS*, Feb. 18, 1907, 3.

59. Ibid.

60. Ibid., Nov. 12, 1906, 1, and May 7, 1907, 11. This unfulfilled allegiance was due to the problems the Maritimes were encountering in commercial baseball leagues while trying to maintain strict amateurism.

61. Annual Report of the CAAU, 1908, 48.

62. For example, see the *Toronto Globe*, March 11, 1906, 8.

63. *Toronto Globe*, April 2, 1907, 8.

64. *MDS*, April 29, 1907, 3. If the Federation had elected to govern professional sport, there is no question that the organization of Canadian sport would have been altered radically.

65. The MAAA fencing team was allowed to register as the Montreal Fencing Club with the CAAU, for example. Ibid., March 11, 1907, 8. For the Ottawa July sports festival, MAAA athletes were to be allowed to compete unattached, but not under MAAA colours. Ibid., July 26, 1907, 3.

66. Ibid., April 29, 1907, 3.

67. Ibid., July 27, 1907, 25.

68. Ibid., July 25, 1907, 3.

69. Ibid., March 12, 1907, 3.

70. Ibid., July 30, 1907, 3.

71. Ibid., July 31, 1907, 2.

72. Ibid.

73. Ibid.

74. *Toronto Globe*, Aug. 2, 1907, 7.

75. *MDS* Aug. 27, 1907, 2.

76. *Toronto Globe*, Sept. 16, 1907, 7. The *Globe* reported verbatim the minutes of the 24th annual meeting of the CAAU. These minutes have been lost in the papers of the collection of the Amateur Athletic Union of Canada.

77. Minutes of the 25th Annual Meeting of the CAAU, Nov. 9, 1908, 4. By November 1909, as the athletic war drew to a close, the CAAU boasted 1 200 affiliated clubs and 75 000 registered athletes. Minutes of the 26th Annual Meeting of the CAAU, Nov. 27, 1909.

78. The annual reports of 1907, 1908, and 1909 all made direct, supported references to this policy and its success.

79. Letters were sent early in the CAAU campaign to all provinces, soliciting support and adherence to its strict amateur principles. See, for example, the *Victoria Daily Colonist*, Oct. 13, 1907.

80. *MDS*, Nov. 16, 1907, 26.

81. Ibid., Dec. 2, 1907, 2, and Minutes of the 25th Annual Meeting of the CAAU, Nov. 9, 1908, 4–5.

82. Ibid.

83. *MDS*, Dec. 21, 1907, 28, and Dec. 19, 1908, 26.

84. The *Toronto Daily Star*, April 24, 1907, contained extensive front page coverage of Longboat's victory parade in Toronto where Longboat was training under Tom Flanagan of the Irish Canadian Athletic Club.

85. Ibid., April 27, 1907, 20. The AAUUS claimed the Toronto City Council award of $500 "worth of education" made Longboat a professional.

86. *MDS*, July 24, 1908, 3.

87. Ibid., July 9, 1908, 2.

88. Minutes of the 25th Annual Meeting of the CAAU, Nov. 9, 1908, 7.

89. Ibid., 8.

90. The *Ottawa Journal*, July 24, 1908.

91. Minutes of the 25th Annual Meeting of the CAAU, Nov. 9, 1908, 14.

92. There were rampant speculations on the reason for Longboat's collapse that ranged from knee injury to fatigue to the claim by the Canadian Olympic team manger, J.H. Crocker, that he had been given an excessive amount of a stimulant, perhaps strychnine. Crocker's report was reprinted in full in the *MDS*, Sept. 2, 1908, 2.

93. *MDS*, Aug. 18, 1908, 2.

94. *Toronto Globe*, Aug. 18, 1908.

95. Ibid. Several times during the athletic war, the CAAU sought alliance with the British governing body of amateurism to counter the Federation's union with the AAUUS. The British had no such articles of alliance.

96. Ibid.

97. *MDS*, Aug. 19, 1908, 2.

98. *Toronto Daily Star*, Aug, 19, 1908.

99. *MDS*, Aug. 25, 1908, 14.

100. Ibid.

101. Ibid., Aug. 27, 1908, 6. The *Star* quoted J.G. Merrick of the CAAU.

102. Ibid., Sept. 8, 1908, 6, and Sept. 9, 1908, 2.

103. Ibid., Sept. 1, 1908, 2. The cartoon showed a very vexed person representing the public motioning two men towards the door of "Dr. Sense, Anti-Foolishness Serum Inoculated." The two men were in heated argument; one man symbolized the CAAU and was shouting, "You shook hands with a man who knows a friend of a pro. The A.A.U. told me — you are disqualified." The other represented the AAFC and was retorting "I disqualify you for breathing the same air as professionals. The A.A.U. told me you did." Mr. Public stated, "Will you gentlemen kindly consult this eminent specialist [Dr. Sense] as quickly as possible. I am very tired of this nonsense."

104. *Toronto Daily Star*, Oct. 19, 1908.

105. Ibid., Nov. 2, 1908, 11.

106. In short, excommunicated by virtue of Boyd's actions in the Olympic marathon. Cited in *MDS*, April 21, 1909, 2, and *Toronto Telegram*, April 22, 1909.

107. See, *MDS*, Aug. 14, 1909, 25, for an extensive review of the athletic war to that point, as well as ibid., Sept. 2, 1909, 2.

108. *MDS*, April 26, 1909, 2. These reinstatements were publicly popular and taken to be a secure sign of peace.

109. Ibid., Aug. 23, 1909, 3.

110. Ibid., Sept. 7, 1909, 2.

111. Ibid., Sept. 10, 1909, 2.

112. Ibid., Nov. 29, 1909, 3, and Minutes of the 26th Annual Meeting of the CAAU, Nov. 27, 1909, 7–20.

113. *MDS*, Dec. 23, 1909, 3.

114. Minutes of the Meetings of the Board of Directors of the CAAU, Oct. 1, 1909, 16–17. This A-B-C amateur definition corresponded to the prevailing Olympic amateur definition with the exception of the corollaries to part C. Minutes of the 2nd Annual Meeting of the AAUC, Nov. 27, 1911, n.p.

115. Minutes of the Meetings of the Board of Directors of the CAAU, Oct. 1, 1909, 17.

116. Minutes of the 2nd Annual meeting of the AAUC, Nov. 27, 1911, n.p.

SOCIAL GOSPEL AND THE YOUNG BOY PROBLEM 1895–1925*

DAVID HOWELL AND PETER LINDSAY

Twelve years have passed since Metcalfe[1] stated in a footnote to his article entitled "Some Background Influences on Nineteenth Century Canadian Sport and Physical Education," that "there is little or nothing written which pertains directly to the relationship between church and ideas influencing attitudes to sport." He went on to say that "sporting activities were a means to an end" and that "even in the liberal portions of the church, recreation and sport had to be justified on the grounds of the attainment of worthwhile ends." An examination of the Social Gospel movement towards the end of the nineteenth century and during the early decades of the twentieth century supports his latter observation. The "worthwhile ends" were the attainment of Christian character and the more practical aim of attracting young men to the Church where Christian influence could be exerted. The attraction was physical recreation programs packaged with a mixture of social and religious attainments.

Under the influence of the social gospel, 1895-1925, Protestantism became more interested in examining the positive social attributes of physical recreation, and in applying the related benefits as a remedy for social ills. Richard Allen, a noted historian of the social gospel movement in Canada,[2] wrote that "fundamentally, the social gospel rested on the premise that Christianity was a social religion."[3] Another prominent Canadian historian, A.R.M. Lower, directed attention to the philosophy of "evangelical protestantism" and its impact on the church goer when he wrote that,

> Not only does it impose the most tremendous of all burdens on him — his own absolute responsibility for his fate, finite

* *Canadian Journal of History of Sport/Revue canadienne de l'histoire des sports* 17, 1 (May 1986): 75–87.

and infinite — but it constantly throws at him the challenge
that he is his brother's keeper, and it makes him feel that the
world's safety and salvation depend not on his rulers or his
boss or his priest but on him.[4]

A feeling of responsibility for society is inherent in this and consequently, human behaviour should be trained to carry out this responsibility. Evangelism stressed free will, an imminent God, restrictive
personal and social morality, and the doctrine of personal perfection,
to name some of the more important tenets.[5]

Allen further wrote:

The Social Gospel that arose in the latter years of the
nineteenth century, developed under influences which encouraged a social concept of man [in contrast to earlier con-
ceptions of man and society which were more
individualistic but without the social appeal] and underlined the social dimension of the Gospel, so that the solu-
tions that appeared to be most useful were those which had
an essentially social character.[6]

The result was the development of interest by the church in Social Darwinism, popularly expressed in the vernacular of the day as an interest in "sociological questions." Darwinism had a profound influence
on the actions and theology of the social gospel, mainly through its
emphasis on the importance of the environment, and particularly on
the environment as a factor in the formation of character, or social behaviour. Adherents to this movement believed that people were influenced not solely by will, but by industrialization and urbanization
in Canada. The social gospel movement, then, was a social movement
in which the influence of modern thinking and modern analytical
methods, represented by Social Darwinism and sociological enquiry,
raised the general level of social consciousness and fostered a realism
which produced a more practical approach by church evangelists and
agencies to solving social ills.[7]

In the quest for social regeneration, the church directed its attention
towards the many church organizations which were a significant
point of contact between church and society as a whole. Church organizations such as Sunday schools, missionary societies, young
people's societies, social welfare councils, temperance societies, and
student volunteer organizations, reached out broadly to the community and, under the influence of the social gospel, were adapted as
agents for social regeneration. These organizations generally fell into
four broad categories, viz., missionary, devotional, educational, and

social, with missionary and devotional interests traditionally dominating. Of particular concern at the turn of the century was the shift of youth away from the church. Young people were seeking more social-oriented activities which the traditional church had failed to provide, and, as a result, organizations of a missionary and devotional nature declined. With a growing sense of alarm, reform committees raised the issue of declining youth membership, particularly boys, in the hope that means could be found to reverse the flow. In the Third Annual Report of the Committee on Young People's Societies to the General Assembly of the Presbyterian Church in 1898, Reverend Fraser stated that "unless some city societies solve more effectually 'the young man problem,' they [the Young People's Societies of Christian Endeavour] will soon be simply Young Women's Societies of Christian Endeavour." Attempts, therefore, were made to capitalize on the increasing emphasis within the various churches upon the social gospel message, bringing about an even greater emphasis on youth, to the gradual neglect of adult programming. Young people's societies, which traditionally had received only limited attention, became the *centre* of attention in the evangelical drive to arrest the debilitating trend of weakened adolescent church membership. For example, Clark writes that "The Epworth League (named in honour of the birthplace of Charles and John Wesley, the 'founders' of Methodism) was designed to close the gap between the Sunday school and the church as a means of checking the heavy loss of support of young people to more aggressive evangelistic religious bodies or to secular agencies."[8] He further points out that the rapid growth of the urban community was having a deleterious effect on young people, and the church, through its failure to develop its own recreational institutions, was losing membership to commercialized forms of recreation.

In the attempt to compete with social programs offered by sects or secular agencies, educational and social interests became the focus of attention for evangelists. Church agencies concentrated upon young membership with such zeal that the concern was transformed into the "young boy problem," a term which came into common usage in the literature. And around this emphasis on youth the church gave strong expression for the value of physical recreation and its usefulness as a social tool. Speaking at a Methodist Epworth League Rally in 1901, Rev. T.E. Egerton Shore gave voice to his thoughts on uniting youth, sport and church, which were illustrative of the rising sentiment:

> At a Conference League Rally held in our city a little over a month ago, the church was packed with 1 800 young people. But they were nearly all young women. Among that crowd

... there were not 100 young men altogether, and most of them were delicate looking specimens of the *genus homo*. Where were the young men of vigor and strength? Where were the young men of athletics and sport? ... Wherever they were, they were not in the church, and they never will be until we go after them, and adapt our methods of work to their conditions and needs.[9]

Anglicans were slower to confront the problem than were the more evangelical, Methodist, and to some extent, Presbyterian denominations, but they were experiencing real declines in church attendance and youth participation in church activities. Liberal Anglicans pushed their arguments forward, emphasizing the attainment of Christian manhood, to which the *Canadian Churchman*, in its efforts to maintain a balanced perspective, reacted that there was too much talk of "manliness," and that the expression "man to man," and the words "men," "manly," and "manliness" were uttered with "wearisome frequency."[10] By 1915, the Anglican Sunday School Commission through its official publication, the *Bulletin*, could recognize that a change of emphasis was taking place not only in its Sunday schools but also in denominational religious education generally:

Never before have "the boy" and what is called "the boy problem" been given so much attention by the leaders in the field of Religious Education and by those institutions which are working in that field. This, in itself, is significant for two reasons:
a) because it shows that there has been, on the part of some, at least, an awakening to a realization that there is a real need;
b) because, along with this realization of the problem, there has come an earnest effort to study it and to seek its solution.[11]

As the young boy problem became more widely discussed, there was increasing interest by the denominations in familiarizing themselves with the literature of social relevance generated through periodicals, books and pamphlets on both sides of the Atlantic. The social gospel was not a unique Canadian movement but was part of a larger and more widespread attempt in Europe and North America "to receive and develop Christian social insights and to apply them to the emerging forms of a collective society."[12] Anglicans, in particular, devoted attention to British publications, while Presbyterians and Methodists concentrated to a greater extent on American literature for information on programs being developed there. Also, very few church or young people's societies were indigenous to Canada. From the United States came the Epworth League, the Christian Endeavour movement and the Brotherhood of St. Andrew, while Britain produced the YMCA, the Boy Scouts and the Boys Brigade. All of these associations, plus literature, conferences, and speaking tours by American and British clerical and secular reformers, contributed to Canadian attempts to solve the young boy problem. Amongst the denominational literature for youth in Canada were to be found the Presbyterian *Pathfinder* for senior youth (aged 15–18), the Methodist *Playmates* for junior youth (aged 6–9) and the *Onward* (aged 10–14), plus the Presbyterian *East and West* (aged 10–14) which provided a good example of morality stories using the motif of sports and games. Anglicans, too, produced similar literature, much of it published by its General Board of Religious Education, and included the *Young Solider and Crusader* aimed at the older boy (aged 15–23 years), and the *Teacher's Assistant* which included the *Commission Bulletin*, the official organ of the Sunday School Commission of the Church of England in Canada. Virtually all of these publications stressed moral teaching through stories, parables, and example of good deeds, and were additional to the adult publications of the church which also carried sections for youthful readers. The more relevant of these latter works to the young boy problem included the Methodist *Christian Guardian*, the Presbyterian *Record*, and the *Canadian Churchman*.

Another factor was the flow of British "muscular Christianity" literature particularly in Canadian Anglicanism with its close ties to Britain. According to the *Canadian Churchman*, the character-forming potential of sport had been responsible for British "stoicism and respect for the rules of the great game of life."[13] Brown[14] has pointed out the impact of men of the cloth who emigrated from Britain to accept positions as headmasters in private schools across Canada, many of which had church affiliation. The successful programs of athletics and perhaps "muscular Christianity" which bloomed under their encouragement did not go unnoticed by the church.

Effects to solve the young boy problem took several forms but first the church needed to determine the needs of young people, as perceived both by adolescents themselves and adult church members. Much persuasion was needed if exponents of change were to convince conservative elements within the church that the new role for Protestantism should be one which developed "a constructive and positive church policy on the question of Recreation and Amusement."[15] Favouring the social survey technique to gather objective data on religious, economic, and social conditions, liberal-minded churchmen sent questionnaires regularly to congregations from coast to coast in order to study attitudes to physical recreation. One thing was immediately evident from the survey results, namely, there was a strong interest in most church communities in athletic sports. The social gospel message that physical recreation had a legitimate place in society, and in church life in particular, was coming out of survey findings. For example, London, Ontario, boasted an interdenominational athletic association with the objective "to unite the young men of the churches of London interested in athletics; to foster amongst them the ideals of amateur sport; to provide for them outdoor recreation according to season and to hold once a year, a field day of track and field events."[16] The social aim of the association was to remedy the two most prevalent evils in sport, viz., that sport was left too much to private enterprise, and too much stress was laid on winning rather than on "the old English ideal of playing the game."[17]

For several reasons survey findings were not always positive towards sports and athletic recreational activities. Those who did not hold the social viewpoint that physical recreation had useful social qualities did not support the growth of sport within the church; those who saw the social potential could also see the social realities of gambling, cheating, and fighting which were sometimes found amongst both players and spectators. Also, many committees had well-developed sports delivery systems which were really beyond the ability of the church to modify or compete with successfully in terms of establishing alternative leagues. But these surveys were important steps in providing the church with the ability to better assess the physical recreation needs and desires of its communicants, and to deliver acceptable physical recreation and athletic programming.

The surveys also pointed out to the church how important the YMCA had become in the delivery of community recreational services. This organization was deeply involved in the message of the social gospel, so it was natural for the more evangelical denominations to want to study the organization and its programs. There was conflict within the church on how to address the young boy problem, and some members felt that the YMCA was best suited to fulfill the physical recreation role. Others felt that the church should become more directly involved in the physical recreation programming. Liberal churchmen saw the potential of the YMCA to attract the young boy and advocated that the church itself should take on the responsibility of providing for youth in a fashion similar to the YMCA. A contributor to the *Era* in 1908 wrote:

> The place for the YMCA is in the church. I believe it is high time for the churches to awake to the fact that young people are demanding that the church be more than an auditorium

for the sermons to tickle the ears of men and women who are content to sit down and listen.[18]

As the debate went on, the church extended its sphere of interest to physical recreation, as did the YMCA, while never losing sight of its central aim of attracting the young boy to the church "through his games":

> The Athletic Club should be subject to the Executive of the [Epworth] League. I am not a sport, and do not play baseball, but I have always permitted myself to be enthused. The best young man I have secured was through his games. Good fisherman try different baits.[19]

The church continued its cooperative effort with the YMCA to bring the young boy under greater Christian influence, as exemplified in a *Report on a Limited Survey of Religious, Moral, Industrial and Housing Conditions* in the St. Catharines District, Ontario, wherein the committee wrote:

> It is surprising that a city with a population of over 17 000 should be attempting to serve its young men with a YMCA building which is without a swimming pool, a running track, boxing or wrestling rooms or lecture hall, and with very limited room in every other particular. This provides a serious handicap to the work which the organizations would like to do.[20]

The point being made was that the church wanted the YMCA to offer a full program because:

> In this way the YMCA would become the recreational centre for all the boy's clubs connected with the churches, as has been so successful in many cities. There is no need of church gymnasiums. One well equipped gymnasium can take care of all the work.[21]

Though there were detractors for the "leave it to the YMCA" philosophy who felt that the YMCA was too concerned with the physical, they were few, and general church opinion was best expressed in the *Presbyterian and Westminister* May 8, 1919: "Let us choose to make it [YMCA] a great instrument for developing in the Canadian nation a strong and clean and Christian manhood." At the Presbyterian General Assembly the following year, 1920, the Committee on

Coordination unanimously agreed that a standing committee be formed to:

> Act in an advisory capacity in all matters affecting the relationship of the YMCA to the churches and of the churches to the YMCA and that a copy of this resolution be sent to each body represented in this conference for their approval and appointment of delegates.[22]

Represented were Baptist, Congregationalist, Anglican, Methodist, and Presbyterian churches, and the YMCA. This resolution did not satisfy all social gospellers, many of whom wanted to go beyond mere encouragement of the physical work program within the YMCA and suggested direct involvement by the church in this area in order to bring more evangelical social influences to bear on the young boy. Ironically, it was YMCA initiative which had produced an earlier compromise program in 1912 acceptable to evangelical and conservative alike, one which attempted encouragement of a basic recognition of all aspects of life — body, mind and spirit — but which offered some flexibility of interpretation.

The compromise program was the Canadian Standard Efficiency Tests, encompassing four categories: Intellectual, Physical, Religious or Devotional, and Social (also referred to as Service). Sunday school associations adopted the program and this helped provide the balanced curriculum which social gospellers were seeking. However, it should be noted that the program was but part of a broader one in which the church was actively searching for appropriate social programming in order to reach larger proportions of the adolescent population. The scheme had only limited success at the Sunday school level, partly because Sunday schools had their own well established tradition. The more evangelical denominations did encourage its adoption by groups other than Sunday schools, for example the Taxis and Trail Rangers, for it was easier to incorporate into the structure of new organizations than into the Sunday school programs. Also, it provided a broadened week-day program within the church, one which continued to expand into the post-war reconstruction period when its name was changed to Canadian Standard Efficiency Training [CSET]. For example, ... Presbyterian Young People's Association membership increased from 42 000 to 97 000 during the period 1917 to 1922, and these figures included only those organizations reported to be conducting mid-week activities.[23] In 1922 the Eleventh General Conference for Methodists also reported considerable optimism: "We rejoice in the increased interest being manifested in week-day religious instruction....The CSET program is most heartily commended for the broad and efficient training which it embodies."[24]

Generally, the program was well received though some Anglicans saw competition with their traditionally favoured Boy Scouts Movement. Numerous articles lauding the advantages of CSET appeared in church literature particularly following the war years, and interest in this social program dominated social editorial interests. And the idea of the CSET program did not limit participation in physical recreation to that prescribed in the tests, as this extract from the *Canadian Churches*, June 21, 1917, testifies:

> I think the reason why so many church clubs fail is because they are only for social amusement, and not aiming at anything higher. The Canadian Standard Efficiency Tests forms a splendid programme....The meeting is opened with prayer and a Bible discussion for half an hour. Afterwards, they come together for a helpful talk, then some tests are taken, or debates on live topics, after which we play games. Once a month we have beans, each group having a table by themselves, so they can give their yells, etc., after which an address is given. During the season the fellows play inter-church and inter-group games of hockey, indoor and outdoor baseball. What is the result? Through the grace of God we are holding our fellows and increasing our attendance 15 percent.

There is no doubt that, for this editorialist, the CSET program was helping to solve the "young boy" problem.

There were four categories to which attention was to be given in the Tests viz., intellectual, religious, Christian service, and physical. For the intellectual standard, career plans, sex education, public speaking, home reading, educational lectures, educational trips and collections, observation and woodcraft, highlighted the main topics of concern. The religious standard included church and Sunday school attendance, morning watch or Bible study, history of religion, and cultural objectives such as music, poetry, art and natural history. The service standard concentrated on the boy in relation to his community and his country, with a wide variety of objectives ranging from increased membership in church organizations to the three C's campaign — clean speech, clean sports, clean habits.

The physical standard drew its rationale from the New Testament I Corinthians 6:19–20: "Know ye not that your bodies are the temples of the Holy Spirit? Glorify God, therefore, in your body." This theme was elaborated upon in the sixth edition of the *Tests*:

> The basis of all development is physical. The muscles are the instruments of the intellect, the feelings and the will. Ninety-five percent of all interests find physical expression. Seventy-five percent of the boy gangs are organized for physical activity. Self control depends upon the proper interaction of nerves and muscles. Adolescence is the age of nerve and muscle education. Flabby muscled boys become pliant men who only talk. Well developed boys become men who will say and act and produce results. Physical training should, therefore, be encouraged, not alone for the sake of the body which is "today grass and tomorrow is cast into the oven", but for the sake of the soul. We must have regard to the body because it is the instrument of the soul.[25]

To accomplish the development of healthy bodies boys were to engage in activities listed under eight headings, viz., Campcraft, Team Games, Group Games, Swimming, Running, Jumping, Throwing and Health Education. Age groups were classified into grades which had progressive standards of achievement, i.e., Grade 1 for 12 or 13 year olds, up to Grade 8 for 20 year olds.

Health Education included both practical and theoretical requirements. For example, during the six month period throughout which observations were to be made in order to pass this athletic standard, the boys were guided to digest such classics as Gulick's *Efficient Life* and *Physical Education by Muscular Exercise*, Muller's *My System*, and Hutchinson's *Exercise and Health*, as well as attend talks on hygiene, the value of bathing, and the effects of alcohol and tobacco. Practical requirements included observance of fixed hours of rising and retiring, drinking specified amounts of water, bathing, and daily teeth cleaning. Endurance tests in chin-ups, rope climbing, cross-country runs, and one-mile walks were to help the leader assess whether or not a boy was living a healthy life.

The Team Games standard exemplified the thinking of the time towards muscular Christianity and the importance of team games in the development of an "upright character." The *Canadian Standard Efficiency Tests* booklet stressed that,

> The altruistic, or "help the other fellow" spirit is strongly developed through team play. As a boy plays so will he live. Play is God's way of teaching him how to live with others. While even unsupervised play may develop many splendid qualities, it is only when a boy's play is guided by a Christian young man who encourages honesty and uprightness

that it becomes one of the greatest of all agencies for character development.[26]

The tests for Team Games involved two parts. First was the requirement that all grades attend a lecture on the character-building value of team games and the oldest boys were required to give a talk on the subject. Second, boys were to participate in a total of fifteen team games (in at least three sports) on separate days during the year. The preferred sports were baseball, lacrosse, hockey, playground ball, rugby, association football (soccer), and cricket, but other sports were accepted, as displayed, for example, by the Excelsior Anglican Club, 1917, when the boys took tests in rowing, basketball, volleyball, and athletics.[27]

Group games for children were also believed to possess similar character-forming qualities to those formed in team games. Such games were spontaneous and often without regard for the number of players. Approved references included Bancroft's *Games for the Playground, Home, School and Gymnasium*, and Chesney's *Indoor and Outdoor Games*. Forty-one games were on the recommended list, of which any ten were accepted as satisfactory participation in this category.

Swimming was considered essential in the complete physical program for the recruit because knowledge of the activity was believed to give the boy self poise and a quiet personal assurance, supposed essential ingredients of a gentleman.[28] Requirements included two 25 yard swims (freestyle and on the back) for grade 1, and 225 yards freestyle plus three lifesaving methods of release and rescue for grade 7.

Athletics, which included the three categories of running, jumping and throwing, were thought of in much the same vein as team games, possessing inherent character building qualities. The *Tests* booklet stated this point clearly:

> The character building influence of wisely conducted athletics is far reaching. Athletic events are thoroughly democratic. They teach self control, and tend to keep one calm when others are excited and alarmed. They help to establish habits of temperance and develop honor, sincerity, honest effort, skills, endurance, courage, perseverance, self-reliance, and other clean-cut manly attributes and ideals.[29]

Once again, it was not the attainment of athletic excellence that guided the CSET organizers but rather a belief in the value of participation for character building and for interesting youth in activities of the church. A handbook for leaders stressed that the boys did not have to be athletes, for effective service, nor was there a need for such, but rather a genuine interest was needed by the leader in the activities and concerns of the boys in order to win their loyalty and fellowship.[30]

The athletic standards included a 60 yard potato race, outdoor sprints, standing broad jump, running high jump, standing hop step and jump, throwing for distance and at a target, pull ups, and shot putting. The majority of these events were classed by weight, and standards were set for each, for example,

Weight	Distance	Time	Pull-up
80 lbs.	50 yards	7.4 secs.	3
95 lbs.	75 yards	10.4 secs.	4
110 lbs.	100 yards	13.4 secs.	6
125 lbs.	100 yards	12.4 secs.	8
Unlimited	100 yards	11.4 secs.	10

To encourage training, "National Athletic Meets" were organized by the National Boys' Work Board, affiliated with the Religious Education Council of Canada since 1917. The requirements for participation in a meet were that an entrant must be an initiated member of a registered CSET group and have attended a minimum number of mid-week and Sunday school sessions,[31] which demonstrates the attempt at encapsulating the participants into the realm of the church.

The CSET program offered the denominations the opportunity to become involved in a structured program suitable for young people's societies in an area of life which they had traditionally believed was best left to the discretion of the individual. Although some critics claimed that it failed to catch on significantly in Sunday school, and proved cumbersome because it tried to encompass all aspects of adolescent development,[32] it nevertheless represented success through a change in church attitude. The denominations had strengthened their Sunday school week-day programs as a result, and later accepted the CSET program as the basis for Trail Rangers (12–14 years) and Taxis (15–18 years) programs, which were interdenominational programs developed under the auspices of the Religious Education Council of Canada. During the period 1918–1921, gains were heralded from CSET with upwards of 25 000 Taxis and Trail Rangers benefitting from this structured program.[33] The CSET program provided the church with a vehicle through which it could encourage athletic sports, sought by the adolescent, in a context suitable to its conservative tradition.

The social gospel message attempted to change the tradition and challenged the church to become more practically involved with youth. The commitment of the social gospel to the social message also gave physical recreation a legitimate place within the church. This idea did not develop quickly but evolved over time, and always in the context of limited traditional experience in this area of life. But the immediacy of the young boy problem was evident, and physical recreation provided one ray of hope of the denominations for attracting the worldly boy's favour. The traditional church was suspicious of influences not under its control and ever mindful of "worthwhile ends."[34] Nevertheless, the church overcame its concerns by adapting the programs offered in its young people's organizations to suit both its needs and those of Canadian youth. The role of the social gospel was an important force in the evolution of ideas within the Protestant churches about physical recreation. In signalling the importance of it as a social benefit, the social gospel established a firm link between the church and ideas influencing attitudes to physical recreation and sport in Canada.

Notes

1. Alan Metcalfe, "Some Background Influence on Nineteenth Century Canadian Sport and Physical Education," *Canadian Journal of History of Sport and Physical Education* 5, 1 (May 1974): 62–73.

2. See Richard Allen, *The Social Passion: Religion and Social Reform in Canada, 1914–1928* (Toronto: University of Toronto Press, 1971).

3. Richard Allen, "The Social Gospel and the Reform Tradition in Canada" in *Prophecy and Protest: Social Movements in Twentieth Century Canada*, ed. S.D. Clark et al., (Toronto: Gage Publishing, 1975).

4. A.R.M. Lower, "Canada: Social and Cultural Institutions" in *Canada*, ed. George Brown (Toronto: University of Toronto Press, 1951), 479.

5. Allen, "The Social Gospel and the Reform Tradition," 45.

6. Richard Allen, ed., *The Social Gospel in Canada: Papers of the Interdisciplinary Conference on the Social Gospel in Canada*, March 21–24, 1973. (Ottawa: National Museum of Man, 1975), 4.

7. Allen, "The Social Gospel and the Reform Tradition," 49.

8. S.D. Clark, *Church and Sect in Canada* (Toronto: University of Toronto Press, 1948), 413.

9. *Canadian Epworth Era* (August 1901), 233.

10. *Canadian Churchman*, Nov. 1, 1900, 661.

11. *The Teacher's Assistant* (The Commission Bulletin) (March 1915), 13.

12. Allen, *Social Passion*, 3–4.

13. *Canadian Churchman*, Feb. 21, 1924, 119.

14. David Brown, "Athleticism and Selected Private Schools in Canada" (unpublished Ph.D. dissertation, University of Alberta, 1984).

15. "Minutes of the Board of Moral and Social Reform (Presbyterian Church)" Sept. 6, 1910, 12.

16. *The City of London, Ontario, Report on a Limited Survey of Educational, Social, and Industrial Life* (Oct.–Dec. 1913), 10. This report was prepared by the Presbyterian Committee on Religious Education, the Methodist Department of Temperance and Moral Reform, and the Presbyterian Board of Social Services and Evangelism.

17. Ibid.

18. *Canadian Epworth Era* (Jan. 1908), 11.

19. Ibid.

20. The Departments of Social Service and Evangelism of the Methodist and Presbyterian Churches, *The St. Catharines District, Ontario, Report on a Limited Survey of Religious, Moral, Industrial and Housing Conditions* (1915), 20.

21. Ibid.

22. *Acts and Proceedings of the General Assembly of the Presbyterian Church in Canada* (hereinafter *APAP*), 46th General Assembly (1920), 239.

23. *APAP*, 50th General Assembly (1924), 218.

24. *Journal of Proceedings of the General Conference of the Methodist Church*, 11th General Assembly (1922), 410. The Canadian Girls in Training (CGIT) was the equivalent program for girls.

25. *Canadian Standard Efficiency Tests*, 6th ed. (Oct. 1914), 34.

26. Ibid., 46–47.

27. *Canadian Churchman*, May 24, 1917, 332.

28. *Presbyterian Record* (Nov. 1912), 502.

29. *Tests* (March 1916), 51.

30. Percy Hayward, *The Mentor's Manual: A Handbook for Leaders. CSET for Trail Rangers and Taxis Boys*, 2nd ed. (National Boys Work Board of the Religious Educational Council of Canada, 1921), 8.

31. *The Canadian Mentor* (April 1925), 5. This was an official organ of the YMCA.

32. David Macleod, "A Live Vaccine: The YMCA and Male Adolescence in the United States and Canada 1870-1920," *Histoire sociale/Social History* 11, 21 (May 1978), 22.

33. *The Mentor's Manual*, 12.

34. *APAP* 51st General Assembly (1925), 221.

SPORTS AND THE DEVELOPMENT OF CHARACTER*

JEAN BARMAN

The unity behind the apparently disparate group of British Columbia [private] boys' schools in operation by the 1920s grew out of the commitment of their individual headmasters to a single educational ideal. These men, frequently physical strangers to each other, came from backgrounds in Britain that predisposed them to act similarly in British Columbia. It was through these agents of cultural transfer that the schools acquired their singular identity.

The founding headmasters of British Columbia's boys' schools possessed as a group three attributes that made them dependable agents of transfer. First, they had come through the British public schools during that system's years of greatest self-confidence in the late nineteenth and early twentieth centuries. A recent historian has argued that "what the public school boy did was to take his school world and its symbolic actions and trappings with him into the outside world."[1] Secondly, these men were almost equally familiar with the calling of the Anglican clergyman, so intimately intertwined in nineteenth-century Britain with that of the private schoolmaster. Of the sixteen British Columbia founding headmasters for whom information is available, three-quarters were either the sons of clergymen or had themselves contemplated taking holy orders. Thirdly, headmasters had generally gone uncontaminated after emigration to British Columbia: they went into teaching or the church, and were not exposed for any length of time to non-British life styles. Those few who had taught in the British Columbia public system usually stayed for so brief a time as to catch only a glimpse of that alien tradition. Almost immediately, they joined the province's private-school

---

* *Growing up British in British Columbia: Boys in Private School* (Vancouver: University of British Columbia Press, 1984), chap. 4, "The Transfer of an Ideal," 63–66, 71–77.

community to be immured among fellow immigrants of similar background.

These men's interest in creating their own schools lay precisely in this common background. Their emigration from Britain had been essentially conservative. They came, not to alter their life style by active participation in a different social order, but to maintain a set way of living. For British immigrants, British Columbia was not alien but a physically distant, minimally presentable outpost of a single Empire whose epicentre they represented. Opportunity lay — as their education had already led them to believe was their special responsibility — in developing that outpost in the context of the larger order. An intimate of British private education might have been describing any of British Columbia's future headmasters when he wrote in 1906 of the typical old boy: "Thus equipped, he goes out into the world, and bears a man's part in subduing the earth, ruling its wild folk, and building up the Empire."[2]

British Columbia's headmasters were greatly aided in the creation of their own schools by the emphasis on replication underlying the process in Britain. Just as it was common practice in Britain for the founder of a school to use as a model the institution he had once attended, so headmasters in British Columbia copied as much as possible from their own experiences. [Kyrle C.] Symons created St. Michael's as a little Dulwich, borrowing its very motto, crest, and school colours, together with as many of Dulwich's practices as were feasible in a school for younger boys. He publicly ascribed any success St. Michael's might have to the influence of his own headmaster; indeed, the lineaments of this august personage graced the flyleaf of the Victoria school's visitors' book.[3] Other headmasters made their relationship with British public schools even more explicit: there was a Cranleigh as well as a Malvern in Victoria. Both [the Rev. Austin C.] Mackie at Vernon and [Charles W.] Lonsdale at Shawnigan copied from their old schools — St. John's Leatherhead and Westminster — the Shrove Tuesday ritual of "tossing the pancake," in which selected pupils scrambled for the largest piece of a pancake tossed in the air. Lonsdale once explained, "Transplanted traditions are hardly traditions, but in a new country they are the next best thing, the only thing possible."[4]

Behind all the rituals so lovingly transferred to British Columbia lay a single educational ideal — that of "building character." To build character was to turn young boys into Victorian "gentlemen." The British public-school phenomenon had sprung from the desire among social groups that had risen in the Industrial Revolution to buy their sons' acceptance into the traditional ruling class. Gentleman status, a prerequisite for membership in that class, summed up their goal. The Rev. Mackie reminded his pupils at Vernon:

> I know no other word which can equal the word "gentleman" as expressing the ideals of courtesy, self-efface-ment, chivalry toward women, honour in business and a sense of noblesse oblige. Therefore my dearest wish will be that each of you may grow up to be a Christian gentleman.[5]

British Columbia headmasters were wedded to this mode of con-struction. At Brentwood's opening in 1923, a principal speaker stressed that "the aim of the college is character building."[6] Writing on "The Joy of Character Building" for the University School magazine five years later, a master rhapsodized: "Is there any satisfaction that can compare with the solid satisfaction and abiding joy of building up a character?"[7] When an advertisement for North Vancouver's Kingsley school asserted, "Character Building Especially Em-phasized," its competitor down the street, North Shore College, countered with "Character Building, Discipline, Physical Training."[8] The Rev. Mackie asserted: "The prime object of this or any other school should be to develop — send out in the world — men of charac-ter."[9] One Sunday in chapel, he counselled his pupils that though their bodies would perish their moral records would adhere to them in Heaven — "hence the enormous importance of developing our charac-ters along the right lines."[10]

The relation between character and leadership was pointed out time and time again. As the speaker at Brentwood's opening stated, "We feel that right here the great men of tomorrow are going to be given their start in life."[11] An early pupil confirmed the school's outlook, recollecting that "it was the quality of leadership that you learnt at Brentwood."[12] A 1925 prospectus for University School explained character "moulding" as "respect for authority and discipline, smart-ness and punctuality, the discovery and development of leader-ship."[13] Lonsdale considered Shawnigan's "prime aim and object" as being to "provide opportunities for developing leadership in the West."[14] A St. Michael's old boy who became a district commissioner in the British Sudan, responsible for training native troops, recalled that when he himself had been drilled by Symons, the instruction was always, "March as if you owned the world and had the receipt in your pocket!"[15] Reflecting after many years as headmaster, Mackie reiterated, "Character will be the deciding factor more than ever — you from your training should take your place as leaders."[16] The final verse in the Brentwood school song summed up the message:

So may all, a hardy breed
To one purpose steady,
By obeying learn to lead,
Self-controlled and ready.[17]

Headmasters in British Columbia as in Britain divided character building into three components — academic, moral, and physical. Speaking to pupils at University School's Christmas ceremonies in 1908, the Rev. [William Washington] Bolton referred to "Matter, Manliness, and Manners": "By Matter he meant ordinary school studies; Manliness was gained in their games and drill; lastly he reminded them that Manners maketh Man."[18] A feature article on Brentwood considered the "three phases of the school's influence" to be "manly character, sound education, and physical fitness."[19] Chesterfield's headmaster described that school's purpose as to "make each boy's body strong and deft; his soul honest and generous; and his mind acquisitive and logical."[20] Malvern House chose "to emphasize building of character through self-reliance, independence of thought, and consideration of others."[21] An editorial in Shawnigan's magazine summed up the three essentials as "manhood, learning, gentleness."[22] The Vernon Preparatory School offered "sound moral, mental, and physical grounding."[23]

...

The most important dimension ... was neither the moral nor the academic, but the physical. The concept was a broad one including all physical activity, with an emphasis on team games. It is hard to overstate the importance that was attached to this aspect of character development. A British observer has suggested that "of the life of the normal schoolboy at least half is devoted to athletics."[24] After all, as one English headmaster put it, "There is usually something which needs correction in the character of a boy who takes no interest in games."[25]

British Columbia headmasters accepted the value their British counterparts assigned to various kinds of physical activity. A hardy life style was the most generalized characteristic. A journalist has written of St. Michael's that "K.C. Symons believed in the Spartan life....He flung windows wide in winter and stripped 'needless' blankets from boarders' beds."[26] Buildings that may have begun crudely out of financial necessity often remained so out of virtue. Outdoor toilets and unheated dormitories were listed among Vernon's "assets" right up to the Second World War. A few of the older boys were selected each winter to sleep out on an open porch with one of the Mackies. One small boy reported home to his mother: "it was 30 below last night and the boys who sleep outside have their sheets and blankets frozen in the morning."[27]

Conditions in the original Shawnigan Preparatory School were similar. A pupil of the 1920s has recalled, "There was no heat in the dormitories, and a window was left open except when rain or snow might blow in....On a long table between the two rows of beds, each boy had an enamel basin and a tin jug of water. It got so cold in winter this water often had ice."[28] Another boy has recalled "outdoor latrines with rows of one holers — all open — each dormitory had its own cubicles — urinal a metal trough which [was] cleaned with disinfectant each day — on wall a list of boys and had to put an "x" when performed — checked periodically — otherwise got medication."[29] A third Shawnigan pupil from these years has added, "Throughout the year we wore shorts with bare knees. My feet used to suffer a lot from chilblains, for which I would rub on coal oil." Yet another has summed up, "You were always hungry, you were always cold." When Shawnigan was rebuilt after its 1926 fire, there was "greater comfort and even luxury," in part perhaps to compete with Brentwood, which had taken over a resort hotel as its quarters.[30]

Opportunities for showing physical manliness were part of the day at every school. At Shawnigan, "the younger ones had to get up to take a cold tub bath....At the same time the older boys took a dive in the lake until it started to freeze over."[31] One year, the "usual keen competition for the honour of being first in — and first out" continued until "the ice is too thick to break." A small boy at Vernon wrote his mother hopefully, "I have a cold bath every day when we get up; do you?" The boys who swam in that school's creek the latest each autumn were "rewarded by a special treat of their own." One Christmas the Vernon magazine noted proudly that three pupils had "continued their icy dips in the creek right up to the end of the Term, despite deep snow, and at times a temperature not far from zero."[32]

The high value placed on hardy conditioning was reflected in the schools' attitudes to health. While accepting the danger and, indeed, the inevitability of occasional epidemics of infectious disease, they remained slightly scornful of routine illness. A woman trained in nursing was part of every boarding-school staff as matron in charge of the boys' physical care. An early Brentwood prospectus assured parents: "The school medical officer visits the College weekly. Boys are carefully examined, general health and development noted, and once a term a Medical Report is sent to parents, who can thus feel assured that no overstrain at games or overpressure at work is allowed."[33] Voluntary complaints of physical discomfort were another matter. Shawnigan's longtime matron is widely remembered for her disinclination to believe reported symptoms. One pupil recorded wryly: "In attendance at the surgery at different hours of the day in the certainty that my temperature was abnormal. Mrs. Stanton adamant. She is more hard-headed even than Pharaoh."[34] Vernon's magazine advised parents "that this climate is not especially fitted for pansy-growing," and reported on another occasion that the victims of a 'flu epidemic were "mainly such as were sadly lacking in intestinal fortitude." Speaking in chapel, the Rev. Mackie informed boys that "nearly all disease comes from over-eating or over-drinking or un-chastity." In sum, ill health implied lack of character.[35]

Regular exercise was integral to the maintenance of a spartan ethos. Each day began with outdoor Swedish drill or "P.T." — physical train-ing. Such activity provided, according to a British exponent, "a mode of expending accumulated energy" which would otherwise lead to "the formation of morbid imaginations."[36] Moreover, as University School informed parents about 1925, "Boys at school, working and leaning over their desks at their daily studies, can be expected in time to develop stooping positions." Thus, "our daily P.T. is really a sys-tem of corrective exercises to bring out Presence of Mind, Absence of Fussiness and Promptness of Action."[37] In inclement weather, P.T. was often replaced by a "long wet run" or "grind," as the carefully marked-out course at Vernon was called.[38] Boys at Kingsley ran up and down the city blocks surrounding the North Lonsdale school.

Organized athletic activities in which pupils participated as in-dividuals rather than as members of a team were considered to have limited character-building value. Boxing had fairly high remedial worth, in one British estimate, because of the "valuable qualities of self-control and resource to be learned through punching and being punched"[39] A number of British Columbia schools, including Shawnigan, Vernon, and University, made regular participation com-pulsory and held annual spring tournaments. The Rev. Bolton's "Ra-tionale for Boxing" was that "boys are combative by nature." If the instinct was suppressed "with a high hand," it "will break out in later years with a virulence in other forms, which is known under the head-ing of Bad Temper." The "corrective" of boxing showed each pupil "the need and value of self-control even in the moment of his fury."[40] Track and field sports were ranked fairly high for their endurance element. Most schools held a Sports Day in the autumn or late spring, to which parents and public were invited and prizes awarded for performance in various events.

Other individual sports that were sometimes available at the dif-ferent schools — tennis, badminton, swimming, golf, archery, skiing, skating, shooting, sailing, riding, fencing — were generally optional, for, as a British headmaster proclaimed, "They have no character-building value."[41] Yet it was recognized that "individualist activities" did provide, in the words of a British Columbia school magazine, "a solution to the problem of occupations on wet afternoons and long winter evenings."[42] Each school came to its own decision about which individual sports to offer. In the late 1920s Chesterfield opted to build an indoor swimming pool and "stabling for six horses."[43] Riding became available at Shawnigan only because a British settler had set up a stable in the area, but the option moved to Vernon when the proprietor and his horses went back to the interior. Fencing was introduced at Shawnigan simply because a master with that expertise joined the staff. The explanation of a leading British headmaster that such activities were "all of them good in their place, good games, but mainly hygienic in their value," was used by Lonsdale in 1930 to explain the school's ad hoc policy.[44]

Participation in individual sports often involved membership in a club with fees to offset costs to the institution. Boys generally had to provide their own equipment. Thus, a Vernon pupil wrote to his mother in great haste: "Please send me a Badminton racquet because the one you gave me broke when I was playing; otherwise I won't be able to play in the tournament."[45] An "official notice" to Vernon parents stated, "Parents wishing their boys to play lawn tennis are asked to send them back both with a racquet and two dollars for the subscription."[46] Even Brentwood, whose reputation was based on its idyllic rural location "tucked away in the remotest corner of a sheltered inlet," organized its celebrated water sports of rowing and sailing on a subscription basis. Pupils owning their own vessels were requested to moor them at the school to help defray expenses.[47]

In both Britain and British Columbia the physical component of character-building centred around team games. Tom Brown [in the famous novel *Tom Brown's Schooldays*] had concluded back in 1856 that soccer and cricket "are such much better games than fives or hares-and-hounds, or others where the object is to come in first and to win for oneself, and not that one's side may win."[48] By late century the catch phrase, "playing the game," had become "the foundation of all that is best in the English character...the real reason why we have been successful in foreign politics and in governing backward races."[49] According to a 1900 British government report, the prime gain from compulsory organized games was "to be willing to sink the personal in the public interest," "to be English-like, or so we fondly imagine."[50]

Lonsdale reported to his new board of governors in 1928: "With regard to games it is well to emphasize the necessity for *Team* games only for *School* games, with individual games such as golf, tennis, squash, etc., for boys' spare amusements."[51] At Malvern House, "games are played every day, including Saturdays."[52] The Rev.

Mackie explained in a sermon why Vernon so strongly supported team games:

> The importance of regular, organized, supervised games cannot be exaggerated; it is on the playing field that a boy learns to play the game of life by giving & taking hard knocks & nasty falls without whimpering or losing his temper, by putting the honour of his side before his own, by scorning to win except by fair means, by disdaining to employ mean or underhand tricks such as tripping or fouling, by taking defeat cheerfully like a good sportsman & by being modest in victory.[53]

So would boys be equipped to "play the Game of Life in the true sporting spirit, struggling to our feet as often as we are knocked down, giving forth every ounce of all that is best in us until the final whistle blows and we leave the ranks of the Church Militant here on earth & join the Church Expectant in the Great Beyond."

Team games formed the heart of school life in both Britain and British Columbia. Every boy played every game. When the school team performed, every single boy not playing was expected to participate by watching. A Vernon old boy still remembers having asked the Rev. Mackie for permission to study during Saturday afternoon cricket matches only to have the headmaster write in his distress to the pupil's father, a well-known Vancouver cricketer. Permission was refused. Details of each school game were the most prominent feature of school magazines, with every individual's contribution to the team analysed in detail. "Sound in the field, a useful change bowler and a fair bat with a weak defence on the leg peg."[54] Cups, medals, and colours were awarded for outstanding performance. In 1925, University School even introduced a Sports Honour Cap — blue velvet with a red tassel — to be awarded to any boy who won his colours in nine out of twelve possible team and individual sports. The headmaster noted proudly that it was, "in measure, like the 'Blue' at Home" — the athletic awards bestowed by Oxford and Cambridge.[55]

The various team games were ranked for character-building value. North American games such as baseball were forbidden, in the words of a former pupil, as "fit only for public school brats."[56] Pride of place was taken by what a British Columbia newspaper of the period called "the traditional games of England."[57] The three principal team games were, in order of increasing importance, soccer, rugby, and cricket. The first two were played in the autumn and the latter in spring and summer. Matches in each of these games were arranged with other private schools. Schools also played against local amateur teams composed of young British settlers and, as time passed, nearby old boys.

From time to time, but not regularly, games were arranged with public schools in the same community. Large schools also set up house teams.

Soccer, known in Britain as "association football," was in decline by the time British Columbia's schools were being established. While it was acceptable for younger boys, its utility in the public school had grown suspect. As a British headmaster commented in 1929, not only did it lack the "speed, endurance, courage, or chivalry" of rugby football, but it was increasingly being played by professional teams, "and professionalism is the complete antithesis of the English tradition of sport."[58] To have value in building character, games had to be played as ends in themselves, for their inherent value as team sports, and certainly not for financial gain. Soccer was, moreover, becoming popular in Britain and British Columbia at all levels of society, including the lower classes, a factor that may have contributed to turning gentlemen against it.[59] Lonsdale faced the soccer issue when Shawnigan expanded after the 1926 fire to include older boys.

> As an old "soccer" player, with a large majority of "soccer" men on the staff, with the "soccer" traditions of the greatest of the old English Public-Schools behind us, it is with extreme reluctance, actuated only by the consideration of the future welfare of our Old Boys, that I have suggested that the school should become a "rugger" school.[60]

North Shore College soon followed Shawnigan's example.

Rugby was valued both for its amateur status and because participants were, it was believed, forced to choose: rugby could be played either with "courage and daring" or in a "'rough' or unfair" manner. Since the second alternative "ruined" the game, the decision itself became "a test for character."[61] In the phrase of a British headmaster, "it is one of its many merits that it can only be played by those who are in the only real sense of the word gentlemen." Every British Columbia boys' school with enough older boys to form a Rugby XV played the game.

Cricket was the aristocrat of team games, not only in British schools but throughout British society. *Tom Brown's Schooldays* described it as "the birthright of British boys old and young, as *habeas corpus* and trial by jury are of British men": "It merges the individual in the eleven; he doesn't play that he may win, but that his side may."[62] A half-century of glorification culminated in the English poet Henry Newbolt's paean of praise with its immortal refrain, "'Play up! Play up! And play the game!'" A modern critic has concluded, "Cricket's influence on the upper-middle-class British mind, with its sense of orthodoxy and respect for the rules and laws and the impartial authority of umpires, can hardly be exaggerated."[63]

No British Columbia headmaster ever even conceived of his pupils, young and old, not being cricketers to a boy. During St. Michael's first year with its meagre numbers and the absence of a playing field, the dearth of organized games was Symons's "main anxiety": hide-and-seek "has never struck me as quite the game to win the battle of Waterloo."[64] By 1925, however, cricket had pride of place with "five nets, all much in use." An old boy of Malvern House has recalled that its head "was very sports minded, and of course, being an Englishman, he was keen on the boys doing well at soccer, gym, and especially at cricket."[65]

British Columbia schools carefully copied the minutiae of cricket ritual that had grown up in their British counterparts. Members of the Cricket XI, or school team, were permitted to wear specially designed blazers and caps in the school colours. At Vernon, "they were optional but it is hoped that parents will sanction the purchase of one or both by boys eligible, as they are a valuable aid to *esprit de corps* and tend to engender keenness." Games were usually held on Saturday afternoons to give every opportunity for attendance by pupils, local parents, and other supporters. A cricket pavilion boarded the field wherever finances allowed. Vernon's included "conveniences for changing, preparing teas, storing cricket appliances, seating spectators." The degree to which cricket permeated the atmosphere of the schools as well as their surrounding communities is indicated by an advertisement in the Vernon magazine, headlined, "Play Cricket": "This expression is significant and has a great deal of meaning. It stands for everything that is straight-forward, honorable, square and fair dealing throughout one's life....The Vernon Garage, Monk Bros., Proprietors, 'Play Cricket.'...Cricket lovers buy Chevrolet and Oldsmobile cars."[66]

The significance of the game for British Columbia boys' schools is well summed up in an intimate, anonymous memoir of Shawnigan, thinly disguised as "Thunderbird School." The day before the game, "the names of the cricket eleven were posed above the mantel" in the assembly hall. Then came Saturday.

> Cricket! To a strange degree cricket represents Thunderbird to me. The general excitement in the school on the morning of a match. The first team looking very attractive in white flannels, black blazers and school or house colours. Special tables in the dining room for the visiting eleven. A leisurely walk up the hill to the cricket field, with an occasional backward glance at the panorama of school buildings and

gardens....Cricket was vital and exciting. Cricket was sportsmanship and fair play. Cricket, I was beginning to realize, was Thunderbird. [67]

A pupil at another school has made the point more succinctly: "The first XI were the Gods."

Notes

1. J.A. Mangan, *Athleticism in the Victorian and Edwardian Public School* (Cambridge: Cambridge University Press, 1981), 145.

2. *The Public Schools from Within: A Collection of Essays on Public School Education, Written Chiefly by Schoolmasters* (London: Sampson, Low, Marston and Co., 1906), 283.

3. Kyrle C. Symons, *That Amazing Institution: The Story of St. Michael's School, Victoria, B.C., from 1910–1948* (Victoria: n.p., 1948), 15; *Colonist* (Victoria), May 31, 1925.

4. *Colonist*, June 7, 1925.

5. The Rev. Austin C. Mackie, Notebooks of sermons delivered at Vernon Preparatory School, vol. 8, Public Archives of British Columbia (hereinafter PABC).

6. *Colonist*, Sept. 23, 1923. General data for this article were taken principally from interviews, school magazines, and newspaper articles.

7. *The Black and Red* (University School Magazine) (hereinafter USM) 54 (1928), 54.

8. *Province* (Vancouver), Aug. 3, 1931.

9. Mackie, Notebooks of sermons, vol. 9.

10. Ibid., vol. 3.

11. *Colonist*, March 3, 1957.

12. *Brentwood College Magazine* (hereinafter BCM) (1944), 47.

13. University School, *Prospectus*, 1925, PABC.

14. *Shawnigan Lake School Magazine* (hereinafter SLSM) (1937), 55.

15. *Colonist*, March 3, 1957.

16. Mackie, Notebooks of sermons, undated notes.

17. *BCM* (1945), 42.

18. *USM* 2 (1909), 3.

19. *Colonist*, Aug. 29, 1931.

20. North Shore Archives, Chesterfield School, *Prospectus*, 1940(?).

21. *Colonist*, Aug. 29, 1943.

22. *SLSM* (1929), 2.

23. *Province*, Sept. 4, 1932.

24. *Public Schools from Within*, 201–02.

25. Alan Rannie, "The Preparatory School" in *The Schools of England*, ed. J. Dover Wilson (London: Sidgwick and Jackson, 1928), 79.

26. *Colonist*, March 31, 1957.

27. Vernon Preparatory School, Letter home from pupil B (unpublished correspondence used with author's permission), Feb. 17.

28. Shawnigan Lake School, "Historical Material" (folder in Shawnigan Lake School Archives (hereinafter SLSA) containing reminiscences gathered in 1974–79, from pupils at Shawnigan Lake Preparatory School, 1916–27.

29. Ibid., and Hugh Lander, taped interview, summer 1980, in SLSA. Identical British practice is described in Tom Driberg, *Ruling Passions* (London: Jonathan Cape, 1977), 13.

30. *SLSM* (1927), 3.

31. Shawnigan Lake School, "Historical Material," and *SLSM* (1924), 15 and (1925), 14.

32. Vernon Preparatory School, letter home from pupil A, Feb. 17, and *The Chronicle of the Vernon Preparatory School* (hereinafter *VPSM*) (Christmas 1931), 6 and (Christmas 1936), 3.

33. Brentwood College, *Prospectus*, 1924(?).

34. *The Millstream* (Shawnigan Lake School pupil literary magazine) 1 (1932), 2.

35. *VPSM* (Christmas 1942), 1, (Easter 1942), 1; Mackie, Notebooks of sermons, vol. 7.

36. *Public Schools from Within*, 183.

37. *USM* 49 (1925), 32; also University School, Prospectus, 1925 in PABC.

38. The "grind" also existed in British school; see Mangan, *Athleticism in the Victorian and Edwardian Public School*, 84–85.

39. Cyril Norwood, "The Boys' Boarding School" in *The Schools of England*, ed. Wilson, 107.

40. *USM* 51 (1926), 6.

41. Norwood, "The Boys' Boarding School," 105.

42. *SLSM* (1923), 4.

43. Frederick K.H. Bates, "The Story of My Life in North Vancouver" (typescript in North Shore Archives).

44. Shawnigan Lake School, *Report of the Headmaster*, 1930, in SLSA.

45. Vernon Preparatory School, Letter home from pupil A, March 8.

46. *VPSM* (Easter 1929), 1.

47. *BCM* (1924), 29; (1926), 21, 25; (1927), 8; (1929), 29.

48. Thomas Hughes, *Tom Brown's Schooldays* (Toronto: Penguin Books, 1977), 271.

49. Alan Rannie, "The Preparatory School" in *The Schools of England*, ed. Wilson, 78.

50. *Preparatory Schools for Boys: Their Place in English Secondary Education*, vol. 6 of *Special Reports on Educational Subjects of Board of Education* (London: HMSO, 1900), 345.

51. Shawnigan Lake School, *Report*, 1930.

52. *Province*, Aug. 20, 1933.

53. Mackie, Notebooks of sermons, vols. 8 and 3.

54. *USM* 48 (1925), 42. Mangan, in his study of athleticism in the British public school, used school magazines to measure its importance. In his sample years from the 1920s, 48 percent of magazine content was devoted to team and individual sports; see *Athleticism in the Victorian and Edwardian Public School*, 243–50. The proportion was even higher in British Columbia: in 1927–28, for instance, 53 percent of Shawnigan's magazine and 59 percent of Brentwood's were given over to sport. In 1934, North Shore College published a school magazine for the first time; fully two-thirds of it was devoted to athletics.

55. *USM* 48 (1925), 8.

56. Jeffry V. Brock, *The Dark Broad Seas*, vol. 1 (Toronto: McClelland and Stewart, 1981), 75. Baseball did receive much emphasis in the British Columbia public system. See, for instance, Vancouver, Board of School Trustees, *Annual Report* (1926), 94 and (1927), 126. In 1926, 70 baseball teams were active in Vancouver schools.

57. Newspaper clipping from the early 1930s in British Columbia, Department of Education, clippings books, vol. 3 (1932–38), in PABC.

58. Norwood, "The Boys' Boarding School," 104.

59. See J.B. Priestly, *The Edwardians* (London: Heinemann, 1970), 104.

60. Shawnigan Lake School, *Report*, 1928.
61. Norwood, "The Boys' Boarding School," 104.
62. Hughes, *Tom Brown's Schooldays*, 271.
63. Corelli Barnett, *The Collapse of British Power* (London: Eyre Methuen, 1972), 35.
64. Symons, *That Amazing Institution*, 15; *Colonist*, May 31, 1925.
65. *Colonist*, Feb. 11, 1973.
66. *VPSM* (Easter 1930), 3; (Easter 1929), 5; (Summer 1935), n.p.
67. "Part of Thunderbird" (anonymous typescript in SLSA), 48-49, 46.

"WE MUST MAINTAIN A BALANCE BETWEEN PROPAGANDA AND SERIOUS ATHLETICS"—THE WORKERS' SPORT MOVEMENT IN CANADA, 1924–36*

BRUCE KIDD

On Saturday evening November 24, 1934, just after supper Tim Buck, the general secretary of the Communist Party of Canada, was quietly released from Kingston Penitentiary and placed on a train for Toronto. He had served almost three years of a five-year sentence (for "seditious conspiracy"), longer than any of the other communists who had been arrested for political activity in the early years of the Depression. During their imprisonment, Buck and the other leaders enjoyed very little news of the outside world and even less contact with their comrades. But if the federal authorities had hoped that jailing the communist leaders would seriously damage, if not destroy, their organization, the show of strength upon Buck's release demonstrated they had been mistaken. Although his parole was to be kept secret — it was timed to miss the Saturday afternoon newspapers — 5 000 people jammed Union Station that evening to meet his train and hear his unrepentant indictment of "bourgeois justice." One week later, 17 000 people attended a rally in his honour at Maple Leaf Gardens, and another 8 000 had to be turned away. Hardly the manifestation of a decimated sect.[1]

At both events, and at smaller rallies around Toronto, Buck was protected by almost 100 athletes. They were all dressed in white, except for a red belt and a red star-shaped crest which read, "Workers' Sports Association" and were accompanied by what appeared to be their youth corps, the similarly clad cadres of the Young Pioneers and the Young Communist League. At the Gardens, they carried him into the arena on their shoulders, as if he was the coach of a successful

* *Proceedings, 5th Canadian Symposium on the History of Sport and Physical Education* (School of Physical and Health Education, University of Toronto, 1982), 330–39.

football team. When he addressed the crowd, among baskets of red roses and carnations and below 30-foot high photographs of Lenin and Stalin, they guarded the podium and kept all but designated officials from approaching. Earlier in the week at the Alhambra Hall, they showed that their muscle was not merely decorative, by performing a series of fast-moving choreographed exercises and human pyramids. They were fit, attractive and moved with military precision.[2] To the sympathetic onlooker, they symbolized the courage and vitality of an organization that had survived five years of state repression. But to others, it might have seemed that the CPC was building a paramilitary unit which would engage in street battles in the manner of la croix du feu, the Red Brigades, and the Stormtroopers of Europe.

Despite their fascination for the parties of the left, Canadian historians have barely noticed the Workers' Sports Association of Canada.[3] Yet during the first two decades of its existence, the CPC sought to develop a national sports movement as an adjunct of its political work. In this effort, it was unique among Canadian political parties. Other parties have sought favourable association with sport by identifying with prominent teams and recruiting outstanding athletes, but none has tried to organize sports teams as a means of training party members, nor to intervene in the affairs of the existing sport structures.[4] Yet that was what the CPC sought to accomplish.

The Workers' Sports Association began as an attempt to transplant the European tradition of class-conscious sport to communities in Canada. Towards the end of the nineteenth century, European socialist groups and trade unions formed gymnastics and sporting clubs, usually as an alternative to bourgeois clubs from which their members had been excluded, but occasionally as a cover for otherwise illegal political activity. By 1913, there were sufficient numbers and interest for five national associations to form an international federation, first known as the Lucerne Sports International (after the site of its successful postwar conference) and subsequently, the Socialist Workers' Sports International. The LSI and its member federations were noted for their attempts to improve the quality of working-class recreation, by providing technical assistance and agitating for improved public facilities and physical education. Between the wars, the LSI staged three Workers' Olympiads, in Frankfurt in 1925, in Vienna in 1931, and in Antwerp in 1937.[5]

But the Workers' sports movement was not without division. In 1921, after the formation of the Communist International, a minority of workers' sports organizations broke away to form the Red Sport International. Whereas the LSI was primarily concerned with the conditions and opportunities for working-class athletes *in sport*, the RSI "wanted to build a sport international that was a political instrument of the class struggle; it was not interested in developing a better sports' system for workers in a capitalist world."[6] Although physical culturists within the Soviet Union hotly debated the proper goal of sport and physical activity for the working class,[7] these discussions rarely filtered through to the deliberations and pronouncements of the RSI. Initially, the RSI sought to win adherents by infiltrating LSI clubs and pushing its own line, without formally affiliating as an organization. When the LSI, understandably, did not invite the RSI to the Frankfurt Olympiad, the RSI tried to stage counter-demonstrations. Only after relations broke down completely did the RSI begin to organize events of its own, beginning with the "counter-Olympic" World Spartakiad in Moscow in 1928. These manoeuvres were conducted within the overall framework of Comintern policies, and the swings or turns occurred as strategy changed in response to internal political struggles and Soviet foreign policy. After the Comintern's Sixth Congress in 1928, for example, it sought "unity from below" and repeatedly attacked LSI leaders as "social imperialists"; after the Seventh Congress in 1935, it sought a "united front against fascism."[8]

The impetus for workers' sports in Canada came from the RSI through the Young Communist League. In 1924, Tom Hill, the Canadian delegate to the Fourth Congress of the Young Communist International, advised Canadian members that "our duty is to work within the workers' sports organizations, mobilizing them against exploitation, militarism and fascism, and for revolutionary understanding."[9] But since "workers' sports organizations" on the European model did not exist in Canada, they had to be created. Shortly afterwards, the league's newspaper, *The Young Worker*, advised every branch to form a Workers' Sport Association:

> Sport, the exercising of the body, and all the mental benefits accruing from sport are an essential part of League work. Baseball should be the most popular, but hikes and runs and boxing and swimming can all be added. But these sports must be turned from commercial antagonistic games into "Red Sports"....They are recruiting agencies because they are beneficial to League membership at large and develop a feeling of comradeship and vitality.[10]

The League intended to build the WSAs into one of the most powerful of the CPC's "mass organizations," designed to win both sympathetic and uncommitted non-party members to the communist cause.[11] WSA members were not required to be communists; the organization was successfully controlled by a "faction" of YCL members acting under party discipline.

The YCL was quick to take up the challenge. In 1925, soccer teams were started in Montreal, Toronto, and Winnipeg (the latter called the "Hammer and Sickle Club") and smaller centres such as Oshawa, Renfrew, Kirkland Lake, Lethbridge, and Drumheller reported field days, team games, boxing clubs, swimming parties, picnics and hikes. In 1926, WSAs were established in 17 centres. The Toronto WSA operated a seven-team softball league, with two teams of cigar makers, one of jewellers, one from the Earlscourt Labour Party, and three WSA teams. The Montreal WSA fielded senior and junior teams in the city soccer and basketball leagues and they attracted a large following. "You didn't have to be a Communist to go to Fletcher's Field on a Saturday afternoon and cheer for the WSA. It was a great morale builder for all the tailors and workers in the area," one participant has remembered.[12] During the 1930s, the Toronto and Montreal WSA soccer teams played each other on an annual basis, and these games attracted crowds as large as 5 000. (Montreal usually won.) Games were followed by speeches, songs, a collection, and an invitation to a WSA dance in the evening.

The WSAs encouraged a diversity of activity, but the staple of most clubs was gymnastics. The great majority of WSA members were eastern European immigrants for whom it was a familiar and favourite form of activity. Gymnastics had the organizational advantage of continuity, as The Young Worker once ruefully admitted: "It must be strictly kept in mind that gymnastic classes and not factory leagues are the basis for workers' sport. In one place a particular WSA branch was organized in the shape of a softball team and when the season finished, the branch was dissolved."[13] In Toronto, a Jewish Workers' Sports Club held competitions, but elsewhere gymnastics was practised for mass exercise and display. Summer and winter, groups would perform long sequences of carefully coordinated floor exercises, and a variety of tumbling and acrobatic stunts. The most frequently performed routine was the multi-person pyramid; the YCL encouraged it because it depicted the importance of working-class solidarity in the class struggle. During the 1930s, the Winnipeg WSA developed gymnastics to such a performance art that many of its members subsequently made careers for themselves as circus and night-club performers. The club held daily classes in gymnastics, strength fitness, boxing, and wrestling; [it also had] weekly dances and choral concerts. Almost every week, its top gym team travelled to small towns in Manitoba, northwestern Ontario and North Dakota staging displays. Twice a year, the club staged a choral and gymnastics festival in the Winnipeg Auditorium.[14]

From the outset, the YCL sought to create a national organization. In 1927, the first attempt to link up the various WSAs failed when no club outside Toronto was able to send a representative to the founding convention. But a second attempt, in 1928, was successful and the Workers' Sports Association of Canada was established. Twenty clubs joined directly and the Canadian Labour Party, the Finnish Workers' Sports Association of Canada, and the Ukrainian Labour Farmer Temple Association joined as affiliates.[15] (Most Ukrainian athletes, however, directly joined the WSAs).[16] In 1929, the national committee began to stage regional and national events.[17] That same year, it affiliated with the RSI. By 1932, the WSAC claimed a total membership of 4 000[18]; by 1933, 5 000.[19] Although turnover was high and the nature of activity varied considerably from club to club, the organization had a foothold in many communities, no mean accomplishment.

The best organized and most athletically gifted members were the radical Finns. The Finns have been deservedly well-known for their enthusiasm for vigorous physical activity and their competitive abilities. In the nineteenth century, despite their inclusion in the Russian Empire where little sport was practised, many Finns adopted the highly organized and sportsmanlike approach to game-contests that had spread from England to other parts of Scandinavia. From the very beginnings of international competition, they excelled. The enthusiasm for sport seems to have been shared by all classes and political perspectives. Workers' sports clubs were formed in Finland by the turn of the century and in 1919, despite the ravages and bitterness of civil war, a national Workers' Sports League was established. It affiliated to the LSI.[20] In North America, left-wing Finns formed sports clubs wherever they settled in numbers; by 1906, there were clubs in Toronto, Beaver Lake, Sudbury, Copper Cliff, Timmins, and Port Arthur.[21] When the Finns joined other organizations, such as the Industrial Workers of the World, they made sporting competitions a regular part of their social activity.[22] In 1924, the clubs in the Sudbury area formed a Central Ontario Gymnastics and Sports Federation and a year later, the northern and northwestern Ontario clubs joined to form the Finnish Workers' Sports Association of Canada. It was closely associated with, but never formally affiliated to, the Finnish Organization of Canada, which was in turn closely associated with the CPC. The first secretary was Hannes Sula, a former Finnish 100-metres champion and the editor of *Vapaus*, the FOC newspaper.[23]

The favoured Finnish activities were track and field, Greco-Roman wrestling, and nordic skiing. No matter where they lived, they usually managed to clear and level enough land for a 300- or 400-metre track, with room for throwing a javelin. They preferred Greco-Roman wrestling (restricted to upper-body holds) because it produced such spectacular throws and falls. In the winter, they practised skiing at night with the aid of miners' lamps and raced on weekends for sweaters and socks — "not that useless bourgeois stuff [medals and cups]." They did not compete in gymnastics, but each year the national executive would determine a new set of routines to be practised by individual clubs and performed *en masse* (with barely a day's practice) at the summer festival. Unlike other WSA groups, the Finns frequently travelled long distances to engage in competition — in rented open trucks or by riding the rails (what *The Worker* described as "the side-door Pullman"). One annual trek is noteworthy. During the 1930s, the clubs around Sudbury and Timmins would each stage a ski race. One week, the men from Sudbury would ski to Timmins, a distance of almost 240 kilometres, stopping at lumber camps along the way; then race and return. Two weeks later, the Timmins men would do the same in the opposite direction. (By comparison, the most celebrated ski marathon in Canada today is from Lachine to Ottawa — a mere 160 kilometres.) The Finns provided WSA with about half of its members, its most experienced organizers, and some excellent facilities. In Toronto, for example, track and field events were always held at the Finnish grounds, either in the Don Valley or at Camp Tarmola, near Woodbridge. In 1932, the Finnish clubs agreed to disband the FWSAC and join as full members.[24] Their presence was always an asset to the organization.

In addition to their athletics, the WSAs supported a number of political campaigns. In 1928, as part of the RSI attempt to discredit "bourgeois sport," the Jewish WSA in Toronto demonstrated against a gymnastics competition at the Canadian National Exhibition because it was conducted under the auspices of the Amateur Athletic Union of Canada.[25] In the years of the IOC's Olympic Games, the WSAs staged counter-Olympic campaigns. In the years of the RSI's Spartakiads, the WSAs attempted to publicize the benefits of these alternative games. WSAs also linked their activity to national and local YCL campaigns. In 1931, for example, the Vancouver WSA took advantage of the drawing power of its baseball league to solicit signatures and contributions in support of the national CPC leaders facing trial in Toronto.[26] In 1932, during a wrestling tournament, it persuaded YMCA members to join it on a march in support of the unemployed.[27] WSA gymnasts frequently performed at rallies and fund raisers. But each of these undertakings was initiated outside the WSAs, either by the YCL or the national WSA office. WSA activities were periodically associated with political struggle, but the focus was unquestioningly on sport.[28]

The YCL never understood the WSAs' reluctance to initiate political activity. Year after year, it berated the WSAs for their "failure to win the majority of the working-class youth over from the influence and leadership of the bourgeoisie" and for pursuing "sport for sport's sake."[29] At the same time, WSAs felt the YCL and the national WSA office were out of touch with their basic sporting needs. Since this basic difference underlay all the difficulties of the WSA, it will be instructive to examine it in detail.

The YCL's approach to sport was fundamentally instrumental. Its resolutions and pronouncements were prompted by the party's analysis of the prospects for revolutionary change. Sport, the communists believed, developed in step with the very conditions of industrial capitalism which gave birth to the proletariat, the revolutionary subject of Marxist-Leninist theory. In its first articles on sport, in which it sought to justify intervention in an activity hitherto scorned as "non-political," the YCL gave primary importance to the connection between sport and industrial capitalism:

> Hundreds of years ago there was no real sports movement in existence, i.e., a movement comprising large numbers of workers. There were merely various clubs of a medieval character, and no large movement as of today.
>
> The development of the proletarian sports movement is connected with the development of industry and its concentration in the large towns.
>
> In Great Britain, which has an old industry, a sports movement developed long ago in the large towns.
>
> America, with its gigantic industry, has possessed an especially large sports movement for a considerable time, corresponding to its industry....
>
> In France, where before the war the petite bourgeoisie dominated, the beginnings of a sports movement developed only towards the end of the last century. The weakness of the movement was evident at international competitions. Belgium, a small country with proletarians, has a huge sports movement.
>
> The end of the war proved quite evidently that the development of sport depends on the development of industry. (The proportion between the two is not always mathematically exact, as there are various factors affecting its development.) In France, where industry took a great step forward during the war, the sports movement increased to a very great extent.

The fact that large masses of peasants have no interest in sport — a result of the nature of their work — also confirms the assertion that industry is the main factor in the development of the sport movement in the capitalist countries.[30]

The YCL believed that workers and their families took part in sport because they had a "natural" desire to do so:

All young workers are naturally inclined to physical recreation. This is the key to the whole matter....Young workers need sports as a recreational factor, as well as to develop their bodies for efficient service in the class struggle. It is only weaklings and morons who decry sports.[31]

Because the natural impulse to physical activity is frustrated by the conditions of modern industry, workers are virtually driven to join sports clubs:

The working conditions of the individual young worker are often very bad. During the week he is bowed over his work or at the machine; his young body is limp and every movement causes him pain; he lives in the unwholesome atmosphere of the workshop; his youth is not yet used to difficult and heavy work, and feels the need for exercise and recovery.

After his working hours, he has to return to the hovel in the overcrowded tenement houses of the proletarian quarter. All these young workers need space, fresh air and exercise. In spite of the systematic misuse of sport in the various sports clubs, the young worker is nevertheless given the opportunity to pass away his leisure time with his comrades; his physical needs induce him to do so. The young worker goes to the sports club to escape from the workshop, to forget it. The Communist Youth can by no means remain indifferent towards this movement.

Two things must be remembered.

Sports result from the physical need of the young worker.

Sports movements, which for a great part are made up of proletarians, grew with the development of industry.

These two facts are significant enough to induce all YCLers to pay greater attention to sports![32]

This syllogism became the basis for all YCL work in sport. Because it never questioned the extent of working-class participation in sport, it was rarely led to examine the conditions underlying participation in Canada, such as the cost of admission to facilities or club membership, equipment, instruction, and travel. In its analysis of other spheres of workers' lives, the YCL was quick to point out the disadvantages faced by the working class — the lack of adequate education and vocational training, the high cost of medical and dental care, low wages and the lack of unemployment insurance, the law prohibiting abortion, as well as exhausting working conditions[33] — but not in sport. Instead it assumed widespread working-class participation and continued to do so, even when, after 1933, it began to campaign sporadically against obvious barriers to participation, such as the fees charged for municipal swimming pools.[34] On this assumption, it defined the primary task as winning back workers' allegiances from the "bosses" or "bourgeois sports organizations." In 1925, the YCL's newspaper, *The Young Worker*, told its readers:

> Sports activity is a means of getting contact with the bourgeois-minded youth. The bourgeoisie has diverted the attention of the toiling youth from his real problems by concentrating his attention upon sports. In one sense this creates difficulty in getting his ear for our propaganda; in another sense it gives us a very fertile ground. After we have organized our sport, selected good baseball teams, etc., we must get contact with the youth of the bourgeois sports organizations by endeavouring to affiliate with them.[35]

A month later in convention, the YCL resolved, "Sports is the stronghold of the bourgeoisie so far as the youth is concerned and our sport must have no other object than the attacking of that stronghold and the capture of it, if possible."[36] Six years later, WSA national secretary Dave Kashtan was still voicing the same line:

> There are thousands of young and adult workers who belong to factory teams in some of the most important industries, where the Party has as yet no contacts whatsoever. These teams are used by the employers as a weapon of keeping down the militancy of the workers and the development of factory workers' sports would assist the Party greatly in coming in contact with them....[37]

Initially, the YCL sought to break bourgeois ideological hegemony in sport by demonstrating that sport was not "neutral," but served to strengthen the ruling class:

To many workers, sports are still neutral, in other words they claim that sports have nothing to do with the class struggle, merely being a very beneficial method of bettering one's physical self, building up a fine body, developing the spirit of fair play and so on ad infinitum. This is certainly false....

The bosses today use sports as a means of drawing the workers away from the class struggle, they use it as a means of drawing the workers into the cadets, preparing them for future wars,...to combat the radicalism of the workers, for increasing productivity by building up stronger bodies, and so on.[38]

The YCL illustrated its attack on "bourgeois" or "bosses" sport by showing the class bias of sports reporting in the daily press,[39] and by attacking the organizations it regarded as competitors: the YMCA and YMHA, the Boy Scouts, the cadet training programs in the high schools, and the AAUC, which at the time was the overall governing body for Olympic sports. The YMCA was repeatedly "exposed" for its "despicable role in suppressing workers in India, China, Korea, etc.,"[40] and in North America, for strike-breaking and masking the fundamental antagonisms of class relations.[41] The Boy Scouts, frequently described as "future White Guards," were [scorned] for their militaristic exercises and their loyalty to British imperialism.[42]

The alternative to "bourgeois sports," the YCL believed, was a militantly partisan working-class movement which would play a leading role in union-organizing, strikes and other mass struggles. All recreational activity, it argued, should advance the class struggle. Games, picnics, and children's camps were to be organized around collective tasks, and the songs and legends of communism. Members were never allowed to forget that these activities had an ultimate, external purpose. "These recreations are serious work," N. Gollam wrote in *The Worker*,

even if the work is done in an atmosphere of laughter and frolic, for social activities tie those who belong to the League in that closer comradeship that comes from common understanding. They keep the youth in contact with the work that is being done for the union of all militant youth into one organization for the great task that lies before the workers of the world.[43]

The best example of socialist sport was provided by the Soviet Union, and readers of *The Worker* and *The Young Worker* were regularly informed about the proletarian sacrifice and class solidarity of athletes in that country. Soviet athletes "vied with each other in raising production."[44] In 1930, a relay of cross-country skiers assisted the Red Army in its offensive against "Chinese Bandits" along the Manchurian border, by delivering messages about the fighting:

> This was no mere "endurance test" as we see in capitalist sports. This was no crazed effort to break a "record." The Soviet sportsmen have given the lie to the empty slogan of "Sports for Sport's Sake"! In all their campaigns, they have taken their full share as the physically most perfect specimens of the Russian working class in the construction of socialism. The working sportsmen of Canada must take their full share also in the struggles of the Canadian working class.[45]

It was the Soviet example which YCL leaders had in mind when they invited WSA athletes to perform at rallies and demonstrations. They enjoyed the gymnastics, but they most appreciated the disciplined display of physical power: they believed it deterred police and fascist disruptions.[46]

In the push for new clubs, Marxist-Leninist analysis plus the Soviet example led the YCL to stress the primacy of "factory leagues." If the revolution was to be made by the industrial working class, it was essential that industrial workers join the WSAs. The YCL tried to discredit company-sponsored picnics and leagues,[47] [to] affiliate [with] existing teams, and [to] recruit new ones. When the Workers' Unity League was founded in 1929, it sought the WSA's assistance, and encouraged its own organizers to develop sport as a means of gaining access to unorganized workers.[48]

No wonder the YCL regarded the WSA as a failure. Despite its slowly growing membership, the WSAs made little impact upon the factories, even less upon the "bourgeois sports organizations." The WSAs are "completely isolated from the general sports activities of the working class youth," Dave Kashtan wrote in a pre-convention article in 1931. "The issue of workers' sports vs. bosses' sports has not been brought out clearly to expose the bourgeois sports organizations....[Many clubs] bear the character of ordinary sports clubs while carrying the name of the WSA."[49] It was a frequently voiced lament.

Not surprisingly, these criticisms did not sit well — to the extent they were understood at all — [with] the members of the local WSAs. They were proud of what they had achieved and resented suggestions they had failed. Few of them shared the YCL's revolutionary aspirations. They were sympathetic to left-wing causes, but their chief motivation in joining the WSA was to participate in physical activity. They were not prepared to drop what they were doing for the unlikely projects the YCL wanted — trying to win members away from the YMCA, or leafletting plant gates in an attempt to establish factory leagues.

If there was no sympathetic "mass organization" in the area, they had to find a facility. In Drumheller, the WSA went inactive the whole winter of 1927–28 when local businessmen refused to rent it enough space.[50] Another shortage was skilled leaders. Clubs lost members to the YMCA because it could offer better coaching.[51] Other needs were equipment, rulebooks, and funds for uniforms and travel. Even in the strongest clubs, the membership constantly turned over, as athletes and instructors moved to find work, or lost interest. In this situation, the YCL polemics were a constant irritant. "We must maintain a proper balance between propaganda and serious athletics," the Alberta secretary wrote *The Young Worker*. "A successful team should give us all the propaganda we care for."[52] On the few occasions it chose to acknowledge these criticisms, the national WSA committee responded by urging more YCLers to engage in sport work.[53] But these pronouncements came to naught.

To be sure, the YCL had other responsibilities and its leaders were frequently in jail.[54] But even if the YCL leaders had had the time, there is little indication they would have addressed the practical needs of the WSAs. The annual resolutions of the YCL and the WSAC stressed the importance of political work. No systematic effort was ever made to pool the talents and experience of the different clubs to strengthen the WSAC *as a sport movement*.

In 1934, after the repression of communist and socialist parties and trade unions in Germany and the spread of fascism in France, the Comintern abruptly changed its strategic line and ordered a new defensive alliance with socialist and liberal-democratic parties, an alliance "united from above" or a "popular front." In sport, the RSI stopped its polemics against the LSI, now the Socialist Workers' Sport International, and sought a joint campaign against the 1936 Olympics in Germany. In France and Norway, workers' sports federations were reunited.[55] In Canada, the WSAC quickly buried the hatchet in its relations with the YMCA and the AAU.

At first the "united front" promised new gains. The WSA announced that it would send a team of 40 Canadian athletes and coaches for competitions and a tour of sports schools, health clinics, factory fitness programs and Young Pioneer summer camps in the Soviet Union. The tour would serve as an advertisement for new members. David Ess of the Montreal WSA wrote in *The Young Worker*:

It would be wrong to take the pathway of least resistance and select members of our own clubs exclusively or merely to extend our invitation to those sympathetic. It should be borne in mind that our delegates will stack up against the renowned Soviet athletes and must therefore be of as high a calibre as possible. We must arouse the interest of bourgeois sports writers and thus secure wide publicity on the sports pages. We must strive for the selection of athletes from the YMCA, the YMHA, high schools, universities and many other independent sports clubs. It may even be possible to get former Olympic contenders to make the trip and compare the true international spirit of the Spartakiad with the chauvinist atmosphere of the bourgeois Olympics.

A firm basis for united front activities can be laid by a careful and correct approach to the young workers who are members of bourgeois sports clubs. Speakers should be sent to address those clubs, and enlist their support for the campaign. Care should be taken to see that our speakers and our printed matter use a type of language that all young workers will understand; our sectarianism can be laid to a great extent to this weakness.

Private negotiations with club executives or athletes should be avoided; our aim is to interest the broad membership in this campaign and have them participate in the selection of delegates, thus ensuring a basis for a series of rallies to greet the delegates on their return and hear their impressions.

A trip to the Soviet Union is something most athletes will strive for. Let us take advantage of the situation and utilize it.[56]

The lure of a free trip to Russia did in fact intrigue athletes and reporters. Despite, or perhaps because of a last-minute decision by the AAU to forbid its athletes to go, the tour generated more publicity in the daily press than the WSA had ever received before. Its campaign against the Berlin Olympics, and its decision to send five non-WSA athletes to the counter-Olympic "People's Games" in Barcelona in the summer of 1936, gave it even more visibility. But in the attempt to prove popular, the YCL and the WSAC gradually abandoned [their] radical programs. At the annual meeting in 1935, the WSA national executive changed its name to the "Canadian Amateur Sports Federation" and encouraged its members to become "Universal Athletic

Clubs."[57] The Winnipeg UAC subsequently described itself as "a non-political independent sports club. Its purpose is to provide physical training and recreation to all young people irrespective of their nationality or beliefs."[58] Newspaper sports columnists switched from Leninist bombast to the sycophancy of the commercial press. *The Young Worker* started a women's fashion page, "Frill and Fancies of the feminine world," and the *Daily Clarion*, which replaced *The Worker*, published uncritical accounts of professional wrestling, Canadian Rugby Union football, and National Hockey League and intercollegiate hockey and began to handicap the horse races.[59] By 1940, when they were shut down by the RCMP because of their ties to the CPC,[60] the Universal Athletic Clubs had abandoned even the ambition of being a revolutionary mass organization.

As a political movement, the Workers' Sports Association clearly failed. Its smartly uniformed athletes may have discouraged Canadian fascists from attacking communist rallies in Montreal, Toronto and Winnipeg, but they did not protect CPC leaders from the police. Although the WSAs supported a number of political campaigns initiated by the RSI and the CPC, they never became a path of recruitment into the party for the unorganized workers and athletes in other organizations they were supposed to approach. Some workers who joined through the Workers' Unity League knew of the existence of the WSAs. So did the AAU athletes and officials who were attracted to their campaign against the 1936 Olympic Games. But for the most part, as *The Young Worker* frequently lamented, "the WSA was too isolated from the masses of the working youth." The reasons for its political failure were complex and include the lack of skilled leadership, the disruptive economic conditions of the period, and police repression. But most significant was the YCL's failure to understand the nature of athletic participation in Canada, an insensitivity best illustrated by the polemic against "sport for sport's sake." For this reason, the WSAs never fully embraced the political ambitions the YCL held for them. Neither leaders nor locals managed to achieve the "balance between propaganda and athletics."

But the WSA was not without accomplishment, even if it did not meet the YCL's goals. It did provide recreation opportunities for a sizable number of people. Participants now fondly remember personal challenge and social interaction, qualities most seek in a recreation program. Although the national events were infrequent and poorly organized, many clubs functioned smoothly and provided a quality of program comparable to other agencies of the day. In the absence of definitive studies of the alternatives — the sports governing bodies, the schools, the youth agencies — it is difficult to judge whether the WSAs provided opportunities would not have otherwise been available. In the case of cross-country skiing and gymnastics, it is likely that they significantly added to what was available.

Nor does the WSA lack historical interest. Historians have become accustomed to noting the ideological nature of social movements such as the YMCA and cultural activities like sport. During the nineteenth century, it is generally believed that most sports in the English-speaking world were organized on strict class lines. Bryan Palmer, in his study of the working class of Hamilton, has argued that "sport could illuminate class inequalities and generate fierce opposition to the fundamental wrongs of the social order."[61] Alan Metcalfe has shown, for Montreal, that sport was almost an exclusive middle-class preserve.[62]

But by the early twentieth century, a profound shift seems to have taken place. As Richard Gruneau, Morris Mott, and others have argued, business, military, church and educational leaders sought to extend sporting opportunities to workers and immigrants as a "solution to the urban crisis" and for other hegemonic ends.[63]

The nature of this transformation — the change in purpose, the means of implementation and the response or resistance the integrative project in sport encountered — has yet to be examined in detail. As studies of other social movements, as well as sport, have shown, at the very least we can expect some regional differences. Although it has been beyond the scope of this paper, the workers' sports movement in Canada provides one measure of the integrative project, from the perspectives of class and ethnicity. Was the YCL's critique of bourgeois domination in sport simply the cut-and-paste reiteration of the RSI's analysis, developed in Europe, or did it reflect despite the Comintern's language, the vestiges of the earlier, indigenous class-conscious perspective in sport? Were there other exponents of this perspective during the interwar years? If the YCL had not been so sectarian, would the WSA have found a more sympathetic audience? What were the attitudes of the workers and immigrants who played for company teams towards their activity? What other immigrant groups struggled to develop their own sports and organizations as an alternative to "Canadian" ones? To the extent that the WSA sought to build an alternative movement, it has pointed the way to the examination of these questions.

Notes

1. *Toronto Daily Star* (hereinafter *TDS*), Nov. 26, 1934; *The Worker*, Nov. 28, 1934; Tim Buck, *Yours in the Struggle* (Toronto: NC Press, 1977), 242–46.

2. *TDS*, Dec. 3, 1934; *Worker*, Dec. 5, 1934. Several photographs of the WSA procession were printed in *Worker*, Dec. 8, 1934.

3. For example, Ivan Avakumovic, *The Communist Party of Canada* (Toronto: McClelland and Stewart, 1965) and William Rodney, *Soldiers of the International: A History of the Communist Party of Canada 1919–1929* mention the WSA but once, and Norman Penner, *The Canadian Left* (Scarborough: Prentice-Hall, 1977) – despite his own membership in the Universal Athletic Club of Winnipeg – Colin D. Grimson, "The Communist Party of Canada, 1922–46" (unpublished M.A. thesis, McGill University, 1966), and Melvyn Pelt, "The Communist Party of Canada" (unpublished M.A. thesis, University of Toronto, 1964), not at all.

4. For example, in 1937, Ontario Premier Mitch Hepburn "encouraged (Lionel) Conacher to use his public appeal to secure the Liberal nomination for the Bracondale riding." Frank Cosentino and Don Morrow, *Lionel Conacher* (Toronto: Fitzhenry and Whiteside, 1981), 52. During the same period, the Ontario CCF sponsored teams, and supported the WSA's opposition to the 1936 Olympic Games. Neither of these parties developed their own sports program.

5. Comité Sportif International du Travail, *50 ans de sport ouvrier international* (Brussels, 1963); Robert F. Wheeler, "Organized Sport and Organized Labour: The Workers' Sports Movement," *Journal of Contemporary History* 13 (1978): 252–65. For an example of the program of one socialist federation see Pierre Marie, *Pour le sport ouvrier* (Paris: Librairie Populaire, 1934). For the Olympic Games, see Erich Kamper, *Encyclopedia of the Olympic Games* (Toronto: McGraw-Hill, 1972).

6. David S. Steinberg, "Sport Under Two Flags: The Relations Between the Red Sport International and the Socialist Workers' Sport International, 1920-1939" (unpublished Ph.D. dissertation, University of Wisconsin, 1979), 44.

7. James Riordan, *Sport in Soviet Society* (Cambridge: Cambridge University Press, 1977), 82–152.

8. Steinberg, "Sport Under Two Flags," 234–70; Bruce Kidd, "The Popular Front and the 1936 Olympics," *Canadian Journal of the History of Sport and Physical Education* 11, 1 (1980), 9–10, has argued that rank-and-file pressure for the "united front" preceded the change in Moscow.

9. *The Young Worker* (hereinafter *YW*), Oct. 1924.

10. *YW*, Feb. 28, 1925.

11. Avakumovic, *Communist Party*, 34.

12. Interview with Dave Kashtan, Oct. 6, 1981.

13. *YW*, Dec. 1927.

14. Interview with Fred Kazor, June 27, 1977 (Kazor dropped the "c" from his surname during World War II); interview with Andrew Bileski and Walter Kaczor, Nov. 3, 1977; Walter Kaczor documents.

15. *YW*, May 1928.

16. In 1924, the YCL had instructed its member leagues to build sports clubs separate from the other mass organizations lest enlarged cultural organizations weaken political and trade union activity. (See Steinberg, "Sport Under Two Flags," 37). In this the Canadian league complied (*YW*, Oct. 1924). Although most WSAs used the facilities of cultural organizations like the ULFTA, they kept a distinct identity.

17. *Worker*, Feb. 2, 1929.

18. Ibid., Oct. 1, 1932.

19. *YW*, July 19, 1933. This figure was the largest claimed by the WSCA; one year later (*Worker*, Nov. 21, 1934) its membership target was 5 000, so we can assume some departures in the interval.

20. Steinberg, "Sport Under Two Flags," 159–61; "Finland and Olympism," *Olympic Review* 103–104 (1976): 252–72; and Finnish Society for Research in Sports

and Physical Education, *Physical Education and Sports in Finland* (Helsinki: Werner Soderstrom, 1979), 9–11.

21. Finnish-Canadian Amateur Sports Federation (hereinafter FCASF), *Canadan Suomalaisten Urheilukiraa* (Sudbury: Vapasus, 1965), 3.

22. Multicultural History of Society of Ontario Archives, Finnish collection, 7387-5.

23. FCASF, 4–8; Edward W. Laine, "Finnish Canadian Radicalism and Canadian Politics: The First Forty Years, 1900–1940" in *Ethnicity, Power and Politics in Canada*, ed. Jorgen Dahlie and Tissa Fernando (Toronto: Methuen, 1981), 96–102.

24. But in 1935, the Finns re-established their own organization; see Bruce Kidd, "The Workers' Sports Movement in Canada: The Radical Immigrants' Alternative" (paper presented to the 9th biennial conference of the Canadian Ethnic Studies Association, Edmonton, Oct. 14–16, 1981).

25. *YW*, Sept.–Oct. 1928.

26. *Worker*, July 4, 1931.

27. *YW*, March 8, 1932.

28. Bruce Kidd, "Canadian Opposition to the 1936 Olympics in Germany," *Canadian Journal of History of Sport and Physical Education* 9, 2 (1978): 20–40.

29. See, for example, *Worker*, July 4, 1931.

30. *Worker*, Nov. 1, 1922.

31. *YW*, May 1926.

32. *Worker*, Nov. 1, 1922.

33. For example, "Political resolution of the National Executive Committee," *YW*, Jan. 1929.

34. *YW*, Nov. 1, 1933.

35. *YW*, June 1925.

36. *YW*, July 1925.

37. *The Party Organizer*, May 1931, 24–25.

38. *YW*, Nov. 1929.

39. For example, *YW*, June 1926, Feb. 1927.

40. *YW*, June 15, 1931.

41. For example, *Worker*, Jan. 12, 1924 and Feb. 23, 1924.

42. For example, *Worker*, May 24, 1924. Scholars have taken a similar view of the Scouts. See, for example, John Springhall, *Youth, Empire and Society* (London: Croom Helm, 1977).

43. *Worker*, Aug. 29, 1923.

44. *Worker*, Oct. 28, 1928.

45. *YW*, June 1930.

46. Interview with Andrew Bileski and Walter Kaczor; interview with Dave Kashtan.

47. For example, *YW*, July–Aug. 1928. The development of company recreation as a means of retaining skilled workers and improving industrial relations seems to have started in the last decade of the nineteenth century; see John R. Schleppi, "'It Pays': John H. Patterson and Industrial Recreation at the National Cash Register Company," *Journal of Sport History* 6, 3 (1979): 20–28.

48. *Worker*, March 28, 1931.

49. *YW*, June 15, 1931.

50. *YW*, Feb. 1928.

51. *YW*, Nov. 1, 1933.

52. *YW*, Oct. 1926. Also interviews with Kazor, Kaczor, and Em. Orlick, Nov. 11, 1979.

53. For example, *YW*, June 15, 1931.

54. For example, Dave Kashtan spent almost half of his two-year stint as national WSA secretary in jail facing charges under the notorious section 98 of the Criminal Code.

55. Steinberg, "Sport Under Two Flags," 234–47.

56. *YW*, Jan. 5, 1935.

57. *YW*, Aug. 31, 1935.

58. Canadian Ukrainian Youth Federation and the Universal Athletic Club, Souvenir Program, Youth Pageant, Dec. 8, 1938.

59. See defence of the new policy in *The Clarion*, July 4, 1936.

60. The details of the seizure and the subsequent defence campaign are discussed by John Kolasky, *The Shattered Illusion* (Toronto: Peter Martin, 1979), 58.

61. Bryan Palmer, *A Culture in Conflict* (Montreal: McGill-Queen's University Press, 1979), 58.

62. Alan Metcalfe, "Organized Sport and Social Stratification in Montreal, 1840–1901" in *Canadian Sport: Sociological Perspectives*, ed. R.S. Gruneau and John Albinson (Don Mills: Addison-Wesley, 1976).

63. Richard Gruneau, "Power and Play in Canadian Society," in *Power and Change in Canada*, ed. R.G. Ossenberg (Toronto: McClelland and Stewart, 1979); Morris Mott, "One Solution to the Urban Crisis: Manly Sports in Winnipeg, 1900–1914" (paper presented to the Canadian Historical Association, Halifax, June 4, 1981); Carl Berger, *The Sense of Power* (Toronto: University of Toronto Press, 1970), 254–57.

THE CONUNDRUM OF CULTURE: SPORT*

JOHN HERD THOMPSON WITH ALLEN SEAGER

Sport illustrates the Canadian cultural conundrum of the interwar period. American peaceful penetration of Canada seemed to be proceeding at an unprecedented rate, as Canadian children "bowed down to Babe Ruth" and professional hockey became continentalized; yet another set of examples could be used to portray the period as the cradle of Canadian cultural consciousness....

America's sports heroes became Canada's also. America's national sport became the Canadian summer game at the same time. As S.F. Wise and Douglas Fisher note bitterly, "mesmerized by baseball's big league glamour, and spoon-fed by the American wire services, sports editors and reporters gave major coverage to baseball at the expense of lacrosse," with the result that both professional and senior amateur lacrosse became extinct in the interwar years. For the participant the basic skills of baseball — or softball, its simpler version — were easier to master than those of lacrosse. It was as a spectator sport, however, that baseball was enjoyed by most Canadians.[1]

Every Canadian community had an amateur baseball team, and many cities and larger towns had franchises in minor professional leagues. "Organized baseball has been a good thing for the towns that have participated," wrote "Knotty" Lee, manager of the Brantford Red Sox of the Michigan–Ontario League. "Baseball, in fact, is one cure for Bolshevism." Baseball was also bicultural. "Your French Canadian citizen likes his *base pelotte*," concluded a Montreal journalist who reported in 1928 that "three or four thousand folks have howled themselves hoarse as a matter of habit every Sunday" at minor league ball games. Larger crowds followed the fortunes of the Montreal Royals and Toronto Maple Leafs, who played in the International League, one

---

* John Herd Thompson with Allen Seager, *Canada 1922–1939: Decades of Discord* (Toronto: McClelland and Stewart, 1985), 186–90.

step below the majors. Toronto's 1926 victory over Louisville in the Little World Series occasioned an outpouring of local and nation al pride, pride accented because one Maple Leaf outfielder, Lionel Conacher, was actually a Canadian.[2]

Yet every Canadian ball fan's deepest love was reserved for the team that he cheered for in the American or National League. Major league baseball recovered quickly from the scandal of the "fixed" World Series in 1919, helped by a livelier ball that increased hitting and by the spectator appeal of homerun champion Babe Ruth and the less charismatic sluggers who imitated him. By the mid-twenties baseball's World Series had become Canada's greatest "national" sporting event, with crowds packed in front of newspaper offices to watch the games charted out on a scale-model diamond, while an announcer with a megaphone recreated the action from a running description provided by the wire services. Before the Cardinal–Yankee series of 1926, the Calgary *Herald* devoted ten column inches of its editorial page to an analysis of "this greatest of all features in the season's baseball program"; an adjacent editorial on the appointment of Lord Willingdon as Canada's new governor general received exactly one inch.[3]

Unlike baseball, Canada's favourite winter sport was more distinctively her own. The annual series of games for the Stanley Cup, symbolic of the championship of Canadian hockey, was the only sporting event that approached baseball's World Series in the excitement it generated among fans. After 1921 the cup was competed for by teams from three Canadian professional leagues: the Pacific Coast Hockey Association, the Western Canada Hockey League, and the National Hockey League. Although the exact format of the playoff varied from year to year, the matching of teams from Central Canada against teams from Prairie and British Columbia cities made Stanley Cup finals a socially acceptable athletic means of releasing regional hostility. In 1923 the NHL Ottawa Senators travelled to Vancouver to eliminate the PCHA Millionaires before defeating the WCHL Edmonton Eskimoes as the last stage of their conquest of the cup. A year later the Vancouver team and the Calgary Tigers journeyed east to take on the Montreal Canadiens. Arthur Meighen dropped the puck in a ceremonial face-off before the decisive game in which rookie Howie Morenz led the Canadiens to the championship with a 3–0 victory over the Tigers.[4]

Wounded Western pride took some comfort in the merger of the PCHA and WCHL to form a single Western Hockey League for the 1924–25 season. The new "major loop," predicted a prairie sportswriter, would "overshadow the present NHL" and become "the predominant hockey league in the world." When Lester Patrick's Vic-

predominant hockey league in the world." When Lester Patrick's Victoria Cougars easily defeated the Canadiens to bring the Stanley Cup to the West, Western editorialists crowed their satisfaction. The days when "the effete East looked down upon the plainsman and the far westerner" seemed to be over, and "the Easterners are learning how hockey should be played from Western teams." But Western arrogance was to melt faster than the natural ice did in most WHL arenas in an unseasonable thaw. The Montreal Maroons took Lord Stanley's silverware back to Central Canada in 1926, and it was not to return for fifty-eight years.[5]

Canadian hockey was revolutionized by American money. In 1924 Boston millionaire Charles Adams was awarded the NHL's first American franchise. Dressed in the brown and gold colours of Adams's grocery chain, the Bruins won only six of thirty games on the ice but were champions at the box office. Before the next season began, bootlegging baron William V. "Big Bill" Dwyer had bought the Hamilton Tigers and moved them into the new Madison Square Garden as the New York Americans. Dwyer's publicity ignored hockey's grace, speed, and finesse to emphasize its violence. The game was played, wrote Paul Gallico in the *Daily News*, by "men with clubs in their hands and knives lashed to their feet"; it was "almost a certainty that someone will be hurt and fleck the ice with a generous contribution of gore." Despite a poor record the Americans attracted 195 579 paying customers to their seventeen home games. In its first season, reported the Edmonton *Journal*, "New York pro hockey outdrew the combined attendance of any four cities of the Western Hockey League." It was painfully obvious that the Regina Capitals or the Saskatoon Sheiks would find the new hockey era too rich for their blood.[6]

Wealthy Americans lined up for a chance at the publicity, prestige, and profit of owning a hockey team. "Will U.S. cash cripple hockey?" asked a Toronto sportswriter. "How long will Canada be able to hold its teams? Our neighbours to the South possess more of that useful commodity, variously known as 'jack' or 'dough' or 'mazuma' than we do [and] the longest purse is bound to win....Star puck chasers will gravitate to the place where they can fatten their exchequers." When the NHL awarded franchises to Chicago financier Frederick McLaughlin, New York coffee tycoon John S. Hammond, and a Detroit syndicate that included a Ford and a Kresge among its members, the less affluent Canadian entrepreneurs who owned the six teams of the Western Hockey League came to the same conclusion. They empowered Frank and Lester Patrick, operators of the Vancouver Millionaires and the Victoria Cougars, to peddle the WHL's most valuable athletic chattels to the NHL before such stars as Eddie Shore, Dick Irvin, and Frank Fredrickson could "jump" of their own accord.

The WHL owners divided the $258 000 the Patricks received from the NHL for their players and quietly hung up their skates. In 1927 the Stanley Cup became the permanent possession of the NHL and so it has remained; first-class professional hockey was not to venture west again for half a century.[7]

When the "National" Hockey League opened its 1926–27 season, Canada's game had been transformed into a continental commercial spectacle. "Hockey," wrote F.B. Edwards in *Maclean's*,

> which began its career as a rough and ready game played by small boys on home-made skating rinks...and grew up to be Canada's national pastime, is Big Business now....Plain, ordinary hockey became Organized Hockey, an air-tight, leakproof, copper rivetted, asbestos packed machine which now controls the professional skate and stick pastime....Millionaires back the organization, fine ladies applaud the efforts of the skating roughnecks with polite patting of gloved palms, ticket speculators buy out the seating accommodations for crucial games and Wall Street commission houses handle bets on the results. Hockey has put on a high hat.[8]

Only four of the ten teams — Montreal's Maroons and Canadiens, Toronto, and Ottawa — were based in Canada, and the NHL's "Canadian" division was brought up to full strength by adding the New York Americans! Ottawa, like the WHL cities, found itself unable to compete with the bankrolls of the new American clubs or to pay for magnificent artificial ice arenas like Montreal's new Forum. Despite laments that it was "a national calamity," Ottawa vanished from the NHL. Only the chutzpah of Conn Smythe saved the Toronto franchise from a similar fate. In 1927 when the St. Patricks were about to be sold to a Philadelphia group for $200 000, Smythe persuaded their owners to accept his smaller offer and kept the team in Canada as the Maple Leafs. Smythe's Leafs, the Maroons, and the Canadiens found it harder to keep the Stanley Cup in Canada. In 1928 the New York Rangers became the first of the American NHL teams to win the cup, and for the remainder of the interwar period the trophy Lord Stanley had donated to honour "the leading hockey club in Canada" spent most of its time in the United States.[9]

Did the continentalization of professional hockey provide further proof that Canada was being turned into a cultural as well as an economic colony of the United States? Virtually all the players of the NHL's American teams were Canadians, and it made little difference to the Canadian identity of a small boy in the Prairies or the Maritimes

Toronto. Canadians still played the best hockey in the world, as the University of Toronto Grads proved at the 1928 Olympics in St. Moritz, overwhelming their opponents by scores of 11–0, 13–0, and 14–0. Amateur hockey thrived in the cities the pros deserted, and local teams from all regions competed fiercely for the Memorial and Allan Cups emblematic of the junior and senior championships.

In many respects sport in Canada was a more effective national unifying influence during the 1920s than it had ever been. National championships were inaugurated in curling, skiing, golf, badminton, and basketball. Canadian rugby football evolved under rules that were unique and distinct from those used in the American game. Canadians were also quick to boast of native sportspeople who won in international competition. Victory was particularly sweet when a Canadian underdog finished ahead of an American favourite, as when Toronto distance swimmer George Young won the Catalina Island race in 1927, or when John Myles of Sydney Mines showed his heels to America's finest distance runners in setting a new record in the Boston Marathon of 1926. The 1928 Olympic team became a similar object of national pride, and every fan knew that Vancouver sprinter Percy Williams, "the World's Fastest Human," had spurned American colleges to train in Canada for his double gold medal performance. Every fan also knew of basketball's Edmonton Grads, the team that won seventeen consecutive North American women's championships, all against the finest the United States could send on to the court, or of the Bluenose, the Nova Scotia schooner with a similar record of confounding her Yankee challengers for the International cup.[10]

Notes

1. S.F. Wise and Douglas Fisher, *Canada's Sporting Heroes: Their Lives and Times* (Don Mills, Ont., 1974), 28–32; R. Terry Furst, "Mass Media and the Transformation of Spectator Team Sports," *Canadian Journal of the History of Sport and Physical Education*, 3, 2 (1972): 27–41.

2. William Humber and Eves Raja, "The Baseball Tradition in Western Canada," *Baseball Research Journal* 2 (1982): 137–41; Nancy Howell and Maxwell L. Howell, *Sports and Games in Canadian Life, 1700 to the Present* (Toronto, 1969), 281–85; George W. Lee, "Baseball in Canada," *Maclean's Magazine* (hereinafter *MM*), May 1, 1920, 64; Leslie Roberts, "Base Pelotte Comes Back," *MM*, July 15, 1928, 16–17, 59; *Canadian Annual Review of Public Affairs* (hereinafter *CAR*), 1926–27, 653.

3. Alexander J. Young, "The Rejuvenation of Major League Baseball in the Twenties," *Canadian Journal of the History of Sport and Physical Education* 3, 1 (1972): 8–27; Calgary *Herald*, Oct. 1, 1926, Oct. 2, 1926.

4. Brian McFarlane, *50 Years of Hockey, 1917-1967: An Intimate History of the NHL* (Toronto, 1967), 30–35; Ronald S. Lappage, "Sport As an Expression of Western and

RECREATIONAL ACTIVITY AT THE HAMILTON VENETIAN CLUB*

ENRICO CUMBO

The Venetian Club is one of the largest and oldest of the Italian ethnic clubs in Hamilton. Although the presence of *alt'italiani* pre-dates the Second World War, the idea of a "Venetian" association was first conceived at a funeral held at St. Anthony's Church in 1946. Upon observing the number of Friulan and northeastern Italians congregated at the funeral, the pastor of the Italian parish approached a prominent member of the Friulan community with the suggestion that a north Italian organization be formed to unite the Friulan and Veneti *corregionali* in Hamilton.[1] Under the aegis of Guglielmo Baldassi and Enrico Travani, an informal, primarily Friulan-based association was formed, consisting initially of sixteen members. Thanks to an extensive membership drive, which was launched within a few weeks of the organization's establishment, some ninety new members were admitted and the club was formally incorporated in April 1947.[2]

The club's primary purpose, as outlined in its constitution, was "the sustenance of fraternal union among its members in order to preserve and to cultivate the language (*l'idioma*), tradition and customs of the Veneto regions and, as an auxiliary function, the provision of moral and material assistance to those of its members that are in need."[3] The cooperation and inter-regional "fraternity" implicit in the statement were apparent from the club's earliest years.

Since the club did not have permanent quarters, the newly formed executive authorized the formation of a building committee to locate and purchase a site for a club hall. In 1949 two adjacent buildings (previously a Jewish community centre) were acquired near the hub of the old Italian enclave in Hamilton's northwest end; the buildings were

* *Polyphony* 7, 1 (Spring/Summer 1985): 59–63.

purchased with the aid of interest-free loans contributed by club members.[4] Although preliminary work had already begun on the property, the rapid influx of Friulan and Trevisan immigrants throughout the 1950s necessitated the extensive renovation and expansion of the building. The degree of the members' commitment may be gauged by the quantity and quality of work done on the property by volunteers (many of the members were, in fact, skilled and semi-skilled workers employed in the local construction trades).[5] A dance hall was built on the second floor, and an extensive, multi-room basement was excavated to house the recreational facilities of the club.

The addition of a basement was particularly welcome in view of the paucity of recreational space. It consisted of a complex of three bocce lanes (the largest indoor bocce facilities in the city), a bar and a series of smaller rooms in which tables were set up for playing cards (*scopa, briscola, tre sette*). Except for special occasions – dances, banquets, the annual Mardi Gras festivities – the club was open to its members one day a week, initially on Saturdays and later on Friday evenings.

These weekly gatherings comprised the only social and recreational activities for many of the members. The exigencies of work and the alien and restrictive nature of the North American values, which informed Sunday laws and the prohibition of informal street congregation, enhanced the importance of the weekly meetings.[6] To a large extent, the club served the same purpose as the *osteria* (the local bar, tavern or cafe) in the old country. Here, young and old, pre- and post-World War Two immigrants, Friulan and Trevisan, congregated. The club served not only as a meeting-place for old friends, but also as the locus for forming new friendships among newly arrived *paesani*. Male sociability played an important part in the recreational activities of the club. In the accommodating atmosphere of the society, men could converse in their own language — variously, Italian, regional dialect, or Italiese — play familiar games, eat familiar foods and consume the drinks purchased by the losers in a friendly match. Recreational activity was conducted without concern for the judgments of non-Venetians or the propriety of formal occasions. As Richard Holt has observed, the sports club "not only offered men enjoyable forms of exertion and emulation through which they could define and develop the qualities of masculinity they admired, they also provided in the club bar a new forum where males could meet for comradeship, conversation and revelry amongst their own sex."[7]

The fellowship at these gatherings fostered not only club or group loyalty, but also a distinctive sense of ethnic solidarity, a trans-regional identity on the part of Friulans, Trevisans and Veneti, as "Venetians." While not unknown in the Old World, given the historical association of the northeastern Italian provinces, this sense of a distinctive "Venetian" identity was particularly acute in Hamilton because of the concentration of many other regional groups of immigrants from Italy in the city's north end. Taking pride in the history and accomplishments of their region, the Venetian Canadians saw themselves as the representative *alt'italiani* of Hamilton's Little Italy.[8]

Besides ethnic pride, the spirit of brotherhood and "mutual respect"[9] which was fostered by the club, provided immediate and very tangible benefits for its members. Club members exchanged information about job possibilities, the availability of work, or the working conditions at a particular work site. There were contractors, craftsmen, salesmen, small businessmen and workers with "connections" and actual or perceived influence at various job sites among them. As Orlando Fava commented, "we all try to help each other."[10]

Of course, as with any other group, cliques and alliances based partly on personal predilection and, to a lesser extent, on sub-regional affiliation, emerged within the club. The informal atmosphere of the gatherings, however, and the way the games were played, helped to alleviate internal divisions. In gathering bocce teams, for instance, a system of selection known as "throwing out fingers" was used, which ensured the aggregation of different players for each game.[11] On rare occasions teams were selected on the basis of sub-regional or town affiliation. Thus, for example, the Paduans played against the Vincenzini.[12] The criterion for association, however, was less the specific regional identity of an individual than his desire to play a match at a specific time, or his willingness to pay the required sum in a game of cards, *morra* or bocce.

Of the various games and sporting activities, bocce playing was especially popular.[13] A familiar and traditional sport, bocce is also inexpensive and not overly taxing; it is a group-oriented activity with stops and breaks allowing for drink and conversation.[14] The popularity of the sport in Hamilton pre-dates the formation of the club. In the 1920s and 1930s, with the first wave of immigrants already well established in their *colonie*, ad hoc bocce lanes were set up in the immigrants' backyards. In the east end of the city, for instance, three bocce yards were installed within a block of each other.[15] Every weekend, friends and acquaintances would meet in these yards in defiance of Sunday laws and Prohibition restrictions to "catch up on the news" and to play bocce for money, beer, or wine. Bootleg liquor was openly sold on these premises, yet only on rare occasions were bocce yards raided by police.[16]

With the formation of the Venetian Club, bocce playing among members was centralized, but it was not restricted to the club. In the summer, the old bocce yards, picnic grounds and city parks were also utilized for play. Whether in the yards or in the club, the atmosphere of conviviality remained unchanged. Neither players nor spectators took the game entirely seriously. The rules were often modified and variations of the play were allowed in accordance with the levity of the occasion. As L. Wylie noted in his study of French *boule*, "the wit, the sarcasm, the insults, the oaths, the logic, the experimental demonstration, and the ability to dramatise a situation give the game its essential interest. Spectators will ignore a game played by men who are physically skilled but who are unable to dramatise their game, and they will gather round a game played by men who do not play well but who are witty, dramatic, shrewd in the ability to out-smart their opponents."[17]

The sport was played "to pass the time" in the "friendly *badinage* of male society."[18] Notwithstanding the informality of play, however, the popularity of these games resulted in the formation of intramural leagues for single and cross-gender competition in bocce, card games and, later, bowling (a game not unlike bocce). Although the competitions were sponsored by local businessmen associated with the club, such as Joe Castel of Primo Salami, or by larger firms, particularly the brewing companies whose sales representatives belonged to the club, the initiative came entirely from the membership. These companies provided trophies and occasionally prize money for the winners.

Sports activity in the club was not restricted to informal and intramural competition. In the late 1950s, a *bocce fila* was started, a quasi-professional association of bocce players affiliated with other Italian-Canadian bocce clubs across the province. The best bocce players in the Venetian Club advanced to represent the club in provincial and national tournaments. In recent years, the success of the club in this field has been so great that a club member is representing Canada in the global tournament. In this context, the game of bocce has, of late, taken on the character of a status sport.

In the last thirty years, the success of the *bocce fila*, the *alt'italianità* of the club and the popularity of its social and recreational activities have enhanced the club's status as one of the more distinctive of the city's social organizations. The club can also claim distinction in a more literal sense. While most of the other ethnic Italian clubs have had to include non-*paesani* in their membership lists (as a consequence of diminishing enrolment), the Venetian Club to this day admits only individuals who were themselves born, or whose parents were born in the "Tre Venete."

The strong sense of regional loyalty which is responsible for the club's vitality, is also apparent in the marriage patterns of immigrants from northeastern Italy. A great many Friulan, Veneti, and Trevisan immigrants, who arrived in Canada in the 1950s and 1960s, married fellow "Venetians" whom they met at the dances and other social activities sponsored by the club.[19]

The ethnic distinctiveness, uniqueness and insularity of the club, however, may be coming to an end. The diminished scale of Italian immigration, the movement of Italian Canadians to the suburbs, the recent formation of a Fame Furlane (Friulan society) in the outskirts of the city, the restricted space in the existing facilities and, predictably, the lack of interest on the part of young people will result inevitably in the gradual transformation of the club. The children of club members, many of whom speak only English, see the traditional recreational functions of the club — Italian card games, bocce, bowling — as outdated and alien. Opinions are legion regarding how best to involve the younger generation in the activities of the club. As yet, however, little has been accomplished in this regard.

If the distant future remains uncertain, the existence of the club in the next few years is very much assured. Every Friday some 200 men continue to gather in the halls and the basement of the complex to play bocce and card games, and to sustain and renew friendships as they have done for the last twenty or thirty years.

Notes

1. "Nascita e Sviluppo del Venetian Club," *Venetian Club of Hamilton, Thirtieth Anniversary, 1946–1976,* n.p.; interviews with Mr. A. Marchetti; Mr. A. Masotti; Mr. O. Fava.

2. "Nascita e Sviluppo del Venetian Club."

3. "Statuto della Societa Veneta," Venetian Club, Hamilton, Ontario, 3, Article I of the constitution reads as follows: "Lo scopo primario della Societa sta nel mantenere l'unione fra in Soci che la compongono, in ordine di preservare e coltivare l'idioma, le tradizioni ed usanze venete ed, in via accessoria, alla mutua assistenza morale e materiale fra i suoi membri."

4. "Nascita e Sviluppo del Venetian Club"; interview with Mr. A. Masotti.

5. Interviews with Mr. R. Santi; Mr. A. Masotti; Mr. O. Fava and Mr. A. Josello.

6. Interviews with Mr. O. Fava; Mr. A. Castellan.

7. Richard Holt, *Sport and Society in Modern France* (Oxford, 1981), 158.

8. The Dante Alighieri Society was for a time based at the Venetian Club. In association with the society and McMaster University, the club through the years has sponsored banquets, classes and special lectures on aspects of Italian culture and language. Recently, the club sponsored a public lecture celebrating the 500th anniversary of Michelangelo's birth.

9. "Onestà, Fratellanza, Rispetto"; observe "Nascita e Sviluppo del Venetian Club."

10. Interview with Mr. O. Fava and Mr. A. Josello.

11. Interviews with Mr. A. Masotti; Mr. L. Mason.

12. Interview with Mr. O. Fava.

13. Besides bocce, soccer was also played by the members of the society. In the early 1950s, Joe Castel, a member of the club and part owner of Primo Salami, founded a short-lived, amateur soccer league consisting largely of Venetians.

14. This was an important consideration in view of the fact that many of the members worked long hours as labourers, factory hands and tradesmen during the week; the weekend was regarded as a time for relaxation and conviviality.

15. In the vicinity of Dickson Street in the extreme north end of the city.

16. Interviews with Mr. A. Masotti; Mr. R. Santi; Mr. A. Castellan.

17. Quoted in Holt, *Sport and Society in Modern France*, 157. Similar attitudes were expressed by Mr. Castellan, Mr. Fava and Mr. Masotti.

18. Holt, *Sport and Society in Modern France*, 158; interviews with Mr. A. Castellan; Mr. A. Masotti.

19. Interview with Mr. and Mrs. Masotti.

MAURICE RICHARD AND FRENCH CANADA*

PETER GZOWSKI

Only one player in the NHL's history of superstars ever really approached [Howie] Morenz's magnetism, and that was the man who succeeded him in Montreal: Maurice Richard. The image that most people who saw Richard play still carry of him is how he looked after he scored a goal, something he did 544 times in regular season play. He would circle under the clock. His stocky body would still be quivering with excitement, and it would not have surprised anyone to see steam coming from his nostrils. From time to time he would glance upward, and even in the least expensive seats in the arena you could see the fire blazing in his eyes. His eyes were his most noticeable feature. They were as dark as coal, and they shone with fissionable power. In conversation they were mesmerizing; when he played they would light up even more fiercely. Glenn Hall, one of the several master goalies of whom Richard in his heyday made dupes, used to say that when Richard broke toward the goal he could see the eyes flashing "like a pin-ball machine."

Unbelievably in view of the records he was to establish, Richard was thought too fragile to last when he first broke into the NHL. He was the oldest son of a machinist from the north end of Montreal. At night, as a boy, he used to listen to the French radio broadcasts of the Canadien games and dream of someday filling the skates of such stars as [Aurel] Joliat, whom he was later to befriend, or Morenz, who was his idol but died when Richard was sixteen. In each of his last two seasons as an amateur he broke bones and, in his first year as a Canadien, he did it again — an ankle this time — after just sixteen games. But in his next year, playing on a line with Elmer Lach and Toe Blake, he scored thirty-two goals; the next season 1944–45, he

---

* *The Game of Our Lives* (Toronto: McClelland and Stewart, 1981), 127–30.

scored fifty in fifty games, an accomplishment that was as meaningful as Babe Ruth's sixty home runs in 1927.

Although many hockey purists insisted that Richard's record was tainted by the wartime absence of too many other premier players — Richard was kept out of the service by his brittle bones — he continued to score at almost as significant a pace throughout his career. From the opponents' blueline to the goal, there has never been anyone to match him; on the attack, he was a man possessed, and some of his most dramatic goals were scored with opponents draped over him like drunks at the end of a party — he would simply carry them home. He seemed to have a special affinity for the Stanley Cup, which the Canadiens won seven times when he played for them. Eighteen times in playoff games he scored the winning goal, six of them in overtime. Seven times he scored three goals in a Stanley Cup game, twice he scored four and in one unforgettable game in 1944 the score was Maurice Richard 5, the Toronto Maple Leafs 1. But, playoffs or not, there was an intensity to his play that transcended statistics. Everything he did he did with incomparable flair; he lifted us from our seats and brought our hearts to our mouths. When Maple Leaf Gardens installed shatterproof glass to protect the well-tailored customers in the front rows, Richard — or the Rocket, as he was by then universally known — shattered it, cartwheeling up against the boards and sending the "impenetrable" barrier onto the ice in a shower of shards and slivers.

He was a national hero in Quebec, bigger than his team, bigger than the game. In "The Hockey Sweater," a story about growing up with the hockey in Sainte-Justine-de-Dorchester, Roch Carrier wrote:

> We all wore the same uniform as he, the red, white and blue uniform of the Montreal Canadiens, the best hockey team in the world; we all combed our hair in the same style as Maurice Richard, and to keep it in place we used a sort of glue — a great deal of glue. We laced our skates like Maurice Richard, we taped our sticks like Maurice Richard. We cut all his pictures out of the papers. Truly, we knew everything about him.

In 1955, an ugly series of events illustrated how deeply the people of Quebec felt toward him. These events began in Boston, on March 13, when the Canadiens played the Bruins in the fourth-to-last game of the schedule. The game was a rough one; tempers and sticks were both high. Late in the third period, Richard was hit across the forehead by the stick of Hal Laycoe, a Bruin defenceman. The hit drew blood. Richard went berserk, charging at Laycoe, taking dead aim and giving him a two-hander over the head. When a linesman wrestled Richard's stick way, Richard picked up another that was lying on the ice — by this time nearly everyone was in the fracas — and then broke *that* across Laycoe's back, too. In the midst of it all, he also struck the linesman. This was not, unfortunately, Richard's first run-in with officials; just after Christmas of the same season he had slapped another linesman across the face with his glove. This time, President Clarence Campbell ruled decisively. Richard, who had been leading the league in scoring at the time of the Laycoe incident, would be suspended not only for the remainder of the season but for the playoffs as well.

That Thursday, St. Patrick's Day, when the Rocket-less Canadiens lined up at the Forum against Detroit, with whom they were now tied for first place, the crowd was seething. Richard took a seat near the Canadiens' bench. In a gesture that seems in retrospect both brave and foolhardy, Campbell showed up too, sitting in his regular box seat, along with his secretary, whom he was later to marry. Throughout the first period, the crowd continued to rumble; someone threw a smoke bomb and the game was delayed. Raw eggs splattered the ice. Somehow, the teams got through the first period. But when it ended, someone got past the policemen who were hovering near Campbell's box and hit him in the face while his horrified fiancée looked on. Pushing and shoving broke out everywhere. The authorities cancelled the remainder of the game, and an announcement to that effect went out over the PA system.

The troubles spilled out of the Forum with the crowd, and through much of the night people went on a rampage in downtown Montreal, hurling bricks through windows, overturning streetcars, setting bonfires; more than $100 000 in goods were looted from stores on Ste. Catherine Street. The city boiled with anger until Richard himself went on the air and asked people to calm down. "I will take my punishment," he said, his eyes burning out of the television screen. "I would ask everyone to get behind the team."

The Richard Riot, as the events of March 1955 came to be called, was, if not the beginning of the Quiet Revolution that was to change Quebec society in the 1960s and 1970s, then at least an important event in its development. Like the Asbestos Strike, which brought together such political figures as Gérard Pelletier and Pierre Elliott Trudeau, then a professor of law at the University of Montreal, or like the bitter strike of radio and television producers against the CBC, the Richard Riot seemed, to its participants at least, to set the French *peuple* — represented in this case by fiery Maurice — against the hated English bosses, as symbolized by the elegant anglophone Campbell. And, later, when the Parti Québécois came to move the Quiet Revolution

A HOCKEY SERIES THAT CHALLENGED CANADIANS' VIEW OF THEMSELVES *

DOUGLAS FISHER

During Team Canada's first [exhibition] game in Stockholm [between the Canadian and Russian segments of the September 1972 series], a nagging apprehension of mine became real. Nothing much could be done about it. Months before, I and other associates in Hockey Canada had compromised our control and direction of the operation in order to ensure that the U.S.S.R.–Canada hockey series took place.

The apprehension was that the behaviour and performance of the Canadian players and team management might be such as to hurt Canadian relations abroad — that what was stock or usual on our hockey scene would be translated as brutish and unsportsmanlike by foreigners. I was mindful of the reigning themes in our hockey, expressed in such popular aphorisms as "Nice guys don't win" or "If you can't lick them in the alley, you can't beat them on the ice."

Stockholm has a stolid and antiseptic air to it. The Johanneshall rink is spacious. The roominess of its aprons and seating run counter to the roaring, cockpit atmosphere of most hockey rinks. Fans need not stand to see incidents anywhere on the ice. Swedish fans are genteel by our standards. Perhaps the high cost of tickets for the Sweden–Team Canada games accentuated the sense of discretion and propriety which our players quickly challenged with vigorous stick-work, elbows and charging. Shortly after a wild scene in the penalty box area with several Canadian stars gesticulating about the ridiculous nature of their penalties and the incompetence of the referees, Alan Eagleson dropped into a seat beside me. He had been sitting several rows above in the distinguished company of ambassadors and ex-ambassadors.

I asked him if the view was better here. He said no, but he could no longer take his diplomatic neighbours' shocked reaction to the Canadians' play.

* *International Perspectives* (Nov./Dec. 1972): 13–20.

Eagleson's Last Word

Team Canada departed Stockholm for Moscow with Mr. Eagleson having the last word, telling the Swedish press that Swedes as players and fans were "chicken," leaving the Canadian Embassy with the aftermath.

This is a rather out-of-context preface to a narrative and appreciation of the U.S.S.R.–Canada hockey series of September 1972. It is unusual in its personal emphasis. I use it to bring you quickly to Mr. Eagleson, executive director of the National Hockey League Players Association, because he symbolized for me the spirit and attitude of the Canadian team. It was his operation. He set its pattern.

If the unbelievable rally in Moscow which aroused Canada, if the certain defeat which became last-minute victory, was worth a lot — as millions seemed to think — then Mr. Eagleson deserves the chief credit. If many others abhor the means or some intrinsics in the behaviour which defeated the Russians, then they must ask themselves whether they are in tune with today's Canadianism. As I expressed my hunch in a newspaper column, Mr. Eagleson is probably more the archetypal Canadian than men like Mitchell Sharp and Maurice Strong.

We in Hockey Canada hoped to have a major international sporting event and a national happening of great interest out of the series. We wanted to establish the principle of "open play" between pros and so-called amateurs in international hockey. We wanted to make big money for furthering Hockey Canada's programs to improve domestic play. We dreamed that from out of the contrasts in style, training and methods offered by the Russians would come lessons for all stages of hockey in Canada.

Federal Role

Success crowned all these hopes and plans. Despite this, other complications, including the tendency to ambivalence about Mr. Eagleson and Team Canada's behaviour, have given everyone I know in Hockey Canada reason to ponder the future of hockey in Canada and elsewhere, and to re-examine the role the federal government may play or should play.

In hockey we do not manifest ourselves as the fair, peaceable, high-minded neutrals projected by men like the late Vincent Massey and Norman Robertson. Some outline of the career of Alan Eagleson may explain this generalization, which most of those who have taken an interest in international affairs would tend to dismiss as unimportant because international sport has only peripheral importance.

Mr. Eagleson is 39 years old. His parents were Irish Protestant immigrants, his father a long-time shop steward and union activist in a Toronto factory. The young Eagleson was a sports enthusiast but a good physique and quickness were not enough to counter smallness and jerky coordination. By the time he reached university he had settled for managing teams rather than playing. At the University of Toronto his classmates came to know him as mercurial and bright, never as interested in good marks or in law as a scholarly field as he was in politics, contacts, and mixing with people.

Mr. Eagleson became a public figure as a Conservative candidate in York West in the federal election of 1963. He lost heavily (and ironically) to the Liberal candidate, Red Kelly, the fine hockey star of Detroit and Maple Leaf fame. At this time the young lawyer was just emerging as the first major agent for professional athletes in Canada. The trend that brought lawyers into bargaining positions for players with owners began to run strongly in the 1950s in the United States during the war between the National Football League and the American Football League.

The huge sums won by high "draft" choices agitated the veteran players into a militancy that turned hitherto bland players' associations in baseball and football into aggressive groups with a willingness to strike in order to get improvements in contracts from owners. This militancy was transferred to the National Hockey League Players Association, which, as a player-run group, had not made much headway with the owners.

In autumn 1963, Mr. Eagleson won the provincial riding of Lakeshore for the Conservatives. He held the seat for only one term, losing in 1967. One of the partisan charges against him in the latter campaign was that he was spending too much time as a wheeler-dealer in sport, not enough in the Legislature and at riding chores.

It was in this period that Mr. Eagleson established his ascendancy as the head of the NHL Players Association. In 1966 he had tied his fortunes to the brightest hockey prospect in generations, Bobby Orr. He dickered with Boston for the first professional contract of this Parry Sound boy. The NHL was a six-team league in 1966; the next year it began to expand, opening up "a players' market."

The first expansion of six teams affronted Canadian nationalism, particularly in Vancouver. All the new franchises were sold to U.S. cities. While Vancouver was admitted two years later (along with Buffalo), one consequence of its first failure was a deepening nationalist antagonism to the NHL. There were increasing complaints that the

NHL dominated all levels of hockey in Canada but was more and more an American entertainment enterprise.

Nationalistic pressure usually finds it focus on the federal government. British Columbia ministers and MPs were demanding action, noting that federal funds had helped build an arena in Vancouver suitable for major league hockey. There was a broad feeling that the NHL held all hockey players 16 years old and older in peonage to a foreign sports industry.

Mr. Eagleson raised another issue with the federal government, asking for the abolition of the "reserve clause," the traditional means in American pro sports by which leagues and teams owned and controlled players.

Election Promise

Out of this dissatisfaction came the Pierre Trudeau election promise, made in B.C., to have sport examined and to develop a stronger federal role in sport than had followed the passage of the National Fitness and Amateur Sport Act in 1960. After the election, a Task Force on Sport, chaired by Harold Rea, a Toronto businessman, was named. It was to make a quick report, announcing its recommendations in May 1969. One of the concerns it tackled was the limping fortunes of the imaginative "Bauer concept." Any understanding of how the 1972 series with the U.S.S.R. came about depends on an appreciation of this noble failure.

Father David Bauer is a member of the noted hockey-playing family from Kitchener. He had been an outstanding coach at St. Michael's College in Toronto. In the early 1960s he had become disturbed by the growing domination of Soviet teams in international hockey and he challenged the values reigning in junior hockey with its emphasis on honing only the very best for a pro career.

Father Bauer believed there should be another avenue open to boys who played hockey, particularly one which gave primacy to education and to nationalism. Rather than challenging or outflanking rules which forbade Canadian national teams to use professionals, Father Bauer planned a national "team-in-being," at a fixed place, with a permanent coach and an association with a university. He won backing for his idea from the federal Health and Welfare Department's Fitness and Sports Directorate, the Canadian Amateur Hockey Association, and from many prominent men, especially in Western Canada.

The CAHA is a federation, the parent body for all amateur hockey in Canada. It held, and holds, the right of representation in the International Ice Hockey Federation. The IIHF has been masterminded since the 1930s by its permanent secretary and treasurer and oft-times president, Bunny Ahearne, a London travel agent.

The "Bauer concept" almost worked. The Canadian national team came close to beating the Russians and the other two European hockey powers, Sweden and Czechoslovakia, both at the annual world tournament and at the Winter Olympics. Father Bauer, working with the CAHA, had to scramble for players. A deepening antagonism toward this initiative came from the NHL, growing out of what that league considered interference with its control of players. Burgeoning costs made it more difficult for the CAHA and private friends of the national team to carry on. One of the underwriters, the federal government, kept hearing complaints that Canada was never going to win this way, that our national honour as hockey's creators and best practitioners was being forfeited in the name of an idealistic but unsuccessful project.

Task Force Proposal

The Task Force on Sport recommended that the federal government sponsor the creation of a new body, Hockey Canada. This non-profit corporation, with representation from all the major hockey interests in Canada, was to have a dual purpose: first, to manage Canadian representation in international tournaments; secondly, to take steps to improve the standards and skills of domestic hockey.

Health and Welfare Minister John Munro accepted this recommendation, guaranteed it federal financial backing until it could raise funds privately and encouraged the Canadian Amateur Hockey Association to devolve its responsibilities and debts regarding the national team on Hockey Canada. The "Bauer concept" was not dead. Rather, it had been put in a larger frame, the hope being that greater co-operation from the NHL representation in Hockey Canada would open up a better player supply for the national team.

By early summer of 1969, Hockey Canada was under way, describing itself as an "umbrella organization for Canadian hockey." On its directorate were nominees from the CAHA, the Canadian Intercollegiate Athletic Association, the NHL Players Association (i.e., Alan Eagleson), the three Canadian teams in the NHL and men from sport and business with a deep interest in the game, including federal nominees.

The CAHA signed a contract with Hockey Canada. The latter took over the national team, including its debts. While the CAHA did not give up its representation in the International Ice Hockey Federation — it's doubtful if it could have transferred this to Hockey Canada —

it agreed to work in concert with Hockey Canada and federal authorities.

The first aim was to get approval from the IIHF for the use of pro players in the world tournament. These, everyone agreed, were our "best." The three Canadian NHL team leaders and Clarence Campbell, the veteran Montreal-based president of the NHL, guaranteed their cooperation. So did Mr. Eagleson, who by this time was the leading agent for hockey players as well as the chief actor in affairs of the NHL Players Association.

The panels of Hockey Canada's umbrella, despite their differing textures, agreed in the determination to assert Canadian supremacy by icing a "national" team which would include the Orrs and Espositos of the NHL.

World Tourney Lost

The first assay of Hockey Canada was diplomatic. The triennial meeting of the IIHF was held in Switzerland in July 1969. There was a narrow failure to get free use of pro players. The compromise resolution would have permitted Canada to use nine non-NHL pros on its national team, then preparing for the 1970 World Tournament, scheduled for the first time in Canada. Late in 1969 the U.S.S.R. forced a review of the compromise, arguing convincingly to spokesmen for countries like Sweden and Finland that playing against such a Canadian team would jeopardize the eligibility of their best players for the 1972 Sapporo Olympics.

Mr. Ahearne agreed with the Russians and, in January 1970, Canada was faced with the choice of giving up the tournament (and missing revenues of some $600 000) or giving up its use of the pros as agreed to in Switzerland. Hockey Canada, after consultation with the CAHA and Mr. Munro, stood firm, lost the tournament, and refused to send a team to the new locale in Sweden.

Shortly afterward the national "team-in-being" was disbanded. From April 1970, Hockey Canada persisted in efforts to get the IIHF to change its ruling on pros. At the same time it approached the U.S.S.R., Sweden, and Czechoslovakia with proposals for round-robin exhibition series in which Canada would use pros.

Annual Draft

The killing of the tournament was especially hurtful in Winnipeg, one of the host cities and the base for the Bauer "team-in-being." The team would have been hard to sustain without any international competition in sight. Aside from the drawback, the expansion of the NHL was creating a mark-up in salaries and opportunities for hockey players with which educational scholarships and mere national representation could hardly compete.

In passing, we should note that out of the Task Force recommendations came an abandonment of the "amateur" farm system of the NHL in Canada and the institution of an annual draft of 20-year-old players. The draft payments went from the NHL to the amateur clubs through which the drafted players had developed. In 1972, this figure reached $1.3 million. Of course, by this time, the NHL was doing an annual business of more than $80 million and its new franchises were costing the successful bidders $6 million each.

While a Hockey Canada-CAHA-federal troika, headed by President Charles Hay of Hockey Canada, worked on his Europeans for games with a team made up of our pros, Mr. Eagleson and his association had contracted with the NHL owners that neither group would enter international hockey competition unilaterally. Indeed, for several years, Mr. Eagleson ranged around Europe trying on his own to set up a series between the NHL players and the Russians.

Mr. Hay believed that co-operation from the Europeans would become a fact once the 1972 Winter Olympics were over. He was right. In April 1972, during the world tournament in Prague, the Soviet sports leaders formally agreed to an eight-game series for September, four games in Canada, four in Moscow. Canada could play anyone it wanted.

No sooner was the coup announced than it became apparent that the NHL owners, particularly the American ones, were much less enthusiastic about the series than was Mr. Eagleson. He used his bond with the players to dragoon the recalcitrant owners into line. One of his persuasive arguments was that half the net revenues of the series would go to supplement the NHL players' pension fund.

The achievement of Russian approval coincided with the appearance in substantial form of a new professional grouping, the World Hockey Association. This impudent rival to the NHL was sponsored by the American entrepreneurs who had launched the American Basketball Association. The WHA committed itself to the placing of four of its 12 franchises in Canada. The WHA insisted it would operate without a reserve clause. This meant a "player war" with the NHL and a fantastic bidding-up of salaries and the value of players as properties. These grand vistas for players were welcomed by the players' champion, Mr. Eagleson. If the NHL owners wished some stability in their labour force during their war with the WHA they needed, at the least, Mr. Eagleson's neutrality. This he gave in a general way and he did not antagonize the NHL by signing many of his own clients to WHA contracts.

Throughout the negotiations planned and completed by Mr. Hay with the Soviets, it had been understood by all the elements in Hockey Canada that the players for the September series would come from the NHL. Mr. Campbell agreed with this. So did Mr. Eagleson. It was also understood that team selection and management would be in the hands of men chosen with the advice of the NHL. It was agreed that Harry Sinden, a former coach of the Boston team, was the best man available to manage, choose and coach the team.

Hockey Canada, through Mr. Hay, conceded that Mr. Sinden should have complete control of the team side of the series. He would be accountable to Hockey Canada only for spending. Hockey Canada would arrange the series in matters involving tickets, television, radio, the U.S.S.R. team arrangements in Canada, the ancillary functions, the refereeing, and the tour in Europe, including a training session and games in Sweden and a game or games in Czechoslovakia.

Eagleson in Control

Unfortunately Mr. Hay took sick shortly after Mr. Sinden was named as manager-coach. Before his future contribution could be determined, Mr. Eagleson took over effective control of the team side of the operation, naming it Team Canada and hiring the trainers and other personnel, choosing hotel and travel arrangements. In effect, Mr. Eagleson, not Mr. Sinden, became the leader of the team. This initiative, quite unexpected by both Hockey Canada and NHL leaders, was given a further force when the time came for consideration of TV contracts for the series.

As a director of Hockey Canada, Mr. Eagleson disagreed with the tentative arrangements it had made to sell the TV rights to "Hockey Night in Canada" for $500 000. When he was challenged to find better alternatives, he asked for time. He constituted a non-profit company in concert with Harold Ballard, owner of the Maple Leaf Gardens and another Hockey Canada director. Their company guaranteed Hockey Canada a minimum of $750 000 for the North American TV and radio rights to the series. The offer had to be accepted, and, given the pervasive influence of TV on hockey arrangements, it put another aspect of series arrangements in Mr. Eagleson's control. The steering committee of Hockey Canada created because of Mr. Hay's illness had Mr. Eagleson as a participant.

Before the team members were announced in early July, Mr. Campbell had reminded Hockey Canada and Mr. Eagleson that the owners understood that candidates for the team must have signed contracts for the next season with their NHL team before they came to Team Canada's training camp. Bobby Hull, one of the ablest and most popular NHL players, had defected from the Chicago NHL team to the Winnipeg entry of the WHA in late June. The whole WHA had underwritten Mr. Hull's massive signing bonus and salary in order to gain the credibility for excellence which he gave to the new league.

Mr. Sinden named his 35 "best" players and included Bobby Hull. A national uproar followed when it was made clear by Hockey Canada that Hull would not be acceptable unless he was signed to a 1972–73 contract with his old club. This seemed to contradict Hockey Canada's much mooted objective of icing "our best." In Western Canada especially, it was seen as another example of NHL domination of Canadian hockey.

As chairman of the ad hoc steering committee for the series, I knew there would be a national hue and cry over the Hull matter if we honoured our understanding with the NHL. If we insisted that Hull should play, we would lose many of the other players whom Sinden had named. Mr. Eagleson could not guarantee that he could provide an excellent team even from his own 25 clients. The best of the latter, Bobby Orr, was a doubtful starter because of a knee operation.

Hockey Canada decided after a long internal debate, political interventions from the Prime Minister and strong disagreement from a minority of its directors to go only with NHL players. The decision was most unpopular with the Canadian public, weakening further Hockey Canada's none too strong reputation.

While the Hull decision was still a public controversy, Mr. Eagleson and his team leaders, including Mr. Sinden, took off for Moscow and Stockholm to line up details on the series, including television coverage, percentages and practice arrangements in the Soviet Union and Sweden. This tour confirmed that he was the executive at the core of almost every important aspect of the series. His leadership was confirmed by the mix of awe and affection which the sporting press of Canada held for him. Most of Hockey Canada's small cadre of permanent people did not qualify as "snowbankers," that is, genuine hockey buffs. And as Clarence Campbell has lamented: "If you're not a snowbanker, you don't rate among Canadian hockey people and fans."

Mr. Eagleson is a fast talker, a fast thinker, one of the best natural salesmen and traders I have ever met. Metaphorically, he was at the throttle of the series juggernaut; we were passengers, waiting to straighten up the accounts after it was all over.

Mr. Eagleson and Mr. Sinden were convinced that the Soviet team would be well-beaten in all eight games. They brushed aside any suggestions from some of us in Hockey Canada that they should con-sult with those who had played and coached against the Russians. We were told with some disdain to "Leave it to the pros" or "Don't bur-den us with bushers." Team Canada was not to be a "chintzy opera-tion." It was to be "first-class all the way" for the 35 players and the other 15 people required to keep them happy and going. All was to befit the best players in the world.

Clearly, here was a man and team heading for a fall, almost deserv-ing it in their cockiness. When the team assembled and began its ex-hibition schedules I realized how in tune with the players Mr. Eagleson was. We began to call him "Big Bird." The players were generally rough and ready, like teenagers in their enthusiasms and in-terests; essentially simple men of instinct, not highly rational. Lusty, capricious, fun-loving and proud, quick to anger, always ready to belly-laugh and clown.

I feel one must note these boyish and unsophisticated qualities of Team Canada, to understand the shock and trauma that it suffered when the Soviet team won two and tied one of the four games in Canada to the accolades of many Canadians, enthused by the Russian speed and pattern-passing. The booing of Team Canada by the Van-couver crowd in the last game in Canada capped the shock. It was a shaken group that went off to Stockholm for a week which had been promised long before as fun and practice before the grimness of Mos-cow and the link-up there with wives and girlfriends.

What renewed old Swedish charges that Canadians were hockey barbarians was a Gethsemane for Mr. Eagleson and the team. Some of the stars were disaffected because they were not being played. Some players were carousing day and night. Others were terribly determined to recover their pride with a comeback in Russia. The Canadian reporters in Stockholm were dismayed by the team perfor-mance there, on and off the ice. The Soviet success had been traumatic for the reporters, almost all of whom had anticipated a Canadian romp. Everyone at home knew Team Canada was in trouble.

The scenario promised to unfold on further disaster in Moscow. One alleviating factor was apparent at once. The group of 3 000-odd Canadians in Moscow for the series brought with it a noisy, militant spirit, all out for the team and determined to cheer it on to victory.

Osmosis of Spirit

While the Soviets won the first game in Moscow with a surprising, late comeback, they had been outplayed for most of the game. Four players from Team Canada reneged on the series and went home. Mr.

Eagleson welcomed these defections: "Now we're getting down to the guys who care." The tactics on the ice stressed more and more what NHL players do best: tough checking, lots of body contact, challenges to the referees, scrambly pressure-plays with lots of shooting. The goal-tending for Team Canada was excellent. There was an osmosis of spirit from the busy, colourful, cheering Canadian fans.

Team Canada turned it around with three hard-won victories in a row. Any neutral would agree that they were outplayed in two of three victories. Breaks, great goal-tending and magnificent opportunism in front of the net did the job. But the most marvellous quality of the team on the ice was simply absolute determination.

Few of us in Moscow — certainly not Mr. Eagleson and the team — really knew how the entire country at home was roused and watching. That realization didn't sink in until they saw the big crowds in Montreal and Toronto to welcome them.

It seems to me that it is stupid to press one's shame too far over the excesses of the players and Messrs Eagleson and Sinden in challenging the authority of the referees and in denigrating the Soviet sports officials.

Of course, the blasts at Soviet society, the maudlin assertions that "We played for democracy" or "We know now what democracy is" were juvenile. I won't forget Mrs. Eagleson, distraught at her husband's seizure by the police, screaming at the Russians around us: "We'll never come back to this bloody dictatorship."

Balance this excess against the long pumping up to high pressure and tension which a desperate Mr. Eagleson and his colleagues had turned to in order to inculcate the determination to win. As one of the Team Canada doctors said to me the morning after the big win:

> This is a powerful country with tough people and a harsh system. They'll respect what the Canadian players and fans have shown here in Moscow. We are not Nice Nellies. We are direct, crude and emotional, easily arrogant, even more easily bitchy and complaining, cherishing a sense of grievance. Before you and others crawl away and hide because of the embarrassment Eagleson and his antics have caused you, think it over: Is there any other way we could have done it and won?

My answer is no, there was no other way, given the similarity in attitudes and values between Mr. Eagleson, Mr. Sinden and most of the players. Their world is a simplistic, emotional one; it is also a very fast-moving one.

Even the self-discovery out of this series that we are among the roughnecks of the world may be useful. There isn't a politician of my acquaintance in Canada who doesn't know that hockey is one of the deepest common denominators we have.

They know, even as the critics such as Dr. Wilder Penfield know, that in the recent series we shared an experience which has turned into a challenge of a long-held view of ourselves. I don't discount the eventual victory with public opinion for the critics of Alan Eagleson. Indeed, by his excesses he has made a future role for himself in international hockey doubtful. The NHL owners may never forgive him. Certainly, they'll never again approve an arrangement which will let him run the whole show. They have had the merit of their product jeopardized. They will resist future contributions to a Canadian "national team." They will go after encounters with the Russians and the other European countries on a basis of club teams against club teams. The Russians will not be anxious to deal with Mr. Eagleson again. Thus we are likely to be left with the memory of a one-shot, unique happening with most of it on our side under the aegis of Mr. Eagleson.

International sport, especially the Olympics, has always had a contradiction in it. The idealists theorize sweetly about the bridging and brotherhood accomplished by the contests and the association of athletes from different countries, unsullied by political motivation. All the while this "the game's the thing" is touted, the emphasis has kept building on winning, winning for national pride, medal totals and point scores. Now we Canadians have shared in this contradiction and found victory most important.

Meanwhile, Hockey Canada and the parts of it are reconsidering the future. What can we do with an even more germane contradiction? Our major sporting interest involves hundreds and thousands of households, it pervades almost every city, town, and village in Canada. But where does the interest lead? Still...to the United States for rewards and glory.

How do we be our own in hockey when the apex of our huge base triangle in hockey is overwhelmingly American in ownership and finances? And much as we know the renewal of a series such as the last one with the Soviets would excite Canada again, it is almost certain to be rare so long as foreigners call the tune. And this brings us back to Alan Eagleson. Now and in potential, he is the only one with the leverage — because almost all the players are still Canadian — to force the re-creation of the Team Canada idea.

Further Readings

International Sports

Trends in sports in Canada usually paralleled or followed, but sometimes anticipated, trends in the United Kingdom, the United States, and some other English-speaking countries. Serious students of Canadian developments should become familiar with the literature on the history of sports around the English-speaking world. Three journals are especially useful: *The Journal of Sport History* (1974–); *The International Journal of History of Sport,* formerly *The British Journal of Sports History* (1984–); and *Sporting Traditions* (1984–). Items in these three journals are not mentioned in the following list of valuable publications.

Adelman, Melvin L. *A Sporting Time: New York City and the Rise of Modern Athletics, 1820–70.* Urbana, Ill.: University of Illinois Press, 1986.

Bailey, Peter. *Leisure and Class in Victorian England: Rational Recreation and the Contest for Control, 1830–1885.* London: Routledge and Kegan Paul, 1978.

Baker, William J. *Sports in the Western World.* Totowa, N.J.: Rowman and Littlefield, 1982.

Baker, William J. and James A. Mangan, eds. *Sport in Africa: Essays in Social History.* New York: Africana Publishing Company, 1987.

Berry, Robert C., William B. Gould IV, and Paul D. Staudohar. *Labor Relations in Professional Sports.* Dover, Mass.: Auburn House Publishing, 1986.

Betts, John Richard. *America's Sporting Heritage: 1850–1950.* Reading, Mass.: Addison-Wesley, 1974.

Brailsford, Dennis. *Sport and Society: Elizabeth to Anne.* London: Routledge and Kegan Paul, 1969.

Cashman, Richard, and Michael McKernan, eds. *Sport in History: The Making of Modern Sporting History.* St. Lucia, Queensland: University of Queensland Press, 1979.

Cashman, Richard, and Michael McKernan, eds. *Sport: Money, Morality and the Media.* Kensington, New South Wales: New South Wales University Press, c. 1980.

Cavallo, Dominick. *Muscles and Morals: Organized Playgrounds and Urban Reform, 1880–1920.* Philadelphia: University of Pennsylvania Press, 1981.

Crawford, Scott A.G.M. "The Game of 'Glory and Hard Knocks'": A Study of the Interpretation of Rugby and New Zealand Society." *Journal of Popular Culture* 19, 2 (1985): 76–91.

Cunningham, Hugh. *Leisure in the Industrial Revolution.* New York: St. Martin's Press, 1980.

Dunning, Eric, and Kenneth Sheard. *Barbarians, Gentlemen and Players, A Sociological Study of the Development of Rugby Football.* New York: New York University Press, 1979.

Fletcher, Sheila. *Women First: The Female Tradition in English Physical Education, 1880–1980.* London: Athlone Press, 1984.

Gelber, Steven M. "Working at Playing: The Culture of the Workplace and the Rise of Baseball." *Journal of Social History* 16, 4 (1983): 3–22.

Gorn, Elliott, J. "'Gouge and Bite, Pull Hair and Scratch': The Social Significance of Fighting in the Southern Backcountry." *American Historical Review* 90, 1 (1985): 18–43.

——————. *The Manly Art: Bare-Knuckle Prize Fighting in America.* Ithaca: Cornell University Press, 1986.

Green, Harvey. *Fit For America: Health, Fitness, Sport and American Society.* New York: Pantheon Books, 1986.

Guttmann, Allen. *From Ritual to Record: The Nature of Modern Sports.* New York: Columbia University Press, 1978.

——————. *Sports Spectators.* New York: Columbia University Press, 1986.

Haley, Bruce E. *The Health Body and Victorian Culture.* Cambridge, Mass.: Harvard University Press, 1978.

Hardy, Stephen. *How Boston Played: Sport, Recreation, and Community 1865–1915.* Boston: Northeastern University Press, 1982.

Henderson, Robert W. *Ball, Bat and Bishop: The Origin of Ball Games.* New York: Rockport Press, 1947.

Henricks, Thomas S. "The Democratization of Sport in Eighteenth-Century England." *Journal of Popular Culture* 18, 3 (1984): 3–20.

Howell, Reet, ed. *Her Story in Sport: A Historical Anthology of Women in Sports.* West Point, N.Y.: Leisure Press, 1982.

Jones, Stephen G. "State Intervention in Sport and Leisure in Britain Between the Wars." *Journal of Contemporary History* 22, 1 (1987): 163–82.

Lucas, John A., and Ronald A. Smith. *Saga of American Sport.* Philadelphia: Lea and Febiger, 1978.

MacAloon, John J. "Olympic Games and the Theory of Spectacle in Modern Societies." In *Rite, Drama, Festival, Spectacle: Rehearsals*

Toward A Theory of Cultural Performance. Ed. John J. MacAloon. Philadelphia: Institute for the Study of Human Issues, 1984.

——————. *This Great Symbol: Pierre de Coubertin and the Origins of the Modern Olympic Games.* Chicago: University of Chicago Press, 1981.

Malcolmson, Robert W. *Popular Recreations in English Society, 1700–1850.* Cambridge: Cambridge University Press, 1973.

Mandell, Richard D. *Sport: A Cultural History.* New York: Columbia University Press, 1984.

Mandle, W.F. "Games People Played: Cricket and Football in England and Victoria in the Late Nineteenth Century." *Historical Studies* 15, 60 (1973): 511–35.

Mangan, J.A. *Athleticism in the Victorian and Edwardian Public School: The Emergence and Consolidation of an Educational Ideology.* Cambridge: Cambridge University Press, 1981.

——————. *The Games Ethic and Imperialism: Aspects of the Diffusion of an Ideal.* Middlesex, England: Viking Press, 1986.

Mangan, J.A., and James Walvin, eds. *Manliness and Morality: Middle-Class Masculinity in Britain and America, 1800–1940.* New York: St. Martin's Press, 1987.

Mason, Tony. *Association Football and English Society, 1863–1915.* Atlantic Highlands, N.J.: Humanities Press, 1980.

McIntosh, P.C. *Sport in Society.* London: C.A. Watts and Company, 1971.

Mellor, H.E. *Leisure and the Changing City, 1870–1914.* London: Routledge and Kegan Paul, 1976.

Metcalfe, Alan. "Organized Sport in the Mining Communities of South Northumberland, 1800–1869." *Victorian Studies* 25, 4 (1982): 469–95.

Mrozek, Donald J. *Sport and American Mentality, 1880–1910.* Knoxville, Tenn.: University of Tennessee Press, 1983.

Phillips, J.O.C. "Rugby, War and the Mythology of the New Zealand Male." *The New Zealand Journal of History* 18, 2 (1984).

Rader, Benjamin G. *American Sports: From the Age of Folk Games to the Age of Spectators.* Englewood Cliffs, N.J.: Prentice-Hall, 1983.

——————. *In Its Own Image: How Television Has Transformed Sports.* New York: The Free Press, 1984.

Riess, Steven A. *The American Sporting Experience: A Historical Anthology of Sport in America.* Champaign, Ill.: Leisure Press, 1984.

Sandiford, Keith A.P. "Cricket and the Barbadian Society." *Canadian Journal of History/Annales canadiennes d'histoire* 21, 3 (1986): 353–70.

——————. "Cricket and the Victorian Society." *Journal of Social History* 17, 2 (1983): 303–17.

——————————. "Cricket and the Victorians: A Historiographical Essay." *Historical Reflections* 9, 3 (1982): 421–36.

——————————. "The Victorians at Play: Problems in Historical Methodology." *Journal of Social History* 15, 2 (1981): 271–88.

Segrave, Jeffrey, and Donald Chu, eds. *Olympism*. Champaign, Ill.: Human Kinetics Publishers, 1981.

Seymour, Harold. *Baseball*. Vol. I. *The Early Years*. New York: Oxford University Press, 1960.

——————————. *Baseball*. Vol. 2. *The Golden Age*. New York: Oxford University Press, 1971.

Somers, Dale A. *The Rise of Sports in New Orleans, 1850–1900*. Baton Rouge, La.: Louisiana State University Press, 1972.

Spivey, Donald, ed. *Sport in America: New Historical Perspectives*. Westport, Conn.: Greenwood Press, 1985.

Staudohar, Paul D. *The Sports Industry and Collective Bargaining*. Itahaca, N.Y.: ILR Press, 1986.

Stoddart, Brian. *Saturday Afternoon Fever: Sport in the Australian Culture*. North Ryde, New South Wales: Angus and Robertson Publishers, 1986.

Vance, Norman. *The Sinews of the Spirit: The Ideal of Christian Manliness in Victorian Literature and Religious Thought*. Cambridge: Cambridge University Press, 1985.

Voigt, David Quentin. *American Baseball*. Vol. 1. *From Gentleman's Sport to the Commissioner System*. Norman: University of Oklahoma Press, 1966.

——————————. *American Baseball*. Vol. 2. *From the Commissioners to Continental Expansion*. Norman: University of Oklahoma Press, 1970.

——————————. *American Baseball*. Vol. 3. *From Postwar Expansion to Electronic Age*. University Park, Pa: Penn State University Press, 1983.

Walvin, James. *Leisure and Society 1830–1950*. London: Longman, 1978.

——————————. *The People's Game: The Social History of British Football*. London: Allen Lane, 1975.

Whorton, James C. *Crusaders For Fitness: The History of American Health Reformers*. Princeton, N.J.: Princeton University Press, 1982.

Canadian Sports

There is no satisfying survey of the history of Canadian sports. Nancy Howell and Maxwell L. Howell, *Sports and Games in Canadian Life, 1700 to the Present* (Toronto: Macmillan of Canada, 1969), and Maxwell L.

Howell and Reet A. Howell, eds., *History of Sport in Canada* (Champaign, Ill.: Stipes Publishing Company, 1981, rev. ed. 1985), are poorly written and contain few passages that try to relate sports to economic, political, and social developments. Some very valuable information and many stimulating ideas are contained in S.F. Wise and Douglas Fisher, *Canada's Sporting Heroes, Their Lives and Times* (Don Mills, Ont.: General Publishing and Canada's Sports Hall of Fame, 1974). This volume attempts to cover sports from "Genesis" to the 1970s, with emphasis on the years after 1840. The biographical approach that is utilized makes personalities come to life but renders it difficult for readers to perceive changes over time in sports and in the contexts in which they were played.

Every issue of the *Canadian Journal of History of Sport/Revue canadienne de l'histoire des sports*, formerly the *Canadian Journal of History of Sport and Physical Education* (1970–), contains at least one valuable item. Articles published in this journal are not mentioned below. The publications listed here attempt to relate the history of sports to broader historical developments. Therefore most of the authors are, or were, academics.

Collections

Cantelon, Hart, and Bob Hollands, eds. *Leisure, Sport and Working Class Cultures: Theory and History. Working Papers in the Sociological Study of Sports and Leisure*. Kingston: Queen's University Centre for Sports and Leisure Studies, 1984.

Cantelon, Hart, and Richard Gruneau, eds. *Sport, Culture and the Modern State*. Toronto: University of Toronto Press, 1982.

Gruneau, Richard, and John Albinson, eds. *Canadian Sport: Sociological Perspectives*. Don Mills, Ont.: Addison-Wesley, 1976.

Harvey, Jean, and Hart Cantelon, eds. *Not Just A Game: Essays in Canadian Sport Sociology*. Ottawa: University of Ottawa Press, 1988.

Proceedings of the First Canadian Symposium on the History of Sport and Physical Education. Ottawa: Department of Health and Welfare, 1970.

Proceedings of the Second Canadian Symposium on the History of Sport and Physical Education. Ottawa: Sport Canada Directorate, Department of Health and Welfare, 1972.

Proceedings of the Second World Symposium on the History of Sport and Physical Education. Edmonton: University of Alberta Faculty of Physical Education, 1971.

Proceedings, 5th Canadian Symposium on the History of Sport and Physical Education. Toronto: University of Toronto School of Physical and Health Education, 1982.

Schrodt, Barbara, ed. *Proceedings, Fourth Canadian Symposium on the History of Sport and Physical Education*. Vancouver: University of British Columbia School of Physical Education and Recreation, 1979.

Sports and Ethnicity. Special issue of *Polyphony, The Bulletin of the Multicultural History Society of Ontario* 7, 1 (1985).

Theberge, Nancy, and Peter Donnelly, eds. *Sport and the Sociological Imagination. Refereed Proceedings of the Third Annual Conference of the North American Society for the Sociology of Sport*. Fort Worth: Texas Christian University Press, 1982.

Young, Louise, ed. *Proceedings from the Third Canadian Symposium on the History of Sport and Physical Education*. Halifax: Sport Nova Scotia, 1974.

Monographs

Auf der Maur, Nick. *The Billion Dollar Game: Jean Drapeau and the 1976 Olympics*. Toronto: James Lorimer and Company, 1976.

Ballem, H. Charles. *Abegweit Dynasty: The Story of the Abegweit Amateur Athletic Association 1899–1954*. Charlottetown: Prince Edward Island Museum and Heritage Foundation, 1986.

Batten, Jack. *Champions: Great Figures in Canadian Sport*. Toronto: New Press, 1971.

————————. *The Leafs in Autumn*. Toronto: Macmillan of Canada, 1975.

Broom, Eric F., and Richard S.P. Baka. *Canadian Governments and Sport*. Ottawa: Canadian Association for Health, Physical Education and Recreation, c. 1979.

Bull, William Perkins. *From Rattlesnake Hunt to Hockey*. Toronto: George J. McLeod, 1934.

Calder, Bob, and Andrew S. Garry. *Rider Pride*. Saskatoon: Western Producer Prairie Books, 1984.

Cochrane, Jean, Abby Hoffman, and Pat Kincaid. *Women in Canadian Sports*. Toronto: Fitzhenry and Whiteside, 1977.

Coleman, Jim. *A Hoofprint on my Heart*. Toronto: McClelland and Stewart, 1971.

————————. *Hockey Is Our Game: Canada in the World of International Hockey*. Toronto: Key Porter Books, 1987.

Cosentino, Frank. *Canadian Football: The Grey Cup Years*. Toronto: Musson, 1969.

Cosentino, Frank, and Maxwell L. Howell. *A History of Physical Education in Canada*. Toronto: General Publishing, 1971.

Currie, Gordon. *100 Years of Canadian Football*. Toronto: Pagurian Press, 1968.

Frayne, Trent. *The Mad Men of Hockey*. Toronto: McClelland and Stewart, 1974.

Frayne, Trent, and Peter Gzowski. *Great Canadian Sports Stories, A Century of Competition*. Toronto: Canadian Centennial Publishing Company, 1965.

Goyens, Chrys, and Allan Turowetz. *Lions in Winter*. Vancouver: Douglas and McIntyre, 1981.

Gruneau, Richard. *Class, Sports, and Social Development*. Amherst, Mass.: University of Massachusetts Press, 1983.

Gzowski, Peter. *An Unbroken Line*. Toronto: McClelland and Stewart, 1983.

——————————. *The Game of Our Lives*. Toronto: McClelland and Stewart, 1981.

Hewitt, Foster. *Hockey Night in Canada: The Maple Leafs' Story*. Toronto: Ryerson Press, 1961.

Hewitt, W.A. *Down the Stretch: Recollections of a Pioneer Sportsman and Journalist*. Toronto: Ryerson Press, 1958.

Humber, William. *Cheering for the Home Team: The Story of Baseball in Canada*. Erin, Ont.: The Boston Mills Press, 1983.

Isaacs, Neil D. *Checking Back: A History of the National Hockey League*. New York: W.W. Norton, 1977.

Jose, Colin, and William F. Rannie. *The Story of Soccer in Canada*. Lincoln, Ont. W.F. Rannie, 1982.

Kearney, Jim. *Champions: A British Columbia Sports Album*. Vancouver: Douglas and McIntyre, 1985.

Kidd, Bruce. *The Political Economy of Sport*. Ottawa: Canadian Association for Health, Physical Education and Recreation, c. 1979.

Kidd, Bruce, and John MacFarlane. *The Death of Hockey*. Toronto: New Press, 1972.

Lenskyj, Helen. *Out of Bounds: Women, Sport and Sexuality*. Toronto: Women's Press, 1986.

——————————. *Women, Sport and Physical Activity: Research and Bibliography*. Ottawa: Ministry of Supply and Services Canada, 1988.

Macintosh, Donald, with Tom Bedecki and C.E.S. Franks. *Sport and Politics in Canada: Federal Government Involvement Since 1961*. Montreal: McGill-Queen's University Press, 1987.

McFarland, Elsie Marie. *The Development of Public Recreation in Canada*. Ottawa: Canadian Parks/Recreation Association, 1970.

Metcalfe, Alan. *Canada Learns to Play: The Emergence of Organized Sport, 1807–1914*. Toronto: McClelland and Stewart, 1987.

Morrow, Don. *A Sporting Evolution: The Montreal Amateur Athletic Association 1881–1981*. Montreal: Montreal Amateur Athletic Association and Don Morrow, 1981.

Redmond, Gerald. *Sport and Ethnic Groups in Canada*. Ottawa: Canadian Association for Health, Physical Education and Recreation, c. 1978.

——————. *The Sporting Scots of Nineteenth-Century Canada*. East Brunswick, N.J.: Associated University Presses, 1982.

Reed, T.A. *The Blue and White: A Record of Fifty Years of Athletic Endeavour at the University of Toronto*. Toronto: University of Toronto Press, 1944.

Roxborough, Henry. *Canada at the Olympics*. Toronto: McGraw-Hill Ryerson, 1976.

——————. *Great Days in Canadian Sport*. Toronto: Ryerson Press, 1957.

——————. *One Hundred — Not Out: The Story of Nineteenth-Century Canadian Sport*. Toronto: Ryerson Press, 1966.

Selke, Frank J., with H. Gordon Green. *Behind the Cheering*. Toronto: McClelland and Stewart, 1962.

Smith, Garry J., and Cynthia Blackman. *Sport in the Mass Media*. Ottawa: Canadian Association for Health, Physical Education and Recreation, c. 1979.

Sullivan, Jack. *The Grey Cup Story: The Dramatic History of Football's Most Coveted Award*. Toronto: Pagurian Press Limited, 1974.

Weyand, Alexander M., and Milton R. Roberts. *The Lacrosse Story*. Baltimore: H. & A. Herman, 1965.

Whitehead, Eric. *Cyclone Taylor: A Hockey Legend*. Toronto: Doubleday, 1977.

——————. *The Patricks: Hockey's Royal Family*. Toronto: Doubleday, 1980.

Young, A.J. "Sandy." *Beyond Heroes: A Sport History of Nova Scotia*, 2 vols. Hantsport, N.S.: Lancelot Press, 1988.

Young, David. *The Golden Age of Canadian Figure Skating*. Toronto: Summerhill Press, 1984.

Young, Scott. *Hello Canada: The Life and Times of Foster Hewitt*. Toronto: Seal Books, 1985.

——————. *War on Ice: Canada in International Hockey*. Toronto: McClelland and Stewart, 1976.

Articles

Abbott, Frank. "Cold Cash and Ice Palaces: The Quebec Winter Carnival of 1894." *Canadian Historical Review* 69, 2 (1988): 167–202.

Batten, Jack. "Sport." In *The Canadians 1867–1967*. Ed. J.M.S. Careless and R. Craig Brown. Toronto: Macmillan of Canada, 1967, 606–20.

Betke, Carl. "The Social Significance of Sport in the City: Edmonton in the 1920s." In *Cities in the West: Papers of the Western Canadian Urban History Conference, University of Winnipeg, 1974.* Ed. A.R. McCormick and Ian MacPherson. Ottawa: National Museum of Man, 1975, 211–35.

————————. "Sports Promotion in the Western Canadian City: The Example of Early Edmonton." *Urban History Review* 12, 2 (1983): 47–56.

Cheska, Alyce. "The Antigonish Highland Games: A Community's Involvement in the Scottish Festival of Eastern Canada." *Nova Scotia Historical Review* 3, 1 (1983): 51–63.

Cosentino, Frank. "Ned Hanlan — Canada's Premier Oarsman: A Case Study in Nineteenth Century Professionalism." *Ontario History* 66, 4 (1974): 241–50.

Culin, Stewart. "Games of the North American Indians." In *Twenty-Fourth Annual Report of the Bureau of American Ethnology to the Smithsonian Institution, 1902–03,* by W.N. Holmes, Chief. Washington: U.S.A. Government, 1907.

Day, Robert D. "Ethnic Soccer Clubs in London, Canada: A Study in Assimilation." *International Review of Sport Sociology* 16, 1 (1981): 37–52.

Franks, C.E.S. "White Water Canoeing: An Aspect of Canadian Socio-Economic History." *Queen's Quarterly* 82, 2 (1975): 175–88.

Hall, M. Ann. "Rarely Have We Asked Why: Reflections on Canadian Women's Experiences in Sport." *Atlantis* 6, 1 (1980): 51–60.

Homel, Gene Howard. "Sliders and Backsliders: Toronto's Sunday Tobogganing Controversy of 1912." *Urban History Review* 10, 2 (1981): 25–34.

Jones, Kevin G. "Developments in Amateurism and Professionalism in Early 20th Century Canadian Sport." *Journal of Sport History* 2, 1 (1975): 29–40.

Lund, Rolf T. "The Development of Skiing in Banff." *Alberta History* 25, 4 (1977): 26–30.

————————. "Recreational Skiing in the Canadian Rockies." *Alberta History* 26, 2 (1978): 30–34.

————————. "Skiing in Canada: The Early Years." *The Beaver* 308, 3 (1977): 48–53.

————————. "Skiing on the Prairies." *Saskatchewan History* 32, 1 (1979): 29–34.

Macleod, David. "A Live Vaccine: The YMCA and Male Adolescence in the United States and Canada 1870–1920." *Histoire sociale/Social History* 11, 21 (1978): 5–25.

McKay, J. "Entity vs. Process Approaches to Ethnic Relations and Ethnic Identity: A Case Study of Ethnic Soccer Clubs in Toronto's Italian

Community." *Canadian Ethnic Studies/Etudes ethniques au Canada* 12, 3 (1980): 56–80.

Metcalfe, Alan. "The Evolution of Organized Physical Recreation in Montreal, 1840–1895." *Histoire sociale/Social History* 11, 21 (1978): 144–66.

——————. "Sport and Athletics: A Case Study of Lacrosse in Canada, 1840–1889." *Journal of Sport History* 3, 1 (1976): 1–19.

——————. "The Urban Response to the Demand for Sporting Facilities: A Study of Ten Ontario Towns/Cities, 1919–1939." *Urban History Review* 12, 2 (1983): 31–45.

McDonald, Robert A.J. "'Holy Retreat' or 'Practical Breathing Spot'?: Class Perceptions of Vancouver's Stanley Park, 1910–1913." *Canadian Historical Review* 65, 2 (1984): 127–53.

Morrow, Don. "Canadian Sport History: A Critical Essay." *Journal of Sport History* 10, 1 (1983): 67–79.

——————. "A Case Study in Amateur Conflict: The Athletic War in Canada, 1906–08." *The British Journal of Sports History* 3, 2 (1986): 173–90.

——————. "The Knights of the Snowshoe: A Study of the Evolution of Sport in Nineteenth Century Montreal." *Journal of Sport History* 15, 1 (1988): 5–40.

——————. "Lionel Pretoria Conacher." *Journal of Sport History* 6, 1 (1979): 5–37.

——————. "The Powerhouse of Canadian Sport: The Montreal Amateur Athletic Association, Inception to 1909." *Journal of Sport History* 8, 3 (1981): 20–39.

Mott, Morris. "Ball Games in the Canadian West: An Historical Out line." *Journal of the West* 23, 4 (1984): 19–25.

——————. "The British Protestant Pioneers and the Establishment of Manly Sports in Manitoba, 1870–1886." *Journal of Sport History* 17, 3 (1980): 25–36.

——————. "Canadian Sports History: Some Comments to Urban Historians." *Urban History Review* 12, 2 (1983): 25–29.

——————. "Flawed Games, Splendid Ceremonies: The Hockey Matches of the Winnipeg Vics, 1890–1903." *Prairie Forum* 10, 1 (1985): 169–87.

——————. "One Solution to the Urban Crisis: Manly Sports and Winnipeggers, 1900–1914." *Urban History Review* 12, 2 (1983): 57–70.

——————. "One Town's Team: Souris and its Lacrosse Club, 1887–1906." *Manitoba History* 1 (1980): 10–16.

Redmond, Gerald. "Some Aspects of Organized Sport and Leisure in Nineteenth-Century Canada." *Loisir et société/Society and Leisure* 2, 1 (1979): 73–100.

Salter, Michael A. "L'Ordre de Bon Temps: A Functional Analysis." *Journal of Sport History* 3, 2 (1976): 111–19.

Schrodt, Barbara. "Sabbatariansim and Sport in Canadian Society." *Journal of Sport History* 4, 1 (1977): 22–33.

Smith, Michael J. "Grateful Athleticism or Robust Womanhood: The Sporting Culture of Women in Victorian Nova Scotia, 1870–1914." *Journal of Canadian Studies/Revue d'études canadiennes* 23, 1 & 2 (1988): 120–37.

Wise, S.F. "Sport and Class Values in Old Ontario and Quebec." In *His Own Man: Essays in Honour of Arthur Reginald Marsden Lower.* Ed. W.H. Heick and Roger Graham. Montreal: McGill-Queen's University Press, 1974, 93–117.

Young, Alexander, Jr. "The Boston Tarbaby." *The Nova Scotia Historical Quarterly* 4, 3 (1974): 277–298.

An honest attempt has been made to secure permission for all material used, and, if there are errors or omissions, those are wholly unintentional and the publisher will be grateful to learn of them.

Morris Mott, chapter from "Manly Sports and Manitobans, Settlement Days to World War One" (Ph.D. dissertation, Queen's University, 1980). Reprinted by permission of the author.

Robert D. Day, "The British Garrison at Halifax: Its Contribution to the Development of Sport in the Community" in *Proceedings, Fourth Canadian Symposium on the History of Sport and Physical Education*, ed. Barbara Schrodt (Vancouver: University of British Columbia School of Physical Education and Recreation, 1979). Reprinted by permission.

Edwin C. Guillet, excerpt from *Early Life in Upper Canada* (Toronto: Ontario Publishing Co., 1933). Reprinted by permission of University of Toronto Press.

Michael Payne, excerpts from "A Social History of York Factory, 1788–1870," Microfiche on file, Canadian Parks Service, Prairie and Northern Region, Winnipeg, 1984. Reprinted by permission of Environment Canada and the author.

Gerald Redmond, "Some Aspects of Organized Sport and Leisure in Nineteenth-Century Canada" *Loisir et société/Society teSocietyand Leisure* 2, 1 (April 1979): 73–100. Reprinted with permission of the journal.

S.F. Wise, "Sport and Class Values in Old Ontario and Quebec" from *His Own Man: Essays in Honour of Arthur Reginald Marsden Lower*, ed. W.H. Heick and Roger Graham (Montreal: McGill-Queen's University Press, 1974). Reprinted by permission of McGill-Queen's University Press.

Alan Metcalfe, "The Evolution of Organized Physical Recreation in Montreal, 1840–1895," *Histoire sociale/Social History* 11, 21 (May 1978): 144–66. Reprinted by permission of the journal.

Ken Dryden, excerpt from *The Game: A Thoughtful and Provocative Look at a Life in Hockey* (Toronto: Macmillan, 1983). Reprinted by permission of Macmillan of Canada, A Division of Canada Publishing Corporation.

Helen Lenskyj, "Femininity First: Sport and Physical Education for Ontario Girls, 1890–1930," *Canadian Journal of History of Sport/Revue canadienne de l'histoire des sports* 13, 2 (Dec. 1982): 4–17; David Howell and Peter Lindsay, "Social Gospel and the Young Boy Problem, 1895–1925," *Canadian Journal of History of Sport/Revue canadienne de l'histoire des sports* 17, 1 (May 1986): 75–87. Reprinted by permission.

Don Morrow, "A Case of Amateur Conflict: The Athletic War in Canada, 1906–08," *The British Journal of Sports History* 3, 2 (Sept. 1986): 173-90. Reprinted by permission of Frank Cass & Co. Ltd.

Jean Barman, excerpt from *Growing Up British in British Columbia: Boys in Private Schools* by Jean Barman, pp. 63–66, 71–77, plus footnotes. Copyright © 1984 by the University of British Columbia Press. Reprinted by permission of the publisher and author.

Bruce Kidd, "'We Must Maintain a Balance Between Propaganda and Serious Athletics' — The Workers' Sport Movement in Canada, 1924–36," *Proceedings, 5th Canadian Symposium on the History of Sport and Physical Education* (School of Physical and Health Education, University of Toronto, 1982), 330–39. Reprinted by permission of the author.

John Herd Thompson with Allan Seager, excerpts from *Canada 1922–1939: Decades of Discord* (Toronto: McClelland and Stewart, 1985), 186–90. Peter Gzowski, excerpts from *The Game of Our Lives* (Toronto: McClelland and Stewart, 1981), 127–30. Used by permission of the Canadian Publishers, McClelland and Stewart, Toronto.

Enrico Cumbo, "Recreational Activity at the Hamilton Venetian Club," *Polyphony* 7, 1 (Spring/Summer 1985): 59–63. Reprinted by permission of the author.

Douglas Fisher, "A Hockey Series That Challenged Canadians' View of Themselves," *International Perspectives* (Nov./Dec. 1972): 13–20. Reprinted by permission.